Fictional Environments

FLASHPOINTS

The FlashPoints series is devoted to books that consider literature beyond strictly national and disciplinary frameworks and that are distinguished both by their historical grounding and by their theoretical and conceptual strength. Our books engage theory without losing touch with history and work historically without falling into uncritical positivism. FlashPoints aims for a broad audience within the humanities and the social sciences concerned with moments of cultural emergence and transformation. In a Benjaminian mode, FlashPoints is interested in how literature contributes to forming new constellations of culture and history and in how such formations function critically and politically in the present. Series titles are available online at http://escholarship.org/uc/flashpoints.

A complete list of titles begins on p. 275.

Fictional Environments

Mimesis, Deforestation, and Development in Latin America

Victoria Saramago

NORTHWESTERN UNIVERSITY PRESS | EVANSTON, ILLINOIS

Northwestern University Press
www.nupress.northwestern.edu

Printed in the United States of America

10 9 8 7 6 5 4 3 2 1

Library of Congress Cataloging-in-Publication Data

Names: Saramago, Victoria, 1985- author.
Title: Fictional environments : mimesis, deforestation, and development in Latin America / Victoria Saramago.
Other titles: FlashPoints (Evanston, Ill.)
Description: Evanston, Illinois : Northwestern University Press, 2021. | Series: FlashPoints | Includes bibliographical references.
Identifiers: LCCN 2020031381 | ISBN 9780810142596 (paperback) | ISBN 9780810142602 (cloth) | ISBN 9780810142619 (ebook)
Subjects: LCSH: Spanish American fiction—20th century—History and criticism. | Brazilian fiction—20th century—History and criticism. | Environmentalism in literature. | Ecofiction—History and criticism.
Classification: LCC PQ7082.N7 S356 2021 | DDC 863.60998—dc23
LC record available at https://lccn.loc.gov/2020031381

For Guillaume and Adrian

Contents

Acknowledgments

I was once advised to create an acknowledgments file in my book manuscript folder to keep track all the people who left their mark on this book. At the time, I was not aware that, like a Polaris or a Southern Cross, this list would gradually become one of the most cherished and reassuring points of reference among the labyrinthine profusion of files that populated my manuscript's folders. Nor was I aware, at the time, that transferring these names from the screen of my computer to the pages of this book would become such a rite of remembrance and gratitude.

This book would not exist in its present form without the feedback of colleagues who read and commented on the current version and previous ones. I am indebted to Dain Borges, Bruno Carvalho, Caroline Egan, Gustavo Furtado, Hans Ulrich Gumbrecht, Gisela Heffes, Ursula Heise, Héctor Hoyos, Alison James, Marília Librandi-Rocha, Rodrigo Lopes de Barros, Agnes Lugo-Ortiz, Paulo Moreira, Sarah Quesada, Andrei Pop, Jorge Ruffinelli, and Carolina Sá-Carvalho. I also thank three anonymous readers who reviewed the manuscript for Northwestern University Press for their combination of enthusiasm and productive feedback.

I am grateful to colleagues who gave me the opportunity to present portions of this book: Leonardo Davino, Davi Pinho, and Andréa Werkema at the State University of Rio de Janeiro, Eduardo Felippe and Ingrid Robyn at the Latin American Studies Association, Alison James and Françoise Lavocat at the Fact and Fiction Workshop at the University of Chicago and at the International Society for Fiction and Fictionality Studies, Lúcia Sá and Javier Uriate at the Brazilian Association of Comparative Literature, Paulo Soethe at the Federal University of Paraná, Pedro Mandagará at the University of Brasília, José Augusto Pádua and Lise Sedrez at the Federal University of Rio de Janeiro, Patricia Vieira at Georgetown University, Laura Colaneri and Krizia Laureano-Ruiz at the Workshop on Latin America and the Caribbean at the University of Chicago, Anna Klobucka and Victor Mendes at the University of Massachusetts at Dartmouth, Oswaldo Estrada at the Modern Language Association convention, Jens Andermann and Gabriel Giorgi at New York University, Paul Firbas and Javier Uriarte at the State University of New York at Stony Brook, Jonathan Aguirre, Marina Bedran, and Rachel Price at Princeton University, Leonardo Tonus at Sorbonne University, Corey Byrnes and Jorge Coronado at Northwestern University, and Aline Araujo, Luciana Namorato, and Estela Vieira at Indiana University, Bloomington. Their comments and insights were invaluable, as were conversations and debates with other colleagues, such as Mark Anderson, Jessica Auerbach, Luca Bacchini, Laura Barbas-Rhoden, Vincent Barletta, Bruno Bosteels, Ximena Briceño, Gustavo Castro, João Cezar de Castro Rocha, Luiz Costa Lima, Regina Dalcastagné, Marcelo Diego, Sandro Dutra, Juan Carlos Galeano, Jennifer French, David Jackson, Víctor Jiménez, José Luis Jobim, Ilka Kressner, Leila Lehnen, Jorge Marcone, Anderson da Mata, John McNeil, Pedro Meira Monteiro, Marcelo Noah, Alexandre Nodari, Mark Payne, Jamille Pinheiro Dias, Mary Louise Pratt, Charlotte Rogers, Gabriel Rudas, Dan Russek, Ignacio Sánchez-Prado, Mario Vargas Llosa, Alberto Vital, and Jorge Zepeda.

I am extremely grateful to my academic community at the University of Chicago; it has provided me with a rich intellectual environment and supported my scholarship on many levels. I thank my friends, colleagues, and students in the Department of Romance Languages and Literatures, the Center for Latin American Studies, the Katz Center for Mexican Studies, the Franke Institute for the Humanities, the Center for the Study of Race, Politics, and Culture, the Workshop on Latin America and the Caribbean, the Fact and Fiction Workshop, and the Climate Change: Disciplinary Challenges to the Humanities and Social Sciences Workshop. Special thanks go to colleagues who provided me with comments on or materials related to my book project, in its earlier forms or the current one: Dipesh Chakrabarty, Daisy Delogu, Sascha Ebeling, Brodwyn Fischer, Edgar Garcia, Benjamin Morgan, Thomas Pavel, Mario Santana, and Mauricio Tenorio. I am also grateful to Frederick de Armas, Noel Blanco-Mourelle, Cesar Braga Pinto, Larissa Brewer-García, Miguel Caballero, Rachel Galvin, Emilio Kourí, Ali Kulez, Ana Lima, Miguel Martínez, Danielle Roper, and Alejandra Uslenghi for making my work as a scholar of Iberian and Latin American studies in Chicago such an exciting endeavor.

As I came to realize, it takes a village to prepare a manuscript for publication. Through her careful editing and insightful comments, Michelle Niemann provided me with the voice I'd like to have in English if I were a native speaker. I am very grateful to Laura Colaneri for her detailed proofreading, and to her, Thomaz Amancio, Isabela Fraga, and Norman Mora Quintero for technical assistance in preparing this manuscript. I also thank Alison Entrekin for making her translation in progress available. It has been a pleasure to work with Anne Gendler, Trevor Perri, and Patrick Samuel at Northwestern University Press, and with Michelle Clayton and Susan Gillman at the FlashPoints Series. I also thank Gianna Mosser for her interest and support.

Likewise, I thank the directors and staff of the Casa de Rui Barbosa, Fundación Juan Rulfo (with special thanks to Víctor Jiménez), the Instituto de Estudos Brasileiros at the University of São Paulo, the Department of Special Collections at Princeton University Library, and the Rockefeller Archive Center (with special thanks to Lee R. Hiltzik). I also thank Marco André Malaquias of the Circuito Turístico Guimarães Rosa and Elson Barbosa of Grande Sertão Veredas National Park's guiding services.

The person who advised me to keep track of people to thank later was my mother, Ligia. For this and so many other wise pieces of advice, as well as for everything else, I thank her, José Augusto, Flora, and Gilberto.

A life spread across different countries and languages made me wonder at some points if I would ever feel at home again. Guillaume and Adrian are my home. This book is dedicated to them.

Fictional Environments

Introduction

The Grupo de los Cien (Group of One Hundred) launched its founding manifesto in March 1985 in the newspaper *Novedades* in Mexico City. Spearheaded by writer and activist Homero Aridjis and signed by about a hundred artists and intellectuals, the manifesto protested the high levels of air pollution in the capital. "Vivimos en la ciudad más contaminada del mundo, y no se hace nada" ("We live in the world's most polluted city and nothing is being done about it"),[1] the Grupo de los Cien contended, while reminding readers of pollution's consequences for public health and its grim implications for the city's future. A landmark in artists' and intellectuals' involvement in the ecological struggles that were then heating up, the Grupo de los Cien's manifesto also highlights Aridjis's environmental work via both literary production and activism. As a vocal leader of the group, he managed to secure compromises from the Mexican government on air pollution and lobbied for the establishment of the Reserva de la Biosfera de la Mariposa Monarca (Reserve for the Biosphere of the Monarch Butterfly) to protect this endangered butterfly, among other efforts. In parallel, his multigenre literary oeuvre has shown a consistent commitment and connection to the ecological causes that have mobilized him. He is, in many senses, a prototype of the ecologically engaged author—a figure that started to take shape in the last decades of the twentieth century.[2]

Less than a decade later, Costa Rican author Anacristina Rossi also combined literary creation with activist involvement. Her novel *La loca de Gandoca* (1992; The madwoman of Gandoca), a novel that had major repercussions in Costa Rica and received relatively significant attention outside of the country, is the semitestimonial account of the author's alter ego in her fight for the preservation of the Refugio Gandoca-Manzanillo, a southeastern coastal area threatened by the Italian company Eurocaribeña's construction of a huge ecotourist enterprise that violated local regulations.[3] The novel attracted public attention to Rossi's legal battle to protect the refuge, which brought her death threats and the arson of her house in San José.[4] Narrating in dramatic tones what seemed to be a lost cause and emphasizing the vulnerabilities of women and Afro–Costa Rican communities, *La loca de Gandoca* remains a paradigmatic case study of environmentalist literature's potential to intervene on behalf of activist causes in Latin America.[5]

Almost twenty years later, Amazonian shaman Davi Kopenawa's testimonial narrative—told to Bruce Albert, published in French in 2010, and made available in Portuguese in 2015 as *A queda do céu* (*The Falling Sky*, trans. 2013)—represented a landmark for testimonial indigenous literature in Brazil. As a member of the Yanomami group in the extreme north of the country, Kopenawa intertwines his life story with the history of the Yanomami and the forest, with a strong focus on their contact with white people who entered the area and deforested it. As such, his account of Amerindian epistemologies goes beyond the human dimension and recounts environmental struggles via a multiplicity of human and nonhuman points of view. From the perspective of this "supernature," Kopenawa reflects on the destructive character of white people's presence and tries to identify some of the causes for such behavior.[6] While the environmental catastrophe in the Brazilian Amazon has been a central focus of the indigenous activist agenda since at least the 1980s, *A queda do céu*, through its breadth and complexity, makes available to the general public a much more compelling account of the movement's philosophical grounding.

Tellingly, these works were released during a period when more varied genres and voices were receiving attention, after the mid-twentieth-century trends and movements and the Latin American Boom of the 1960s that had given the region's literature a specific profile. As part of this increased diversity, indigenous and female voices have become more prominent, and *testimonios* and postmodern narratives are challenging the High Modernist orientation that characterized so much of the region's mid-twentieth-century production. Concomitantly, Aridjis, Rossi, and Kopenawa are clearly concerned about the imminent risk of environmental loss in the areas about which they write, and their involvement in activist struggles in these regions goes hand in hand with the diffusion of their works among a broader reading public. Such committed reading is facilitated by and partially dependent on the flourishing of environmental movements that, beginning with Rachel Carson's *Silent Spring* (1962) and especially from the 1970s on, have reframed environmental crises in public debate and prompted a body of ecologically committed literature.

Since the 1990s and, on a larger scale, the 2000s, the new academic field of ecocriticism has focused on analyzing this expanding corpus through a diverse range of approaches to the relationship between literary works and environmental issues, including their authors' activism and how these works might help protect the environment. As such, the tight connection between these works' appeal to the reading public and their appreciation as literary works tends to paint in explicit, dramatic colors the process of ecological change they narrate. But how is this contrast constructed and felt in the larger tradition of Latin American environmental writing that predates the development of an explicit ecological awareness framed as a project in literary works? How has the reception of such writing interacted with environmental transformations over the decades? What forms can the relationship between fiction's enduring worlds and the drastic transformations of real biomes take? What theoretical and methodological challenges arise from an examination of fictional works' role in the conservation of certain environmental images and, occasionally, in the very management of environmental realities?

FICTIONAL ENVIRONMENTS

Delving into this complex interaction between enduring representations and changing real environments before and during the momentum gained by ecological movements, *Fictional Environments: Mimesis, Deforestation, and Development in Latin America* investigates how fictional works have become sites for the production of knowledge about, imaginations of, and interventions in Latin American environments. Focusing on a period of accelerated urbanization and deforestation from the 1940s to the 1960s, it explores the role of fiction in developing environmental imaginaries and establishing environmental policies through readings of novels by Alejo Carpentier on the Venezuelan Gran Sabana, João Guimarães Rosa on the Brazilian backlands, Clarice Lispector on urbanizing suburbs in Brazil, Juan Rulfo on the Mexican countryside, and Mario Vargas Llosa on the Peruvian Amazon.

In the mid-twentieth century, Latin American literature began to attract unprecedented attention. Strikingly, these and other writers started to reach a larger public and garner international interest; the best-seller status and international acclaim of Gabriel García Márquez's *Cien años de soledad* (1967; *One Hundred Years of Solitude*, trans. 1970) is an emblematic example. While critics and specialized journals were announcing the advent of the "new novel" as early as the 1950s, in the 1960s the Latin American Boom heightened the profile of this literary production worldwide and augmented its power to shape transnational imaginaries of the region. The enduring fame that these authors have enjoyed from the 1950s and 1960s to the present through a plethora of translations, literary prizes, and media attention has also brought spaces such as the Amazonian forest, the Mexican plains, the Brazilian backlands, and urbanizing capitals to an international literary marketplace.

In a Latin American context, the idea that the region's literature had attained a "precious maturity," Idelber Avelar proposes, was grounded on a compensatory dynamic by which literary achievement counterbalanced socioeconomic "backwardness,"[7] at the same time as developmentalist projects spread across the region, under either democratic governments or dictatorial regimes.[8] The 1960 inauguration of Brazil's new capital, Brasília, combined the desire for modern architecture and car-based urban planning with the country's political and economic integration. Meanwhile, food production in Mexico, Colombia, and other Latin American countries boomed during the Green Revolution in spite of the environmental and public health challenges its methods entailed. In the transnational space of the Amazon, the extraction of natural resources and accelerating deforestation set the stage for grassroots environmental movements from the 1970s on, from Brazil to Ecuador. All these transformations, and others, were based on the dominant underlying assumption that the Americas had an unending supply of forested and semiforested areas, all potentially exploitable and ready to be occupied.[9] This book engages with the symbolic dimensions deforestation has taken on in the context of Latin American developmentalism, either as a necessary and sometimes welcome step in national development and integration or as a painful predicament that causes change and suffering, to which responses range from nostalgia to conservationist activism.

"Paradoxically, then, regionalism returned to prominence in Latin America because modernization had begun to penetrate regions that were isolated, paralyzed, or in decline after one of the continent's typical boom-and-burst economic cycles."[10] Under the rubric of narrative transculturation, Ángel Rama proposes his influential yet contested reading of how some mid-twentieth-century authors modernized Latin American narrative by rearticulating autochthonous components not as picturesque pieces of data, like in earlier regionalist fiction, but as fundamental factors informing style, narrative voice, and what Rama calls "cosmovision."[11] Usually unnoticed in the criticism focused on Rama's concept of narrative transculturation is the importance of environmental change to his formulation. These areas that he called "paralyzed" due to their relative isolation were, according to Rama, on the verge of being deeply transformed by the opening of roads, industrialization, and urban growth—in sum, the range of policies that, in a number of Latin American countries, took shape under the guise of developmentalism form the context in which the conditions for Rama's transculturation flourished. The combination of enthusiasm for the "cultural plasticity" that allowed these communities to be "unfrozen" by modernizing winds and enter into a lively mestizo cultural economy, on the one hand, and the nostalgic tone of his assessment of how these "submersed" communities emerged, on the other, lends to Rama's work an ambivalence that, as I aim to show, mirrors the fundamental ambivalence about the cultural and environmental changes of the 1950s and 1960s displayed by the authors analyzed in this book.[12] While some keep an ironic distance, as does Lispector through her fictional town of S. Geraldo, these authors do participate, to varying extents and sometimes with open enthusiasm, in euphoria about the ideals of progress and modernization fostered by developmentalist policies across the continent. Some of these authors were themselves agents in this process—as was the case with Rulfo, who served on the commission for building the Papaloapan dam—while others for the most part commented on such efforts in their fictional, essayistic, and journalistic works, as does Vargas Llosa. However, even a radical advocate for development at any cost like Vargas Llosa conveys a certain fascination with imposing Amazonian nature and its cultural specificities in his novelistic depictions of the forest. This kind of affective attachment or "loving attention to the local,"[13] which is very clear in the works of Guimarães Rosa and Carpentier, for example, often manifests as nostalgia and as a yet-unrecognized desire for conservation that, in the case of some of these authors, became more explicit in subsequent decades.

In this sense, the very concept of fictional environments encodes some of these ambiguities, as it refers simultaneously to the fictionality of novels as they create their environments and to the fact that, as many of these environments disappear in real life, the way they are collectively perceived may remain tied to their depiction in fictional works and other cultural objects. The widening gap between these environments' changes in real life and their unchanging presence in fictional works is the subject of *Fictional Environments*. By arguing that these literary sites of knowledge remain active and impact the perception of actual social and environmental transformations, this book examines, for example, how novels have inspired the establishment of protected areas such as national parks, have offered a counterpoint to desires for agricultural modernization or urbanization, and have even, in one counterintuitive case, advocated against indigenous land rights.

Consequently, *Fictional Environments* makes the case for an ecocritical methodology that emphasizes literature's agency in certain sociocultural contexts. I contend that, in particular circumstances, literary works not only represent specific environments but also help forge and negotiate public perception of these environments. To read novels for their fictional environments means combining close readings with a broad view of reception history as it intersects with discourses and policies about the regions in which they are set. As Corey Byrnes writes in his study of how the long and powerful cultural history of the Three Gorges region in China provided the horizon of possibility for a dam-building project, "Poems do not build dams, but this book shows that the Three Gorges Dam would not exist as we know it without them."[14] *Fictional Environments* seeks to show that entanglements between the trajectories of fictional works and the fates of the environments they depict over the decades, when considered in this methodological light, prompt us to reexamine the interplay between textual realism and referential reality. The approach I advocate also demands a reconsideration of the embattled category of canonicity: after all, the wider the reach of a given work, the greater its potential to perform some type of environmental agency.

Within the dynamics analyzed here, the very notion of referent becomes slippery, due both to the relative remoteness of represented areas and to the slow collective grasping of their sometimes rapid transformations. In this sense, if ecocritics are to understand fictional works as cultural objects that interact with and intervene in environmental awareness when they are published and afterward, we must take into consideration the mimetic relations implicated in these exchanges. In other words, the mimetic status of environments conserved in fiction vis-à-vis the changing environments of referential reality constantly readjusts as the collective perception of change becomes more acute. Often in a nonlinear and irregular fashion, this perception of loss grows along with environmental awareness, either through direct experience or, more frequently, through diverse media images of areas undergoing deforestation and other environmental transformations, as well as through the attention garnered by local and activist groups. *Fictional Environments* shows how such tension is also visible in the case of celebrated, canonical pieces that have enjoyed a continuing presence in certain cultural frameworks, either through spontaneous reading, required reading in schools, filmic adaptations, or other engagements.

MIMESIS, FICTION, REALISM

The intricate mimetic relationship between literary works and referential realities was at the core of early debates in ecocritical studies. Lawrence Buell explored the issue in nineteenth-century American nature writing in his foundational *The Environmental Imagination* (1995), where he shows that "outer mimesis," applied primarily to nonfiction narratives, establishes a stronger connection between text and context and allows readers to have a special type of reading experience. By approaching texts from an environmental perspective that takes into consideration the referential realities being represented, Buell's work drew attention to the fact that ecocritical readings, especially of nonfictional texts, are marked by a "dual accountability" to both scientific and aesthetic dimensions.[15] Such a view was vigorously contested by critics such as Dana Phillips, whose assessment of the state of ecocriticism at the time found a target in Buell.[16] Two major points of Phillips's critique were precisely that his work focused on a past in which an unstained nature was presumed to have existed, and it assumed that literature would somehow bring about a closer proximity between such a nature and representation—that is, between world and text.[17] Timothy Morton revisited the issue a few years later, ironically employing the term *ecomimesis* to convey this unachievable desire to connect with nature via literature and other cultural forms.[18]

Phillips and Morton's critique constitutes an important turning point in the reassessment of the status of mimesis in environmental writing. Can or does literature, then, develop or expand ecological agendas or, more broadly, increase environmental awareness among a general public? In a more recent phase of this debate, Christine Marran discusses "how fundamental the natural world is to producing cultural and political collectivities."[19] In response to what she terms "biotropes"—tropes that refer to the natural world in order to produce cultural identity—*Fictional Environments* asks how the cultural identities that fuel and are fueled by these tropes and other discursive strategies interact with perceptions of environmental change.

This sequence of responses to Buell's work brings to the fore, in a few words, some of the main theoretical issues associated with the mimetic implications of ecocritical readings: anxieties about the desire to reach a nature "out there," even if it is via the mediation of literature and other arts rather than direct contact (also a problematic notion); the documentary value of fiction and nonfiction in transmitting information to a larger audience; and realistic representation's ability to create consensus about how certain environments are or ought to be. The first problem stems precisely, as Morton argues, from the impossibility of accessing such a sublime or ineffable nature. Recognizing this impossibility leads to a form of engagement with the environment that he calls "dark ecology." Second, texts arguably become more important as sources of information when they reveal details about remote areas that the general public cannot visit in person. To a certain extent, such a documentary capacity corresponds to the role of fiction as "a true form of research and discovery of the country,"[20] as Antonio Candido characterized early novelistic writing in nineteenth-century Brazil,[21] to the point that, according to Flora Süssekind, the Brazilian novel itself developed out of numerous travels accounts that sought to discover and catalog the country's specificities, including its flora and fauna.[22] Such accounts were coupled, as Jens Andermann has shown in the case of both Argentina and Brazil, with a visual apparatus composed of, among other items, photographs, maps, and objects cataloged and displayed in museums, which would assert different forms of national authority over these areas.[23]

In terms of the third theoretical issue, while mid-twentieth-century fiction in Latin America had already taken a much more complex turn in the diversity of its themes and forms, mimesis's most basic function as an imitation—a "mirror of reality," to echo the gospel of literary realism—remains an important component in the reception of the works analyzed here, especially when a substantial portion of the reading public lives far away from the places represented and is unlikely to ever visit them. The number of actual visitors to the Amazonian rain forest, for instance, is significantly smaller than the number of people who want to know more about the region through films, articles, and books, and who donate to help preserve species and places they will likely never see in person.[24] Thus realism as a narrative strategy is crucial in allowing the novels discussed here, and many others, to convince readers of their own referentiality, to the point where readers perceive them as reliable, accurate images of the environments where they are set. This is the case even for novels that are not, in a strict sense, considered realist: despite fantastic elements and surrealist-inspired descriptions in the works analyzed in the following chapters, the reality effect they produce, in the sense Roland Barthes defines it, has been often perceived as an authentic, direct channel to the real spaces they depict.[25] Yet one must ask: What do these real spaces, given their constant processes of change and the arbitrariness of their borders, actually consist of?

A large body of scholarship has already studied the stylistic conventions that shape general notions of textual realism. Erich Auerbach's classic 1946 study on mimesis, for example, questions the notion that realism directly reflects extranarrative worlds by analyzing the myriad forms realistic conventions have taken over the centuries in Western texts, arriving at the "serious, problematic, and even tragic representation" of ordinary individuals and their daily lives in modern realist fiction from early nineteenth-century French literature on.[26] A couple of decades later, Roland Barthes went farther in questioning the reality of the referent as an independent entity by defining the real as "a code of representation."[27] If the referent takes shape through fictional narratives, fiction organizes and gives an identifiable face to the disorderly multitude of the real. I contend, however, that rather than disappearing or being "de-depicted,"[28] referential reality may remain a spectral presence throughout a work's reception history. In unnatural narrative theory's more recent reassessment of classical narratology, Maria Mäkelä has shown that, even in the modern realist novels that Auerbach analyzes, a "cognitively estranging" effect evoked, for example, by disparate elements in long descriptions, questions the "cognitively familiar" with which readers associate realism and through which they will make sense of the text.[29]

If there is anything that ties together this large body of scholarship, it is the insight that textual realism is a stylistic convention like any other, but one that denies its own artificiality to the point where readers acculturated to the convention misperceive it as a direct channel to reality. Such denials become especially significant in the case of canonical novels that constitute major gateways to perceiving certain environments: more than being taken as mirrors of what reality is, in specific contexts such works provide images of what reality *should* be. Thus, I argue that realism takes on a normative dimension that goes beyond the general understanding of realistic narratives as faithful descriptions of a given reality. This normativity is particularly evident in the chapter on Guimarães Rosa, but it is also implied when, for example, Rulfo's work is read as representing the quintessential Mexican countryside or Vargas Llosa suggests the immutable alterity of the Amazon by describing it as immersed in the Stone Age.

To be sure, these fictions interact with myriad sources of differing degrees of fictionality, including nonfictional forms. By fiction I understand, quite simply, works identified as such, from novels to fictional films and TV series. Fiction may be perceived as departing from referential reality even while it has elements that, because they are recognizably based on a given context, readers understand as documentary.[30] This is why, for example, Guimarães Rosa's *sertão* or Carpentier's jungle is perceived as conveying valuable information about these real places to readers, in spite of the fact that their novels entail so many fantastic, supernatural, or even innacurate elements.

Fictionality, in turn, is not dependent on the genre of fiction but, as Richard Walsh pragmatically puts it, works as "a communicative resource, rather than an ontological category":[31] "The rhetoric of fictionality is brought into play whenever a narrative is offered or taken as fiction, regardless of issues of form, style, or reference."[32] The very perception of fictionality consequently relies on a cultural frame of reference that deems a text or a portion of a text fictional, regardless of its genre. Such a distinction is relevant to *Fictional Environments* in its use of sources categorized in the genre of fiction, mostly novels, alongside a series of other documents—from newspaper articles to official reports and sociological studies to advertising—that occasionally make use of fictionality as a communicative resource without being labeled fictions. I am interested in how environmental configurations are negotiated among fictional and nonfictional forms.

Connected to the terms *fiction* and *fictionality* but not dependent on them, *mimesis* is understood here as the interweaving, by readers and authors alike, of often disparate perceptions of certain environments that stem from an equally heterogeneous set of sources. Beyond Barthes, the referent's elusive status has prompted a number of theorizations in which it fades out of the picture in a variety of ways, from Jacques Derrida's view of mimesis, based on Mallarmé's *mimique*, as an imitation that never had a referent,[33] to Jean Baudrillard's simulacra, which have "no relation with reality whatsoever."[34] It is not by chance that early ecocriticism, going against the grain of poststructuralist and postmodern thought and often identified as antitheoretical, was so committed to bringing back to literary studies a strong sense of referentiality.[35] "As a critical stance, it [ecocriticism] has one foot in literature and the other on land,"[36] says Cheryll Glotfelty in her oft-cited introduction to *The Ecocriticism Reader* (1996). Taking "land" as a theoretical problem and complicating its relationship with "literature," *Fictional Environments* follows Glotfelty in arguing for an extratextual approach to the referent. Rather than being inherent to the sign, the referent's spectral quality as I explore it here emerges as an increasingly uncomfortable result of the very fact of deforestation, urbanization, and other consequences of the politics of development. The progressive disappearance of environmental components referred to in fictional works takes on this spectral quality, which is painful and which people often actively fight against as it becomes more evident.[37]

I contend, consequently, that growing recognition of the deleterious effects of the planetary ecological crisis effectively fuels a mimetic rift that results from the threatening, painful perception of environmental loss, often codified in narrative modes such as elegy and tragedy, as Ursula Heise has demonstrated, and that strengthens the public's nostalgic engagement with these places.[38] This is where fictional environments become concrete: they are found in the tense relationship between fiction's lasting imaginaries and the unavoidable predicament of ecological change. The documentary dimension of mimesis becomes nostalgia as its referents fade, and the desire for a reversal of mimesis by which these referents might somehow be recovered and maintained takes a variety of forms. *Fictional Environments* engages with three of these, each corresponding to one section of the book: (1) public policies that, to different degrees, directly intervene in certain sites in order to recreate environments as they are portrayed in fiction or by a broader imaginary in which fiction participates; (2) increasing awareness of ecological change as fictional representations of environments dialogue with or offer alternative narratives for understanding these changes; (3) in a fundamentally opposed move, a celebration of the autonomous existence of fictional representations of environments in an explicit, almost welcome affirmation of this mimetic rift as a necessary condition for economic development.[39] Thus this book brings to light the changing interactions among novels, their reception histories, and the environments they fictionally conserve. Intervening in the ecocritical debate outlined above, *Fictional*

Environments focuses on the outcomes of the impossible desire for a fusion between text and context, as well as for fiction-based assumptions about how certain regions should be, in the face of their impending transformation. Mimesis, then, becomes a dynamic movement that projects itself back onto referential reality at the same time as it enhances the role of novels as carriers of environmental memories.[40]

As Luiz Costa Lima defines it, mimesis is the production of difference against a background of similitude. Through the similitude of the copy to what is copied, mimesis makes evident the shadows, the unperceived sides of reality that are at once revealed and called into question by the representational object. As such, mimesis never has a stable meaning but rather operates as a folding of the real that shapes the way in which it is perceived.[41] *Fictional Environments* emphasizes this instability and the constant production of new meanings that emerge at the intersection of environmental changes, the unequal and nonuniform spread of awareness and concern about them, and the role of fiction in providing images of a (sometimes recent) past that may be projected into a desired future. Such projections may certainly be accompanied by an array of discourses and objectives, from commercial enterprises based on sustainable tourism, to nationalistic celebrations, to an unapologetic defense of natural resource exploitation.

Going back to the example of the Amazonian forest, the fact that it mobilizes so much more attention than other areas as harshly degraded as, for instance, the *cerrado*—to which chapter 1 is devoted—shows that readers' interest in literature's documentary function depends, to a large extent, on the affective dimension of mimetic engagement with environmental works. Drawing on cognitive science to understand how readers respond to environmental writings, Alexa Weik von Mossner has proposed that "the embodied simulation of a protagonist's conscious experience allows readers to get a sense of *what it is like* to be in that environment, leading to an empathetic affective response" that, I contend, may serve as a first step on the way to activism.[42] Such engagement can be formulated as a desire to rupture the boundary between text and context so as to let descriptions of nature somehow replace physical presence, as Morton's concept of ecomimesis proposes. As Jean-Marie Schaeffer shows, readers do understand the difference between fictional narratives and other types of accounts and are cognitively able to separate them,[43] but fictional images nevertheless enter a broader economy of symbols that, especially in the case of remote areas, often serve as proxies for what a given reality should look like. This is the case, for example, with the enduring idealized views of tropical forests fostered by novels, travel accounts, films, TV series, and many other cultural materials: readers and viewers typically engage with these forests through such cultural products rather than through direct contact. The same can be said of pastoralized views of rural Latin American life, which are persistently attached to regionalist novels even when these same works make evident the harshness of that life.[44]

If, following Michel-Rolph Trouillot, history produced inside and outside of academia is recreated from a present position that refers to the past from its own standpoint,[45] then a compelling historical narrative that portrays these environments not as idealized paradises but as areas facing environmental loss, even with occasional apocalyptic undertones, necessarily clashes with these past fictional accounts. But these novels, rather than constituting painful images of collective trauma, such as the transatlantic slave trade or the Holocaust, figure as the opposite: as reminders of increasingly nostalgic views of environmental realities prior to accelerated deforestation, the mechanization of agriculture, or the rise of megalopolises. The novels discussed in this book, most of them canonical and often with large national and international audiences, thus become part of a culture of memory with globalized contours. These contours, like the Berlin described by Andreas Huyssen, reveal the presence of the past in the form of a palimpsest—but a palimpsest that mixes idealized and catastrophic narratives perceived through collective imaginaries and carefully negotiated by the touristic gaze.[46] As such, this globalized cultural memory points to a fear of the future that, contrary to the collective traumas mentioned above, does not derive from the past, at least not from a human-led past.

As a result, nostalgia takes on a prominent role in shaping the ways in which fictional environments are perceived. Nostalgic feelings are intimately connected to the transformations wrought by developmentalist policies and accelerated modernization. Svetlana Boym claims that "nostalgic manifestations are side effects of the teleology of progress."[47] Nostalgic undertones are already at work in some of the novels discussed here when they describe rural and forested areas as already threatened—and at times mourned—by the characters themselves, who notice the impact of modernizing forces. Interestingly, this awareness of change coexists, in many novels, with a certain reaffirmation of the slow or nonexistent pace at which these places were developed, as if they were too removed to be absorbed by waves of progress. This is especially evident in Guimarães Rosa, Carpentier, and Rulfo, and to a lesser extent in Vargas Llosa. Already present in nationalistic discourses as their nations' emblematic landscapes, the *sertão*, the Gran Sabana, and the rural landscapes of the *Llano*, for example, become what Giorgio Agamben calls capitalist museums.[48] Alongside parks and nature preserves, I argue, are environments conserved in fiction.

In summary, nostalgia manifests in the contexts studied here as a double vector that seems to shield environments depicted in fiction from impending changes at the same time as it surreptitiously introduces the possibility of change. This simultaneous museification and modernization dramatizes, in the very literary works themselves, the multiple and often contradictory processes undergone by their referential realities as conservation efforts clash with deforestation and other forms of environmental loss.

DEFORESTATION AND DEVELOPMENT

Forests and processes of deforestation are not easy to define, and definitions of them have changed significantly over the decades. Current definitions refer not only to the expected association of forests with trees but also to the minimum tree density required to constitute a forest and the amount of tree loss that qualifies as deforestation. According to the most recent "Forest Resources Assessment: Terms and Definitions" report produced by the Forestry Department of the United Nations Food and Agriculture Organization in 2018, a forest is defined as "land spanning more than 0.5 hectares with trees higher than 5 meters and a canopy cover of more than 10 percent, or trees able to reach these thresholds *in situ*. It does not include land that is predominantly under agricultural or urban land use."[49] This and other definitions provided by forestry institutions often prove insufficient depending on a number of factors,[50] including the differences between deforestation and forest degradation,[51] environmental policies, and the different stages and types of reforestation.[52] We might also ask about the place of forests in the Western imagination, as Robert Pogue Harrison has done in his literary and cultural history of them: forests, though understood as marginal to and outside of civilization,[53] have more recently "come to assume powerful symbolic status in the cultural imagination to the degree that they provide a compelling paradigm for the notion of earth as a single, complex, integrated ecosystem."[54]

Whichever definition is adopted, two facts are clear: the twentieth century saw an unprecedented acceleration of deforestation on a global scale, and tropical forests, many of which are located in Latin America, were the main focus of this destruction. According to John McNeill, about one-third of the tropical forests that covered 1.5 billion hectares of land around the world were gone by mid-1990, and "most of this forest removal—over an area about the size of India—occurred between 1960 and 1990."[55] This shift occurred mostly as the depletion of forests in Europe and North America led to logging in former colonies, and as developmentalist policies in Latin America across the twentieth century promoted deforestation for both resource extraction and land occupation.[56] At the same time, forested areas across the world started to be more closely scrutinized in the first decades of the twentieth century in order to understand the resources they offered and the impacts of their loss.[57]

Latin America—more specifically, the Amazonian region—may be considered a special case because of the international public attention it has received and its unique place in global conservationist imaginaries. As Candace Slater shows, the Amazon has mobilized global popular environmental imaginaries from multiple angles, with different degrees of accuracy and according to a myriad of agendas.[58] "America's Neotropical nature is still strongly imbued with the symbolic association of paradise, pristine and unsullied," says Shawn Miller.[59] In fact, the Amazon, formerly known in popular culture as the "lungs of the world" and still perceived as a vast area of untouched, paradisiacal tropical nature, has remained central to global environmentalism, even if its real condition has changed significantly in the past century. In parallel, the forest's mysteries, including unknown fauna and tropical diseases, have contributed to an image of it as a "green hell." These jungle horrors went beyond such environmental factors to include crimes perpetrated by human hands: rubber exploitation at the turn of the twentieth century led to torture, slavery, and a wide range of abuses that Roger Casement, for example, denounced following his visit to the Putumayo region in the Peruvian Amazon. Previously perceived as *threatening*, the region is now conceived of as *threatened*; this transition, coexisting with its characterization as a lost paradise, has played a significant role in transnational perceptions of Latin American environments, as Claudia Leal shows.[60] Similar processes have taken place in other regions of tropical forest, such as Central America's forests and the Lacandon forest in southern Mexico, and in a range of other biomes.

Images of burning trees, huge plantations being sprayed with agrotoxins by planes, the building of hydroelectric dams, the complete erasure of towns and woods for mining and oil extraction, birds and fish dying in oil spills, or melting ice in the Andes: from Patagonia to the Rio Grande, the radical environmental changes the region has undergone in the past half century have created a sense of nostalgia and loss permeated by an awareness of the urgency of preserving the remaining areas. Even when awareness of these changes is absent, either due to denial or lack of information, this sense of nostalgia has still been slowly finding a place amid the resilient images of pristine landscapes that increasingly survive primarily in protected areas and in tourist brochures.

In the period on which *Fictional Environments* focuses, such environmental transformations were largely supported by the developmentalist policies taking shape across the region, often as part of postwar efforts to integrate Latin America and other developing regions into the global economy—efforts that were also encumbered by a paradigm of sociocultural westernization. In this context, the creation of CEPAL (Comisión Económica para América Latina y el Caribe, or Economic Commission for Latin America and the Caribbean, ECLAC, in English) in 1948 provided an institutional basis for a generation of economists such as Raúl Prebisch to advance the notions of development and underdevelopment that guided many developmentalist-oriented governments in the period. The faith in modernization underlying the "discourse of development,"[61] in Arturo Escobar's terms, has devastating, enduring ecological consequences that have also uprooted and profoundly changed the lives of local communities, whose sacrifice in the name of development, progress, and modernity was perceived in almost religious terms.[62]

To ignore the many forms of resistance to this forced modernization and to deem the relations between local communities and their environments "primitive" or ineffective is, according to Fernando Mires, "a bad reading of Latin America's own history."[63] Joan Martínez Alier and Ramachandra Guha coined the term "environmentalism of the poor" to describe such popular forms of environmentalist resistance, which are not dependent on the concepts and values of environmental movements in the global north but instead develop autochthonous modalities of activism framed by local cultures and the specificity of their challenges.[64] As the stories of these other varieties of environmentalism have come to the fore in the form of testimonies, scholarly studies, journalistic articles, or narrative pieces, they have become much more visible than in the mid-twentieth century. Having published their works before developmentalist frenzy started to be critically reassessed, the authors analyzed in this volume manifest a certain ambivalence toward its effects, ranging from enthusiasm to a latent nostalgia. As environmental degradation affects vulnerable communities through what Rob Nixon terms processes of slow violence, "a violence that occurs gradually and out of sight,"[65] forms of narrating and representing these processes also emerge, often in the figure of the writer-activist. While this mid-twentieth-century generation falls largely outside Nixon's characterization of such writers—Aridjis, Rossi, and Kopenawa would certainly make better examples—the reception of their novels over time, I argue, has contributed to their inclusion in an environmental imaginative framework that often dovetails with environmentalist agendas.

Published around the time accelerated deforestation was verified in the second half of the twentieth century, and integrated into national and regional canons during the decades when devastated lands began to replace forests in both reality and cultural imaginaries, the novels examined in this volume find themselves on the threshold of real environmental changes. The history of their reception coincides with increasing ecological awareness fostered by the rise of environmental movements worldwide and institutionally recognized by events and treaties from the First Earth Summit in Stockholm in 1972 to the 2015 Paris Climate Accord.[66] Thus, even if many of these authors do not explicitly depict processes of slow violence, their novels tend to participate retrospectively in the collective perception of such modes of violence. One of the questions this book seeks to answer concerns not only how issues of environmental justice in novels are seen at the time of their publication but also how these perceptions evolve over time. As such, *Fictional Environments* addresses both the environmental perspectives present in these canonical texts and the new nuances they take on as their public's horizon of expectations changes.[67] At this juncture, we find a reverse mimesis by which the representation has an impact on what is being represented. In other words, the environmental fictions analyzed here come to create fictional environments. Fictional environments remain at work in broader imaginaries and are dramatized by their contrast with actual environmental loss. In the era that Amitav Ghosh has called the "great derangement," in which the forms of the modern novel are still at odds with the specific uncanniness of climate change,[68] I contend that the trajectories of the novels analyzed in this book offer ways not only to understand how fiction might gradually absorb this uncanniness but also to reassess the role, in this process, of novels written before terms such as the Anthropocene or the Great Acceleration were proposed.[69]

Finally, what does *nature* itself mean to the authors approached in the next chapters, and what does that term stand for in this book? No single answer can fit the semantic multiplicity of *nature* at stake in these authors' works. They seem, to different degrees, to bring together a variety of notions that Kate Soper identifies in ecological discourses of nature: the metaphysical, which asserts the exceptionality of human nature vis-à-vis the nonhuman; the realist, which refers to the physical world as conceived by the natural sciences;[70] and the "'lay' or 'surface' concept, . . . [that is] the nature of immediate experience and aesthetic appreciation,"[71] or the "natural" world as opposed to urban environments. While questioning the divide between humans and nonhumans is central to Lispector's work, novels closer to the genre of the *novelas de la selva*, such as Carpentier's and Vargas Llosa's, evoke the surface effect of nature, usually with intricate dynamics involving the indigenous and other human populations living there. Nature also appears as the personified entities that Raymond Williams describes, as a single or abstract form or principle, or as a manifestation of fate. Rather than working with a singular definition of nature, *Fictional Environments* uses the term as it is embedded in these literary works and the cultural frameworks that shaped their reception. Crucial for understanding the mediated character of conceptions of nature in the novels at stake are the connotations of the term in Latin American literary history, in which the environmental components used to define whole genres—*tierra*, *selva*, *seca*.

LATIN AMERICA

Although the model of ecological awareness dominant in contemporary literature set in forested and rural areas is hardly noticeable in earlier fiction, nature has played a role in the very definition of the Latin American novel. Since the beginning of the colonial period, Latin America has been associated with vast natural areas with little to no human presence,[72] an association that was given new vitality by nineteenth-century travel writing, especially that of Alexander von Humboldt, and which took new forms early in the twentieth century.[73] The first decades of that century saw the rise of *novelas de la tierra* (novels of the land), *novelas de la selva* (novels of the forest), and *romances da seca* (novels production of the 1920s and 1930s, which, as Carlos Alonso shows, expressed an anxiety about affirming the region's identity in the face of the United States' growing influence. As part of this "wider search for an autochthonous literary expression,"[74] these genres all challenge the very category of nature as a mere setting in which human-driven events unfold.[75]

The antagonistic role that rainforests, plains, and semiarid regions played in relation to human protagonists led scholars at the time to theorize nature as a major force in defining the Latin American novel. As early as 1936, Puerto Rican critic Concha Meléndez noted, of José Eustasio Rivera's iconic jungle novel, *La vorágine*, that "the jungle avenges itself by driving the most expert guides crazy" and added that in Rómulo Gallegos's classic *novela de la tierra*, *Doña Bárbara*, "the landscape, the environment, continues to be here the central character, elaborator of the characters, cause of the conflicts."[76] Venezuelan critic Pedro Grases reflected this position when, in a 1949 essay, he wrote that "nature, better Nature—capitalized—imposes itself majestically upon the human element, with a decisive and overwhelming potential. . . . Neither a man nor humanity is any longer the fundamental protagonist of the American novel. Its greatest characters are "vitalizations" of Nature."[77] In the same year, Mexican critic Ángeles Mendieta Alatorre explained how prosopopoeia became central to understanding the role of nature in early twentieth-century Latin American literature. Through this figure of speech, novelists make readers forget characters "in such a way that in some cases only the sour taste of some of the aspects of the American land stay with us."[78]

Though described by such critics as a highly innovative or even foundational aspect of authentic Latin American narrative, the overwhelming presence of nonhuman elements and nonurban settings in these genres nevertheless met harsh criticism from the Boom writers of the 1960s, who considered this and other aspects of the fiction produced in previous decades outdated and in contrast with their own self-proclaimed novelty.[79] Carlos Fuentes's 1969 *La nueva novela hispanoamericana* (The New Spanish American Novel) recalls *La vorágine*'s closing sentence, "Se los tragó la selva" ("The jungle swallowed them up"), to note how often characters were devoured by natural elements in Latin American novels published in the preceding century.[80] A few years later, José Donoso described this earlier fiction as "parochial."[81]

Yet forests and rural areas continued to populate Boom novels. Chapter 5 resumes this discussion of the novelistic role assigned to nature by Boom authors, in particular Mario Vargas Llosa. For now, it suffices to note that the depiction of nature was central to the contrast they set up between their own work and previous fictional trends. Sometimes formulated as a conflict between regionalism and cosmopolitism and focused on other issues, this contrast, rather than actually marking a significant departure from previous understandings of nature's role in narrative, instead underscores the extent to which nature persisted as a concern.[82] And it remained present as the Boom authors expanded their reach in the international literary market, with huge sales as well as a critical consecration that, in the following decades, made magical realism almost a synonym for Latin American literature for a nonspecialized public.[83]

Critical reassessments in the following decades ranged from John Beverley's characterization of the Boom as having an "adult, white, male, patriarchal 'lettered' subject,"[84] to Idelber Avelar's description of it as mourning for the impossibility of restoring "the auratic against the grain of a secular, modernized world."[85] But I evoke the way in which the Boom was hailed as foundational and quasi-messianic by its authors and early critics in the 1960s and early 1970s in order to ask how the unprecedented attention and swift canonical status these novels received may have shaped views of Latin American environments beyond the literary sphere. This process is not limited to Gabriel García Márquez, Julio Cortázar, Carlos Fuentes, and Vargas Llosa, but also includes writers of the *nueva novela* who began publishing earlier, such as Guimarães Rosa, Carpentier, and Rulfo,[86] as well as those who, having entered the international market via other paths, were nonetheless classified as "los olvidados del *boom*" ("the Boom's forgotten ones"), such as Clarice Lispector.[87]

Beyond the inexhaustible debates about its definition, applicability, and comprehensiveness—debates in which I do not seek to directly intervene—the constellation of ideas, themes, and debates surrounding the Boom during and after its key years offers a privileged viewpoint on the imbrication of environmental change with novelistic production. For this book's corpus is situated at the crossroads of styles, disputes, and changing contexts of reception, where the line separating avant-garde experiments from a thoroughly criticized documentary tone was extremely thin, if not indiscernible. These are, moreover, works by mostly canonical authors who have helped create an idea of Latin American literature based primarily on the Modernist paradigm of literary autonomy. This paradigm—though challenged by a number of literary works and trends in recent decades, such as the testimonial and semitestimonial narratives discussed in the introduction to this book—has remained predominant in general conceptions of the Latin American canon. Far from disputing critiques of the Boom's idea of what can be included in the category of literature, *Fictional Environments* takes them as a point of departure. In other words, this volume seeks to understand how the canonicity and auratic aspirations of these novels have led to the types of cultural and environmental agency analyzed in the following chapters. What is at stake here is no longer the place of these titles in a broad literary economy but what may arise from this place once it is identified and established.

To discuss the role of the environment in twentieth-century literature therefore means more than marking how an uncritical condition in which environments are mere backgrounds gives way to contemporary ecological concerns. It means, rather, considering the complex trajectories of the categories of nature, jungle, city, and desert, among others, in the dynamics of literary production and criticism throughout the century.[88] Long before contemporary environmentalism started to appear in fiction, the environment was already a theoretical problem at the very heart of attempts to define what a specifically Latin American novel might look like and, later on, how a modern Latin American novel should respond to those earlier works. A historical revaluation of this discussion is therefore a key point of departure for the readings proposed in *Fictional Environments*: all the novels discussed here, to different degrees, engage with traditions and genres that generated theses on the centrality of nature for Latin American fiction around the time many of these works were released.

CHAPTER SUMMARY

Fictional Environments is divided into three parts, each focused on a relevant set of policies, attitudes, and trends that have, in different ways, affected processes of deforestation in Latin America and the imaginative framework attached to them. Part 1, "Conservation," focuses on the relationship between fiction writing and conservationist policies in the region. Together with films, photographic and journalistic materials, TV shows, and other cultural objects, novels have played an important role in shaping views of areas that, in spite of their remoteness, have come to have symbolic importance and have helped inspire conservationist initiatives.

Few novels in the region have had as much impact on specific realities as João Guimarães Rosa's *Grande sertão: Veredas* (1956; trans. *The Devil to Pay in the Backlands*, 1963). A landmark of Brazilian literature, it epitomizes a long tradition of intellectual and literary reflection on the country's backlands, reconfigured in this novel via a Modernist style with a wide range of references in world literature, but remaining deeply grounded in the specificities of local environments and ways of life. Chapter 1 investigates some fundamental ways in which this novel has functioned as a social and environmental agent by inspiring a number of conservationist projects in the region and setting symbolic standards for what referential reality should be. Drawing on theories of fiction and artistic agency, the chapter lays the foundation for understanding key aspects of the convergence between fiction and environmental conservation explored in part 1. It does so by analyzing projects that explicitly attempt to recreate and evoke the novel's settings in the Brazilian backlands: the Grande Sertão Veredas National Park, the Guimarães Rosa Touristic Circuit, and the Manuelzão Project.

Chapter 2 continues and expands this comparative approach to fiction and conservation, now transported to the forests of Venezuelan Guiana, and most specifically to the area known as Gran Sabana (Great Savannah). The Gran Sabana has been an object of attention in international popular culture since the early twentieth century, from Arthur Conan Doyle's books to Disney-Pixar movies; it and other portions of the Guiana region are also the setting for Cuban author Alejo Carpentier's *Los pasos perdidos* (1953; trans. *The Lost Steps*, 1956). This novel, as well as some of Carpentier's journalistic pieces and his concept of the *real maravilloso* (the "marvelous real"), were written and developed after environmental protection initiatives started in Venezuela but before they gained momentum. This chapter argues that Carpentier's portrayal of the forest as a self-sufficient microcosm provides a fictional template for ideas of environmental conservation in the region. In fact, many of the most significant places in *The Lost Steps* would be declared national parks and natural monuments in the 1960s and 1970s. This chapter shows how Carpentier's work participates in a broader environmental imaginary that results in national parks and the fictionalizing operations that are necessary to establishing and maintaining them.

Part 2, "Development," focuses on policies adopted by a number of governments, especially in the second half of the century, that sought to foster social and economic growth in the region. The two chapters composing this section investigate how fictional works have reflected on and offered counterpoints to developmentalist waves in Mexico and Brazil, through agricultural programs and urban expansion, respectively.

In this vein, chapter 3 examines divergent views of modernity in mid-twentieth-century Mexico by focusing on Juan Rulfo's *Pedro Páramo* (1955; trans. *Pedro Páramo*, 1959) and the deep transformation of agriculture and food production in the country. From the early 1940s on, the so-called Green Revolution greatly increased agricultural production in Mexico through the introduction of hybrid seeds and chemical inputs. Before the high environmental and public health costs of the program became known, the Mexican model was considered a success to be copied worldwide. In parallel, the literary modernity so celebrated in the early reception of Rulfo's novel was permeated by images of the place where *Pedro Páramo* is set: a devastated, empty, dry countryside in the wake of the Cristero War. This chapter examines the contrasts between the Green Revolution's celebration of modernized, self-sufficient agriculture and the paradigmatic desertified lands of Rulfo's fiction. It argues that Rulfo's fictional modernity, in connection with the powerful tradition of the *novelas de la Revolución* with which his work engages, offers a critical counterpoint to desires for and expectations about a modern agricultural prosperity whose risks were underestimated.

Going beyond transformations of rural and forested areas, chapter 4 examines the expansion of some of Latin America's largest cities around the time developmentalism started to gather momentum in public debate. Specifically, it focuses on the urbanization of a Brazilian suburb near a capital probably inspired by Rio de Janeiro in Clarice Lispector's third novel, *A cidade sitiada* (1949; trans. *The Besieged City*, 2019). Based on new materialist theories of nonhuman agency, the chapter shows how lengthy descriptions of the fictional suburb of São Geraldo enable Lispector to relativize human agency on the grammatical and narrative levels. In a novel heavily populated by objects, machines, streets, animals, and other nonhuman agents positioned as syntactical subjects, the narrative hierarchy between an environmental background and a foreground populated by human characters becomes blurred. By reading the novel against developmentalist theories of social and economic progress in mid-twentieth-century Brazil, this chapter treats *A cidade sitiada* as a locus for intense reflection on the potential and limits of urbanization in Latin America. Through a comparison with Lispector's novels from the 1940s to the 1960s, this chapter explores links between nonhuman agency on a narrative level and the accelerated processes of urbanization and deforestation Brazil underwent during this period.

The last part, "The Rights of Nature, the Rights of Fiction," makes an argument about how to reconcile increasing environmental awareness and the reading public's resulting demands with conceptions of literary creation that are not necessarily in line with those demands. While all the previous chapters presupposed a strong affinity between authors and the environments about which they wrote, chapter 5 challenges the common assumption that writers necessarily defend such environments and the interests of their local populations. An intriguing example is that of Mario Vargas Llosa. The author of paradigmatic novels on the Peruvian Amazon, such as *La casa verde* (1966; trans. *The Green House*, 1968) and *El hablador* (1987; trans. *The Storyteller*, 1989), among others, Vargas Llosa has nevertheless, in his essays and political activities, repeatedly defended extensive exploitation of Amazonian natural resources at the expense of indigenous rights and environmental conservation. Such positions have led to public confrontations with indigenous and nonindigenous leaders, activists, and intellectuals. This chapter revisits his novels, writings about fiction, and positions as a public intellectual and politician from the 1960s to the 1990s in order to understand the place of the Amazon in his work. By connecting writings from across his career and ideological trajectory, it underscores a theory of mimesis, present in his work as early as the 1960s, that suggests the independence of the fictional text from the referential reality it represents and its conservation of past realities. This chapter argues that this independence also goes in the opposite direction: Vargas Llosa's fictional environments do not owe anything to the actual environments and imaginaries they mobilize.

In order to capture the multiplicity of mimetic relations implicated in perceptions of environmental permanence and change, each chapter explores the issue from a different angle. The actual impact of novels on real-world projects and policies is most concrete in the first chapter, which advances the argument that *Grande sertão: Veredas* performs a reversal of mimesis in northwestern Minas Gerais. Still examining the effect of fiction on conservation initiatives, the second chapter treats Carpentier's novel as one of a series of works influencing environmental imaginaries of the Gran Sabana. The enduring impact of environments depicted in novels is the subject of the third chapter, in which Rulfo's representations of rural areas are contrasted with the changing landscapes of the Green Revolution. The fourth chapter looks at a variation on such interactions between novels and developmentalist waves as Lispector traces an alternative, nonanthropocentric account of industrialization and urbanization in Rio de Janeiro that contrasts with interpretations provided by the flourishing social and economic theories of the time. Finally, the nontransitive notion of mimesis advanced by Vargas Llosa as an affirmation of aesthetic autonomy gradually takes on reactionary undertones in the context of changing expectations during the 1980s and 1990s.

PART I

Conservation

CHAPTER 1

The *Sertão* Reconstructed

João Guimarães Rosa's Grande sertão: Veredas

When the Brazilian Academy of Letters elected João Guimarães Rosa a new member in 1963, journalist Pedro Bloch tried to interview an author clearly reluctant to speak.[1] After a few questions that received short answers, Bloch asked Guimarães Rosa, "João, como é que você, que fala com essa absurda simplicidade, usa todo aquele 'rebuscamento' para criar um conto?" ("João, how is it that you, who speak with this absurd simplicity, use all that 'adornment' to create a story?"). Guimarães Rosa answered:

> Você conhece os meus cadernos, não conhece?—faz ele. Quando eu saio montado num cavalo, por minha Minas Gerais, vou tomando nota de coisas. O caderno fica impregnado de sangue de boi, suor de cavalo, folha machucada. Cada pássaro que voa, cada espécie, tem voo diferente. Quero descobrir o que caracteriza o voo de cada pássaro, em cada momento. . . . Não há nada igual neste mundo. Não quero palavra, mas coisa, movimento, voo.
>
> You've seen my notebooks, right? he said. When I go out on horseback through my Minas Gerais, I take note of things. The notebook becomes filled with ox blood, horse sweat,

> crushed leaves. Every bird that flies, every species, has a different flight. I want to discover what characterizes the flight of every bird, in every moment. . . . There's nothing else like it in the world. I don't want words, but things, movement, flight.[2]

These notebooks were a fundamental component of Guimarães Rosa's travels in the early 1950s to the backlands of northwestern Minas Gerais, where he collected the names of places, people, animals, and plants, as well as songs, anecdotes, and other pieces of information he later used to compose the novel *Grande sertão: Veredas* (1956; trans. *The Devil to Pay in the Backlands*, 1963) and other novellas and short stories. Tainted by the cattle's blood, the horse's sweat, or the crushed leaves, these notebooks and notepads are evidence of the author's recurrent concern with literature's potential ability to bring words and things together, or, in his words in a later interview with Günter Lorenz, to enact the idea that "literatura tem de ser vida" ("literature must be life").[3] These referential traces, as Clara Rowland has shown in her study of the material poetics of his published works, were absorbed into the materiality of his writing.[4]

Since its publication in 1956, the success of *Grande sertão: Veredas* has been coupled with concrete environmentalist attention to the referential area in which the novel is set; such work simultaneously reverberates with and deviates from Guimarães Rosa's own care for the region.[5] The birds, cattle, and horses that once filled Guimarães Rosa's diaries remain powerful elements of the Rosian *sertões*, characterizing the landscape that a tourist visiting the Circuito Turístico Guimarães Rosa (Guimarães Rosa Touristic Circuit) expects to see, in spite of the extensive plantations of soy and eucalyptus now covering the area. The social and environmental Projeto Manuelzão (Manuelzão Project), named after the legendary cattleman in Guimarães Rosa's fiction, is dedicated to providing a platform for researching the impact of pollution and water contamination in the das Velhas river basin, educating the local population about environmental risk, and highlighting local cultural production. The Parque Nacional Grande Sertão Veredas (Grande Sertão Veredas National Park) works to preserve birds, *buritis* (an indigenous type of palm), and *veredas*,[6] all described in Guimarães Rosa's works, from devastation caused by monoculture and uncontrolled urban growth.

These and other initiatives celebrate and seek to maintain a certain version of the Brazilian savannah biome known as the *cerrado*—one that necessarily conflicts with sharp transformations in the region. Either through a pragmatic approach to the environmental problems the region faces or through an idealized gaze that systematically turns the tourist's eyes away from what does not fit in a Rosian landscape, these projects point to the persistence of an environmental imaginary, based on fiction, that resists and sometimes denies the transformations that have been taking place in the region since the novel's publication. By different means, they aim to make the region imitate the *sertão*, or backlands, of Guimarães Rosa. While such cultural and environmental projects need not depend on a fictional framework, the fact that some of them do challenges the very notion of literary representation as a one-way process.

In this chapter, I propose that Guimarães Rosa's work—especially through his only novel, *Grande sertão: Veredas*—has been operating as an environmental agent in the northwestern *sertão* of Minas Gerais over the past few decades. As such, his work constitutes a paradigmatic example of the normative realism discussed in the introduction, in which fiction sets standards for a reality perceived as lost—and incessantly pursued through restoration efforts—in an area of accelerating environmental change such as this one. This novel's agency is not separable from the prestige of Guimarães Rosa's work in Brazil and abroad, nor can it be understood without attention to the author's intervention in the complex and multifaceted meaning the term *sertão* has acquired in Brazil. What many critics consider the "universality" of his fiction has played a real role in the conviction that its referential area of northwestern Minas Gerais should be preserved. These efforts to keep Guimarães Rosa's *sertões* alive have led, I argue, to a reverse environmental mimesis, in which particular interventions in current realities aim to mimic fictional worlds. To talk about the *sertão* of Minas Gerais as a fictional environment thus means to consider how expectations about the *sertão* based on its representation in Rosian works, as well as in a whole repertoire of cultural products on the many Brazilian *sertões*, dovetail with sustainability and environmental management projects that use these works as a symbolic justification for addressing the effects of deforestation and urbanization. As such, these projects make evident the many possible connections between fiction and conservation on which this and the following chapters focus.

THE NOVEL: BETWEEN DOCUMENTS AND METAPHYSICS

Running to nearly six hundred pages, *Grande sertão: Veredas* is one of the longest books in the Brazilian canon. Without chapters, fragments, or subdivisions, it develops in one narrative block, divided only into paragraphs, as the farmer and former bandit Riobaldo recounts his life history to an educated man from a big city. The numerous *veredas* of Riobaldo's life detail his childhood memories as an orphan living with his wealthy godfather; his wanderings across the *sertão* with a group of *jagunços* (bandits), first led by the strong leader Joca Ramiro and, eventually, by Riobaldo himself; his struggles to avenge the murder of Joca Ramiro; an unconfirmed pact he might have made with the devil; and most importantly, his conflicted love for his friend and coconspirator Diadorim in a context of absolute hostility to homoerotic desire. The multiplicity of plots is matched by the plethora of novelistic genres that the narrative takes up. A bildungsroman, a queer novel, an epic, a regionalist novel, a Faustian novel, an existential novel, a chivalric novel: *Grande sertão: Veredas* easily fulfills these and other labels, as David Arrigucci has shown.[7]

Echoing this narrative profusion is a geographic profusion. Alone or with his group, Riobaldo's constant travels through the region shape a dazzling geographical web that spreads into three states and encompasses hundreds of toponyms, a complex hydric system, and a number of named plants and animals. Through his blend of existing toponyms with other named geographical markers whose veracity cannot be confirmed, the geography of *Grande sertão: Veredas* draws the reader into a labyrinth.[8] "O senhor sabe o mais que é, de se navegar sertão num rumo sem termo, amanhecendo cada manhã num pouso diferente, sem juízo de raiz? Não se tem onde se acostumar os olhos, toda firmeza se dissolve. Isto é assim. Desde o raiar da aurora, o sertão tonteia. Os tamanhos. A alma deles."[9] ("Do you know what it is like to traverse the endless sertão, awaking each morning in a different place? There is nothing to which to accustom the eyes, all substance dissolves.")[10]

From this excess of toponyms, displacements, and unknown localities, *sertão* emerges as a powerful term that not only encompasses and emphasizes the immensity of this space and its social, economic, and political marginality in relation to the rest of the country but also gives it an existential connotation. This is, after all, a work in which the words *sertão* and *sertões* are repeatedly invoked, defined, and redefined. Two of the novel's most widely known definitions of the backlands are "O sertão é do tamanho do mundo" (65; "The sertão is the size of the world")[11] and "O sertão é sem lugar" (323; "The sertão has no place"). While such definitions are instrumental in making the *sertão* transcend geography, they also periodically affirm the *sertão* as a vast yet specific space, whose existential and geographical dimensions coexist and are sometimes indissociable. Thus, together with the maze of complex plots and toponyms, the constant gesture of redefining the *sertão* underscores its exceptionality.[12]

As such, the Rosian *sertão* combines a metaphorical projection of human soul onto a spatial category with a metonymic reaffirmation of the region's reality.[13] When Günter Lorenz asked if *Grande sertão: Veredas* was, to a certain extent, an autobiographical work, the author first called it an "autobiografia irracional" ("irrational autobiography"),[14] then promptly agreed with Lorenz's suggestion that "talvez a culpa disso caiba à mistura de elementos realistas e daqueles que você costuma chamar 'metafísica' ou 'irracionalidade'" (94; "Perhaps that's the fault of the mixture of realist elements and those that you are accustomed to call 'metaphysics' or 'irrationality'"). "Realist elements" can be understood as those that refer to the local reality of Minas Gerais's backlands and that attest, via the conventions of realist narrative, to the close proximity of life and literature, as argued above.

On the one hand, Guimarães Rosa, in letters and interviews, repeatedly spoke of the *sertão* as the space par excellence of a conception of poetic creation based on the primacy of intuition. As Rosa states in a famous letter to his Italian translator, Edoardo Bizzarri, "Ora, Você já notou, decerto, que, como eu, os meus livros, em essência, são 'anti-intelectuais'—defendem o altíssimo primado da intuição, de revelação, da inspiração sobre o bruxulear presunçoso da inteligência reflexiva, da razão, a megera cartesiana" ("Look, you've already noted, certainly, that, like myself, my books, in essence, are 'anti-intellectual'—they defend the highest primacy of intuition, of revelation, of inspiration over the flickering presumption of reflexive intelligence, of reason, that Cartesian shrew").[15] It is not by chance that Guimarães Rosa's notion of metaphysics is to be found at the threshold of rationality, if not in fact in the realm of the irrational, the purely intuitive.[16]

On the other hand, in the same letter to Bizzarri, Guimarães Rosa insists on the "authenticity" of the *sertão*: "O sertão é de suma autenticidade, total. Quando eu escrevi o livro, eu vinha de lá, dominado pela vida e paisagem sertanejas. Por isto mesmo, acho, hoje, que há nele em *Grande sertão: Veredas* certo exagero na massa da documentação" ("On the other hand, the *sertão* is of complete authenticity. When I wrote the book, I was coming from there, dominated by the life and landscape of the *sertão*. It's due to this, I think, today, that there is in *Grande sertão: Veredas* a certain exaggeration in the mass of documentation").[17] This "mass of documentation" stems from the regular, intimate contact Guimarães Rosa had with the region, from his childhood to the 1952 journey following a *boiada* (cattle herd) that culminated in the notepads mentioned in the opening paragraph of this chapter. It also stems from the author's careful study of the area's history and geography, as attested by the multitude of books and documents on related topics in his personal library.[18] The documentary orientation that permeates Guimarães Rosa's work—perhaps most visible in his 1956 texts, *Corpo de baile*'s novellas and *Grande sertão: Veredas*—is, then, an indissociable component of the metaphysics of language that fuses life with literature. In the novel, documentation appears in the form of numerous lists of toponyms, names of plant and animals, and descriptions of local habits. It is also thematized via the notepad of Riobaldo's interlocutor, the man from the city who listens to his narration and possibly transcribes it: "O senhor enche uma caderneta. . . . O senhor vê aonde é o sertão?" ("You're filling up a notebook, sir. . . . Do you see where the *sertão* is?").[19]

It is thus through the interdependence of documentary and metaphysical elements that, in Guimarães Rosa's poetics, the figure of the *sertão* becomes capable of unifying and absorbing the array of conceptions of literary creation at stake in his statements: "Levo o sertão dentro de mim e o mundo no qual vivo é também o sertão. . . . Acho que Goethe foi, em resumo, o único grande poeta da literatura mundial que não escrevia para o dia, mas para o infinito. Era um sertanejo" ("I carry the *sertão* within myself and the world in which I live is also the *sertão*. . . . I think that Goethe was, in short, the only great poet of world literature who wrote not for the day but for the infinite. He was a *sertanejo*").[20] By configuring this door to the infinite, the *sertão* provides the conditions under which literature can "become life." But this notion of infinity is also at work in the *sertão* in a different yet connected way: the Portuguese colonial enterprise imagined the *sertão* as a land of infinite potential, and as such, it remains a powerful geopolitical category in independent Brazil.

THE *SERTÃO*

The term *sertão* was commonly used in the enterprise of Portuguese maritime expansion to designate inland areas not yet reached by the Portuguese; as such, it reflected a prospective view of territorial occupation still in a state of potentiality. As the colonial frontier advanced, the *sertão* came to be considered the opposite not only of the coast and coastal towns but also of inland cities. During the gold rush in Minas Gerais in the eighteenth century, for instance, the state's nonurbanized areas surrounding mining towns were thought of as *sertões*—some of them Guimarães Rosa's *sertões*. The malleability with which the term was applied shows the extent to which it was not a fixed category but rather a relational term or, as Antonio Robert de Moraes puts it, a "geographical ideology."[21] The *sertão* resists exploration, though it is constantly about to be explored and absorbed by urbanization. Once the *sertão* is reached and colonized, it ceases to be *sertão*. This is why Haruf Salmen Espindola defines it as "a landscape built to be extinguished."[22] The *sertão* of a certain region is usually a mobile category, as the expansion of nearby cities necessarily shrinks its original space. The term's character is not specific to Brazil; in fact, the *sertão* has a transatlantic reach linked to the history of Portuguese colonization.[23]

This colonial background notwithstanding, the *sertão* continued to be a dominant term in Brazilian intellectual history following independence in 1822. Its dichotomous relationship with the country's big coastal cities fed the *sertão*'s association with barbarism and backwardness.[24] In the twentieth century, the term became increasingly attached to a specific image of the interior of northeastern states, in which severe cyclical droughts and misery in predominantly rural communities coexisted with generations of *cangaceiros* (bandits) and messianic movements. A touchstone of the geographical stabilization of the term *sertão* in the northeast was Euclides da Cunha's *Os sertões* (1902; trans. *Rebellion in the Backlands*, 1944), whose portrait of *sertanejos* (backlanders) as an ambivalent symbol of backwardness and national authenticity remained influential for decades to come. Akin to Carpentier's Gran Sabana or Rulfo's plains, the *sertão* generated enduring national icons exhaustively portrayed in the country's cultural production from 1930s northeastern novels to a number of twentieth- and twenty-first-century soap operas and TV series, in addition to apparel and craftsmanship associated with the region. Such cultural products are, as Durval Muniz de Albuquerque shows, the result of an extensive process of fashioning a northeastern sense of regional identity, a "construction of a political-cultural totality."[25] The *sertão* from which these productions and symbols radiate is that of the northeast's inland areas, thus at a geographical distance from Guimarães Rosa's *sertão*. But these northeastern *backlands* are important to the broader imaginary economy that the term *sertão* has invoked in Brazilian culture in the past century.

The connections between *Os sertões* and *Grande sertão: Veredas* are numerous and have received critical attention beginning with the latter's early reception, such as in Antonio Candido's "O homem dos avessos" (1957).[26] In spite of approaching two geographically distinct *sertões*, both works are in many senses indebted to long-standing rhetorical tropes according to which the *sertão* consists of a harsh, impenetrable, and hardly mappable environment, resistant to exploration as much as to urbanization, yet full of potentialities to be eventually brought to light.[27]

In the years following the publication of *Grande sertão: Veredas*, the *sertão* of Brazil's *cerrado*, where most of the Rosian *sertão* is to be found, was profoundly changed by the transfer of Brazil's capital from Rio de Janeiro to Brasília. Guimarães Rosa's subsequent book, *Primeiras estórias* (1962; First stories), registers this transformation's earlier moments. The relocation of the capital city had been considered repeatedly, beginning in the eighteenth century, and was finally carried out as part of President Juscelino Kubitschek's "fifty years in five" plan. This transfer had, as one of its major goals, the development of the country's vast *sertões* and the promotion of stronger social, economic, and political integration on a national level: "The whole discussion was based on the assumption of the radiating, civilizing role of a capital in the backlands of the country," affirms Nísia Trindade Lima.[28] As Brasília's construction began in the same period as the publication of *Grande sertão: Veredas*, this timely event influenced the reception of the novel and of Guimarães Rosa's other works.

Vastness, indeterminacy, tense potentiality, and inexorable extinction are fundamental aspects of the Brazilian *sertão* that were synthesized and reshaped by Guimarães Rosa. His engagement with the term in fact expanded the already wide range of meanings it had historically taken on: on the one hand, his works deepened the existential, philosophical, religious, and magical connotations previously attached or easily attachable to the *sertão*, and on the other hand, they contributed to a celebratory image of the backlands as productive of national identities.[29] The Guimarães Rosa Touristic Circuit draws on this broad imaginary to shape the expectations of its audience.

EXAMPLE 1: THE GUIMARÃES ROSA TOURIST CIRCUIT

Since 2001, the village of Andrequicé, in northwestern Minas Gerais, has been the home of the Museu Manuelzão, a museum devoted to Manuel Nardi, the real man who was friends with Guimarães Rosa during the writer's trips to the region as well as one of the most characteristic examples of the cattle ranchers and storytellers so common in Guimarães Rosa's fiction and the protagonist of one of his novellas, "Uma estória de amor" (A love story). The museum, which occupies the house in which Manuelzão lived for a good portion of his life, displays his personal objects, mostly related to his rural work on horseback, as well as a large number of photographs and texts of his songs and stories.

More than half a century after the novel's publication, Andrequicé's little downtown has not drastically changed. However, the village's rural outskirts—where Soropita, the protagonist of the novella "Dão-lalalão," wandered—are no longer made up exclusively of cattle ranches, small- to medium-size plantations, *buritis*, *veredas*, and fruit trees. A labyrinthine sense of profusion is conveyed through other means: these outskirts are now covered with eucalyptus plantations, which form a true maze of perfectly identical rows of trees in large swaths and produce charcoal to fuel the state's mining industry.[30] Along with soybeans, corn, rice, and other monocultures, these extensive eucalyptus plantations have changed the landscape of the municipalities included in the Guimarães Rosa Touristic Circuit.

The circuit is mostly located in the biome called *cerrado*, a type of savannah characterized by low grasslands and seasonal rains. The *cerrado* spreads across the western portion of Minas Gerais and most of central Brazil. While it is a biophysical category and not a sociocultural one, parts of the *cerrado* are sometimes referred to as *sertões*. Large landholders began expanding monocultures throughout the *cerrado* not long after the publication of *Grande sertão: Veredas*, when, in 1965, a policy of subsidized credit for wealthy farmers stimulated the production of large-scale commodity crops, notably soybeans and corn, in the region. Monoculture expansion was also fostered by programs such as the Program for the Development of the Cerrado (POLOCENTRO) and the Brazil-Japan Cooperative Program for the Development of the Cerrado (PRODECER), initiated in 1975 and 1979, respectively.[31] Soybeans adapted to the local climate were developed in collaboration with North American researchers,[32] and they, along with the large-scale introduction of pesticides and fertilizers, made Brazil part of the Green Revolution.

While chapter 3 analyzes in more detail the beginnings and effects of the Green Revolution in developing countries, it must be noted that, in both Brazil and Mexico, the growth of a highly mechanized agricultural industry set the stage for today's agribusiness model. As in Mexico in the late 1940s, in Brazil this shift benefited large farms and export producers to the detriment of local small farmers, leading to land concentration and increasing rural inequality. At the same time, while the Amazon about which Vargas Llosa writes mobilized strong international support for conservation efforts, "the native cerrado had little apparent economic value," and its grasslands were not perceived to be as unique and precious as the rainforest.[33] The *cerrado* thus suffered more from agricultural expansion, which "may be an undesirable side effect of the pressure by national and international organizations to halt deforestation in Amazonia."[34] Although it has "a unique fauna and the largest diversity of savanna floras in the world,"[35] the *cerrado* faces deforestation that accelerated in the 1960s and, if it continues at this pace, could lead to the biome's disappearance around 2030, according to 2004 estimates.[36] It is in the context of these transformations, as well as of conservation initiatives discussed further below, that tourism in the area has been taking shape.

Although they draw small crowds compared to Minas Gerais's historic cities of Ouro Preto and Mariana, modalities of literary tourism related to the work of Guimarães Rosa have been developing in the region since the foundation of the Guimarães Rosa House Museum in 1974.[37] Located in the house where the author grew up in Cordisburgo, the museum contains personal objects, original furniture, and a growing library. Together with the Academy of Letters of Cordisburgo, since 1989 it has sponsored the Semanas Rosianas (Rosian Weeks), an annual cultural festival that combines talks with plays, concerts, art workshops, craftsmanship and book fairs, and "Eco-Literary Hikes" to places that appear in the Rosian works. Tourism in the region was given a jolt of new energy in 1994, when Elisa Almeida founded the Association of the Friends of the Museum.[38]

In the early 2000s, Rosian tourism took a decisive turn with the creation of the Guimarães Rosa Literary Circuit. Established in 2003, sponsored by the Minas Gerais State Tourist Office since 2005, and popularized during the celebrations for the fiftieth anniversary of *Grande sertão: Veredas* in 2006, the circuit links a number of towns in a joint effort to increase literary tourism to the area.[39] Not all of the towns mentioned in Guimarães Rosa's work are included—Andrequicé is not, for example—but all the towns on the circuit, or at least their original area, figure to some extent in his fiction. Besides providing information, maps, and routes for tourists inspired by Rosa's literary works, the circuit supports and publicizes events and organizations related to Guimarães Rosa, such as the Rosian Weeks, the Grupo Miguilins (Miguilins Group), and the Grupo O Caminho do Sertão (The Path to the Sertão Group).[40] Moreover, a new initiative will establish visual continuity among the participating cities by installing gates at the entrance of each one with information on the circuit, as well as signs on the roads and on the path Guimarães Rosa took in 1952.[41] Along with the activities promoted by the Casa da Cultura do Sertão (Cultural House of the Sertão), located in the circuit's hosting city, Morro da Garça, the circuit has helped cultivate a literary perception of the region's geography.

Perhaps the circuit's major challenge, then, is to harmonize the Rosian geography and landscape with the environmental transformations the region has undergone over the decades. In other words, the problem seems to be how to guide tourists in adjusting their eyes so that they can see Guimarães Rosa's *sertão* within the circuit's perimeter. These tensions are also evident in the map of the circuit provided to travelers and available on the circuit's website. By combining actual toponyms, some of which were nonexistent when the texts were published (such as Presidente Juscelino), with imaginary literary toponyms (such as Liso do Sussuarão), the map helpfully identifies the geographical areas where *Grande sertão: Veredas* and *Corpo de baile* are set while giving travelers some reference points. It also uses cow head icons to indicate the path taken by the author on his 1952 trip. Scattered across the map, images of *buriti* trees evoke the style of drawings by the Brazilian artist Poty for the cover of the novel's second edition. In fact, there are still a number of such trees in the region, as well as large areas devoted to raising cattle. However, the tourist will be unable ignore the plantations of soy, eucalyptus, and oranges mentioned above, whose expansion started long before the 2003 establishment of the circuit but which are curiously omitted from its map and from the information on its website. Instead, the website's undated text attests that

> pelos caminhos do sertão podemos apreciar o engenho e a arte de viver do sertanejo; os sons das violas e dos berrantes; as festas tradicionais, religiosas e populares; cavalgadas; passeios de barco pelo rio São Francisco; capelas e fazendas; cafés sertanejos; "causos," estórias e belas caminhadas lite-

> rárias com contadores que narram trechos da obra de João Guimarães Rosa.[42]

> throughout the paths of the sertão we can appreciate the ingenuity and art of the *sertanejo*'s lifestyle; the sound of the guitars and horns; the popular, religious, and traditional festivals; the cavalcades; the boat rides down the São Francisco River; the chapels and farms; *sertanejo* coffee; anecdotes, stories and beautiful literary excursions with storytellers that narrate parts of João Guimarães Rosa's work.

Such a description is not altogether inaccurate. Most of these peoples, places, and traditions can to some extent still be found, some of them having changed little over the past several decades. It is not as if the circuit aimed to recreate the *sertão*'s reality independently, as a hyperreality like Disneyland, wax museums, or the reproduction of historical villages in the United States, which Umberto Eco understood as an obsession with creating "a 'real' copy of the reality being represented."[43] Instead, the circuit is based on the traveler's willingness to ignore the elements of today's *sertão* that do not fit into the Rosian universe. By emphasizing the aspects that remain, such as the *buriti* trees, the cattle pathways, and to some extent, the *veredas*, the circuit cultivates a selective mode of perception in which Rosian or traditional elements are gathered up and savored while signs of environmental degradation and cultural change are discarded and ignored. Realism, in this case, sorts and selects the building blocks not only for restoring reality to how it should be but also for perceiving it. In a 2006 report on the circuit published by the prestigious journal *Estudos Avançados* as part of a dossier on Guimarães Rosa in celebration of *Grande sertão: Veredas*'s fiftieth anniversary, Marily da Cunha Bezerra, president of the Association of Friends of the Casa da Cultura do Sertão, and Dieter Heidemann, geography professor at the University of São Paulo, underline this point. In a description redolent of the idyllic, genuine, uncorrupted countryside that, as Raymond Williams showed, remains a powerful convention that contrasts with ever-changing urban spaces, Bezerra and Heidemann write, "What happens in these places that attract every year more people from outside the region? Certainly they are outsiders that have the *sertão* within themselves. . . . They're people who are nostalgic for a life they never lived and thirst for a primordial, uncorrupted world, where there is still something to be done."[44]

This pastoralist nostalgia for an uncorrupted world therefore does not so much intervene in referential reality as shape perceptions of it. This attitude would probably not have been possible, however, without the canonical position that the Rosian work has occupied since its inception, as the paradigm of a Brazilian universality that would eventually carve out its place in what Pascale Casanova called the "world republic of letters."[45]

A REGIONAL QUEST FOR UNIVERSALITY

The emergence of the Rosian *sertão* as a literary category that has an impact upon referential reality is a multifaceted process that entails the history of Guimarães Rosa's critical reception and his work's growing prominence. His fiction, translated at a relatively fast pace into French, English, German, Italian, and Spanish, garnered international interest that paralleled and resonated with his critical reception in Brazil. If, as Casanova argues, translations are "the greatest proof of literary consecration, bordering the definition of literary art itself,"[46] this international acclaim attests to what has usually been called the universality of Guimarães Rosa's work.

As early as 1946, the publication of the author's first volume of prose fiction, *Sagarana*, led the critic Álvaro Lins, in the article "Uma grande estreia," to comment: "He presents a regional world with the universal spirit of an author who has experienced a highly exquisite and intellectualized culture."[47] Even after Lins's work was rejected by pioneers of academic literary criticism,[48] universalism and regionalism remained a common conceptual pair in criticism of Guimarães Rosa over the following decades, as well as in the critical reception of other authors discussed in this book, most notably Rulfo. An influential example is Antonio Candido's 1970 essay "Literatura e subdesenvolvimento," in which he discussed the progress and shortcomings of regionalist fiction from the nineteenth century to Guimarães Rosa's generation. The endpoint in Candido's teleology is a superregionalism in which Guimarães Rosa's work participates and in which "what we see now, beneath this appearance, is a novelistic flowering marked by technical refinement, thanks to which the regions are transfigured and their human contours are subverted, causing the previously picturesque details to be stripped away and acquire universality."[49] Another good example is the volume *Guimarães Rosa*, edited by Eduardo Coutinho in 1983, which remains one of the most comprehensive collections on the author. An obsession with reading *Grande sertão: Veredas* as the Brazilian equivalent of James Joyce's *Ulysses* (1922) and with comparing Guimarães Rosa's work to other classics of European literature runs through the volume; these themes serve to legitimize what critics have seen as his universality.[50]

These "cosmopolitan desires," as Mariano Siskind has named the ways in which "Latin American intellectuals and texts articulated the possibility of a cosmopolitan modernity,"[51] are part of a broader debate about cosmopolitanism and universalism versus localism and regionalism that has marked Latin American literary and cultural historiography. My intention is not to revisit these contestations in detail, but rather to show how fictional works deemed "universal" may have unintended consequences for, and indeed effects on, referential local realities. Such indisputable prestige, on the one hand, keeps alive an understanding of the *sertão* permeated by Guimarães Rosa's work and, on the other, gives legitimacy to projects that aim to preserve the Rosian *sertão* in real life. Therefore, the uniqueness of the author's *sertão*, validated by critical and international acclaim, is projected back onto the referential reality of northwestern Minas Gerais. In a reversed modality of mimesis, it is this area that represents the Rosian *sertão* and not the other way around. But this reverse mimesis is not motivated exclusively by a nostalgic desire to recover a lost world. It is also strategically mobilized to bring financial revenue to the area as well as attract attention to and resources for social and environmental initiatives. Culture here becomes advantageous, in George Yúdice's terms, to the extent that it becomes a resource that makes action and recognition possible: "In our era, representations of and claims to cultural difference are expedient insofar as they multiply commodities and empower community."[52]

If Silviano Santiago has recently criticized scholarly work on *Grande sertão: Veredas* for trying to domesticate the monstrous, ingenious complexity of the novel,[53] the projects at stake here also have, to a certain extent, tried to "domesticate" the novel for their own ends. The violence of banditry, for example, is largely absent from their vocabulary, and so are discussions of the novel's homoeroticism and its transgender character, of Riobaldo's possible pact with the devil in exchange for power, and indeed of all other aspects of it perceived as potentially uncomfortable for a broad, heterogeneous public. In this sense, the novel's agency upon the region has been mostly effective in the environmental components it has helped make visible, as well as the desire to conserve local cultural traditions. This reverse mimesis should consequently be understood as a selective process by which fiction makes visible and acts upon some strategic issues, rather than as a uniformly comprehensive effect involving all of the novel's numerous topical strands.

LITERATURE AS POLITICS

A desire for universality has been one of the central tenets of the extensive criticism on Guimarães Rosa's work; critics have highlighted the universal dimension the author gives to a distinctively regional setting. This regionalism in turn invokes a large body of Brazilian literature, at the same time as it expands its reach so as to transform our very understanding of the *sertão* as a concept. This strange cocktail is further complicated by the Rosian *sertão*'s existential and metaphysical dimension, which contributes to the trope of universality developed by his critical corpus.

While developing an understanding of the *sertão* on the national and metaphysical levels, Guimarães Rosa simultaneously stages the specific region of northwestern Minas Gerais, where most of his works are set, as a land of vivid contours and inexhaustible profusion. In this sense, his works reconfigure the *sertão*'s role within the distribution of the sensible, which is, in Jacques Rancière's words, "a general law that defines the forms of part-taking by first defining the modes of perception in which they are inscribed."[54] If politics is to be understood as "the cluster of perceptions and practices that shape this common world," literature does politics inasmuch as, by being "involved in this partition of the visible and sayable,"[55] it allows specific data to appear in the common sphere of experience. This is the way in which Guimarães Rosa's fiction shapes the *sertão*, and it is dramatized in the novel through Riobaldo's constant engagement with his urban interlocutor, who, in many senses, stands for Guimarães Rosa's reading public: "Que tal, o que o senhor acha?" (*Grande sertão*, 75; "So, what do you make of it, sir?); "O senhor é bondoso de me ouvir" (89; "You're kind to listen to me, sir"); "O senhor conhece, o senhor sabe" (549; "You know, sir, you've seen it"). I want to propose that, by making this region visible and sayable in the perceptions and practices that constitute politics, Guimarães Rosa provides space for a political dimension of the *sertão* to emerge, through which this space participates in the framing of a polemical "common world." Consequently, the politics of Guimarães Rosa's aesthetics contributes to the reconfiguration of Minas Gerais's *sertão* as a region of universal contours.

Yet, the assumed universality of this *sertão* depends on maintaining and highlighting specific characteristics of the region, such as its *veredas*, *buritis*, farms, cattle, and rivers. But how can these features be kept in a space that, as Espindola noted, is built to be extinguished? Since the novel's publication in 1956, major transformations have indeed taken place. The inauguration of the new national capital only four years later was a predictable magnet attracting a larger population to the area. In addition, monocultures expanded, roads were built, the Três Marias dam was constructed in 1961, cities such as Januária, Corinto, Curvelo, and Pirapora grew in the following decades, and in the late 1960s and 1970s, southern migrants arrived in the north of the state, now known as Chapada Gaúcha.

At the same time, especially since Brazil's redemocratization after the two-decade-long military dictatorship ended in 1985, this visibility of Minas Gerais's *sertão* through Guimarães Rosa's fiction has resulted in a series of past and ongoing efforts with social and environmental impacts on the region. These efforts do not depend on Guimarães Rosa's work for their existence, nor would the area necessarily lack conservation projects otherwise. Still, they do rely on the Rosian aesthetic and popularity as a symbolic justification for their existence. They constitute an homage to a local author, yet the level of influence exercised by his work makes these actions more than mere homages. In many cases, they understand the visible and sayable *sertão* of fiction as a parameter for what social and environmental realities should be.

To show that fiction can have such a concrete impact on the area in which it is set means going beyond the politics of literature. More than breaking down the barriers between art and life or regarding art as a form of life, as Guimarães Rosa did, what is at stake here is the agency of his work as it affects the realm of social and environmental policies. More than representing reality, fiction becomes reality's endpoint. The impossibility of bringing Guimarães Rosa's *sertão* back to life does not prevent such initiatives from having this as a stated goal and an object of nostalgia. This is a case in which manifestations of nostalgia move beyond their potentially reactionary tonalities to effectively foster social and environmental change, as Jennifer Ladino has shown.[56]

The touristic circuit described above is a first example of how Guimarães Rosa's readers and admirers have to negotiate the many contradictions stemming from, on the one hand, their desire to see the literary landscape as it was when his works were written and, on the other, their encounters with evidence of numerous transformations that have irrevocably altered referential reality in the region. In contrast to the touristic circuit, the projects described in the following sections propose not so much to shape the viewer's gaze as to actually intervene in these realities. One of the most successful of these undertakings is the Manuelzão Project.

EXAMPLE 2: THE MANUELZÃO PROJECT

Predictably, the Manuelzão Project was inspired by both the character and the man on whom he was based, who supported the project until his death a few months after it began. Launched in January 1997 by the School of Medicine of the Federal University of Minas Gerais (UFMG), it first aimed to improve the sanitary conditions of the Rio das Velhas basin through the promotion of antipollution, public health, and environmental education initiatives. Since then, its scope has broadened through a series of multidisciplinary projects and partnerships with other institutes inside and outside UFMG, as well as with municipal and state governments.

Among the main activities and projects sponsored by Projeto Manuelzão is the Núcleo Transdisciplinar e Transintitucional pela Revitalização da Bacia do Rio das Velhas (Transdisciplinary and Transinstitutional Center for the Revitalization of the das Velhas River Basin), also known as NuVelhas, which fosters "research activities in diverse areas such as biomonitoring, geoprocessing, and the recuperation of riparian forests."[57] Another initiative, created in 2005, is that of the Núcleos Manuelzão (Manuelzão Centers), local councils that provide forums for discussion of "water management, environmental education, and also participation in the formulation and evaluation of public policy for watersheds" (*Projeto Manuelzão*). As environmental education is a central component of the project, it runs a series of initiatives directed at students and teachers in the region. For example, the Centro Itinerante de Difusão de Ciência e Ecologia (Itinerant Center for the Diffusion of Science and Ecology) visits school groups for talks, and the project offers courses such as Capacitação em Gestão de Projetos (Training in Project Management), Treinamento em Biomonitoramento (Training in Biomonitoring), e Capacitação em Educação Ambiental (Training in Environmental Education), as well as publications on methods for environmental education, such as *Uma viagem ao Projeto Manuelzão e à bacia do rio das Velhas* (A voyage to the Manuelzão Project and to the das Velhas River basin) and the *Programa de Gestão Ambiental Integrado—PGAE* (Program for Integrated Environmental Management). Building on its focus on the people of the region and on raising awareness of cultural and environmental resources, since 2005 the project has also hosted the FestiVelhas, a cultural festival held periodically in the area, which includes poetry, theater, music, and workshops. In partnership with the School of Communication at UFMG, the project also sponsors the *Revista Manuelzão* (Manuelzão magazine), which has published more than eighty issues on the project's activities and news about the region, environmentalism, education, and related topics since December 1997.

Far from ignoring the environmental changes and threats the region has been facing, the Manuelzão Project is primarily focused on researching them, bringing them to public attention, and proposing or developing interventions. FestiVelhas and other cultural activities, in this sense, show how regional themes and traditions are in dialogue with urbanization, pollution, the expansion of monoculture, and so on. In other words, a number of hybridization processes, to use Néstor García Canclini's terminology, are shaping the notion of culture Projeto Manuelzão seeks to convey.[58] The Rosian *sertão* is invoked as part of this hybrid culture and serves symbolically as the environmental parameter based on which the project takes action.

Manuelzão, in this case, brings together the fictional *sertão* of Guimarães Rosa and the transformations that are taking place in today's referential *sertão*. In spite of being four years older than Guimarães Rosa, Manuelzão outlived him by thirty years and saw the landscape change in ways the author himself might have had trouble imagining. The first issue of *Revista Manuelzão* featured an article on him and his friendship with Guimarães Rosa, and later documents that the project produced about Manuelzão also recalled their connection. For instance, in this passage from 2005, UFMG School of Medicine professor and coordinator of the project, Apolo Heringer Lisboa, explains the choice of Manuelzão as its patron:

> [Manuelzão] vivera no sertão mineiro, conhecendo o cerrado antes dos cortes para a produção do carvão das usinas siderúrgicas e do desmatamento generalizado para o plantio de eucaliptais, soja e outras monoculturas extensivas. Abominava esse tipo de progresso sem conservação, que aniquila as

> veredas, a fauna dos Gerais, desfigurando suas características naturais e o modo de vida sertanejo. A linguagem de outro sertanejo, João Guimarães Rosa, é toda impregnada da relação homem natureza e o contador de histórias Manuelzão materializava essa situação e linguagem. Conheceu veredas no grande sertão e a força das águas do São Francisco com seus peixes, e não aceitava a destruição desses ecossistemas.[59]
>
> [Manuelzão] lived in the *sertão* of Minas Gerais and knew the *cerrado* before its trees were cut down to produce charcoal for the steel mills and before the general deforestation to make way for the planting of eucalyptus, soy, and other extensive monocultures. He detested this type of progress without conservation, which annihilates the *veredas* and the animals of Gerais, disfiguring its natural characteristics and the *sertanejo* way of life. The language of that other *sertanejo*, João Guimarães Rosa, is entirely filled with the relationship between man and nature, and Manuelzão, the storyteller, embodied this situation and language. He knew the *veredas* of the great *sertão* and the strength of the waters of the São Francisco River with its fish, and he didn't accept the destruction of these ecosystems.

The dramatic situation of the northwestern *sertões* in Minas Gerais is thus made material in the figure of Manuelzão, a major Rosian protagonist and a real cattleman who represents the threshold between past and present *sertões*, between the fictional character who lives in works still read in today's Brazil and the real person who "detested" the cutting down of actual *sertões* that nevertheless persist in fiction. The figure of Manuelzão operates, in this case, as something close to an ambassador both of an existing fictional reality and of a lost referential environment.[60] Thus Manuelzão's double existence—in fiction and in reality—becomes a powerful means for fostering the kind of local initiatives on which the project relies.

RIOBALDO'S ENVIRONMENTAL VIEWS

Although Guimarães Rosa did not engage in environmentalist advocacy in his prose in the way that such advocacy came to be understood from the 1970s onward, the notion of environmental change was not absent from his work. If some transformations are more clearly dramatized in short stories on the building of Brasília, such as "As margens da alegria" ("The Margins of Happiness") and "Os cimos" ("Treetops"), both from *Primeiras estórias*, even in *Grande sertão: Veredas*, Riobaldo recounts such changes from the time of his youth up to the moment of narration. Urban growth, economic integration on state and national levels, the building of roads, the election of lawmakers from the *sertão*, entrepreneurial initiatives, the increasing presence of soldiers, judges, and policemen: in spite of seeming to be an isolated, self-sufficient, labyrinthine microcosm, the novel's *sertão* runs up against Riobaldo's occasional yet definite suggestions that its present features are bound to meet their end in a not-very-distant future.[61]

The modalities of such transformations, however, clearly differ depending on whether they take place in Riobaldo's narration of his present or his past. When describing the past, to which the vast bulk of the narrative is devoted, Riobaldo portrays the conflict-ridden integration of the *sertão* into the nation on mostly political and military levels. One of the major forces driving these changes involves the soldiers who occasionally intervene in *jagunços*' affairs. While they embody federal intentions to establish some orderly control over the *sertão*, their status as third parties unable to understand the area's internal conflicts and interact meaningfully with its principal actors results in misplaced interventions. For example, when, after Zé Bebelo's judgment, "aquela soldadama viera para o Norte era por vingar Zé Bebelo" (*Grande sertão*, 276; "all them soldiers had come to the North to avenge Zé Bebelo"), the soldiers, out of ignorance, end up fighting the man they were supposed to defend: "Mas, quem era que podia explicar isso tudo a eles, que vinham em máquina enorme de cumprir o grosso e o esmo, tendo as garras para o pescoço nosso mas o pensante da cabeça longe, só geringonciável na capital do Estado?" (276; "But who could explain all this to them, who had come like an enormous machine to crush and destroy us, with their claws on our throats but their thoughts off in the rattletrap capital of the State?").[62] Another force driving these transformations is a desire that some characters—most prominently the same Zé Bebelo, one of the *jagunços*' bosses—express for political representation on the state and federal levels through the election of deputies and the creation of an almost oxymoronic "sertão nacional" (80; "this *sertão* of ours"): "Ao que Zé Bebelo elogiou a lei, deu viva ao governo, para perto futuro prometeu muita coisa republicana" (121; "At which Zé Bebelo praised the law, in-gloried the government, promised a whole bunch of things for the republic in the near future").

Interestingly enough, when Riobaldo mentions the transformations that the *sertão* is undergoing in the narrative present, or at least since he left banditry and started a peaceful life as a farmer, these are more often environmental changes stemming from urban growth: "Ah, tempo de jagunço tinha mesmo de acabar, cidade acaba com o sertão. Acaba?" (152; "Ah, the outlawing days had to come to an end, the city puts an end to the *sertão*. Doesn't it?") or "Diz-se que o Governo está mandando abrir boa estrada rodageira, de Pirapora a Paracatu, por aí" (23; "They say the government's clearing the way for a good truckway, from Pirapora to Paracatú, thereabouts"). It is unsurprising that he was more concerned about military presence in the past, when soldiers actively affected his activities as a *jagunço*. Yet, because his worry over the *sertão*'s landscape does appear in the narrative, this sense of ongoing environmental change in the present should not be overlooked. Instead, it suggests specific awareness of an irreversible process of urban growth that would presumably continue after Riobaldo's narrative present—in fact, culminating a few years after the publication of the novel in the inauguration of Brasília. Guimarães Rosa was aware of these changes and mentions them in some of his notes, as Monica Meyer demonstrates.[63]

The shrinking of the *sertão*'s frontiers is therefore portrayed as a multistage process that starts with police forces occupying territory to stop banditry and continues with the building of roads and the expansion of cities, projects that signal the end of the *sertão* as a microcosm resistant to modernization. This sequence is outlined in Zé Bebelo's vision in which the end of the *jagunçagem* will be followed by urbanization. According to Zé Bebelo, "Dizendo que, depois, estável que abolisse o jaguncismo, e deputado fosse, então reluzia perfeito o Norte, botando pontes, baseando fábricas, remediando a saúde de todos, preenchendo a pobreza, estreando mil escolas" (119; "Saying that, afterward, firm that he'd abolished outlawry and was a congressman, the North would shine in perfection, making bridges, housing factories, fixing folks' health, filling in poverty, opening a thousand schools"). While the environmental changes wrought by bridges and factories are entangled with broader social changes that have an immediate impact on health and education, it is worth noting that the poverty which the *sertão*'s national integration is to overcome needs to be "preenchida," or "filled." This singular lexical choice for characterizing solutions to the social problem of poverty seems to allude to the view of the *sertão* as an empty space to be filled so prevalent in justifications for building Brasília and occupying the west. The phrase thus links this view of the *sertão* as an empty space with the developmentalist view, mentioned in the introduction, according to which underdevelopment is understood as a condition of lack that must be filled with modernization projects.

This extensive reflection upon the potentialities and limits of the *sertão* as articulated in Guimarães Rosa's work, then, draws upon and intervenes in multiple debates on the role of the *sertão* in mid-twentieth-century Brazil. As proposed above, the recovery of the fictional landscape of the Rosian *sertão* in the referential area where it is set has been a significant component of social and environmental projects in the region. One of the initiatives that most radically and problematically tries to achieve this aim is the national park.

EXAMPLE 3: THE GRANDE SERTÃO VEREDAS NATIONAL PARK

The Grande Sertão Veredas National Park was created in 1989, amid the country's redemocratization and only a few months after Brazil's current constitution went into effect. While a number of national parks to protect the *cerrado* biome, where Brasília is located, were established during the new capital's construction and first year, most of the *cerrado*'s national parks were founded during redemocratization in the mid-1980s or afterward.[64] Grande Sertão Veredas is but one example. What is unique about this park is its mission to emulate the landscape of a fictional narrative, an objective not only expressed in the park's name but repeated in official documents and reports.[65]

One of the most emblematic of such documents is the national park's lengthy *Plano de manejo* (Management plan), which details the region's history and geophysical characteristics, its flora and fauna, and the park's future directions. Produced in 2003, it dates from about a year before the park's area was more than doubled in May 2004. The frequent references to Guimarães Rosa and his work in the management plan indicate the role they played in the park's inception and development. In a section titled "Descrição da área da influência" (Description of the area of influence), the report notes that "Toda esta região é amplamente citada na obra de Guimarães Rosa, *Grande Sertão: Veredas*" ("This whole region is widely cited in the work of Guimarães Rosa, *Grande Sertão: Veredas*").[66] A later section, "Os cenários de Rosa"

(Guimarães Rosa's setting), elaborates, "O cenário do romance é o norte de Minas e mais especificamente os cerrados das margens direita e esquerda do Rio São Francisco, cujas tipologias encontram-se quase todas preservadas no Parque Nacional" (48; "The setting of the novel is north of Minas and more specifically the *cerrados* of the right and left banks of the São Francisco River, whose typologies are found nearly completely preserved in the National Park"). It is not surprising, in this case, that a description of the use of hydric resources in the area is reinforced with the phrase "conforme registrado na literatura de Guimarães Rosa" (78; "as registered in the literature of Guimarães Rosa"), or that the first item in a list of "Objetivos específicos do Parque Nacional Grande Sertão Veredas" (Specific objectives of the Grande Sertão Veredas National Park) is "Conservar a paisagem dos Gerais, cenário da obra de Guimarães Rosa, com destaque para as exuberantes veredas" (167; "Conserve the landscape of Gerais, setting of the work of Guimarães Rosa, especially the exuberant *veredas*").

While there are references throughout the plan to the literature of Guimarães Rosa and its role in determining how the area should be experienced and conserved, the section titled "Aspectos culturais e históricos" (Cultural and historical aspects) provides a short yet comprehensive history of the area from the seventeenth century up to the period in which the novel is set. This historical overview is followed by a study of *Grande sertão: Veredas* itself, with a summary of it and commentary on the historical and geographical background of the novel. Also covered in this section are accounts of nineteenth-century travelers to the region, the context of the park's creation, and local festivities, gastronomy, craftsmanship, and architecture.

This rich historical and cultural contextualization of the region in a management plan is thus permeated by a desire to make the park's landscape represent the one in Guimarães Rosa's fiction as closely as possible. This attention to the region's referential and fictional pasts notwithstanding, the very category under which the national park is classified—an "unidade de conservação" or "conservation unit"—precludes human dwellers in the park area. Their removal is only the most recent episode in a series of restrictions in access to land that the local population, also known as *veredeiros* in a reference to the *veredas*, has endured since the 1970s. Geraldo Inácio Martins identifies four moments in this process;[67] the first two are tied to the agricultural and occupational changes mentioned above. The first is essentially the situation in which the novel is set, in which large tracts of unoccupied and ownerless land serve as pasture. Second, in 1966, when the state government established the Rural Minas foundation, these areas began to be privatized in generous programs for migrants and entrepreneurs that prompted impressive expansion of monocultures, especially soy and sugarcane. At the same time, Rural Minas participated in the creation of the Programa de Assentamento do Vale das Araras (PADSA; Araras Valley Settlement Program), which brought migrants from the south of Brazil to the northwest of Minas Gerais. Each family received a small-to-medium portion of land (two hundred to seven hundred hectares) and helped increase demographic density in the area. These initiatives significantly limited the area available for pasturing cattle, upon which the *veredeiros* had traditionally depended.

The third moment began with the creation of the Grande Sertão Veredas National Park in 1989. The Fundação Pró-Natureza (Pro-Nature Foundation), which had advocated for creation of the park since 1986, was mostly concerned about the quick spread of extensive soy plantations in the area, as well as artificial pasture, which threatened not only the region's natural resources but also the small-scale agriculture of local families. Albeit aimed at protecting the area from the environmental impact of monoculture, the park ironically excluded the *veredeiros* who already lived there. Many left gradually over the following decade, although as late as 1997 there were still 390 people living in the park. As the management plan describes, from 1997 to 2002 an initiative was developed to remove these *veredeiros* and give them the choice of receiving either a monetary indemnification or twenty-five hectares of land in the nearby municipality of Formoso. Most opted for the second, and from 2003 onward they began to be resettled. This process of resettlement marks what Martins classifies as the fourth moment. Yet, as of June 2003, as the plan indicates, only 21 percent of the park's area had been restored according to conservationist standards.[68] The park's expansion in 2004 made the process of resettlement and land restoration even more complex.[69]

The long process of establishing the park and the destiny of the *veredeiros* underscores the conflict between local populations and conservation areas since the inception of national parks. On the one hand, the Grande Sertão Veredas National Park aims at restoring the environments that characterized the region in Guimarães Rosa's time, before the changes that started in the 1960s. On the other, national parks are par excellence spaces without human inhabitants. Since the world's first national park, Yellowstone, was created in 1872 in the United States, there has been a constant tension between parks as wilderness areas to be kept free of human presence and as institutions that serve the nation through science and tourism. The absence of human inhabitants has been at the root of some contradictions noted in classic scholarship on national parks. In Roderick Nash's "The American Invention of National Parks" (1970), for example, the United States' democracy is named as a crucial impetus for the creation of national parks in their current form, but this democracy seems to include the middle-class tourists who visit the parks, while excluding local, often Native American populations, who are expelled from them.[70] Such displacements, not always conducted in a fair or smooth fashion, have had a deep effect on these groups' lives. In spite of the environmental impact of tourism, after all, national parks usually imply a concept of nature as a pure, Romantic wilderness "out there," untamed by human hands, which does not fit well with the reality of people living and working in these spaces. Such a view of nature obscures what Marcus Colchester has called the "unhappy truth which conservationists have only recently come to admit, [which] is that the establishment of most national parks and protected areas has had negative effects on their prior inhabitants."[71]

Brazil partially adopted—although it did not always enforce—the North American model in the initial decades after the creation of its first national parks.[72] The 1937 founding of the first Brazilian national park, Itatiaia, embraced the North American template: in its creation decree, then-president Getúlio Vargas stated that the land would be transformed into a national park "para que possa ficar perpetuamente conservada no seu aspecto primitivo" ("so that it might remain perpetually conserved in its primitive appearance"), even though it would allow human presence for "necessidades de ordem científica" ("necessities of a scientific order") and tourism.[73] However, the expulsion of local dwellers, as well as of larger property owners, was not enforced for decades in the country's parks. According to Frederico Freitas, such enforcement did not start in Brazil until the 1970s—in Iguaçu National Park, which had been created in 1939.[74] With the 1979 Plan for Brazilian National Parks, explains José Augusto Drummond, a major restructuring of the Brazilian national park system led to increased control over conservation units, a more uniform distribution of units over territory, and a more comprehensive system for determining whether to allow people to live in or visit particular units according to their conservation status.[75]

The case of Grande Sertão Veredas has been one of progressive expansion of the park, more and more removal of local populations, ongoing

Figure 1: Sign at the exit of the Grande Sertão Veredas National Park. Photograph by Elson Barbosa.

construction of infrastructure for tourism and scientific research, and most notably for the present discussion, increasing use of Guimarães Rosa's work to mediate visitors' experience of the area. When the park's first trail for tourists opened in 2015, it was lined with signs about the flora that included passages from *Grande sertão: Veredas* in which they are mentioned. In what might seem the inverse equivalent of the author's desire to bring horses' sweat and crushed leaves materially into his notepads, here the textual environment is literally inscribed onto the real one, as if to affirm the reverse mimesis in which the actual *sertão* represents the fictional one.[76]

As such, this park aims at re-creating an original landscape that in fact invokes two contrasting origins: a time before the area was shaped by human activity and the time of Guimarães Rosa's work. Caught in between these two ideals, the *veredeiros* and their relocation demonstrate how problematic it is to imitate a fictional landscape marked by human presence with the conceptual tool of a national park. It is not by chance that the management plan devotes significant attention to local cultures while it narrates the very process of removing them from the park. At the same time, the existing tourist infrastructure inserts textual representations of fictional environments into real ones. The novel thus operates as a kind of Trojan horse: if, on the one hand, it provides a legitimized model of landscape that the park's managers are to follow, on the other it undermines the very premise of empty, untouched space on which the park depends.

This disjunction is a preliminary factor to note when considering the relationship between fictional environments and conservation initiatives. As the next chapter shows in the case of the Canaima National Park, such a connection often relies on conservationist narratives constructed to defend the creation of conservation units. Such narratives tend to make use, whenever possible, of cultural memories built on a repertoire of novels and other works, insofar as they underscore the larger significance of the areas to be conserved. That the primary aim of creating Grande Sertão Veredas National Park was to promote environmental conservation in the *cerrado* is undeniable. Nevertheless, the park's name and the repeated references to Guimarães Rosa in its management plan put into relief how the Rosian *sertão* symbolically justifies the endeavor. A two-way process is at stake here: those who have read the author's work find reality faithful to his stories, while those who have never read his books enter for the first time into his reality.

LITERARY AGENCY

A touristic circuit in which travelers are invited to turn a carefully cultivated selective gaze on the areas where most of Guimarães Rosa's works are set, in an effort to recreate a vanishing Rosian *sertão*. A longstanding project covering a wide range of areas that, based on the Rosian universe epitomized in the character and the person of Manuelzão, aims at promoting conservation and well-being in social, environmental, cultural, and scientific domains. A national park that, located in a peripheral place in relation to the Rosian settings, aims at maintaining an almost untouched landscape, at the price of expelling rural families and in expectation of increasing tourism and scientific research. These are three initiatives, among others, in which an array of projects and objectives are combined with the desire to keep Guimarães Rosa's *sertão* alive. Such a desire, one might argue, works mostly as a convenient framework for projects that would exist independently. But would they? For one could also argue that these and other projects are grounded in a Rosian cultural imaginary from their very inception. Their appeal depends, to a significant extent, on the larger symbolic background upon which they act and that acts upon them.

One might ask how Guimarães Rosa's works are capable of influencing these initiatives. After all, reading *Grande sertão: Veredas* or any of his works is not really a prerequisite for engaging with this world and participating in it. It might even be unsurprising if most of the workers involved in these projects have never opened a book by Guimarães Rosa.[77] Yet, his works act on and intervene in local realities. More than that, these projects attempt not only to improve such realities socially and environmentally but also to mimic the fictional *sertões*. A twofold process becomes apparent, in which a deaestheticization of Guimarães Rosa's work leads to social and environmental change through these projects, which subsequently result in the reaestheticization of today's *sertão* as shaped by these same projects.

Deaesthetization, simply put, presupposes that the imaginary linked to by Rosa's work can affect referential reality. Reading the book is thus not a requirement for working on these projects. In order to understand art's diversity of functions beyond Western aesthetics, Alfred Gell's anthropological theory of art defines it as "the outcome and/or the instrument, of social agency."[78] Artifacts come to have social impacts, as "whoever allows his or her attention to be attracted to an index, and submits to its power, appeal, or fascination, is a patient, responding to the agency inherent in the index. This agency may be physical, spiritual, political, etc. as well as 'aesthetic'" (31). The aesthetic power of a work is, then, only one of the dimensions through which it can exercise agency over a wide range of patients that may include not only spectators and artists themselves, but also prototypes—that is, the objects or contexts represented by artifacts. By representation, Gell means both mimetic artifacts, such as a realistic painting, and artifacts that stand for something else, such as a nonmimetic object—a stone, for example—that stands for a god: "The ideas of 'representing' (like a picture) and 'representing' (like an ambassador) are distinct, but none the less linked" (98). In spite of the Western emphasis on the former, both are equally capable of agency.

In a process that includes yet goes beyond the role of the Rosian *sertões* in the distribution of the sensible, an understanding of *Grande sertão: Veredas* as capable of becoming a social agent implies precisely a provisional abstraction of its aesthetic dimension in favor of its diplomatic function in negotiating social and environmental frameworks in contemporary northwestern Minas Gerais. The novel acting on these situations is less a literary work to be read by a collectivity than it is an object imbued with an almost magical power that inspires and sets standards for action in real life. The human agents who work for or participate in the initiatives described above, in spite of potentially never having read Guimarães Rosa's novel, adopt it as a representation, in the mimetic and diplomatic senses, of the *sertão* they seek to conserve or restore.

Toponyms, characters, and landscapes crisscross and weave the many layers—imagined, fictional, real, or desired—of the area at stake. Among the profusion of toponyms in Guimarães Rosa's works are the ones that make up the touristic circuit. As little points that guide the reader/traveler across space, they are only the most prominent signs of a vast web of toponyms—most of which are already lost or always fictional—that the reader/traveler may attempt to discover. Something similar can be said of Projeto Manuelzão, whose more complex notion of representation involves an array of actions in different domains, all of them aiming at "keeping alive"—which is nothing less than imitating—the social, cultural, and environmental world of Guimarães Rosa, be it through initiatives to keep the Rio das Velhas clean or through theater performances of the author's works. It is not by chance, then, that the project, with its focus on the human component, is called Manuelzão, as an homage to the man who was, perhaps, most successful in transitioning between an imitative reality and a realistic mimesis. Finally, the Grande Sertão Veredas National Park makes visible a concern not so much about human presence as about the geophysical, botanical, and animal particulars that make up the *veredas*' landscape within the broader *sertão*. Previously described as little oases punctuating a drier area of low vegetation, not only do the *veredas* integrate the rich web of spatial metaphors developed in the novel, but they also present an impressive biodiversity that the park seeks to preserve. In all these cases, the influence that Guimarães Rosa's works exert on the area correspondingly rebounds in the opposite direction—that is, attempts to keep the *sertão* as it was indeed create new ways of experiencing it aesthetically. Admirers of Guimarães Rosa's works, who are especially but not exclusively his readers, may seek out this "thirdspace," to use Edward Soja's concept,[79] which brings together fictional, imagined, and referential realities in a whole whose parts demand constant negotiation but can nevertheless be recomposed as Guimarães Rosa's *sertão*.

In a region marked by the steady expansion of monoculture, as well as mechanized agriculture, industrial activity, urbanization, and contamination on several levels, this imagined recomposition is not only necessary but increasingly challenging. The very term *sertão*, understood as a vast nonurbanized area, is more and more inadequate and rarely used in the region's everyday vocabulary. The initiatives discussed in this chapter and others like them demonstrate the extent to which today's *sertão* performs a complex mimesis of the Rosian *sertão* for the many travelers who wish to see the landscapes they read about in fictional narratives, as well as for those who never go to the area, and perhaps do not even read the books, but still wish to believe in and imagine the current existence of a *sertão* as portrayed in *Grande sertão: Veredas*: a place "onde os pastos carecem de fechos; onde um pode torar dez, quinze léguas, sem topar com casa de morador; e onde criminoso vive seu cristo-jesus, arredado do arrocho de autoridade" (5; "where pastures have no fences; where a man can go fifteen, twenty miles without coming to a single house; where outlaws live out their hallelujah, in the yonder beyond the law").

While the numerous changes the region is undergoing progressively jeopardize this mimetic reconstruction of the fictional *sertão* in the real geographic region, the existence of actual projects, travels, and other initiatives attests to the resilience of the Rosian landscape. The social agency of Rosian works—manifested in desperate, hopeful, maybe even naive attempts to keep this *sertão* "alive"—has yielded positive consequences in the actual results of such projects, while simultaneously attempting to bring together the two sides of a rift only bound to grow with time.

CHAPTER 2

Narrative Conservation and Conservationist Narratives

Alejo Carpentier's Gran Sabana

Published in 1957, the book *Jungle Oil: The Search for Venezuela's Hidden Treasure* aimed to give a North American public a sense of one of South America's major oil-producing areas. Filled with photographs by the Creole Petroleum Corporation, the Ford Motor Company, and US Steel, *Jungle Oil* narrates a triumphant history of the fossil fuel's extraction in Venezuela, from its geological formation to the construction of a modern nation fueled by it. Targeting young adults, the book concludes with a description of the Gran Sabana, or Great Savannah, the "land of mystery" in Venezuela's southeast,[1] which the book conceptualizes as occupying the whole southern portion of the country.

A "vast, mysterious territory" is also the way *Petroleum Geography of Venezuela* describes the Venezuelan Guiana,[2] where the Gran Sabana is located. This 1957 booklet, by none other than then-director of the Creole Petroleum Corporation, Guillermo Zuloaga, offers an overview of the country's regions. The Gran Sabana is home to the world's highest waterfall, Angel Falls, and the large, remarkable table rocks known as tepuyes; it is located far away from oil production sites. These publications portray the region generally referred to as the Gran Sabana as of interest due to a combination of its economic potential, its impressive natural settings, and a sense of adventure akin to that of Arthur Conan Doyle's novel set in the region, *The Lost World* (1912).[3]

Textually and thematically separated from Venezuela's oil production, the chapters devoted to the Gran Sabana attest to the area's enduring power in shaping transnational views of South America. In fact, a few years later, in 1962, Canaima National Park was created to protect a portion of the region. The park expanded to encompass savannah areas in 1975 and subsequently become a UNESCO World Heritage Site in 1994,[4] besides inspiring a number of cultural products exploring the Gran Sabana and its landmarks, including novels, travel accounts, films, TV programs, publicity pieces, and the two books mentioned above.

The year before they were distributed, a quite different publication brought the Gran Sabana's landscapes to the attention of English-speaking readers following its successful reception in Latin America and Europe. I am referring here to the Cuban author Alejo Carpentier's *Los pasos perdidos* (1953), whose English translation by Harriet de Onís, *The Lost Steps*, was first published in 1956. Albeit connected to the aforementioned publications through their common fascination with the Guianan region and, specifically, the tepuyes of the Guiana Highlands, the novel contrasts starkly with them. Rather than representing the area as empty land awaiting Western exploitation, Carpentier's fictional forest conserves a complex web of human and nonhuman interactions barely accessible to outsiders. The array of analogies through which the novel understands this web underscores Carpentier's attempt to develop a "literature that could encompass the historical processes whereby cultural forms had been uprooted, transplanted, and reconstituted in New World contexts."[5]

Carpentier moved to Caracas in 1945 and took his first trip to the Venezuelan Amazon two years later, in July 1947. It lasted a few days and included flights over the Gran Sabana and the Orinoco River, in addition to two days in Santa Elena de Uairén. Mesmerized by the experience, the author went again a year later, in September 1948. This time, he traveled to the western portion of the Venezuelan Amazon, first by bus from Caracas to Ciudad Bolívar and then down the Orinoco River, with some detours in the country's southwest, passing by Mount Autana and the Caño de Guacharaca.[6] Readers of *Los pasos perdidos* may recall the "Nota" appended to the novel, in which these real names replace the fictional toponyms in a sort of geographical roman à clef: the *caño* is the place where the three *V*s were inscribed in a tree trunk "señala la entrada del paso secreto" ("marking the entrance to the secret channel"),[7] and Autana is the Capital de las Formas (Capital of Forms), among others. Carpentier did, indeed, repeatedly evoke memories of this deeper exploration of the jungle and of his plane travel the year before in later writings, both in the series of newspaper articles *Visión de América* (Vision of America) and in many other essays, talks, and journalistic contributions.

Many of these pieces—and especially *Los pasos perdidos*—present the Venezuelan Guiana as enclosed and self-sufficient, with a sharp alterity operating in opposition to an oil-fueled modernity. While Carpentier famously called the Orinoco "una materialización del tiempo" (a materialization of time) in a lecture in Caracas in 1975,[8] the novel's compartmentalization of historical periods in the spaces of the jungle also dovetails with a certain environmental stasis. In other words, the jungle that encompasses different times, from Romanticism to the Neolithic, is a jungle relatively invulnerable to change from the outside. But how would this world "de muy pocas puertas" (*Los pasos perdidos*, 164; "with few entrances," 126) be opened to urbanization, natural resource extraction, and deforestation? Moreover, how does the novel, with its tropes and descriptions, participate in and contribute to an environmental memory of the Venezuelan Guiana, more specifically of the Gran Sabana?

The environmental changes wrought by extractivist activity and technology in the Orinoco River Basin, as Charlotte Rogers discusses in detail, alarmed the author and are visible in the novel through, for example, the presence of an airplane as well as mentions of mining and oil drilling.[9] The contrast between such elements and the novel's representation of the jungle as an immutable reality akin to that of Genesis dramatizes the multifaceted, at times ambiguous set of assumptions and desires upon which Carpentier's fictional Gran Sabana is built. After all, Carpentier's years in Venezuela and his writings on the Amazon coincide with the country's early steps toward conservation initiatives, initially led by the Swiss naturalist Henri Pittier and culminating in the creation of its first national park. On the other hand, there is no indication that Carpentier had any direct involvement in such initiatives or in other conservation movements. In a global context of deep uncertainty regarding the nuclear threat after Hiroshima and Nagasaki, Carpentier's environmental concerns instead belonged to a planetary scale. He fully shared the nuclear anxieties of the time, as a number of his newspaper articles show—including some of the most pessimistic he ever penned. Side by side with his worries about impending nuclear catastrophe was a curiosity about flying saucers and the possibility of communication with alien forms of life. To a certain extent, one might suppose this interplanetary reality to be as marvelous as the American one in his theory of the *real maravilloso* (marvelous real), with the nuclear counterpart as its dystopian facet.

Taking all these factors into consideration, the present chapter investigates how Carpentier's writings in his Venezuelan years, especially *Los pasos perdidos*, helped shape and were shaped by an environmental imaginary of the Gran Sabana. More specifically, I propose a parallel between the history of environmental conservation in the Venezuelan Amazon and the way *Los pasos perdidos* "conserves" that forested area, both through its representation of the forest as a static, autonomous realm and through its contact points with conservationist initiatives. If the Gran Sabana's transformation into a national park and later into a UNESCO World Heritage Site is also the result of its recognizable cultural status as a precious "lost world," this chapter analyzes how fiction, by symbolically conserving specific environments, plays a role in shaping their referential areas as recognizable sites of memory that must be conserved in real life through the creation of national parks and other conservation units. In the case of a landscape that, like the Gran Sabana, has been imprinted on an array of cultural objects, I argue that the consensus about the need to preserve it partially depends on its persistent portrayal as a pristine wilderness of exceptional beauty in novels, travel accounts, films, TV series, and so on. While this is certainly a much more indirect process than that via which João Guimarães Rosa's work informs Grande Sertão Veredas National Park, what is at stake here is a larger circuit of many actors, of which Carpentier is but one—albeit a non-negligible one. Yet, there is a certain "structure of feeling," in Raymond Williams's terminology, underlying the forms of engagement with these areas through cultural products. Moreover, the very way these areas are managed may be, I argue, conditioned by certain fictionalizing operations implied in the concept of conserved areas itself—which these novels both support and critique. At the same time, Carpentier's proto-ecological thought developed alongside his period's enthusiasm and ambivalence about discourses of social and scientific progress prevalent in the period, from the central place of oil in an understanding of Venezuelan modernity to the atomic threat on a global level.

LO REAL MARAVILLOSO, OR SEEING A FLYING SAUCER FROM THE ORINOCO

"¿Pero qué es la historia de América toda sino una crónica de lo real-maravilloso?" (But what is the history of all the Americas but a chronicle of the real marvelous?).[10] The final sentence of the famous "Prólogo" to the 1949 novel *El reino de este mundo*, first published as an independent piece on April 8, 1948, in the Venezuelan newspaper *El Nacional*,[11] synthesizes the main elements of the influential concept Carpentier proposed in 1948–49 and took up again later. In a few words, it argues that America's actual reality has a marvelous component that Europe can represent only incompletely through art and literature. This ontologization of the marvelous in the continent's reality presupposes that the American uncanny transparently reveals itself to the eyes of the beholder. The narrators of America, as the passage above makes explicit, are merely chroniclers, whose primarily documentary function suffices to convey to the reader a marvelousness that their European counterparts only achieve through artistic artifice. Consequently, a very specific notion of mimesis is also presupposed here: mimesis in the realms of the *real maravilloso* is no more than a direct rendering of referential reality.

As a concept geared to the American reality, the *real maravilloso* necessarily had a continental dimension. In fact, a turning point in Carpentier's formulation of the *real maravilloso* was his 1943 visit to Haiti, a country that deeply impressed him and became the setting for *El reino de este mundo*.[12] Nonetheless, "la magia de la vegetación tropical, la desenfrenada Creación de Formas de nuestra naturaleza" ("Prólogo," 9; "the magic of the tropical vegetation, the uncontrolled Creation of Forms in our nature," 29), as represented in Wifredo Lam's paintings, also enables the emergence of a marvelous reality. Carpentier again took up the very idea of "Creación de Formas" with a few variations in *Los pasos perdidos*, the novel in which he fully developed an environmental version of his key concept. But beyond its continental scope, how can the *real maravilloso* be understood environmentally? If we pursue this reading, to what extent does the marvelous real admit environmental change, including urbanization and deforestation?

Key elements that appear later in *Los pasos perdidos* are already clearly recognizable in an important early text, the collection of short essays *Visión de América*. Carpentier was then living in Caracas, having accepted Carlos Frías's invitation to work at the Venezuelan company ARS Publicidad. *Visión de América* first appeared in the form of weekly articles published between October and December of 1947 in *El Nacional* and republished in the Cuban magazine *Carteles* during the first half of 1948. This collection of essays narrating his travels to the Amazon, fundamental to understanding the genesis of *Los pasos perdidos*, was to have formed part of an unfinished book, "El libro de la Gran Sabana" (The Book of the Great Savannah), which Carpentier abandoned to compose the novel.[13] These articles describe different portions of the eastern part of the Venezuelan Amazon that he visited in 1947.

Narrating in the first person, Carpentier gazes down from the height of an airplane and describes the tepuyes, the "alucinante mundo geológico de la Gran Sabana"[14] (the hallucinatory geological world of the Great Savannah), with an emphasis on landmarks such as Mount Roraima and Angel Falls (also mentioned in *Jungle Oil* and *Petroleum Geography of Venezuela*), in addition to the city Santa Elena de Uairén, the inspiration for Santa Mónica de los Venados in *Los pasos perdidos*. The accounts of all these places converge on a single conclusion: in the Gran Sabana, time passes in a rather peculiar fashion. In front of the tepuyes, "el tiempo estaba detenido ahí, al pie de las rocas inmutables, desposeído de todo sentido ontológico para el frenético hombre del Occidente. . . . No era el tiempo que miden nuestros relojes ni nuestros calendarios. Era el tiempo de la Gran Sabana. El tiempo de la tierra en los días del Génesis" (*Visión de América*, 20; "time had stopped, at the foot of the immutable rocks, devoid of all ontological sense for the frenetic Western man. . . . It was not time as measured by our clocks nor our calendars. It was the time of the Great Savannah. It was the time of the earth in the days of Genesis").[15]

It is not that time does not pass in the Gran Sabana, but that it passes in a different way—as it might in Genesis: in a time before history. A few pages later, in his account of Santa Elena de Uairén's foundation, yet another past is similarly actualized: "En 1927 surge, pues, una ciudad nueva en América, exactamente como pudo nacer con igual proceso de formación la de Santiago de Cuba, en 1514" (*Visión de América*, 24; "In 1927, a new city arises in America, exactly as Santiago de Cuba was born in 1514—with the same process of formation"); and this city needed to have a Calle Mayor "como hiciera Pizarro en Lima" (25; "as Pizarro had done in Lima").

In other words, the foundation of Santa Elena is understood as reenacting the founding of the first cities of Spanish America, just as the immutability of the tepuyes reenacts Genesis. Both fulfill certain *figurae* in Erich Auerbach's sense: "Figural interpretation establishes a connection between two events or persons, the first of which signifies not only itself but also the second, while the second encompasses or fulfills the first."[16] This 1938 definition of *figura* is built on the classic case of the Old Testament prefiguring the New Testament. In accordance with Auerbach's definition, the Gran Sabana, as the fulfillment of a series of *figurae*, cannot be understood as a strict allegory, inasmuch as its own historical existence is recorded and documented. Yet, it also participates in an alternative temporality that becomes the basic standpoint from which *Los pasos perdidos* sees it. An environmental reading of Carpentier's *real maravilloso* thus presupposes a specific notion of time: it is apparently still, but those who know it may identify its movements, which are sometimes predetermined and sometimes unpredictable, and mark the forest dynamics of the novel.

The particular temporality in which the Gran Sabana operates becomes more vivid when Carpentier comments that Santa Elena's founder, Lucas Fernández Peña, did not want to accumulate wealth, aware as he was of "la inutilidad del oro para todo individuo que no aspira a regresar hacia una civilización que no sólo inventa la bomba atómica, sino que halla, además, justificaciones metafísicas a su empleo" (*Visión de América*, 26; "the uselessness of gold to any individual who does not aspire to return to a civilization that not only invents the atomic bomb but also finds metaphysical justifications for using it"). In a text published only two years after Hiroshima and Nagasaki, the mention of the bomb as an example of the suicidal meaninglessness of "Western civilization" highlights the contrast between a marvelous reality apparently immune even to the atomic threat and the deep uncertainty surrounding the postwar period.[17]

Yet, if withdrawal from the appeals and threats of modernity indeed suggests some form of escape from atomic holocaust and the then-isolated forested area provided this site of protection via the trope of return to nature, the tone of apprehension in Carpentier's nonfiction only betrays the fictionality implied in his representation of the forest as a real shelter. Interestingly, while the idea that any place can be completely isolated seems necessarily fictional today, the period in which Carpentier expressed his most acute concerns about the atomic threat was also the period in which the myth of isolated places justified the United States' unprecedented nuclear testing in the Pacific Ocean's Marshall Islands—via concepts such as the isolate that also fostered, ironically, the development of modern ecology through the increasingly popular notion of ecosystems, as Elizabeth DeLoughrey shows.[18] As such, Carpentier reaffirms the understanding of the jungle as an isolated space that nevertheless inverts that of the Marshall Islands: instead of providing an ideal laboratory for nuclear experiments, it might represent a possible shelter against them.

This early reference to the atomic bomb is but one in a larger group of texts in which Carpentier's environmental views may be traced. After *Visión de América*, from 1951 to 1959, Carpentier also wrote a column in *El Nacional* called *Letra y solfa*, where his views on many subjects, especially those related to literature and the arts, found expression. Published about a year before *Los pasos perdidos*, in August 1952, the *Letra y solfa* piece "Platillos sobre el Orinoco" ("Flying Saucers above the Orinoco") makes an uncanny connection between the author's trip to the Orinoco in 1948 and outer space when he affirms, "Hace cuatro años, vimos platillos voladores sobre el Orinoco"[19] ("Four years ago we saw flying saucers above the Orinoco"). While at first Carpentier thought they were meteorites, after he saw a representation of flying saucers in *Life* magazine, he changed his mind.

Although irony, of course, cannot be ruled out as a possible interpretation of Carpentier's declaration about flying saucers, this piece is somewhat of an exception among those published in *Letra y solfa*, in that it does connect the local realities of the Orinoco River to anxieties about the global future. In fact, the postwar years and the atomic threat of an emerging Cold War yielded a number of disillusioned articles for this column. Only four months after publishing his piece on flying saucers, Carpentier wrote, "Ante las informaciones que hablan de nuevas pruebas atómicas, de velocidades supersónicas, de bombas de hidrógeno, el hombre moderno se muestra más melancólico que maravillado" (*Letra y solfa*, 138; "In the face of news about new atomic tests, supersonic speeds, hydrogen bombs, modern man finds himself more melancholic than amazed"). By April 1954, his fears had not abated: "Se nos dice que los científicos, situados en auténtico plano de Apocalipsis, se entregan a experimentos cuyas consecuencias finales no pueden preverse" (180; "They tell us that scientists, fully situated on the plane of the Apocalypse, throw themselves into experiments whose final consequences cannot be predicted").

Such worries shared space with some enthusiasm for what Carpentier saw as mounting evidence that flying saucers actually exist and for the possibility of space travel in the relatively near future, especially after an aeronautics conference held in 1956, which he repeatedly invoked. Nevertheless, these remarks do configure a whole arena of concern regarding the future of the planet that is quite distant from America's marvelous reality. To a certain extent, the reality of flying saucers, the atomic threat, and space travel could itself be considered marvelous, and Carpentier often expressed his amazement at it, albeit usually in a dystopian fashion. What this reality does not share with the American marvelous reality, however, is the unpredictability of its future consequences. These planetary concerns mark a horizon of uncertainty in Carpentier's writing—a realm of fear, speculation, and hope. As such, his combination of enthusiasm for and pessimism about a future guided by technical progress reinforces the constitutive ambivalence, in his fictional and essayistic writings, of praise for the persistence of an isolated area in an increasingly integrated world. Such ambivalence is at play in the very title of *Los pasos perdidos*, where the fact that the "steps" are lost, at least to the inhabitants of a claustrophobic modernity, means both that such realities are safe from harm and that it is impossible for such outsiders to reach them. While the marvelous reality of Haiti, the Mexican ruins, or the Venezuelan jungle of *Los pasos perdidos* all seem sheltered from outside interference and its risks, the fact that the steps of the title are lost adds to this invulnerability a dimension of fictionality: because they cannot be found anymore, they must live only in the pages of the book.[20]

Before this fictional dimension attained its more sophisticated version in the novel, however, its features started taking shape in the author's journalistic articles. In the 1952 piece "El Mundo del Tiempo Detenido" ("The World of Stopped Time"), some motifs of *Visión de América* and *Los pasos perdidos* appear in the form of the indigenous musical instruments that Carpentier saw in the Exposición Médico Etnográfica (Medical-Ethnographic Exhibit) in Caracas's Museum of Natural History: "Todo esto, fascinante, misterioso y magnífico, es la Gran Orquestra de la Selva, la que escucharon nuestros antepasados más remotos, un poco después del Sexto Día de la Creación, que sigue sonando en el Mundo del Tiempo Detenido" (*Letra y solfa* 117; "All this, fascinating, mysterious, and magnificent, is the Great Orchestra of the Jungle, the one heard by our most remote ancestors, a little after the Sixth Day of Creation, that keeps sounding in the World of Stopped Time"). Any changes this world may undergo thus follow a predetermined order from which they usually cannot deviate: they exist in a state of isolation whose doors, like those of the novel's jungle, are seldom open to the reality of deforestation and exploitation in the region.

The Venezuelan Guiana and forested portions of the Orinoco were present in Carpentier's column from its inaugural moments in 1951. These areas appeared more frequently in 1952, when Carpentier was arguably more connected to them during the composition of *Los pasos perdidos*. In these articles, Carpentier makes a series of references to more recent works on the forest, thus offering a different archive than the colonial chronicles and nineteenth-century accounts privileged in the novel and prevalent in criticism of it.[21] Articles by New York's *Geographic Magazine* on Angel Falls, Arthur Conan Doyle's *Lost World*,[22] an exhibit by Caracas's Natural Science Museum (*Visión de Venezuela*, 4), Jules Verne's novel *The Mighty Orinoco* (1898; 29–31), the account of Alain Gheebrant's travels in 1948–50 (33–38): all make up the alternative, more recent cultural history of the Guiana that Carpentier outlined in his column.[23]

These columns also suggest how Carpentier's views made their presence felt in a Venezuelan realm. Published in the widely circulated *El Nacional*, these almost daily columns were easily available for a much larger public than the limited reading audience of *Los pasos perdidos*, originally published in Mexico and received with suspicion by Venezuelan critics and intellectuals.[24] While the novel enjoyed a successful reception elsewhere and even prompted Tyrone Power's attempted Hollywood film adaptation, Carpentier's scattered yet persistent articles on the Venezuelan Guiana in *Letra y solfa* provided a parallel environmental imaginary of the region specifically for Venezuelan readers.[25] Considering his eccentric position as a foreign author working as an advertising executive, this column constituted a privileged place from which to circulate his views, seven decades after another Cuban, José Martí, had also had a newspaper column in Caracas.[26] Carpentier's case is different from that of Clarice Lispector (see chapter 4), a Ukrainian who immigrated to Brazil at an early age and, having written all her work on Brazil, saw her foreignness often linked to her singular style. Coming from a nearby country with the same language, Carpentier's foreignness probably would not have allowed him to write a national classic as Rómulo Gallegos did, yet he was not perceived as exotic in the way Lispector was.

But the Venezuelan Guiana was not the only area that drew Carpentier's attention: pieces on Caracas were perhaps even more frequent, and also reflected the divergence noted above between the author's anxieties on a planetary level and lack thereof on a local one. In the short piece "El clima y las modas" (Climate and fashion), published in the same year as the novel, Carpentier notes the apparent change in temperature over the decades in urban centers such as Caracas and Havana due to urban growth, potentially because of deforestation, the increasing number of cars and heat-accumulating materials, rivers drying out, and so on. In spite of that, "cuando cotejamos los índices de temperatura y humedad, . . . observamos, con alguna sorpresa, que las cifras han sufrido muy pocas modificaciones—cuando aparece alguna" (*Letra y solfa*, 168; "when we compare temperature and humidity rates, . . . we realize, somewhat surprisingly, that the figures have suffered very few changes—if any at all"). There is no record of what sources he might have consulted, if any. Yet, he concludes, "Esto nos lleva a preguntarnos si esa noción de que la temperatura de las ciudades nuestras 'era más fresca en otros tiempos,' no proviene de una disposición física que el hombre ha ido perdiendo con los años" (168; "This begs the question of whether this notion that the temperature of our cities 'used to be cooler,' does not result from a physical disposition that man has been losing with time"). If this conclusion that recent generations are simply more sensitive to heat, rather than that temperatures are rising, would please not a few of today's climate denialists, in Carpentier's context it does not go beyond a witty commentary on a problem still relatively small. Ironic or not, this piece gives a sense of how distant local realities were from global ones in the author's writings, even when known processes of local environmental degradation are explicitly mentioned, as in "El clima y las modas."

All these pieces suggest a disjuncture between Carpentier's "sense of place" and his "sense of planet," to use Ursula Heise's terms to describe the tension "between the commitment to a planetary vision and the utopian reinvestment in the local" that marks modern environmental movements and is implied in a number of cultural objects.[27] This tension is, in its own way, latent in Carpentier's fictional and nonfictional writings. While the planetary concerns discussed here were largely relegated to the background, American forests as a whole are an integral component of his intellectual project through the concept of the *real maravilloso*. In this context, the forests' particular temporality, functioning, and closed nature, which are at odds with the pace of modern cities and military uncertainties, allowed a powerful imaginary framework of tropical nature as static and self-sufficient to take hold even as this image was occasionally tainted by the intrusion of modernizing forces. As such, the jungle provided a counterpoint to another natural resource that played an instrumental role in the political and social dynamics of Venezuela from the early twentieth century to the present. That resource is oil, and it has shaped the narratives of both progress and prosperity. Oil is the natural body fueling the political body that, as Fernando Coronil has showed, powered the image of a magical state covered in petrodollars: "The Venezuelan state has presented itself as the miracle worker that could turn its dominion over nature into a source of historical progress."[28]

LOS PASOS PERDIDOS

In 1953, Alejo Carpentier revisited the *novelas de la selva* genre by taking his unnamed protagonist to a compact, independent, forested world where, as a result of the area's often unpredictable dynamics, cities and other human settlements might just as easily disappear as grow.[29] As "novels of the jungle" do, *Los pasos perdidos* draws on the way the jungle fascinates and changes human characters.[30] Carpentier tells a story of a Latin American man living in a metropolis in the Northern Hemisphere, who, after traveling to the depths of the tropical jungle, supposedly to collect indigenous musical instruments for his former mentor's ethnographic collection, tries to leave everything behind to live and compose music there but is prevented from doing so by circumstances both from the metropolis and in the forest. Throughout this narrative, Carpentier provides profoundly rich, attractive descriptions of the mysterious, mesmerizing world of the jungle. Moreover, he manages to dramatize the tense opposition between the metropolis and the forest in a way that reflects on claustrophobic life in modern cities and the need for escape, unattainable as it may be. The novel thus emphasizes the impossibility of evading modern life or finding permanent shelter from it. But how does the image of the forest in *Los pasos perdidos* contribute to a discourse of environmental conservation in Venezuela?

> Cubriendo territorios inmensos—me explicaba—, encerrando montañas, abismos, tesoros, pueblos errantes, vestigios de civilizaciones desaparecidas, la selva era, sin embargo, un mundo compacto, entero, que alimentaba su fauna y sus hombres, modelaba sus propias nubes, armaba sus meteoros, elaboraba sus lluvias: nación escondida, mapa en clave, vasto país vegetal de muy pocas puertas. (*Los pasos perdidos*, 164)

> Despite the vast area of the jungle—he explained to me—embracing mountains, abysses, treasures, nomad peoples, the remains of lost civilizations, it was, nevertheless, a world compact, complete, which fed its own fauna and its men, shaped its own clouds, assembled its meteors, brought on its rains. A hidden nation, a map in code, a vast vegetable kingdom with few entrances. (*The Lost Steps*, 126)

The references to immensity, the "vegetable kingdom" with its mountains, all correspond to a Romantic notion of wilderness quite common in nineteenth-century accounts of European travelers in America. This Romantic allusion is underscored by Carpentier's mentions of European travelers in *Visión de América*, most notably the Schomburgk brothers and Alexander von Humboldt.[31] Wilderness here means a world relatively untouched by human presence, a world before humans, or, as William Cronon somewhat ironically puts it, "the last remaining place where civilization, that all too human disease, has not fully infected the earth."[32] In this Carpentier follows another powerful trope of the *novelas de la selva* according to which the jungle, as Fernando Aínsa proposes, is "a closed and therefore mysterious world, . . . a conflict-filled space par excellence,"[33] where poetic creation is enhanced.

Such isolation, however, does not preclude past and present human occupation, even though both the "remains of lost civilizations" and "wandering peoples" who are presented in a stylized fashion clearly contrast with the reality of the Pemon and other indigenous groups actually living in the area at that time and today. This same contrast can be identified in the analogical web through which parts of the jungle materialize particular periods of world history or, still according to Aínsa, "diverse historical periods that coexist in separate compartments."[34] Human presence and the compartmentalization of time complicate the dynamics of stability and change in the forest, which are both understood as independent of outsiders' interference and, to a certain extent, independent of any human action at all. Such representations reinforce the view of the forest as a microcosm easily detachable from the rest of the country and, indeed, the world. As I will propose, this view coincides with and contributes to the conservationist narrative of Venezuela.

Crucial to the gaze developed in *Los pasos perdidos* is the narrator's analogical eye, which constantly draws parallels between either the jungle and Western cultural objects or the jungle and periods of "world" history as conceived in the West:

> Allá, detrás de los árboles gigantescos, se alzaban unas moles de roca negra, enormes, macizas, de flancos verticales, como tiradas a plomada, que eran presencia y verdad de monumentos fabulosos. Tenía mi memoria que irse al mundo del Bosco, a las Babeles imaginarias de los pintores de lo fantástico, de los más alucinados ilustradores de tentaciones de santos, para hallar algo semejante a lo que estaba contemplando. (223)

> Beyond the gigantic trees rose masses of black rock, enormous, thick, plummet-sheer, which were the presence and the testimony of fabulous monuments. My memory had to recall the world of Bosch, the imaginary Babels of painters of the fantastic, the most hallucinated illustrators of the temptations of saints, to find anything like what I was seeing. (171)

Analogy is unavoidable, yet its power is limited. It is often the only tool the narrator has at hand to make sense of the world around him. More than that, the forms of the jungle, its "roots" in their literal and metaphorical senses, all seem to suggest these analogies and to offer themselves up as the equivalents of recognizable styles, allusions, and myths. Even though this analogical operation does not always suffice, such as in the moments when the narrator recognizes its limits in the face of the marvelous forest, it remains a basic mechanism for making sense of the jungle environment.[35] Moreover, the narrator's analogical gesture attempts to assert some form of control. As such, it implies a precariousness that mirrors what Mark Millington has called the performative dimension of a masculine ego in crisis:[36] the narrator styles himself "an 'hombre macho' in the jungle, [but] his gender identity is more precarious than that of any other character in the novel."[37] If Lesley Wylie has pointed out how frequently a character such as Rosario is associated with "nature" through a telluric vocabulary in the novel's criticism,[38] I contend that the way in which this character's behavior constantly both reaffirms and questions the narrator's ability to perform a hypermasculine self is echoed by his incessant yet necessarily incomplete attempt to make the jungle familiar through analogy.[39]

These analogies coexist with the other major analogical gesture of the novel, according to which the novel becomes, in the words of González Echevarría, "a compendium of world history read backwards."[40] In other words, the deeper the narrator goes into the forest, the farther back he goes in time until he reaches "el mundo anterior al hombre" (*Los pasos perdidos*, 241; "the world that existed before man," *The Lost Steps*, 186). His slow progress by boat is quickly reversed on his way back to the country's capital, after he boards the airplane sent to the jungle to rescue him:

> Los cincuenta y ocho siglos que median entre el cuarto capítulo del Génesis y la cifra del año que transcurre para los de allá, pueden cruzarse en ciento ochenta minutos, regresándose a la época que algunos identifican con el *presente*—como si lo de acá no fuese también el *presente*—por sobre ciudades que son hoy, en este día, del Medievo, de la Conquista, de la Colonia o del Romanticismo. (299, Carpentier's emphasis)
>
> One hundred and eighty minutes, returning to the epoch some identify with the present—as though this were not the *present*, too—flying over cities that today, at this very time, belonged to the Middle Ages, the Conquest, the Colony, or the Romantic era. (234, Carpentier's emphasis)

This coexistence of temporalities, a major mark of the *real maravilloso* for Carpentier, unfolds in a reasonably linear fashion, as successive periods of time occupy contiguous spatial units of the forest.[41] Formed by an organizational pattern rooted in a static past, this "compendium of world history read backwards" conveys a sense of the forest as a container for an already crystallized world history that it constantly reenacts.

This analogical operation could arguably be read, on the contrary, as an extreme example of Timothy Morton's ecomimesis, as it unsuccessfully attempts to represent a nature "out there" in textual space and tries to make sense of this nature by invoking the very categories that only announce, from the beginning, its nonexistence in a pure state.[42] Without denying that there are examples of ecomimesis in the novel, it is worth asking to what extent this "world history compendium" anticipates Morton's objection to environmental literature and criticism in the period before the early 2000s. After all, if the narrator admittedly cannot convey a sense of the immediacy of nature without relying on Western categories to quite artificially organize it, isn't he already taking a step beyond the ecomimesis that Morton criticizes? Isn't Carpentier already, in an instance of what Morton calls critical ecomimesis, questioning "the gap between content and frame" (*Ecology without Nature*, 144)? Consequently, though the novel relies on Romantic tropes in its moments of nature writing, that does not erase the ironic dimension of this gesture; through the temporal encapsulation of spatial units, Carpentier makes evident his awareness of the impossibility of making nature transparent via text. In fact, in *Visión de América*, the author refers to "las rutinas imaginativas de mi cultura occidental" (21; "the imaginative routines of my Western culture") to mark the impossibility of representing American nature as it is; he still alludes to a nature "out there" more fit for other eyes but establishes a layer of mediation between his descriptions and what he sees.[43]

Beyond the "compendium of world history read backwards," there are also in the novel points of convergence between the forest and its cities that challenge the view of the jungle as a purely "virgin world." From the suburbs of Los Altos to the lack of urban areas as the group travels deeper into the forest, many layers of villages, ruins, and settlements suggest a parallel environmental history of the Amazon that denies neither human inhabitation nor human disappearance in past historical periods.[44] This long history of human and nonhuman interactions functions as a powerful critical tool against the drawbacks of a conservationist view based on the idea of an untouched "lost world."

At the same time, the interactions between humans and forest unfold at a slow, almost imperceptible pace, especially as the narrator approaches its deeper reaches. At numerous moments, in fact, stasis is overwhelming: "Todo era silencio e inmovilidad. Era como si una civilización extraña, de hombres distintos a los conocidos, hubiera florecido allí, dejando, al perderse en la noche de las edades, los vestigios de una arquitectura creada con fines ignorados" (*Los pasos perdidos*, 179; "All was silence and repose. It was as though some strange civilization of people different from those we know had flourished there, leaving, as they were swallowed up in the night of ages, the vestiges of an architecture designed for unknown purposes," *The Lost Steps*, 138). This passage is telling, insofar as it emphasizes both the unchanging nature of the forest and the broader history of human presence gradually taken over by it. In either case, the result is the forest as an independent microcosm that, from an outside perspective, appears static. If, on the one hand, "la selva era el mundo de la mentira, de la trampa y del falso semblante" (215; "the jungle is the world of deceit, subterfuge, duplicity," 166), when the narrator pays closer attention to them, the general feeling of stillness pervades and gives an architectural aspect even to the clouds in the sky: "Esas nubes, rara vez enlazadas entre sí, estaban detenidas en el espacio, como edificadas en el cielo, semejantes a sí mismas, desde los tiempos inmemoriales en que presidieran la separación de las aguas y el misterio de las primeras confluencias" (217; "These clouds, rarely joined together, were as though suspended in space, as though part of the sky, resembling themselves since time immemorial, when they watched over the separation of the waters and the mystery of the first coming together of the rivers," 167).

If, in this passage, the denotational and metaphorical branches of the narrator's perception of the jungle seem to converge, in others they are sharply divergent. A significant moment takes place in Santa Mónica de los Venados, the would-be city where the narrator would have established his new home had circumstances permitted him to stay. Santa Mónica is a village composed of a dozen huts that, nevertheless, has a Plaza Mayor and a Casa de Gobierno (*Los pasos perdidos*, 245); its leaders live in a state of legislative frenzy even as a church is being built. While this might seem an indisputable sign of growing urbanization in the area, when the narrator asks the founder, Adelantado, "qué haría si viese aparecer en Santa Mónica, de pronto, a algún buscador de oro, de los que manchan cualquier tierra con su fiebre. 'Le daría un día para marcharse', me responde. 'Este no es sitio para *esa gente*', acota Marcos" (269, Carpentier's emphasis; "I asked the Adelantado what he would do if one day a gold-hunter were to appear in Santa Mónica, one of those who spread their fever wherever they go. 'I would give him one day to get out,' he answered. 'This is not the place for *those people*,' added Marcos," 209, Carpentier's emphasis). In fact, the Adelantado carefully conceals Santa Mónica from the gold hunter Yannes before returning to the city in chapter 5. As with the figural dimension of Santa Elena de Uairén, Santa Mónica's founders seek development that moves teleologically from village to colonial town and involves establishing a bureaucratic order. As this passage suggests, however, Santa Mónica's development is closed to and does depend on one of the most typical sources of urban growth in the Amazon in the first half of the twentieth century: the exploitation of gold and diamonds that, as Rogers explains, was instrumental in Santa Elena's expansion from the late 1930s on and that Carpentier noted in his trip to the city.[45] In "este continente de naturaleza todavía invencida por el hombre" (244; "this continent on which nature had not yet been subdued by man," 189), a city could exist only as long as it "no figure en los mapas, que se sustraiga a los horrores de la época, que nazca así, de la voluntad de un hombre, en este mundo del Génesis" (244; "did not appear on maps, was withdrawn from the horrors of the epoch, was born of the will of a man, in this world of Genesis," 189). Resonating with what Carpentier has written about Santa Elena's founder, Lucas Fernández Peña, this reference to "los horrores de la época" seems to allude to the atomic threat and reinforces the disillusionment with modern life expressed in the author's articles, complemented by Santa Mónica's near nonexistence for outsiders as a town that does not appear on maps, a town on the verge of being fictional.

The town's failure to appear on maps notwithstanding, the novel progressively effaces geographical referents as it portrays the forest as a separate world. After leaving the town of Los Altos to start the journey on behalf of the Museo Organográfico that would eventually lead him to the forest, the protagonist arrives in the Valle de las Llamas, which corresponds to the El Tigre region that Carpentier visited on his second trip, one of the first and main areas of oil extraction in the Orinoco basin:[46]

> Ya me habían hablado algunos, durante el viaje, de la población nacida allá abajo, en unas pocas semanas, al brotar el petróleo sobre una tierra encenagada. . . . Sobre una llanura pelada, era un vasto bailar de llamaradas que restallaban al viento como las banderas de algún divino asolamiento. Atadas al escape de gases de los pozos se mecían, tremolaban, envolviéndose en sí mismas, girando, a la vez libres y sujetas a corta distancia de los mechurrios. (132)

> I had already been told, during the trip, of the town that had sprung up here in a few weeks when oil began to gush from the marshes. . . . A bare plain was the setting for a vast dance of flames crackling in the wind like the flags of some divine conflagration. Run up by the escaping gases of the wells, they fluttered, came together, swirled, coiled around themselves, free and yet joined to the exhaust pipes. (101)

This is a border region between the forest and the countryside areas visited earlier in the novel. It does accommodate rapid urban growth, as the passage above shows, yet this description of the oil fields does not exactly emphasize the oil-fueled modernity that El Tigre was to make possible. Instead, they constitute a picturesque spectacle, with a long description of dancing flames whose magical aspect still does not point clearly to the state as a "great alchemist" that transforms oil into wealth.[47] If the mere presence of oil fields may sound uncanny in a novel like *Los pasos perdidos*, Carpentier's description ties them more to the separate world of the jungle than to Venezuela's economy at large, as in *Jungle Oil* or *Petroleum Geography of Venezuela*. This transformation of oil fields into a marvelous event in a village that has rapidly sprung up marks a threshold, an entrance into the forest whose dynamics seem detached from those of the nation.

A double movement can thus be identified here, through which the jungle spatializes temporal units that correspond to stages of world history, while it also has its own, independent history, one that outsiders, who often mistake it for a static landscape, can only perceive in glimpses. This landscape is not devoid of human presence: cities are founded here, and natural resources are exploited. Yet, these interactions seem to occur in a parallel realm quite independent of their ramifications in the reality outside the forest. Both movements add an allegorical layer to the forest, yet allegory is not enough to explain the author's assumptions about the Amazonian environment.

As a spatialization of time, a key word for understanding the forest's functioning and organization is *conservation*, but not exactly conservation in the sense that the environmentalist movement later used the word, as Carpentier was not advocating an environmental agenda when he published this novel. Rather, the narrative conservation I refer to here has two elements. The first is the preservation of a collective environmental memory through descriptions of the forest. The second is the representation of the forest as a self-sufficient microcosm that conserves spatialized layers of world history while allowing for a dynamic of change that most outsiders do not notice. While deforestation is hardly present in Carpentier's vocabulary as either a novelist or a journalist, the narrative conservation of the jungle in *Los pasos perdidos* coincides with the development of a history of environmental conservation in Venezuela.

LOS PASOS PERDIDOS IN VENEZUELA'S HISTORY OF ENVIRONMENTAL CONSERVATION

In February 1992, two years before UNESCO declared the Gran Sabana a World Heritage Site, 1,800 experts on conservation and related areas drafted the Caracas Declaration, a plan and manifesto to raise environmental awareness and urge governments, companies, local authorities, organizations, and individuals to push for more protected areas. Formulated a few months before the United Nations Earth Summit in Rio de Janeiro, the Caracas Declaration was the offspring of the Fourth World Congress on National Parks and Protected Areas.[48] These fruitful years for conservation in Venezuela were nevertheless part of a longer history.

Early environmental conservation efforts were fundamentally indebted to Swiss naturalist Henri Pittier, who moved to Venezuela in 1917 and remained there until his death in 1950. As a result of his "intense conservationist movement," which eventually received the support of then-president Eleazar López Contreras, the first Venezuelan national park was created in February 1937.[49] Originally named Rancho Grande, it was later renamed Henri Pittier. A second park in a nearby area, Agustin Codazzi, was created in Aragua State in July 1944, a few months before Carpentier arrived in the country.[50]

The author enjoyed traveling to this region, as his *Letra y solfa* essay on the Valles de Aragua, "La jornada del estrépito," shows. In this piece, he complains about changes modernization has brought to the area, although not so much to the landscape as the soundscape: the jukeboxes that allowed people to listen to fashionable tunes were ruining the majestic atmosphere of the valley (*Letra y solfa*, 157–58). A more interesting piece is "Los nuevos vándalos," in which the author complains about tourists who were beginning to visit "una maravillosa y escondida playa del litoral venezolano" (148; "a marvelous and hidden beach on the Venezuelan coast," 148) where he used to spend weekends. He stopped going there when "la arena se llenó de latas vacías, de papeles grasientos, de frutas podridas, de basuras de toda índole" (148; "the sand became filled with empty cans, greasy papers, rotten fruit, garbage of all types"). He further criticizes this irresponsible behavior by mentioning that the United States was then spending $228 a day to keep Yellowstone National Park clean—at that time, this was a sizable amount. The trash and the jukebox were, for the author, "una odiosa plaga, demasiado frecuente en nuestra época" (149; "an odious plague, too frequent in our time"). These pieces and the writings analyzed above suggest Carpentier's views about Venezuela's environment. His enthusiasm for it is evident, and he expresses environmental concerns on a local level, insofar as degradation affects him and other visitors in search of aesthetic experiences of nature. However, this does not seem to translate into more substantive environmentalist principles or actions.

In 1941, after participating in the 1940 Washington Convention, Venezuela formalized the juridical status of the national park and established a common nomenclature for preserved areas, such as national reservations, natural monuments, and reservations of virgin regions, through a series of laws that allowed for the creation of new protected areas.[51] By the time *Los pasos perdidos* was published, besides the aforementioned parks, Venezuela had created a third in 1952, the Sierra Nevada National Park, and two natural monuments, Alejandro Humboldt (Cueva del Guácharo) and Arístides Rojas (Morros de San Juan), both in 1949.[52] The establishment of protected areas gained momentum from the 1970s on, especially with the formal creation of the Sistema de Parques Nacionales (National Park System) in 1973.[53]

The development of a conservationist structure was thus still in its infancy when Carpentier lived in Venezuela. In fact, no national parks or natural monuments were established in the Amazonian region until Canaima National Park was founded in 1962, three years after the author's return to Cuba. Until then, all the preserved areas were located in the north and northwestern portions of the country. *Los pasos perdidos* therefore should be seen not as a result of a broader movement of environmental protection and awareness, but rather as an early piece that may have contributed to the very development of such a movement.

The 1940s and 1950s were a crucial period for the expansion of both oil production and its associated environmental effects.[54] While national parks were concentrated in the north, the devastation resulting from intense oil extraction had caused complaints for decades in the Maracaibo Lake region.[55] These environmental effects occurred alongside and often paled in comparison to the dominant place of oil in Venezuelan ideas of progress throughout the twentieth century—an ambiguous progress, it must be said, that has often put into question the country's sovereignty given the persistent presence of foreign oil companies, mostly North American, since Juan Vicente Gómez's dictatorship from 1908 to 1935.[56]

Venezuelan intellectuals and politicians had repeatedly warned against excessive dependency on oil; Arturo Uslar Pietri's 1936 pledge to "sembrar el petróleo" ("sow the oil") was a particularly successful motto. According to Uslar Pietri, oil should not constitute Venezuela's main source of revenue but rather provide the means to enable a more diversified version of progress: "Urge aprovechar la riqueza transitoria de la actual economía destructiva para crear las bases sanas y amplias y coordinadas de esa futura economía progresiva que será nuestra verdadera acta de independencia" ("It is urgent to take advantage of the transitory wealth of the current destructive economy in order to create the healthy, comprehensive, and coordinated base of that future progressive economy that will be our true act of independence").[57] Interestingly, this sentence follows his statement of concern about the uncontrolled cutting of balata trees to provide coal, so that his critique brings together the environmental and economic impacts of overreliance on oil.

Meanwhile, the Amazonian region had been suffering other kinds of exploitation. In the Bolívar state where the Gran Sabana is located, this took the form of logging, dam building, the extraction of gold and diamonds, and polluting rivers, including the Orinoco, with the mercury used to pan for gold.[58] Resources particularly targeted were iron, bauxite, gold, and diamonds. This area was already very fragile due to poor soil and the high concentration of endemic species.[59] It was therefore especially vulnerable to environmental loss due to extractive activities.[60]

While the effects of human activity have become more visible in recent decades, this intensive exploitation of Amazonian resources was seen as a strategic way of reducing the national economy's excessive dependence on oil by politicians such as Rómulo Betancourt, president of Venezuela from 1959 to 1964.[61] In fact, less than a month after he created Canaima National Park, Betancourt announced the beginning of steel production in the Guiana by the Siderúgica del Orinoco program, which would free Venezuela from "la peligrosa situación de país cuya economía y finanzas públicas dependen casi exclusivamente del petróleo" ("the dangerous situation of the country, whose economy and public finances depend almost exclusively on oil").[62] A typical example of Betancourt's perspective on the Guiana can be seen in the speech he gave at the inauguration of the Universidad de Oriente in Cumaná in May 1960: "La Guayana de los próximos años ya no será la Guayana de los carreros de Upata, de Guayana del balatá y de la sarrapia, sino la Guayana del hierro, del acero, del aluminio, la Guayana donde fabricaremos tractores y automóviles, la Guayana que se convertirá en el epicentro de la industria nacional" ("The Guiana of the next few years will no longer be the Guiana of the cart drivers of Upata, the Guiana of balata rubber and the sarrapia tree, but rather the Guiana of iron, of steel, of aluminum, the Guiana where we will manufacture tractors and automobiles, the Guiana that will be transformed into the epicenter of national industry").[63]

Amid these industrializing projects, Canaima National Park was created on June 12, 1962, through a decree, signed by Betancourt, in which the tropes of beauty and uniqueness are the only reasons cited for the park's creation: "Una zona de incomparable belleza destacándose en ella el Salto Ángel y el grupo de montañas conocidas como Tepuis" ("A zone of incomparable beauty in which Angel Falls and the group of mountains known as the Tepuyes are highlights").[64] Beyond the importance of the deity Canaima in the Carib tradition, the park's name is also an obvious homage to Gallegos's eponymous novel.[65] One of the most prominent writers in Venezuela and onetime president of the country, Gallegos was Betancourt's political ally in the Acción Democrática. Carpentier was well aware of Gallegos's work, and even based his character Marcos on *Canaima*'s protagonist Marcos Vargas, as González Echevarría shows,[66] besides mentioning this novel in his typed travel notes about the trip.[67] In spite of the relative prestige he enjoyed in Caracas, Carpentier, as a foreigner working in advertising, could not rival a writer-statesman like Gallegos in his influence on the establishment of national landmarks.

More important, however, is the geographical location of the park. *Canaima* is set in the region of Ciudad Bolívar and Upata, to the north and west of the park's actual location. Although the jungle where Marcos Vargas gets lost is southeast of these cities, it most likely is not far south enough to be within the park's current limits. In contrast, a significant portion of the plot of *Los pasos perdidos* unfolds within the area later devoted to the park and its surroundings. Carpentier himself indicates this in the novel's closing "Nota" when he mentions the Gran Sabana, "cuya visión se ofrece en distintos pasajes de los Capítulos III y IV" (358; a vision of which is to be found in different portions of chapters 3 and 4," xvi), and clarifies that Santa Mónica de los Venados is based on the actual city Santa Elena de Uairén, which now borders the park, in its early days. Even though it is not possible to affirm in objective terms that the novel and Carpentier's newspaper articles inspired the creation of the park, it is undeniable that *Letra y solfa*'s popularity, as well as the broad dissemination of *Los pasos perdidos*, with numerous editions and translations coming out in the years following its publication, contributed to the fame of the area, whose literary resonances are clearly stated in the park's name.

All these factors suggest that *Los pasos perdidos* arose at something close to a turning point in the history of conservation and environmentalist awareness in the region. It was published when conservation initiatives that would later expand were slowly developing. The novel thus acted as another element in that expansion, insofar as it helped give visibility to areas that would be protected later on. The many conservationist narratives at stake in the expansion of such initiatives, I contend, feed on the larger set of images, affects, and curiosity inspired by the forest conserved in fiction.

NARRATIVE CONSERVATION

In his study of how nonliterary archives shaped the modern Latin American novel, González Echevarría dubs *Los pasos perdidos* "the founding archival fiction": "*Los pasos perdidos* is an archive of stories and a storehouse of the master-stories produced to narrate from Latin America."[68] As Lúcia Sá has demonstrated and as the articles in *Letra y solfa* suggest,[69] the scope of the novel goes beyond the colonial chronicles and nineteenth-century travel diaries that formed its archive for González Echevarría: a variety of indigenous and nonindigenous sources participate in the continuous creation and reformulation of a repertoire on the Guiana and specifically on the Gran Sabana region. In the twentieth century, this repertoire included sources from popular culture, among them novels, films, and TV series. To a certain extent, *Los pasos perdidos* offers a critical counterpoint to the most openly neocolonial components of these materials while partially participating in a certain neocolonial attitude that, as Mary Louise Pratt has argued, enables "a unique self-creation rather than a poor reflection of Europe."[70] In one way or another, González Echevarría's image of a warehouse is useful for making sense not only of the archive identified by the Cuban critic but also of the broader range of materials on the Guiana that the novel activates and is activated by. These materials, I argue, are crucial to the formation of an environmental memory of the Gran Sabana that—though partially constructed outside of the area itself—nonetheless affects it through environmental policies.

In his discussion of the term *environmental memory*, Lawrence Buell has pointed out "the possibility that literature and other expressive media might act as carriers of environmental memory over against the inertial force of what the environmental psychologist Peter Kahn, Jr., has called 'environmental generational amnesia.'"[71] Literary mimesis is thus put in the service of conserving certain views of the environment that may offer a counterpoint to perceived degradation. In cases where generations see their local realities undergo drastic transformation, literary works, especially when seen as realistic portrayals of these areas, can have the role of "dramatizing reality,"[72] to use Luiz Costa Lima's term, inasmuch as they contrast different temporalities.

One might ask how literary mimesis can conserve environmental memory in cases where readers are distant from, or completely unfamiliar with, the referential reality of represented environments. After all, such a major landmark of the Gran Sabana as Angel Falls was not photographed from the ground until 1949, when Ruth Robertson did so in an expedition that for the first time took precise measurements of the falls' length and allowed pictures of it to circulate around the world following their publication in *National Geographic* in November of that year.[73] In the broader realms of national and transnational perceptions of the Gran Sabana, "environmental memory" is fundamentally indebted not so much to direct experience as to mediation through an array of works, from travel diaries to novels, films, and TV series, that have made and continue to make possible an imaginary of the region. This memory remains visible even in works that, like *Jungle Oil* and *Petroleum Geography of Venezuela*, demonstrate an internal conflict between attraction to the idea of wild nature and the desire to see it exploited. This heterogeneous and evolving set of materials, whose political and social agendas may conflict, points nonetheless to a certain mode of experience of the area, scattered and sometimes hardly perceivable, yet common to the environmental perspective of these works. They may be read as parts of a structure of feeling as Raymond Williams understands it: as social experiences "at the very edge of semantic availability,"[74] which do not conform to "fixed forms and units" (130), which may indeed pose challenges to "formally held and systematic beliefs" (132), yet are lived just as much by those who read Richard Schomburgk's travel account and those who watch Disney's 2000 movie *Dinosaur* as by those who founded Canaima National Park and those who visit it.[75] All those readers, visitors, and spectators are presented with an image of the forest as precious, which, I argue, reinforces the case for maintaining it in its current state.

Nonetheless, contrasts persist and abound. For example, a reader of *Los pasos perdidos* might be surprised to learn that Santa Elena de Uairén, the real city behind the bucolic village of Santa Mónica de los Venados, is now an island of relative prosperity amid the current economic crisis in Venezuela, largely due to the illegal reselling of Venezuelan oil to Brazilians who cross the frontier in search of cheaper gas.[76] Not a few readers might also be surprised to find out that the tepuyes of Mount Autana mentioned in the novel remain reasonably preserved, not due to some form of mysterious isolation in which they are still immersed but rather because of the creation of conservation units, such as natural monuments, to protect them.[77]

If Kahn's "environmental generational amnesia" is indeed in for a shock when it runs up against the realities represented in fictional works, such friction between represented and referential realities would be minimal, if not entirely lacking, in the absence of a referential reality to make the comparison possible. In other words, it does not matter that a movie such as the 2009 Disney-Pixar production *Up* still represents the twenty-first-century Gran Sabana as a nineteenth-century traveler might have seen it, since most of the film's viewers do not have a sense of the twenty-first-century Gran Sabana and thus cannot question *Up*'s portrayal of it.[78] But what is a national park if not a real-life attempt to conserve an area in a way somewhat similar to that of literary conservation?

Let us summarize and expand some points about the nature and definition of national parks presented in the previous chapter. National parks were created to preserve certain environments due to either their beauty or the need to address the degradation of vulnerable areas. They are meant to preserve or re-create a nature untouched by humans, at the same time as they are used for the enjoyment of humans—especially white humans. As Alison Byerly shows, the paradox is clear, since an area that receives visitors will necessarily no longer be devoid of humans. A wilderness such as Yellowstone National Park "designates an area that 'appears' to be affected primarily by nature, one in which man's imprint is present but 'substantially unnoticeable.' It describes an image, not a reality."[79]

Consequently, national parks try to re-create environments as they would have looked before deforestation or human presence. This is the case even in parks such as Canaima, which allows Pemon villages to persist inside the park's boundaries, allowing, according to a 2000 estimate, "the approximate presence of 95 indigenous communities and possibly more than 8,000 inhabitants."[80] At the same time, most parks also allow nonindigenous people to enter for scientific research and tourism. Therefore, national parks aim to recreate the appearance of an untouched nature and, in doing so, to recover an environmental memory of a certain area before the arrival of nonindigenous humans. Even when there are indigenous groups in the area, they are often seen through an idealized gaze that, as Luis Angosto Ferrández shows, insists on ignoring their gradual inclusion in capitalist economies and instead relegates them to an ancient temporality, in what Johannes Fabian has called a "denial of coevalness."[81] Instead of what Pierre Nora has coined *lieux de mémoire*, national parks are *lieux avant la mémoire*.[82]

This reconstruction, of course, would not be possible without the careful work of environmental engineering that manages and maintains this supposedly untainted nature. An example can be found in Canaima's 2007 Final Plan, where the difficulty of accessing certain areas is presented as a problem that the park's maintenance department needs to address. If the plan were really to keep it a "lost world," wouldn't this difficulty of access in fact qualify it as an "untainted" area? National parks, in this sense, constitute an effort to "civilize nature," as proposed by Bernhard Gissibl, Sabine Höhler, and Patrick Kupper: "This established notion of civilization as human progress through growth-oriented development at the cost of nature was countered by a conservationist view of civilization as an idealist endeavor that respected the aesthetic, ecological and social value of wild nature. Protecting and valuing nature in its raw, untransformed state became a property of being civilized."[83]

I argue that this maintenance of an "untransformed" appearance entails a fictionalization of the protected area through which a certain environmental imaginary is applied to it and becomes its aim. In *Fictional Worlds*, Thomas Pavel proposes understanding fictions as secondary universes that integrate a dual structure, whose base or primary universe is the real world: "I shall call *salient* structures those dual structures in which the primary universe does not enter into an isomorphism with the secondary universe, because the latter includes entities and states of affairs that lack a correspondent in the former."[84] These secondary universes are understood as possible worlds in the terms of modal logic, that is, as alternative states of affairs that maintain a certain relation with other possible worlds, including the real one or *base*.[85] Religion is a good example of this dual structure and shows that such possible worlds are not necessarily understood as fictions. Fictional texts also work, although differently, as salient worlds that may include components that do not exist in the real world or that shed light on some aspect of it that is not usually perceived.

The question to ask in the case of a national park in a remote area like Canaima—and it was even more inaccessible when the park was first created—is the degree to which the secondary, fictional universe might shape the very notion of the primary universe.[86] In other words, to what extent is the area upon which the imaginary boundaries of the park are to be set seen as "raw nature" precisely because of the continuous portrayals of this area in cultural products *as* "raw nature"? In the absence of access to a primary, existent world, the secondary, fictional world takes precedence in determining how the primary universe looks and should continue to look. If the idea of establishing a protected area already implies a certain view of nature to which referential reality has to conform, this process becomes even more dependent on external perspectives in the case of an area both hard to access and frequently portrayed in cultural objects, like the Gran Sabana. Therefore, the antithetical combination of cultural attention and difficulty of access puts this salient, fictional world of the Gran Sabana in a privileged position to intervene in the expected state of affairs in the real world.

The specific impact of a single work on consequent policies may vary significantly. In the case of Grande Sertão Veredas National Park, its imaginary was problematically built on its namesake novel as well as an ideal of untouched nature. Unlike *Grande sertão: Veredas* and its park, *Los pasos perdidos* did not directly inspire the creation of Canaima National Park. Official documents about the park do not mention the novel, and its influence may be perceived only indirectly, especially in areas with notable landmarks not mentioned in the book, such as Angel Falls and Mount Roraima. Yet the numerous descriptions analyzed above of the forest, either within or outside of the Gran Sabana area, as marvelous and uncanny may well work as carriers of a specific view of the region that the novel both participates in and propagates. More than that, *Los pasos perdidos* clearly places the forest in a separate realm, where self-sufficiency is coupled with an apparent stasis that only obscures a series of cycles and transformations hardly perceptible to outsiders. Not only is the jungle mimetically conserved in the novel, but there seems to be a fairly clear border dividing its domain from the rest of the world.

Nonetheless, the appearance of stillness does not mean an actual pause. As shown above, Carpentier's jungle finds itself in perpetual motion, which often reveals a long history of exchanges and mutual interactions among human and nonhuman actors. These changes include the destruction as well as the creation of cities, in a deviation from the common understanding of deforestation and urbanization as unilinear phenomena. Moreover, their manifest randomness and relative indifference to the purposes of outsiders become evident when the narrator, after having gone back to the northern metropolis, is prevented from returning to the forest by a flood that has covered the marks in a tree trunk signaling the entrance to Santa Mónica de los Venados.

The analyses of two novels and two national parks undertaken in the previous chapter and in this one show how narrative conservation and conservationist narratives complement each other. Narrative conservation encompasses the representation of environments in fictional works. Narratives such as *Los pasos perdidos* and *Grande sertão: Veredas* thus become carriers of environmental memories that remain active through generations and may reverberate in other cultural objects and projects. All the cultural objects about a certain environment compose a structure of feeling, a set of lived experiences that advocates for keeping it as it is or re-creating it as it once was.

In their turn, conservationist narratives are the fictionalizing operations by which parks come to be seen as "raw, untransformed" nature, even when this pristine state is only achieved through comprehensive interference in the area, whether through the removal of local populations and destruction of settlements, fire management, animal and plant control, or trail and road construction. These two modalities of interpenetration between conservation and fictionality mutually benefit each other. Fictional narratives may raise environmental awareness and promote conservationist initiatives, while national parks and other conservation units fuel the environmental imaginaries of these areas. At the same time, *Los pasos perdidos* and other novels may introduce critical parameters that allow readers to perceive, for example, a longer history of human and nonhuman interaction, rather than assuming that these environments are simply "untouched."

By making this argument about the relationship between national parks and fictions, I surely do not mean to imply that national parks are fictions, or that they have any undesirable artificiality that should be rejected, or that they lack any form of legitimacy. To be sure, cultural objects do not have the same kinds of effects as does the actual maintenance of parks, which is a fundamental form of twentieth- and twenty-first-century environmental policy. Fictional works do not have the power to establish and alter policies and management practices, nor do they intervene directly in the referential reality of the park.

Yet fictional works may help in developing a set of fictionalizing operations that justify the objectives of parks, legitimize their existence, and make them more visible. This is especially true in a park of literary inspiration such as, again, Grande Sertão Veredas, but a similar conservationist mentality not seldom based on fictionalized images of pristine environments is at work in virtually any park.[87] In fact, even parks that do not have cultural objects specifically attached to them, that are not portrayed in books, films, or TV series, and that may even be known only to a small portion of the local populations also benefit from this broader environmental imaginary that fuels a longing for untouched nature to exist.

The years Carpentier spent in Venezuela were preceded and succeeded by a series of conservation initiatives in the country, yet conservationist discussions were not widespread enough to capture the attention of a writer otherwise quite interested in the Venezuelan Guiana, not only as a source of personal fascination and delight but also as one of the major sites for the development of one of his most influential concepts, the *real maravilloso*. In this sense, Carpentier's writings on the Guiana, and especially *Los pasos perdidos*, participate in a transnational imaginary of the Amazonian forest and the Gran Sabana not many years before actual steps to conserve the area started to be taken, and have, together with other cultural products, contributed to the appreciation of its "incomparable beauty," which justified the creation of the park.

While the previous chapter traced a direct connection between a novel and specific conservationist efforts and institutions, this chapter has shown how narrative conservation develops in Carpentier's Venezuelan writings and, in doing so, converges with the conservationist narratives that grounded and fostered the expansion of protected areas worldwide. The novel reinforces a view of the jungle as a self-sufficient world separate from larger urban areas—a view that was and would continue to be of paramount importance for the very concept of national parks and protected areas—at the same time as the novel's dimension of change and interaction between humans and nonhumans offers a critical counterpoint to this idea. In parallel fashion, conservationist narratives depend on fictionalizing operations that benefit from environmental archives, of which Carpentier's writings are a component. His and other words attest, in different forms and with different objectives, to how the Gran Sabana, isolated from a world marked by strong desire for social and economic development as well as by anxiety and uncertainty amid the atomic threat and the space race, remains an enduring presence in a global environmental imaginary.

PART II

Development

CHAPTER 3

Juan Rulfo's *Pedro Páramo* and the Green Revolution

Modern Literary and Agricultural Dilemmas

In 1955, *Pedro Páramo*, Juan Rulfo's only novel, was published by the Fondo de Cultura Económica. That same year, Rulfo worked as a photographer during the shooting of Roberto Gavaldón's film *La escondida* (*The Hidden One*) in the state of Tlaxcala. One of Rulfo's on-set photos from the film show the protagonist, played by actor Pedro Armendáriz, among maguey leaves, wearing a traditional Mexican outfit and staring at the sky meditatively.

Three years later, a similar picture, *Beans, Corn, Wheat*, was taken by the Rockefeller Foundation as part of the Mexican Agricultural Program (MAP) it had sponsored in partnership with the Mexican government since 1943. Instead of replicating Armendáriz's contemplative gaze, the rural worker in this picture smiles at the camera as he presents a bag of potatoes, ostensibly harvested as part of the increasingly modernized agricultural infrastructure in certain areas of Mexico where the MAP conducted research. Interestingly, he and his bag of potatoes are not set in a field where such a harvest might have taken place, nor are they in front of a warehouse or truck where potatoes might be stored or transported. Instead, the image includes the same elements that compose Rulfo's photograph of Armendáriz: the beautiful forms of the maguey

Figure 2: Actor of *La escondida* among maguey leaves. Courtesy of Fundación Juan Rulfo.

leaves, a relatively arid countryside, and some mountains in the background. The title of the picture alludes to *milpa*, a traditional method of rotating corn, beans, and squash, but in this instance squash is replaced by the MAP's star crop, wheat.[1] The man's outfit is more contemporary than that of Armendáriz's character, yet it includes traditional elements. The men in both images are relatively displaced: the center of Rulfo's picture is occupied by the maguey leaves that also cover the left half of it, whereas the second photograph centers the bag of potatoes.

While *Beans, Corn, Wheat* was almost certainly not inspired by Rulfo's photographs of *La escondida*, the image's semiotic components make visible a desire to integrate a recently developed agricultural modernity with what were seen as traditional elements of Mexican culture and landscapes. But how does this project look when placed alongside

Figure 3: *Beans, Corn, Wheat*. Photograph. Rockefeller Foundation Records. Courtesy of Rockefeller Archive Center. https://rockarch.org/.

a broader cultural imaginary and iconography of the Mexican countryside? Rulfo's works provide a productive standpoint from which to approach this question: both his on-set images and the MAP photograph resonate with *Pedro Páramo*'s landscape and with the dry, melancholic tone of the novel's characters. While *La escondida* is considered part of the Golden Age of Mexican cinema, *Pedro Páramo* constituted a landmark of Mexican literature and was perceived as a key work for understanding the "new novel" in Latin America, as well as the Boom literature that brought the region to the center of an international literary market in the following decades. Meanwhile, the so-called Green Revolution promoted by the pioneering MAP had a profound, albeit ambiguous, impact on food production in Mexico and in a number of other countries in the mid-twentieth century, leading to what Angus Wright has called the "modern agricultural dilemma,"[2] to which the title of the present chapter alludes.

The literary modernity so celebrated in Rulfo's early reception was permeated by images of a devastated, empty, dry countryside in an early-twentieth-century revolutionary and postrevolutionary Mexico, which, in *Pedro Páramo*, was contrasted with the verdant, fertile lands prior to the fall of the cacique (local boss) and of Porfirio Díaz.[3] In parallel, before the MAP's high costs to the environment and public health became obvious, the Mexican model was considered a success to be copied worldwide. On the one hand, a prolific output of literary works, films, and other cultural products had for decades powerfully reflected on Mexican rurality. On the other, the promise of prosperous agricultural production fueled dreams of a future that would diverge strikingly from the Mexican landscape as it was portrayed in these very works. As with Carpentier and the history of conservation in Venezuela explored in the previous chapter, *Pedro Páramo* and the Green Revolution illuminate some common dilemmas and address related contexts even though the link between them is not direct. The novel and the project of agricultural modernization both participated in shaping ambivalent ideas of Mexican rurality as a locus for social and technical modernization and as an enduring emanation of the imagined community of Mexico.[4]

While the previous two chapters explored fictional works, conservation efforts, and the fictionalizing operations that connect them, the second part of this book focuses on the relationship between fiction and processes of environmental change—specifically, between *Pedro Páramo* and agricultural modernization in this chapter, and Clarice Lispector's *A cidade sitiada* and urban growth in the next chapter. The mimetic dynamics at stake here do more than generate spectral archives of ways in which referential reality might be accessed and nostalgically preserved or recovered, as in the first two chapters. The spectral quality of mimesis in *Pedro Páramo* and *A cidade sitiada* instead interplays with the proleptic movement of developmentalist utopias: among the ghosts and ruins of *Pedro Páramo*, a past perceived as archaic also announces, and to a certain extent warns against, a future in the making. This catastrophic prolepsis, activated in different yet parallel ways in *Pedro Páramo* and in *A cidade sitiada*, leads to scenarios of confinement and ruin from which living beings are expelled. The novels' counterpoints to and points of convergence with the Green Revolution or urban growth may offer what Gabrielle Schwab has called an "imaginary ethnography of the future"[5] that continually reshapes social and psychic realities. Fictional environments, in this sense, emerge as nonactualized realities that question and haunt the painful realization of irreversible processes of environmental loss.

Usually understood and described under the broad rubrics of progress, modernity, and especially, development, the processes of urbanization and agricultural industrialization were both widely welcomed and sorely feared by the groups directly involved in them. The Green Revolution conjured up developmentalist perspectives in the agricultural arena, at the same time as the genre of the *novelas de la Revolución* (novels of the Mexican Revolution), as well as the larger body of works dealing with this moment and its aftermath, such as *Pedro Páramo*, both built on and contested postrevolutionary nationalist narratives. Views of agrarian Mexico took their most paradigmatic form in the context of the land reform implemented during the presidency of Lázaro Cárdenas (1934–40) and continued to evolve during the so-called Mexican miracle from the 1940s to the 1970s. Although *Pedro Páramo* and MAP did not stem directly from these ideas of rural Mexico, the novel's reception and the MAP's ramifications respond to them. This chapter compares their trajectories and the parallel views of modernity they convey on aesthetic and technical levels. By weaving together these key actors in the development of a Mexican Modernism and Mexico's modernization, this chapter, like the next one, explores the relationship between novels and transformations of the environments they represent through the lens of mid-twentieth-century Latin American developmentalism.[6]

THE WRITER, THE TRAVELER

The film *La escondida* is an adaptation of Miguel N. Lira's 1947 novel of the same name, a later example of what came to be known as the *novelas de la Revolución*. *Pedro Páramo* was published in a literary context of simultaneous exhaustion of the genre and stabilization of a canonic corpus in the 1960s.[7] A diverse range of authors with differing levels of education and literary recognition penned works dealing with the revolution, including its origins and aftermath, during the deepening of conflict in the 1910s and throughout the decades that followed. This genre represents, in Max Parra's words, "a novel process of social introspection, which begins to provide patterns for cultural recognition, marks of identity for a country that was in the process of reconstituting its social fabric."[8] In the 1930s and 1940s, the *novelas de la Revolución* were increasingly recognized as part of a nationalist cultural imaginary also made up of the visual arts, especially *muralismo* and the period known as Golden Age of Mexican cinema, but the genre's codification took a decisive turn with the 1960 publication of the anthology *La novela de la Revolución mexicana* (*The Novel of the Mexican Revolu-*

tion), edited by Antonio Castro Leal.[9] A commercial success with numerous reprints, this anthology not only helped keep the genre alive in readers' minds but also established a more precise canon. While Castro Leal set a chronological limit of 1947 that excluded Rulfo's works, it is worth noting that the genre was in vogue and receiving much attention when *Pedro Páramo* was published.[10]

The inclusion of Rulfo's work among the *novelas de la Revolución* has been a contentious topic due to its formal innovation, which was perceived at the time as another type of revolution: the prime example of a Modernist Mexican literature seen as diverging from the documentary tone usually associated with revolutionary novels.[11] Regardless of where Rulfo's fictional works are placed in literary periodizations, they do closely engage in dialogue with the genre that constitutes an important background for his early reception.[12] The same can be said of novels based on agrarian conflicts whose tone and style connect them to this tradition, such as José Revueltas's *El luto humano* (1940; *Human Mourning*, 1990) and Agustín Yáñez's *Las tierras flacas* (1962; *Lean Lands*, 1968), or even novels of the Boom's later wave that nevertheless are (partially) set in revolutionary times, such as Carlos Fuentes's *La muerte de Artemio Cruz* (1962; *The Death of Artemio Cruz*, 1964).

While in conversation with and read against the background of this larger corpus that constructs a national identity based on the revolutionary event,[13] *Pedro Páramo* also draws upon and seems to allude to a later context. In his famous interview with Luis Harss published in *Los nuestros*—a volume that helped establish the canon of the *nueva novela hispanoamericana* in the 1960s—Rulfo often brings up rural workers in Jalisco abandoning the countryside and migrating to larger cities. While mentioning major contributing factors such as human displacement during the revolution and the Cristero War and injustices in land distribution during the 1930s land reform,[14] he pays special attention to soil erosion due to unsustainable agriculture practices. Right after referring to Jalisco as the country's biggest producer of corn, Rulfo notes, "El maíz es un gran destructor de la tierra. Entonces, la tierra está destruida. A grado tal que en ciertas regiones ya no hay tierra. Es una erosión completa" (63; "Corn is a big destroyer of the soil. So, the earth is destroyed. To such a degree that in some regions there is no soil. It's total erosion"). This phenomenon is, for Rulfo, one of the primary causes of the state's rural depopulation: "Había un río. Nosotros nos íbamos a bañar en tiempos de seca en el río. Actualmente ese río no trae agua. . . . Los bosques en las montañas que rodean el pueblo—

encierran toda la zona en una herradura monolítica—han sido talados. Casi todo el mundo ha emigrado" (64; "There was a river. When there were droughts, we used to go bathe in the river. Now this river doesn't bring any water. . . . The forests in the mountains that surround the town—they enclosed the whole zone in a solid horseshoe—have been chopped down. Nearly everyone has emigrated").[15] Rulfo expressed similar environmental concerns about pollution in Mexico City when, at the end of his life, he signed the manifesto of the Grupo de los Cien mentioned in the introduction.

Far from being merely old memories of a Rulfo who had been installed in Mexico City for years by that point, these impressions of Jalisco came from someone who, for most of his life and most intensely in the years prior to writing *Pedro Páramo*, traveled around the country. From 1947 to 1952, Rulfo traveled constantly as a tire salesman for the Goodrich Euzkadi Company,[16] an opportunity that seemed to fit well with his interest in Mexico's history and geography. Besides work-related travel, he was also a hiking and mountaineering enthusiast, belonged to the Everest Club, and climbed some of the country's major summits.[17]

Rulfo quit his job at Goodrich Euzkadi to accept a fellowship from the recently created Centro Mexicano de Escritores (Center for Mexican Writers; CME), which provided him a precious opportunity to focus solely on writing from 1952 to 1954.[18] Directed by U.S. writer Margaret Shedd and initially financed by the Rockefeller Foundation, CME became one of liveliest literary institutions in Mexico in the 1950s and remained so throughout the next couple of decades. Despite being financed in part by the Mexican government and in part by the Rockefeller Foundation, and later by the CIA-connected Farfield Foundation in an effort to promote non-Communist writers during the Cold War, the center's fellows remained reasonably independent both of the United States' anti-Communist agenda and of pressure from the Mexican government.[19] Its explicit agenda in its inaugural years, as Patrick Iber shows, was to promote high-quality, distinctively Mexican literature using the model of the creative writing workshop and creative writing techniques popular in the United States. "Shedd also tended to identify 'technique' as one of the major 'American contributions to the Centre,'" writes Patrick Iber, who notes that the foundation paradoxically did not at first want to give the center an obvious U.S. imprint.[20] By sponsoring the development of specifically Mexican literary work with formats and techniques from the United States, therefore, the CME's initial model was intriguingly similar to that of the MAP itself and conforms to the idea of an export literature, as described in the introduction. The results of the two programs, however, clearly diverged, given the stylistic independence and diversity, as well as the various political agendas, of the CME's actual fellows and their literary works.

In 1955 and 1956, Rulfo was a member of the Comisión del Papaloapan, a large-scale water management initiative that sought to control floods while generating hydroelectric energy.[21] After signing the con-

Figure 4: In a report written during his time at the Papaloapan Commission, Rulfo twice mentions the ecological problem of the slash-and-burn practice that was widespread in the region, since the slopes were eroding rapidly. One of the commission's objectives was to end this practice and replace it with irrigated agriculture in the low and flat lands. Photograph by Juan Rulfo documenting the problem. It was supposed to appear in a commission magazine, edited by him, that never came out. Courtesy of Fundación Juan Rulfo.

tract to join the commission as *Pedro Páramo* was being printed, Rulfo, as Víctor Jiménez relates, devoted a good portion of 1955 and 1956 to a project in which his environmental concerns took on their most concrete dimensions.[22] The commission was fundamentally occupied with the consequences of deforestation in the region under the "roza, tumba y quema" system (slash-and-burn agriculture), which quickly erodes the soil, making it unproductive after a few harvests, and causes land sedimentation, flooding, and uncontrolled fires.[23] The group tried to put in place alternative agricultural practices to address these problems. As a member Rulfo documented this situation both through reports and photographs, in which he registered the devastation wrought by slash-and-burn practices.[24] This and other works place Rulfo at the crossroads of modernizing projects in Mexico, contributing to them at the same time as he pointed out their shortcomings.[25] In a certain sense, his views sketch what could be considered, in contemporary vocabulary, an earlier form of sustainable development.

At the same time, Rulfo remained keenly interested in Mexican history, as a number of interviews and accounts, as well as the volumes in his personal library, show. Some examples of interest for the present discussion are the texts, compilations, and pictures that Víctor Jiménez collected in *Juan Rulfo: Letras e imágenes*.[26] By copying descriptions of religious buildings from catalogs such as the "Catálogo de construcciones religiosas del estado de Hidalgo (1940–2)," Rulfo not only gathered representations of landscapes similar to that of *Pedro Páramo* but also added sentences to these passages that make them further resemble Comala, the town in the novel. Recurrent additions to the original text that mention ruins and destruction are evidence of Rulfo's interest in the degraded state of the buildings in such catalogs. While writing about the church of Tlayacapan, for example, he notes that "las celdas y otros compartimentos presentan un aspecto *de la más desoladora destrucción, y la obra ruinosa de los años deja ver sus huellas en este enorme conjunto almendrado*" (Rulfo, *Letra*, 36, Jiménez's italics; "The cells and other compartments present an aspect *of the most desolate destruction, and the ruinous work of the years shows its tracks on this enormous ornamented edifice*").

From such a setting emerges *Pedro Páramo*. The story of the landowner and cacique Pedro Páramo, who sought to establish complete control over his estate of Media Luna, the neighboring farms, and the nearby town of Comala, ends with his ruin after the loss of a son and the unhappy death of his insane childhood sweetheart, Susana San Juan.

Years later, the son he never met, Juan Preciado, travels to Comala in search of his father, only to find an abandoned, deserted place populated by ghosts, and with the whispers of the dead, whom Preciado will soon join, echoing in its walls. The contrast between fertile, prosperous Comala and the ruined land "en la mera boca del Infierno" (Rulfo, *Pedro Páramo*, 67; "at the very mouth of hell," 6), with "el puro calor sin aire" (119; "pure, airless heat," 5) forms the novel's spatiotemporal organization.

Pedro Páramo therefore responds to a much broader spectrum of concerns than merely those of the narrow time frame in which it is set. It resonates with Rulfo's thoughts about rural depopulation due in part to soil erosion caused by intensive, unsustainable agricultural practices. It incorporates Rulfo's firsthand experience as a traveler around the country. Finally, it takes a broad view of Mexican history as well as the ruinous remnants of forgotten pasts, among other historical elements. Because, as Rulfo said in interview with Joseph Sommers, "los muertos no tienen tiempo ni espacio" ("the dead have neither time nor space"),[27] the dead of Comala also inhabit an unspecified temporality of weak historical contours and wide temporal resonances. Consequently, *Pedro Páramo* combines elements of a genre that was received and publicized as emblematic of Mexican identities with an atemporal, insular perspective on the Mexican countryside, which echoes Rulfo's specific contemporary observations and concerns but seems to transcend temporal and spatial boundaries.[28] The documentary tone of its realistic conventions is tainted here by a spectral quality that makes the novel not only a commentary on the past and the present but also a potential warning about the near future. This amalgam of temporalities is at the core of what so many readers and critics, such as Silvia Lorente-Murphy and Manuel Ferrer Chivite, consider the novel's discussion and embodiment of the very idea of *mexicanidad*.[29] Besides initially aiming to address some of these same problems, the MAP also tried to speak the same cultural language as *Pedro Páramo*.

AGRICULTURAL MODERNITY ACCORDING TO THE ROCKEFELLER FOUNDATION

The trope of the dry, empty, devastated land, relatively common in the tradition of the *novelas de la Revolución*, is exacerbated in *Pedro Páramo*.[30] In spite of gloomy predictions about the fate of Mexican food production toward the end of Cárdenas's presidency, however, this view of the landscape as a desert stood in stark contrast to expectations for its bountiful agricultural production at the time of the MAP.[31] This program, whose international version would later be known as the Green Revolution, began in 1943 as a partnership among the Mexican and American governments and the Rockefeller Foundation, after U.S. vice president Henry Wallace visited Mexico. The MAP sent U.S. scientists hired by the Rockefeller Foundation to Mexico to improve agricultural productivity through research; this project was carried out in conjunction with the Secretaría de Agricultura y Ganadería (Secretariat of Agriculture and Cattle Raising). In this initial stage, the program began in a limited fashion. It received some land and personnel to develop laboratories, including its main headquarters in Chapingo, which was subsequently transformed into the International Center for Wheat and Maize Improvement (CIMMYT) in 1966.[32]

From its early years, the program had two objectives. The first was to eradicate hunger and fight poverty by investing in crops traditionally tied to subsistence in Mexico, most notably corn. As Olsson shows, the scientists brought in by the MAP were, for the most part, sensitive to the specificities of the country and not simply eager to import U.S. methods.[33] The second objective, however, was more in line with the development of Mexican agriculture for international export—which privileged wheat—in order to help the country industrialize, especially during the presidency of Miguel Alemán (1946–52).[34] The two crops on which the MAP's research focused, corn and wheat, thus reflected this double objective.[35] In fact, as Olsson shows, then-current racial theories, to which agriculture secretary Marte Gómez was sympathetic, suggested that a corn-based diet was responsible for poor health and lower levels of development among populations of indigenous origin, whereas wheat would provide the strength and health associated with white Americans.[36]

Another basic goal of the MAP was to develop insecticides. This effort relied on widespread use of DDT and was undertaken by a team of entomologists committed to eliminating a variety of common plagues and diseases, with an emphasis on wheat rust. Further chemical interventions mostly relied on nitrogen and phosphorous-based fertilizers capable of improving crop quality. The use of pesticides, which Rachel Carson had already denounced in the United States in *Silent Spring* (1962), would be key to later criticism of the program, such as in Angus Wright's work. Ultimately, advancing research was difficult, and small farmers and *ejidatarios* (owners of communal lands devoted to agriculture) resisted the improved seeds, fertilizers, and pesticides because of the vulnerable position in which distribution of such products placed them. All this led to the privileging of wheat as the MAP's centerpiece in the late 1940s and early 1950s; under the leadership of Norman Borlaug, the program developed quickly in larger commercial farms, especially in northern Mexico.[37] This was the model that prevailed and gradually replaced small and communal farms as the rural exodus and land concentration intensified in the following decades.

Increasing use of the MAP's technologies converged with and depended on a series of environmental changes stemming from attempts to reshape the country's agrarian structure and use of forests. From 1940 to 1970, the rate at which conservation units were created fell drastically compared to that of Cárdenas's presidency in the 1930s.[38] At the same time, laws and codes to regulate the management of unprotected forests were aimed at supporting rapid economic growth and industrial development. Some woods were conserved in areas near recently built dams, such as the Papaloapan project on which Rulfo worked, to help maintain them. While some dams were built to generate hydroelectric energy, others were built for large-scale irrigation projects that, in the end, favored the big farms in northwestern Mexico that had adopted the MAP's products more broadly than small farms and *ejidos*.[39] Artificial irrigation was considered a solution to a serious problem that Ávila Camacho's presidency had already tried to tackle in the early 1940s: soil erosion. Unfortunately, during his and subsequent governments, insufficient efforts and decreasing budgets did not properly address the problem. In the words of Lane Simonian, "Government officials decried soil erosion as a national tragedy but were not willing to make the prevention of soil erosion a national priority."[40] The period in which the Green Revolution flourished was also one of failed attempts to contain increasing deforestation and the soil erosion that alarmed Rulfo, particularly in areas with more vulnerable populations.

Let us return to the late 1940s and early 1950s in order to understand the prevailing MAP discourse, both of the U.S. outpost and of the Mexican agencies that managed seed and chemical distribution. A crucial agency is the Comisión del Maíz (Corn Commission), created in 1947 by Miguel Alemán's government.[41] This commission, in charge of distributing hybrid corn seeds to campesinos, attempted to convince them to adopt the new seeds by at times evoking a postrevolutionary rural iconography within a discursive framework of modernization and progress.

Figure 5: Agricultural show put on by Rockefeller Foundation, Cuernavaca, 1954. Photograph. Rockefeller Foundation Records. Courtesy of Rockefeller Archive Center. https://rockarch.org/.

The Rockefeller Foundation and the Comisión del Maíz published technical bulletins and informative pamphlets, organized agriculture days where rural workers could learn more about the program, put on exhibits such as those in Cuernavaca and Jalisco in 1954, and produced advertisements for the "sementes mejoradas" (improved seeds) designed by the highly esteemed Taller de Gráfica Popular [Workshop for Popular Graphic Art]. As Joseph Cotter notes, the initiative "did attract much attention [from Mexican farmers]. Attendance at MAP and SAF [Secretaría de Agricultura y Fomento, Ministry of Agriculture and Development] demonstrations grew from tens to hundreds to 1,000 to 2,500 per meeting as the Green Revolution spread."[42] At these exhibitions, explanatory tables and pictures were accompanied by baskets full of samples of the improved varieties of corn and wheat, in an attempt to make potential successes more palpable to the campesinos.

Complementing these initiatives is a series of woodcuts by the Taller de Gráfica Popular,[43] in which scenes of rural workers contemplating cornfields, holding large corncobs in their hands, or examining the harvest in front of a shack with a wife and child sitting by the door, were published alongside slogans such as "Si empleas la semilla híbrida que te proporciona la Comisión del Maíz, tendrás mejores resultados" ("If you use the hybrid seed that the Corn Commission provides you, you will have better results"); "Con igual área / con igual trabajo / con mejor semilla: / mayor producción" ("With the same area / with the same work / with better seed: / greater production"); "Las semillas mejoradas de maíz afirmarán tu futuro" ("The improved corn seeds will affirm your future"); "Puedes sembrar con mal suelo / Puedes sembrar con mal cielo / Puedes sembrar con agua / Puedes sembrar sin agua / NO PUEDES SEMBRAR SIN SEMILLA" ("You can plant with bad soil / You can plan with bad weather / You can plant with water / You can plant without water / YOU CAN'T PLANT WITHOUT SEED"; flyer's emphasis).[44] These pieces clearly intend to keep smallholding property owners as the protagonists of Mexican agricultural modernity. What needs to change is not the relations of production themselves but the very forms of production. These and other pieces suggest that the types of vulnerability feared by a *Pedro Páramo* character like Fulgor Sedano and always looming in Comala and Media Luna will no longer threaten future crops.

In fundamental ways, the narrative surrounding the Rockefeller Foundation's actions involves a discourse of modernization also employed in publicity pieces for non-Mexican audiences. Specifically, it is a typical narrative of modern rupture with a primitive past. "Blueprint for Hungry Nations," a *New York Times* article published on the first day of 1950 by Rockefeller employee George W. Gray, notes that

> Mexico was predominantly agricultural. . . . And yet, most of Mexican agriculture was operating at a miserably low level. . . . What to do, then, to help Mexico pull herself out of the agricultural doldrums? . . . They felt that the situation required a group of experienced agricultural specialists in full time Mexican residence "to cooperate with and advise the Mexican Department of Agriculture in its various activities."[45]

The image of a concise but efficient initiative touching off a revolution in production levels runs through the whole article and sets a very specific objective: for the corn grown in Mexico to look like the corn grown in Iowa.

In the same vein, *Mexican Agricultural Program*, an institutional short film commissioned by the Rockefeller Foundation in 1950, redirects its audience's expectations about Mexico by showing imposing landscapes that are replaced by fertile fields as the narrator speaks: "But this is not a visionary story of beauty and color, but a realistic effort to set down some hard facts of Mexican life and to trace a project that is dealing with these facts. That's why we go now from the snow-capped mountains to the hard-worked land below."[46] As a rural worker exposes a corncob and breaks it in half to pull off some kernels, the narrator continues: "His varieties of seed have not improved and his corn in some cases, like this primitive brown-seeded popcorn, is still the same corn which his ancestors grew centuries ago" (2). This display of Mexican corn's weakness and vulnerability to disease is followed by an explanation of how hybrid seeds developed by crossing different varieties of corn had resulted in the improved seeds that were revolutionizing Mexican agriculture. The hybrid seeds' curious name, Rocamex (a combination of Rockefeller and Mexico), suggests the foundation's desire to integrate its brand as a synonym for innovation with an affirmation of the seed's Mexican origin.

As these examples attest, the MAP fostered a narrative of agrarian modernization connected to a range of traditional motifs that took different forms depending on the audience. For a Mexican audience—specifically, for rural workers who might use the hybrid seeds—the idea of modernization was folded into a positive portrayal of the campesinos through the use of traditional images and an implicit defense of small farms and *ejidos*. For a foreign audience, however, the MAP emphasized the contrast between Mexican agriculture trapped in primitive methods and the revolutionary potential of technology. *Pedro Páramo* draws on similar images of the peasantry, both through its story of desertification that results from unsustainable practices and through its sympathetic representation of local populations. As the MAP increasingly privileged large properties and, as agronomist Jesús Uribe Ruiz puts it, "deformed and even worse de-Mexicanized agricultural research,"[47] the rift between the visions of modernity at stake in the novel and in the program only expanded.

AGRICULTURE: NARRATIVE AND DOMINATION

At first glance, *Pedro Páramo* might, in a number of senses, appear to provide a welcome complement to the narrative of modernization promoted by the MAP and the Mexican agencies sponsoring it. On one hand, the novel's literary modernity, which was so celebrated throughout its reception history, does make it a cultural counterpart of the Mexican Miracle insofar as it is a highly Modernist take on the *novelas de la Revolución* that, like *Grande sertão: Veredas*, was from early on conceived as universal.[48] On the other hand, the novel is permeated by images of an empty, dry countryside devastated by *caciquismo*'s abuses and unsustainable practices as well as by rural people abandoning the fields due to the Mexican Revolution and the Cristero War—in other words, images of the very conditions the MAP sought to address. If, as Marcos Natali concludes, thematically it is a story of death and devastation as much as "a portrait of a triumphal moment of the expansion of capitalism";[49] the novel also constitutes a groundbreaking moment in the very perception of a Latin American literary modernity.

In a recent article, Kerstin Oloff proposes reading *Pedro Páramo* as a gothic representation of the Green Revolution's rural exploitation. If, as Oloff proposes, "the anxieties that the gothic mode registers thus revolve around reorganizations of nature-society relations,"[50] the forms of environmental awareness implied by *Pedro Páramo*'s gothic tropes make visible what Oloff classifies, paraphrasing Fredric Jameson, as an "ecological unconscious."[51] *Pedro Páramo*, as a symbolic act that promotes a "rewriting or restructuration of a prior historical or ideological subtext,"[52] encodes contradictions arising from divergent perspectives on what constitutes a Mexican modernity. Going beyond this first horizon, the next section shows how the dialogic dimension of this symbolic act was "significantly modified and enlarged"[53] as the novel's reception in the following decades built on a process of "cultural 'universalization'" (72) that gave it hegemonic contours in a national framework. First, however, this section explores how *Pedro Páramo* offers a multifaceted view of agricultural modernization that makes it simultaneously a cautionary tale and an antithesis to the MAP's policies. In other words, the novel can be interpreted both as a parable of immeasurable hubris regarding land exploitation and a portrait of the failure of old agricultural modes in the context of land concentration.

Pedro Páramo embodies, first and foremost, the archetypical figure of the cacique—those who concentrated latifundia and local political power during the Porfiriato, some of whom resisted postrevolutionary efforts at agrarian reform. According to Rulfo's comments on his character, however, this *caciquismo* was at work even centuries prior to the arrival of the Spanish in America and then throughout the colonial period via the *encomenderos* (Spaniards who, in first decades of the colonial period, were granted the right to exploit natives' labor in a form of communal slavery).[54] Pedro Páramo thus incarnates the archaic yet resilient figure of the landowner who will exploit all the resources available, including humans, and will steal neighboring lands if their owners cannot properly defend them.[55]

As a cacique "made possible by uneven and combined development,"[56] Pedro Páramo determines the destiny of Media Luna and Comala and decides to take as much as possible from the land and its people.[57] Environmentally, he exploits resources seen as "cheap nature," in Jason Moore's terms.[58] Beyond this exploitation, however, a homological relationship between the cacique's body and his land becomes evident. Elsewhere I have proposed that the textual materiality of *Pedro Páramo* corresponds to three forms of spatial organization in the novel: the dry, infertile landscapes; the soundscapes of the dead's whispers; and the bodyscape of the cacique.[59] This last form is marked by the notable homology between the cacique's body, the land of Media Luna, and the text, in which the cacique's final fall—"se fue desmoronando como si fuera un montón de piedras" (Rulfo, *Pedro Páramo*, 178; "He fell to the ground with a thud, and lay there, collapsed like a pile of rocks," 124)—is equivalent to the fall of the land and to the end of the book. In other words, when Pedro Páramo, disillusioned by the fact that the Comala townspeople heard the bells announcing the death of Susana San Juan as festive, decides that "me cruzaré de brazos y Comala se morirá de hambre" (171; "I will cross my arms and Comala will die of hunger," 149), the town has no option but to follow suit.

The town's population, moreover, is connected to Pedro Páramo by blood, as many of its inhabitants are illegitimate children of the cacique: "Y es de él todo ese terrenal. El caso es que nuestras madres nos malparieron en un petate aunque éramos hijos de Pedro Páramo" (68; "He owns every bit of that land. We're Pedro Páramo's sons, all right, but, for all that, our mothers brought us into the world on straw mats," 7), says Abundio Martínez in the beginning, jumping from a description of the land to a direct reference to Pedro Páramo's fathering. Not only is he the owner of the area's main plantations, but his semen is also responsible for an apparently significant portion of its human inhabitants. The hypermasculine image conveyed by the cacique, in contrast to the precarious masculinity performed by the narrator of *Los pasos perdidos*, implies a convergence of sexual politics and land politics through which Pedro Páramo's control of Media Luna's female characters is equivalent to his control over land, so that his ascendancy over Media Luna's male inhabitants becomes genetically literalized.

In fact, the genetic influence of the cacique is but one component of the intimate connection between his body and the land that affects the very chemical composition of the soil, which acquires some of its owner's bitterness. "Allá en Comala he intentado sembrar uvas. No se dan. Sólo crecen arrayanes y naranjos; naranjos agrios y arrayanes agrios. A mí se me ha olvidado el sabor de las cosas dulces" (130; "I've tried to grow grapes in Comala. They don't bear. Only guavas and oranges: bitter oranges and bitter guavas. I've forgotten the taste of sweet fruit," 72), says Father Rentería to the priest before they comment that the land belongs to Pedro Páramo. In the same way, Susana's father warns her about what to expect upon a possible return to Comala: "Aquí en cambio no sentirás sino ese olor amarillo y acedo que parece destilar por todas partes. Y es que éste es un pueblo desdichado" (140; "Here there's nothing but that sour, yellowish odor that seems to seep up from the ground. This town is cursed," 83). Although the personality of the cacique permeates the very taste and smell of his land, his greed curiously does not seem to translate into a concern for his crops, delegated to his manager and *capataz*, Fulgor Sedano—who is well aware of the perils of unsustainable agriculture.

After Sedano's first meeting with Pedro Páramo upon the death of his father and the beginning of his ascent, in which it becomes clear that the orphan will do anything to increase his revenues, the manager leaves the hacienda asking himself whether he should keep his position at Media Luna. "Pero le tenía mucho aprecio a aquella tierra; a esas lomas pelonas tan trabajadas y que todavía seguían aguantando el surco, dando cada vez más de sí" (98; "But he loved that land: the barren hills that had been worked year in and year out and still accepted the plow, giving more every year," 38). *Lomas pelonas*, or "barren hills," alludes to natural or artificial elevations around the contours of which rows of crops are planted. Due to erosion, the top of the hill is the first portion to become unproductive—hence its baldness. Through Sedano's realization that the hills keep coping with the furrows and giving more and more of themselves, this passage underscores both the dangerously aggressive methods of farming in Media Luna and the threat of production shortages due to the exhaustion of fertility. The concerns Rulfo expressed in his conversation with Harss about severe soil erosion in Jalisco likely find an early iteration here.

If Pedro Páramo's apparent lack of concern about the limits of his land's productivity suggests unsustainable agricultural practices, he is equally unconcerned about harvest management. In the fragment where his only recognized son, Miguel Páramo, recruits Dorotea to find women to fulfill his sexual desires in exchange for food, Sedano listens to the young Páramo declaring that Dorotea will be as well fed as he himself. Shortly after, the manager goes to the barn to check corn storage levels:

> Llegó a las trojes y sintió el calor del maíz. Tomó en sus manos un puñado para ver si no lo había alcanzado el gorgojo. Midió la altura: "Rendirá—dijo—. En cuanto crezca el pasto ya no vamos a requerir darle maíz al ganado. Hay de sobra."
>
> De regreso miró el suelo lleno de nubes: "Tendremos agua para un buen rato." Y se olvidó de todo lo demás. (124)

> Fulgor went to the storage bins, where he could feel the warmth of the maize. He took a handful and examined it to see whether it had been infested with weevils. He measured the height in the bins. "It'll do," he said. "As soon as we have grass we won't have to feed grain anymore. So there's more than enough."
>
> As he walked back he gazed at the overcast sky. "We'll have rain for a good while." And he forgot about everything else. (65)

This type of calculation brings to light uncertainty about threats to crop storage. For Media Luna's harvest is, indeed, vulnerable to pests such as the weevil as much as to lack of rain. Mitigating this dependence on sheer luck, especially in regard to pests, was one of the major goals of the Mexican Agricultural Program. The fact that Media Luna ultimately depended on chance in feeding its own inhabitants gives a sense of how welcome pesticides were on large estates when the novel came out in 1955. But were Sedano's fears of food shortage well founded in a land like Media Luna, which was bound to follow its owner?

The uncanny relationship between the cacique and his land, as suggested above, shapes a parallel regimen of agricultural production in the novel. On the one hand, cultivation methods and external factors such as pests and droughts do pose risks to crops. On the other hand, given an owner so dominant that even his feelings are somehow reflected in the land, his moods and disillusionment constitute a distinct modality of threat. These two sources of degradation come together following Pedro Páramo's decision to abandon his land and burn his belongings after Susana San Juan's death: "Desde entonces la tierra se quedó baldía y como en ruinas. Daba pena verla llenándose de achaques con tanta plaga que la invadió cuando la dejaron sola" (137; "From that day on the fields lay untended. Abandoned. It was a sad thing to see what happened to the land, how plagues took over as soon as it lay idle," 80). The land is overcome not only by pests but by aches and pains resembling those of Pedro Páramo's elderly body. Moreover, the land is left in ruins, just like the religious buildings in Hidalgo that interested the author. These two conditions account for the two regimens to which the land responds: external factors intervening in it and Pedro Páramo's dominating influence.

Pedro Páramo is a story of excess. Its protagonist struggles for total domination over nearby lands, the local population's behavior, and even their feelings, besides expecting the land to keep yielding food despite methods that exhaust its fertility. His downfall is, then, also a failure of productivity reflected in the images of wasted land that permeate the novel. *Pedro Páramo*'s excess expresses itself through two vectors: the uncanny domination of a place through the homological relation between land and the landowner's body, and the rationalization of production under Sedano's management. Through the almost magical power concretized in the symbiotic relation between the land and its owner, Páramo reinforces a dictatorial authority over both things and people frozen in the same distant, objectified position.[60]

But what offers an example of the belief in total control over nature through science if not the Mexican Agricultural Program and the Green Revolution? The basic assumption underlying the MAP, after all, was not that the Mexican lands were good but underexploited, but rather that any land is potentially productive with proper management: that scientific progress is capable of canceling out agrarian limitations and making almost any land potentially fertile. As mechanized agricultural modernity gave rise to larger and larger conglomerates with transnational reach, domination over local populations that resulted in excessive exposure to pesticides, with all of its subsequent public health consequences, was but another facet of the same process of land control.

Comparing the novel *Pedro Páramo* with the Green Revolution thus underscores a common premise motivating both the cacique and the scientists: that the inevitable uncertainty of natural phenomena *can* be escaped through control over agricultural production. In other words, Pedro Páramo's political and economic influence over territory, as well as his magic control over land, finds some parallels in the forms of scientific control that the MAP developed. The two offer distinct yet concurring views about how land management can overcome nature's unpredictability.

The ironic underside of these examples is that both are also stories of how such control reveals a disturbing fragility manifested in its very practice. In the case of *Pedro Páramo*, his deliberate abandonment of Media Luna and Comala and their resulting desertification are the cacique's last acts in his desperation over the impossibility of dominating the only thing beyond his control, which is the heart of Susana San Juan. In the case of the Green Revolution, the intensive agriculture practiced in large areas of Mexico led to severe soil erosion and dependency on chemicals, such as fertilizers and ever-stronger pesticides. In this sense, during a peak period for the MAP, in which production was booming and the Rockefeller Foundation was promoting it as a model for other countries, *Pedro Páramo* offered a representation of devastated land as an alternative outcome, which, I contend, could be regarded as a cautionary tale for the program, rather than merely an antipode to agricultural modernity and a description of primitive methods to be overcome.

THE DECADES THAT FOLLOWED

The year 1970 brought important awards to two figures who helped shape twentieth-century views of the Mexican countryside: Norman Borlaug, who won the 1970 Nobel Peace Prize for helping eradicate hunger in the world by exporting the Mexican model to a number of developing countries in an effort to ensure North American control in a Cold War context;[61] and Juan Rulfo, who won the Premio Nacional de Literatura (National Literary Prize) that year. While Borlaug's Nobel prize was fiercely contested because of numerous environmental problems and social imbalances that were quite evident at the time, Rulfo's award could be seen as unsurprising for an author who, many claimed, also deserved the Nobel Prize in Literature.

The two prizes show how *Pedro Páramo*'s reception and the MAP continued evolving and gained new dimensions from the 1960s to the 1980s. Agricultural programs based on the MAP took more decisive, dramatic turns, while the novel grew in importance to become, more than a late classic of the *novelas de la Revolución* or an early classic of the Latin American Boom, a paradigmatic view of the rural Mexico that had been forgotten by central authorities and persisted in spite of twentieth-century land reforms. The cultural hegemony of *Pedro Páramo* and the agricultural hegemony of the Green Revolution carved different paths that nevertheless kept influencing perceptions of and dilemmas about the Mexican countryside. In the context of the "Mexican Miracle," the MAP's results, as Joseph Cotter notes, "produced food for industrial workers" and allowed "others to grow export crops to pay for imported machinery."[62] Around the time *Pedro Páramo* was published, the MAP was in its heyday: in 1956, Mexico became self-sufficient in wheat, and corn self-sufficiency followed shortly after. In the same period, the publication of *El Llano en llamas* and *Pedro Páramo* prompted a similar euphoria about the country's literary production. Jorge Zepeda shows how concerns about poverty and inequality as portrayed in Comala persisted in the novel's early reception together with attention, either enthusiastic or critical, to the formal novelties of these works. According to Zepeda, the major common point in early Mexican reviews and comments was "the constant reference to the updating of narrative techniques in order to effectively express the Mexican *reality*."[63]

The social and formal concerns of the novel's reception, whether on a national or Latin American level, took on new variations in the 1960s and the 1970s, as the novel was gradually incorporated into the canon of the "new novel" even as it continued offering powerful images of agrarian realities on a regional level. As early as 1960, for example, Peruvian novelist José María Arguedas found in Rulfo's work a model Peru ought to follow to give a literary voice to underrepresented populations. The Uruguayan writer Mario Benedetti expressed a similar opinion, praising Rulfo's literary works as "simultaneously 'modern' and 'committed.'"[64] In the same vein, an early collection of essays edited by Antonio Benítez Rojo in Cuba in 1969 included several pieces connecting Rulfo's fiction to the revolutionary spirit so prevalent in that context.[65]

This evolving critical corpus was coupled with the growing significance of Rulfo's novel in the cultural life of the country. After the initial publication of 5,000 copies in the 1950s by the Fondo de Cultura Económica (FCE), the first half of the 1960s saw 7,000 copies printed per year on average, a number that jumped to 16,000 copies per year from 1965 to 1969, 40,900 copies per year in the 1970s, and 44,500 copies per year in the 1980s.[66] These numbers refer only to the copies printed by the FCE and circulating in Mexico, and do not include other Spanish-language editions and translations.[67] They attest to the unique position that *Pedro Páramo* occupies—even in a study that aims to rethink the impact and consequences of canonicity for social and environmental purposes, as this book does. Among the works discussed here, Rulfo's novel is probably the one whose presence and influence is most insistent for the general public.

Such large print runs make sense, as the book became required reading in Mexican schools. For example, Daniel Sada, a writer deeply influenced by Rulfo, would later comment:

> In the 60s, I was living in Mante City, Tamaulipas, and there I read *Pedro Páramo*, in secondary school. The students talked a lot about the novel among themselves. We were around thirteen or fourteen, and they began to introduce it in our literature courses. It was one of my first incursions into the canon of Mexican literature. At that time, no one talked about other Mexican writers; Rulfo was the center of attention.[68]

According to Víctor Jiménez, this was around 1966 or 1967.[69]

Concurrent with this sharp increase in the number of copies of *Pedro Páramo* circulating in Mexico was the adaptation of Rulfo's work for the cinema. The novel was adapted twice, in 1967 and 1976, by Carlos Velo and José Bolaños, respectively. It is indeed curious that, in the former, Pedro Páramo, played by John Gavin, first appears dressed in a remarkably modern suit and tie that resemble those of modernizing agents decades later rather than the traditional outfits Gavin wore in the remainder of the film. A number of short stories and combinations of stories from *El Llano en llamas* were likewise translated to the screen: *Talpa* in 1955 (by Alfredo B. Crevenna) and *Los confines* (*The Confines*) in 1987 (by Mitl Valdez), as well as "*El gallo de oro*," adapted in 1964 by Roberto Gavaldón and again in 1985 by Arturo Ripstein as *El imperio de la fortuna* (*The Realm of Fortune*), among others.[70] Besides the cinematic spread of his work, Rulfo's photographs began to be gradually discovered; their exhibition at the prestigious Palacio de Bellas Artes in Mexico City in 1980 reinforced the images of rurality already present in his literary work.

These widely circulated Rulfian views of the countryside were often regarded as indices of Mexican rural landscapes in general. This trajectory is perceptible in the work of the aforementioned critics, as well as in influential essays such as Carlos Blanco Aguinaga's "Realidad y estilo en *Pedro Páramo*" ("Reality and Style in *Pedro Páramo*") or Rama's *Writing across Cultures*. For Neil Larsen, these and other works attest to the cultural hegemony of Rulfo's work, which dehistoricizes and neutralizes the possibility of historical change and in which the state is invisible "except in the negative image of its Other."[71] While I argue that this reading is not attributable to the "Rulfian narrative" itself [72] as much as to critics, readers, and epigones over the course of the decades, Larsen's study delineates a horizon of expectation on the part of the reading public, as well as nonreaders of Rulfo who might still be familiar with his fictional universe, in which his works provide direct access to a certain experience of culture that had become hegemonic.[73] The "universality" and unquestionable modernity of *Pedro Páramo* blended into a lasting image of Mexican reality. This understanding of the novel combined an ahistorical perspective on rural society as unchanging since colonial times with a dislocated view of Comala and Media Luna, which were transposed from the state of Jalisco to represent rural areas across the country. I propose that this reading remained a powerful aspect of the Rulfian imagination in the decades after the novel's publication, even as its plot allowed readers to position it in relation to historical events and linked it more broadly to the *novelas de la Revolución*.[74]

As shown above, the MAP's narrative was one of rupture with primitive agricultural techniques and with the uncertainty that pests and other external factors brought to production. In this sense, *Pedro Páramo* fit well into the MAP's perspective, as the novel represented old ways of farming and offered evidence that modernization was needed. The fear of food shortages, the hunger that some of Comala's residents faced, and low-yield crops were all issues that the MAP sought to address. The public face of the program, whether through fairs or intermediaries such as the Comisión del Maíz, counterpointed an appeal to traditional representations of Mexican campesinos with an emphasis on the need to adopt new techniques, as in the pamphlets discussed above and their images of rural workers and their families. As such, the MAP found in these motifs a language in which the progress and productivity of the *ejidos* emerged from uniting technological innovation with national tropes.

As the program developed and changed its focus from *ejidos* to big farms, and as its environmental costs and health problems related to agrochemical exposure became more obvious, the triumphal narrative of rural technological revolution began to unravel. The issue became more contentious as similar programs expanded to the different areas of the world as part of the Green Revolution. The case of Mexico remains emblematic: from the late 1940s onward, according to Raj Patel, "technocratic concerns trumped considerations of power and knowledge. The apparatus of the Green Revolution was an anti-politics machine."[75] While the increasing concentration of new pesticides, fertilizers, and hybrid seeds on larger farms, especially in the northern states, eventually led to the development of the contemporary agribusiness model, the expansion of the Green Revolution to Colombia, Brazil, India, Pakistan, and the Philippines, among other countries, took different forms that nevertheless resulted in similar patterns of land displacement, deforestation, and local exposure to agrochemicals.[76] The depoliticization of such initiatives on the local level, however, occurred alongside a larger U.S. geopolitical policy to shore up its influence around the world in the context of the Cold War.[77] The very name Green Revolution, coined in 1968 by William Gaud, an administrator at the U.S. Agency for International Development, was opposed to the Red Revolution in the socialist block and the White Revolution in Iran.

Yet resistance persisted in a variety of contexts. In Mexico, rural workers' rejection of MAP technologies was a major obstacle to its initial growth, as previously shown. In the late 1980s and early 1990s, publication of major critiques of the Green Revolution made more information accessible to a wider public. A vocal critic of the process in India has been Vandana Shiva, whose extensive work—debuted in the groundbreaking *The Violence of the Green Revolution*,[78] first published in 1989—has shown the harms and inequities the program inflicted on the Punjab region. The case of Mexico found its classic in *The Death of Ramón González*, in which Angus Wright traces possible links between the use of agrochemicals and the death of the eponymous worker in the region of Culiacán, in order to unfold a whole history of modern agriculture in Mexico and arrive at the "modern agricultural dilemma" that not only Mexico but any modernizing nation faces: "Can the pursuit of economic prosperity be made consistent with ecological health and some reasonable degree of human equality?"[79] This crucial question would continue to be present, even if in an implicit fashion, in most studies on the topic in the following decades.

FICTIONALIZING THE COUNTRYSIDE

As the Green Revolution and controversies about it became more evident and acute across a variety of social and environmental contexts,

Rulfo's works also came to influence broader layers of Mexican cultural life. While the novel obviously did not participate in the deleterious effects of the program described above, it offers approaches to how this fictional environment ought to be negotiated. Perhaps what is so powerful about Rulfo's work and the Green Revolution in Mexico is the extent to which they act upon a space, the Mexican countryside writ large, that has been such a crucial stage for postrevolutionary projects and desires. If the *novelas de la Revolución* have had an important role in shaping paradigmatic images of this space due to their typical focus on rural areas and small towns, both Rulfo's work and the Green Revolution in Mexico activate and reshape some of these images. As such, they were but two of the many layers of a space produced, in Henri Lefebvre's terms, through the superimposition of symbolic meanings, geographical factors, social interactions, and networks. As part of this larger lived space, both the novel and the program respond to two key issues that permeate traditional tropes of the countryside as well as modernizing projects for it. The first is land distribution, which is broadly explored in *Pedro Páramo* and which, in the form of concentration of land in large estates, uncomfortably accompanied the Green Revolution. The second is land fertility, a subject that haunted public debate about land reform, also extensively present in Rulfo's work, from the deserted landscapes of the novel to short stories such as "Nos han dado la tierra" ("They gave us the land"), and which was the MAP's primary target both as a scientific and, initially, a social problem.

Consequently, comparing Rulfo's work and the Green Revolution reveals a multifaceted view of a Mexican countryside carefully produced as a fictional reality capable of fueling a powerful range of imaginaries. From the implacable tyranny of the prerevolutionary caciques to the authentic yet modern Mexico cherished by nationalistic projects throughout the twentieth century; from hopes for a modernized agricultural bonanza that would also bring about social equality through a functional model for the *ejidos*, to the increasing land concentration, resistance to pesticides, and soil erosion that called into question the viability of the Green Revolution: all these vectors are mobilized by multiple views of what a Mexican rural modernity might look like. These periodically reenacted dilemmas point to the many narratives that give substance to these imagined and lived realities and, conversely, to how these realities continue fueling such narratives.

Such realities, however, do not remain the same over time. The environmental and social rift between *Pedro Páramo*'s images of rural

Mexico and the results of the Green Revolution as it unfolded over decades has thus seemed to widen over time but in a problematic fashion. The collective perception of *Pedro Páramo* as a repository of Mexican identities—in opposition to the mechanization of the countryside and the disintegration of the *ejidos* and other small farms—has contributed to this gap. As it promotes the image of a "archetypical town" among cornfields,[80] *Pedro Páramo* offers an imaginary counterpoint to these and other bitter aspects of rural change, one whose spectral quality questions and anticipates the dilemmas such change entailed.

Though the land was later devastated, Comala's past is also framed by a pastoral narrative of verdant fields and abundance won through a simple life and traditional agricultural techniques, which is in stark contrast with the agrochemical-dependent farms that came to symbolize the Green Revolution and, in a parallel movement to the one Raymond Williams analyzed, remains an appealing yet problematic trope for readers usually not well acquainted with rural realities.[81] Like the projects described in the first chapter, the rural images and contradictions mobilized by *Grande sertão: Veredas* as well as by *Pedro Páramo* give rise to the nostalgic view of a simpler, more authentic life in the countryside that persists across a range of historical periods, conflicts with the city, as Williams showed, and reveals the neocolonial exploitation of labor and environment taking place in the developing world.[82]

The Comala and Media Luna of the past thus seem to constitute a powerful chronotope, as Mikhail Bakhtin conceptualized it, corresponding to a "folkloric time" in which nature is "a living participant in the events of life,"[83] and not merely a "landscape, . . . [an] immobile dead background."[84] Albeit only part of the story, this nostalgic perspective remains, in my view, even though, as Beckman shows, "the social space of the novel is *already* modern,"[85] and it persisted in other literary developments after the collapse of the revolutionary agrarian project, such as the *narconovelas* narrating rural narcotrafficking-related violence in Mexico from the 1980s onward, which, as Paul Goldberg shows, describe the countryside in pastoral terms.[86] In consequence, the rift between the novel's fictional environment as understood in a broader cultural imaginary and the ongoing social and environmental transformations in an expanding portion of Mexico's rural areas is bound to grow.

Antithetical as the Green Revolution's purposes and *Pedro Páramo*'s exhausted land may seem, they find some points of contact. If the MAP initially aimed to put an end to the problems plaguing rural populations such as that of Comala, the novel offers a never-ending reflection on the limits of such a project. Moreover, the novel resists being read as merely setting the stage for the fulfillment of the Green Revolution's triumphal narrative. For as long as generations of readers reenact the novel's misery, exploitation, and desertification—as long as they continue to see it as a portrayal of a Mexican rurality that persists in changing contexts across the decades—*Pedro Páramo* and *El Llano en llamas* will remain anticipatory, critical commentaries on some consequences of the Green Revolution, as *Los pasos perdidos* and *Grande sertão: Veredas* are for conservation projects. As such, they become "a form of imaginary ethnography of the future." To return to Gabrielle Schwab's work: "Literature provides us with the supplementarity we need to cope with the traumatic belatedness of human temporality."[87] When it comes to *Pedro Páramo*, what critics have seen as the ahistorical character of Comala, or the suspended temporality in which the novel takes place, become visible instead as a lasting imaginary of the past that has been historically transposed into a frustrating perception of the present and near future.

In the absence of projects such as those examined in the first chapter, the fictionalizing operations involved here take many shapes. Such fictionalizing maneuvers include the belief that the novel's settings still exist in an unchanged fashion; they may be fueled by a nostalgic perspective that resists change, or they may fully embrace the MAP's developmentalist orientation and be unaware of the fictionality that characterizes many of its cherished images. In any case, the fictionalization of the Mexican countryside is to be found in these diverse ideas of what this space is or should be, fostered by discursive formations built on a heterogeneous set of landmarks, such as Rulfo's novel and the Mexican Agricultural Program.

A novel and a process of agricultural change cannot be understood on the same level. They act in different fields, they activate different affective dimensions, and they project different sets of desires. This distance notwithstanding, they do both participate in the long and heterogeneous negotiation over how the postrevolutionary countryside should be conceived in Mexico. In doing so, they both constitute projects of rural modernity—either with respect to the cultural imaginary surrounding it, in the case of the novel, or through gradual yet accelerating changes in its social organization and environmental impact, in the case of the Green Revolution. The topics and anxieties associated with these projects are sometimes in direct opposition and sometimes assume an uncanny complementarity. The rift between them may continue to grow as the novel remains a powerful reminder of changes taking place now, or the novel may offer a commentary on these changes based on shared points of contact. In one way or another, these fictionalizing operations, by an actual fictional work or by unfulfilled promises following moments of apparent prosperity, have participated in shaping the lived space of the Mexican countryside for a significant portion of the twentieth century.

CHAPTER 4

Besieged Plots

Nonhuman Agency in Clarice Lispector's A cidade sitiada

Previous chapters have dealt with classics of twentieth-century Latin American literature. *Grande sertão: Veredas*, *Los pasos perdidos*, and *Pedro Páramo* fundamentally contributed to lasting environmental perceptions of the Brazilian *sertão*, the Venezuelan Gran Sabana, and the Mexican countryside, respectively, even as these referential areas have undergone significant changes. While these fictional environments have remained relevant to collective perceptions of these places largely because of the enduring prestige and canonical status enjoyed by these novels and other works by the same authors, the current chapter on Clarice Lispector, by contrast, describes alternative dynamics between author, work, and the reading public. Though her work has received increasing attention over the past few decades, and she indisputably figures in the Brazilian literary canon today, Lispector had a more tortuous career and more periods of obscurity than her male counterparts, and some of her novels are still quite unknown. In a literary market traditionally less attentive to female voices, these variations are certainly not random. They do, however, affect the impact that Lispector's work has had on environmental imaginaries in Brazil. Rather than establishing correlations between such imaginaries and her work's reception history, this chapter will address environmental aspects of her production not yet fully visible in the critical corpus on some of her early novels.

Lispector's career began with the publication of *Perto do coração selvagem* (1943; *Near the Wild Heart*, 1990), which was well received but then followed by a long and uncomfortable relative silence that lasted until the publication of the short stories in *Laços de família* (1955; *Family Ties*, 1984) and later of her masterpiece *A paixão segundo G.H.* (1964; *The Passion according to G.H.*, 1988). Her prestige as a protagonist of Brazil's literary scene solidified in the 1960s and 1970s. French feminist writer Hélène Cixous, who read her as a major example of her concept of *écriture féminine*,[1] gave Lispector a decisive international profile whose growth gained new momentum with the publication of Benjamin Moser's biography and the recent republication of her work in English. Although the environmental domain has been absent from criticism of her work for the most part, the nonhuman dimensions of so much of her writing have received reasonable attention, and in the past few years scholarship framing her work within animal studies and posthumanism, by Gabriel Giorgi, Evando Nascimento, and Alexandre Nodari, among others, has gained traction.[2] One need only remember the linguistic and existential tour de force involving G.H.'s encounter with a cockroach in her apartment in the novel *A paixão segundo G.H.* or Ana's epiphanic moments among the lush of plants and fruits in Rio de Janeiro's botanical garden in the short story "Amor" ("Love"), to mention some of Lispector's best-known pieces, to have a sense of how often human and nonhuman subjects interact in her work.

Despite a level of interest that has gradually made Lispector a key name in Brazilian literature, her prominence in feminist studies, her groundbreaking experimentations in narrative form, and the philosophical resonances of her existentialist prose, a group of her early novels remains understudied. They are *O lustre* (1946; *The Chandelier*, 2018), *A cidade sitiada* (1949; *The Besieged City*, 2019), and to a lesser extent, *A maçã no escuro* (1961; *The Apple in the Dark*, 2009). Published when the young Lispector was not yet fully established as a writer and was living abroad as a diplomat's wife, they combine some characteristic traces of Clarician prose, such as clear dialogue with a genre that critics and scholars do not typically associate with her: regionalist fiction. Critics noted her presumed break with earlier regionalist fiction, which was so prevalent in Brazil, even in their reception of her first novel, *Perto do coração selvagem*.[3] While the three novels that followed do not feature the realist prose and documentary concern usually attributed to the genre, they still engage with topics dear to twentieth-century regionalist fiction, such as life in rural areas and small towns, the conflict between such places and urban centers, and a critique of rural exploitation alternating with an almost pastoralist emphasis on the countryside. This chapter builds on Luís Bueno's argument that, far from constituting "absolutely isolated cases,"[4] Lispector and Guimarães Rosa respond to and continue trends and themes already present in regionalist fiction, especially through their approach to diverse forms of social alterity. *A cidade sitiada* tells of a suburban area still dotted with rural pockets that transitions into an urban center; the novel recovers some regionalist tropes even while narrating their very extinction as a series of developmentalist policies, fostered by Getúlio Vargas's government from 1930 to 1945 and intensified in the 1950s, marked a decisive turn in Brazil's environmental, social, and economic history.

This chapter reassesses *A cidade sitiada* as an alternative chronicle of developmentalism in Brazil from the viewpoint of those left on the discursive margins by these policies: nonhuman actors, often in their relationship with female characters. By examining the intersection between the agency of things and the social relations implicated in their circulation, I follow Héctor Hoyos, who, in proposing the concept of transcultural materialism, integrates historical and new materialisms.[5] I investigate how *A cidade sitiada* conveys a sense of environmental transformation by relativizing human agency and presenting an alternative account of Brazilian urbanization under developmentalist policies. Published in 1949, a few years after the author had left Brazil for what would be a seventeen-year absence, Lispector's third novel narrates the saga of urban growth in a suburban town that is leaving behind its pastures to embrace viaducts. As an evolving classification that includes urban, rural, and even forested components, the category of the suburban challenges simple dichotomies between forest and city or country and city. The city—in this case the changing city of S. Geraldo—replaces one set of peoples, animals, and objects with another.[6] As she brings the topic of urbanization to the forefront of her narrative, Lispector interrogates the role of description by destabilizing the distinction between description and narration and the primacy of human-led plots. Far away from the deep countryside of *Pedro Páramo*, it is in this urbanizing space, where multiple referents and alternative histories find their voices, that the fictional environment of the novel reshapes the very notion of development.

SUBJECTS

Clarice Lispector once classified *A cidade sitiada* as "um de meus livros menos gostado" ("one of my least appreciated novels"), adding that "no entanto relendo-o as pessoas passam a gostar dele" ("but people start liking it after rereading it").[7] In fact, the novel was not greeted with the same enthusiasm that many of Lispector's novels enjoyed, with critics commenting on how its long descriptions of the town of São Geraldo resulted in a stylistically excessive narrative.[8]

At first, *A cidade sitiada* may seem overly descriptive, and its characters may not appear much more prominent than the streets on which they walk or the glasses with which they drink water. I propose here that these numerous, lengthy descriptions are not so much technical problems of composition as a way of relativizing human agency on both grammatical and narrative levels. By constantly placing objects, machines, streets, animals, and the weather in the position of subjects in the sentences of the novel, Lispector makes evident a broader web of nonhuman agents whose insistent presence throughout the narrative questions the very centrality of a human-led plot.[9] While, as Lucia Villares has proposed, the objects' agency stems from their fetishization as commodities, I contend that the agency assigned to diverse categories of nonhumans is also part of Lispector's broader narrative experiment in destabilizing human exceptionalism.

Told by a third-person narrator who combines frequent use of free indirect discourse with occasional sarcastic comments about the characters, *A cidade sitiada*'s plot is simple: in the small suburban town of S. Geraldo, probably in Brazil's southeast, the young woman Lucrécia Neves lives with her mother and has some unspecific dreams for the future. She then marries an older man, moves to a big city for some time, goes back to S. Geraldo with her husband, becomes a widow years later, and finally decides to leave S. Geraldo for good when her mother brings up the possibility of finding another husband for her in a different town. But there is actually another plot, a plot as important as Lucrécia's life story: a small suburban town starts growing and becomes a city. Some elements of the little town remain as the streets become avenues, the horses are replaced by cars, and the hills and pastures on the skyline are replaced by viaducts and towering plants and factories, in a transformation that, as Benedito Nunes has proposed, actually conditions the plot centered on Lucrécia.[10] She watches this growth as much as she watches her life—"sua modesta função que era: olhar" ("her modest function which was: to look")[11] in a town that "era explorável apenas pelo olhar" ("was exploitable only with the gaze").[12] In one of the most comprehensive studies of the novel, Regina Pontieri investigates this peculiar gaze in which "subject and object, rearranged in different polarities . . . are two sides of the same reality. Hence the search for integration that is coterminous with the consciousness of separation."[13]

S. Geraldo's development is filtered through, but not reduced to, a character's gaze, even in a novel heavily based on observation through free indirect discourse. For example: "Duas ruas além três mulheres de pedra sustentavam a porta de um edifício moderno. Os fios telegráficos fremiam em pontos e traços. . . . Num salto Lucrécia Neves estava à varanda, as mãos contendo contra as pernas a camisola que o vento soprava" ("Two streets down three stone women were holding up the door of a modern building. The telegraph wires were trembling in dots and dashes. . . . With a leap Lucrécia Neves was at the balcony, her hands holding in check against her legs the nightgown that the wind was blowing").[14] The three stone statues of women, the telegraph, and the wind act—just as Lucrécia acts by leaping onto the porch. Grammatically, they are all in the subject position and in the active voice. The reference to Lucrécia's jump is the most direct assertion of her movement in a sentence where she is the subject of the verb *estava*, meaning "to be, to stay, to linger." Even her hands as they hold her gown seem independent from Lucrécia herself. The references to the modern building and the telegraph may remind the reader of the vivid descriptions of cities so typical of Modernist fiction.[15] Yet, *A cidade sitiada* does not reserve this disorienting intensity only for signs of an urban modernity in S. Geraldo. Instead, the whole novel is permeated by passages that emphasize the agency of objects, animals, sounds, streets, houses, and parts of bodies by making them the subjects of sentences where there is very little space to frame them within human perception. While Lucrécia remains the main narrative focus through which human and nonhuman actors become visible, their level of grammatical and narrative independence is remarkable and often destabilizes any possible hierarchical relation between them and Lucrécia's gaze. Instead, her gaze and these nonhuman actors are, to a certain extent, equivalent, as Evando Nascimento proposes when he calls the gaze a "thinking thing."[16]

Lispector's affirmation of nonhuman agency through syntax is the first strategy I want to point out. It makes evident what Jane Bennett has defined as *thing-power*, or "the moment of independence (from subjectivity) possessed by things, a moment that must be there, since things do in fact affect other bodies, enhancing or weakening their power."[17] The independence of things is indeed the very means by which the city grows, not with the help of the human protagonist's gaze but in spite of it: "E a dureza das coisas era o modo mais recortado de ver da moça. Da impossibilidade de ultrapassar essa resistência nascia, de fruto verde, o travo das coisas firmes sobre as quais soprava com heroísmo esse vento cívico que faz tremer bandeiras!" ("And the hardness of things was the girl's most clipped way of seeing. From the impossibility of overcoming that resistance was emerging, in green fruit, the tang of firm things over which was blowing with heroism that civic wind that makes flags flutter!").[18] A vocabulary of warfare, so appropriate for a novel whose title refers to a besieged city, here reaffirms the power of things to resist Lucrécia's gaze and, in doing so, to create a unified sense of what an unconquerable city should be. "Tudo o que tombasse naquela cidade se materializaria em coisa?" (49; "Would everything that tumbled into that city materialize into a thing?," 45), the character asks herself in her often unsuccessful yet continuous struggle for visual apprehension of things. The result is a novel heavily based on visuality that, at the same time, repeatedly points to its limits, both through passages, like the ones quoted above, that highlight those limits and through sentence structures that privilege the grammatical independence of things from the human gaze. Such a strategy, as the last section of this chapter will further discuss, is an example of how, according to Bill Brown, "the task of dramatizing the thingness of objects . . . is rarely the task of theory, let alone of philosophy. It is the task of art."[19]

DESCRIPTIONS

The second strategy addresses the very definition of these representations of nonhuman acts as "descriptions." Almost necessarily understood via its connection with or dependence on narration, the descriptive mode, which Lispector uses often in this novel, destabilizes the flow of events and, therefore, the distinction between description and narration itself. "The essence of description," says Philippe Hamon, "if there ever was one, its effect, would be an effort—an effort to resist the constraining linearity of the text, the post hoc ergo proctor hoc of the narrative algorithms, the channeled dynamism of every written text."[20] If they are understood solely as descriptive material, the nonhuman agents of *A cidade sitiada* are supposed to merely set the scene, so to speak, in which human characters, most notably Lucrécia and her interlocutors, act. But these nonhumans are quite numerous and occupy a significant portion of the text, from beginning to end. This unending parade of objects and animals moreover changes over the years and thus slowly becomes a narrative account of the urbanizing town. Seen from this perspective, such passages are not, as Gérard Genette puts it, descriptions in which "a given segment of narrative discourse corresponds to a null diegetic duration."[21] More than extra pieces of information that facilitate understanding but do not really contribute to the unfolding of events, these prolific descriptive segments break the linearity of the human-led plot even while they gradually constitute a plot of their own, a plot marked by a multiplicity of actors with varying origins, not necessarily interacting with each other and, above all, usually indifferent to what human characters may be doing or feeling.

A good example of how the novel challenges traditional definitions of description and narration appears as early as the first chapter, when Lucrécia and one of her suitors, Felipe, stroll in a crowded street fair. The initial scene provides readers with a good sense of who the human and nonhuman characters are, leading us to expect a focus on Lucrécia, the protagonist, in the sequence. What happens, however, is the exact opposite: Lucrécia disappears momentarily, relinquishing space to a long description of the suburban town of S. Geraldo, and she only reappears when this other protagonist—the town and the things in it—is sufficiently vivid for the reader.

Readings that try to find a slim plot in a sea of descriptive material, however, are only justified by the anthropocentric lens they bring to the task, in which the novel's actors ought to be human characters. Yet, as Bruno Latour and others have shown, actors go far beyond the human. In his attempt to redefine the concept of the social in response to sociology's limitations and abstractions, Latour's actor-network theory (ANT) "simply says that no science of the social can even begin if the question of who and what participates in the action is not first of all thoroughly explored, even though it might mean letting elements in which, for lack of a better term, we would call non-humans."[22] Latour's effort to "extend the list of participants" in what he calls a sociology of associations finds in literature a privileged way of imagining how such a broader notion of the social might work.[23]

A cidade sitiada provides precisely such a means of making the agency of things, and their effects on both humans and nonhumans, palpable narratively and grammatically.[24] Their numerous "moments of independence" make them more than mere objects that assist and enhance human action; instead, they seem to have a certain resistance, a certain ability to react, and an independent existence that leads them to challenge human characters rather than be challenged by them. For example, "Também no aposento os objetos, de forma constante, tornaram-se insuportáveis além de alguns segundos—a moça estava sempre de costas para alguma coisa; o quarto já se precipitara, pesado de ornamentos" ("Also in the room the objects, in a constant way, had become unbearable beyond a few seconds—the girl always had her back turned to some thing; the room had already rushed ahead, heavy with ornaments").[25] If the eclectic range of theories included under the rubric of new materialisms, such as Bennett's and Latour's, have brought greater scrutiny to the diverse configurations of these nonhuman modalities of agency, *A cidade sitiada*, as well as other works by Lispector, offers an earlier example of how grammatical and narrative structures can explore similar questions. By playing with well-established notions of description and narration and disrupting them, Lispector turns what we might call the novel's descriptions into speculations about how things and animals think—how they resist the human gaze and gaze back.

WOMEN, HORSES, CITIES

Once the novel is no longer besieged by anthropocentric readings, *A cidade sitiada*'s alternative plot becomes clear: it is a tale of human and nonhuman interactions as part of a broader process of urbanization and environmental change.[26] From the beginning of the novel, this transformation is taking place: "O subúrbio de S. Geraldo, no ano de 192 . . . , já misturava ao cheiro da estrebaria algum progresso" ("The township of São Geraldo, in the year 192 . . . , was already mingling some progress with the smell of the stable"),[27] even though "Apesar do progresso o subúrbio conservava lugares quase desertos, já em fronteira com o campo" (19; "Despite the progress the township retained almost deserted places, right on the border of the countryside," 12). Meanwhile, the nonhuman actors in the city keep changing, as its narrow streets and green hills give way to broad avenues and industrial towers. Lucrécia senses this change sharply upon her return from the big city: "Aproveitando sua ausência, S. Geraldo avançara em algum sentido, e ela já não reconhecia as coisas. Chamando-as, estas não mais respondiam—habituadas a serem chamadas por outros nomes" (129; "Taking advantage of her absence, São Geraldo had advanced in some sense, and she was already not recognizing things. Calling them, they would no longer answer—accustomed to being called by other names," 133).[28] Perceived with excitement, indifference, or sometimes nostalgia, these signs of change possess neither positive nor negative vectors. They remain mostly a means through which nonhuman actors—and, we might add, people—are replaced as part of the city's transformation.

Tellingly, the novel concludes with the protagonist's decision to leave a city she no longer recognizes, "de onde os últimos cavalos já haviam emigrado, entregando a metrópole à glória de seu mecanismo" (191; "from which the last horses had already emigrated, surrendering the metropolis to the glory of its mechanism," 201). This is the moment when "fora levantado o sítio de S. Geraldo" (191; "the siege of São Geraldo had been lifted," 201). That is to say, the town has surrendered to modernizing forces from outside, it no longer belongs to anyone, and its former inhabitants—horses, widows, and others—have no option but to desert the conquered city. Although the trope of the dehumanized metropolis overtaken by technology may lend itself to spectacular representations, the gradual expulsion of things and characters in *A cidade sitiada* constitutes what Rob Nixon refers to as slow violence: "A violence of delayed destruction that is dispersed across time and space, an attritional violence that is typically not viewed as violence at all."[29] This process, already latent in the novel, is made suddenly obvious when the town's inevitable defeat is recognized and Lucrécia leaves.[30] Of course, Lucrécia's behavior and even Lispector's differ sharply from that of the writer-activists Nixon analyzes—the women who led the Green Belt Movement in Kenya, for example—and Lispector's work is distant from contemporary environmental justice movements. Yet *A cidade sitiada* does challenge the "representational bias against slow violence" insofar as, by narrating urbanization, it brings to light the "casualties most likely not to be seen, not to be counted," whether human or not.[31]

The novel's final paragraphs, in which the meaning of *siege* becomes clear, also suddenly reveal the resistance to urbanizing forces that has shaped the two plots—that of S. Geraldo as a modernizing suburb and that of Lucrécia in her trajectory as a woman. Horses are significant to this resistance; they are recurrently mentioned in the novel, and equine qualities occasionally figure in descriptions of Lucrécia herself. Horses were a continuous source of fascination for Lispector and appear in her work through her final novels.[32] They often imply a hidden force of character in humans and are specifically tied to her protagonists' femininity. This identification usually takes place when women observe horses and then merge with them spiritually, such as in the short story "Seco estudo sobre cavalos" ("Dry Sketch of Horses"): "Já me relacionei de um modo perfeito com o cavalo. . . . Pela sua agreste crina agressiva. Eu me sentia como se algo meu nos visse de longe—Assim: 'A Moça e o Cavalo'" ("I have related perfectly to a horse before. . . . Over its rustic aggressive mane. I felt as if something of mine were watching us from afar—Thus: 'The Girl and the Horse'").[33]

The horses in *A cidade sitiada* are often presented in a similar fashion and with a similar vocabulary; they surround Lucrécia and figuratively pervade her character through descriptions that make use of equine metaphors: "[Lucrécia] estava excitada, de quando em quando dava uma rabada com uma das pernas na cauda ausente" ("She was all worked up, now and then she'd give a kick with one of her hind legs at her absent tail");[34] "Tudo parecia esperar que também ela batesse firme breve com a pata" (75; "Everything seemed to be waiting for her too to stomp firm and fast with her hoof," 73).[35] More importantly, like Lucrécia, horses mark the transformation of development and the consequent loss of control over urban space when they are replaced by cars. While horses embody a form of wild and vivid strength with which Lucrécia is identified, their continuous presence makes them builders and keepers of the city: "A moça e um cavalo representavam as duas raças de construtores que iniciaram a tradição da futura metrópole, ambos poderiam servir de armas para um seu escudo. A ínfima função da mocinha na sua época era uma função arcaica que renasce cada vez que se forma uma vila, sua história formou com esforço o espírito de uma cidade" (21–22; "The girl and a horse represented the two races of builders that had initiated the tradition of the future metropolis, both figure on its coat of arms. The measly function of the girl in her time was an archaic function that is reborn every time a town is formed, her history formed with effort the spirit of a city," 15).

In this passage from the first chapter, the woman and the horse take on a constructive role in the development of the city, as forces that imbue it with its first impetus. In spite of the way Lispector refuses to relegate nonhuman agency to mere description in the background of the narrative, as I argue above, passages like this suggest that horse and women nevertheless perform a secondary, "irrelevant" function in urban development, in Val Plumwood's terms. This kind of backgrounding consists of the "treatment [of women and nature] as providing the background to a dominant, foreground sphere of recognised achievement or causation."[36] Moreover, Lucrécia's unmistakable identification with horses points to the underlying assumption in the West that women and nature share some special connection that both makes them irrational and justifies their subjugation.[37] *A cidade sitiada* remains ambivalent on this point, insofar as it seems to simultaneously reinforce and undermine the presumed link between women and nature. On the one hand, Lucrécia is indeed inextricably attached to the horse as a symbol of natural force; both are "domesticated" throughout the novel, and both represent an initial impulse for development that nevertheless remains marginal in the face of urbanization's novelties. Far from being segregated from or marginalized by industrialization, however, the woman and the horse are the very forces propelling this process. They serve as agents of development, but not exclusively of Brazil's twentieth-century development: they are, rather, "archaic" agents of the continuous creation of villages and their transformation into cities from time immemorial.

Their function, however, becomes more ambivalent as they fit less and less into the growing city. A sentence added to the 1964 edition of the novel reinforces this feeling, stating that "elas [as mulheres] tinham medo da cidade que nascia" (20; "they [the women] were afraid of the city that was being born," 13). As S. Geraldo turns into a metropolis toward the end of the book, Lucrécia does not recognize objects in the new city anymore, as in the passage quoted above, and the horses, like the woman, find no place there: "Havia mesmo planos de construção de um viaduto que ligaria o morro à cidade baixa. . . . Os terrenos do morro já começavam a se vender para as futuras residências: *para onde iriam os cavalos*?" (138, my emphasis; "There were even plans to build a viaduct to connect the hill to the lower city. . . . The plots on the hill were already beginning to be sold for future residences: *where would the horses go*?" 143, my emphasis).

In the development of urban space, women and horses are interchangeable and function as simultaneously progressive and regressive forces. While they enable progress in the initial moment of establishing a village or town, they turn gradually to a position of resistance, until they seem to try to shield it from urbanization. Not by chance, Lucrécia concludes that the city is surrounded and harassed by forces beyond its walls: "Mas não havia como sitiá-la [a cidade]. Lucrécia Neves estava dentro da cidade" (71; "But there was no way to besiege it [the city].

Lucrécia Neves was inside the city," 69). As a result, all that women and horses can do is resist the external siege of modernization and flee when it has finally succeeded.

Two readings emerge from this disturbing connection between horses and women and their roles and displacement in relation to urban growth. The first revolves around Lucrécia as a female protagonist who explicitly lacks much of the reflexive power and subjective depth of most of Lispector's other main characters. In a certain sense, she resembles Macabéa from *A hora da estrela* (1977; *The Hour of the Star*, 1992), whose narrator reaffirms, as does that of *A cidade sitiada*, the main character's dullness and limited understanding of the world. It is thus through this disturbing irony that Lucrécia's flatness and her connection with the nonhuman world, most completely achieved through her equine metamorphoses, are to be understood.

If we consider the problem from a nonanthropocentric perspective, however, we face Lispector's radical narrative experiment of using both her human protagonist and nonhuman actors to tell a story of transformations of social space. Lucrécia then becomes, just like the things that surround her, a complete exteriority: "Tudo o que Lucrécia Neves podia conhecer de si mesma estava fora dela: ela via" (68; "Everything that Lucrécia Neves could know of herself was outside her: she was seeing," 65). Rather than constituting an inferior condition, this seems to be the very state Lispector herself wished to achieve, haunted as she was during the writing process by intellectual and emotional conflicts.

Representing women and horses simultaneously as agents of urbanization and elements of resistance thus leads to two conclusions. Firstly, there is a near equivalence between women and horses that gives them an archaic and unrecognized, yet essential, role in the building of a city, which will lead to Lispector's expanded portrait of developmentalism. Secondly, rather than taking a unidimensional view of the already multispecies conjuncture of Lucrécia and the horses, Lispector opts to present them as challenging the chains of causes and effects that directed developmentalist narratives during and after the Vargas years, in which most of the novel is set. As a result, the plot that centers on Lucrécia reveals itself to be one of environmental change and negotiation over who will remain, who will arrive, and who will have to leave—regardless of their status as human or nonhuman. This is the fictional environment Lispector crafts through a number of strategies that give it narrative prominence and make evident the impacts that the perception of environmental change may have upon narrative form.

REFERENTS

The process of urbanization, suburbanization, and industrialization in Brazil sped up sharply not only in the 1920s, when the first part of the novel is set, but also in the late 1930s and early 1940s, when Lispector lived in Rio de Janeiro before moving to Europe, where she wrote *A cidade sitiada*. Although the location of the fictional S. Geraldo is not specified in the novel, the reader learns that it is within driving distance of one of the country's biggest cities, where she can go "ao Museu, ao Jardim Zoológico, ao Aquário Nacional" ("to the Museum, to the Zoo, to the National Aquarium"),[38] with "national" hinting that this is the federal capital, Rio de Janeiro. Although there is no indication that S. Geraldo is a coastal city, the reader also learns that it is relatively close to the sea, as there is a nearby island—referred to simply as "the island"—where Lucrécia lives for a short period of time. These pieces of information suggest that S. Geraldo is in the state of Rio de Janeiro, even though it resembles many towns across Brazil that are similarly situated.

The demographics of Rio and the Federal District, among other factors, provide statistical support for the fictional narrative. According to the 1920, 1940, and 1950 censuses made available by the Brazilian Institute for Geography and Statistics, in the state of Rio and the federal capital together, the number of factories grew to 9,699 in 1950 from only 2,037 in 1920. The urban population more than doubled, from 1.3 million people in 1940 to 2.7 million in 1950, whereas the rural population decreased slightly, from 1.4 million to 1.3 million. Interestingly, the suburban population declined more sharply, from 833,000 in 1940 to 684,000 in 1950.[39] These numbers point to an increasingly urban population as suburban areas were absorbed by bigger cities, probably driven by the quadrupling of industrial companies.[40]

Urbanization and industrialization in Rio de Janeiro and its suburbs led, predictably, to environmental consequences, including deforestation of the remaining Atlantic forest that originally covered most of the country's eastern coast. Early twentieth-century industrial activity, as Warren Dean states in his history of the Atlantic forest, "continued to depend for fuel primarily on its immense standing stock of native wood resources."[41] Consequently, the deforestation of Atlantic coastal woodlands, which had been taking place since the beginning of Portuguese colonial rule in the sixteenth century, continued to be essential to industrial growth during the time period in which the novel is set. Although the novel does not narrate this process of deforestation, it is, to a certain extent, connected to the broader transformation portrayed in the book.

In short, the census data and the area's environmental history contribute to an ecological and demographic picture of S. Geraldo as an industrializing suburb that has become a city by the end of the book. While it would be easy to assume a simple mimetic relation between the fictional town and a number of towns in the state of Rio during this period, a closer look at the novel's composition may reveal that, just as in Lefebvre's social spaces, mimetic relations in fictional spaces also "interpenetrate one another and/or superimpose themselves upon one another."[42]

S. Geraldo may not look Swiss, yet its accelerating transformations find an unexpected parallel in the city of Bern, where Lispector lived for approximately three years between 1946 and 1949, and where she wrote *A cidade sitiada*. After shorter periods spent in Naples, Italy, during the last moments and aftermath of World War II, the author found herself profoundly bored by and exasperated at what she considered Bern's tranquillity and lack of personality. In April and May of 1946, she wrote: "Berna é um túmulo, mesmo para os suíços" ("Bern is a tomb, even for the Swiss"); "Esta Suíça é um cemitério de sensações . . . só Deus mesmo sabe que tempo cinzento eu tenho passado, que falta de tudo, e de esperança" ("Switzerland is a cemetery of sensations . . . only God knows the gray time I've been facing, what a lack of everything, and of hope"); "Berna é de um silêncio terrível" ("Bern lives in a terrible silence"); "É uma pena eu não ter paciência de gostar de uma vida tão tranquila como a de Berna. É uma fazenda" ("It is a shame I don't have the patience to enjoy a life as peaceful as the one in Bern. It is a farm").[43] These and other comments in letters indicating Lispector's distaste for Bern are complemented by passages in which she describes her difficulties writing there and the long hours she wasted doing nothing but waiting for time to pass.[44]

In his biography of Lispector, Benjamin Moser establishes parallels between the author and her protagonist, Lucrécia. For Moser, Lucrécia is what Lispector desperately wanted, yet could not manage, to be: a person who "is content not to see beyond the surface of things."[45] At the same time, the two women both lived in somewhat oppressive small towns with some periods in bigger cities.[46] These parallels, however, are not confined to the human dimension: S. Geraldo's transformations allude to an urbanizing Brazil and distinguish it from the medieval, sepulchral Bern. While at first glance the two cities clearly resemble each other in their rural feel and pervasive sense of stillness, of resistance to novelties, S. Geraldo is progressively dissociated from this characterization and becomes less and less recognizable. Yet, as Lispector states in another letter to her sisters: "Os outros [S. Geraldo's residents except for Ifigênia] sentiam o perigo em S. Geraldo progressista, e já tinham um pouco a nostalgia da 'volta' à rusticidade" (136; "The others [S. Geraldo's residents except for Ifigênia] felt the danger in a progressive S. Geraldo, and already had some nostalgia for the 'return' to rusticity"). This nostalgia, as the novel shows, coexists with a desire for modernization: the inhabitants of S. Geraldo dream of having a subway, as the novel's last sentences make explicit.

The fictional town thus responds to a double referentiality. It represents generic yet real changes faced by a series of small towns and suburbs close to Rio de Janeiro around the time the book was written. Her representation of this urbanization nevertheless also reflects and reacts to the immutability of Bern, a city that was comfortable in resisting the siege of progress and remaining attached to its old habits, in Lispector's view. The novel's commentary on Brazil's urbanization works, then, as a countercommentary about the exasperating tranquillity of a city immune to both progress and war—contrary to the intellectually stimulating albeit deeply affected postwar Italy where Lispector lived right before her stay in Bern.

As the previous chapters have shown, such conflation of multiple referential sources results in fictional environments that address and depict local, concrete situations while simultaneously responding to a series of more or less persistent anxieties about what these spaces could or could not be. Thus, the fact that "the city besieged" by factories and viaducts represents urbanizing areas in the state of Rio de Janeiro somewhat precisely does not exclude a siege's martial dimensions, especially for an author who lived through the end of the war in Italy and then faced the stagnation of Bern.

The multiple meanings of *siege*—by urban growth, by stagnation, and quite literally by war[47]—turn *A cidade sitiada*'s environment into a patchwork. While this multiplicity of referents might initially seem to weaken the novel's power to make a specific commentary on the local level, I argue that, on the contrary, it makes the environment of S. Geraldo more recognizable from a literary perspective. In fact, the referential porosity of which the text is composed seems to permeate the porosity of the city itself, in Bruno Carvalho's sense; he understands parts of Rio de Janeiro as a "porous city" in its "mixtures and encounters" and also as marked by urban divisions.[48] The diverse historical and social layers that compose the urban tissue of S. Geraldo, however, are besieged by modernization, which constantly decides who leaves, who stays, and who arrives—and in which, in Gabriel Giorgi's words in his biopolitical analysis of Copi's *La ciudad de las ratas* (1979; The city of rats), "The distinction between humans and animals does not reflect a species ontology, but a politics of the body."[49] More than providing empirical data on a referential context, *A cidade sitiada* participates in the creation of a literary imagination about an urbanizing and industrializing Brazil in the first half of the twentieth century.

DEVELOPMENTALISM

This literary imagination about urbanization and industrialization had been gaining traction not only in metropolises such as Rio but also in the work of writers located in other areas of the country, such as Graciliano Ramos in *Angústia* (1936; Anguish), set in the northwestern capital of Maceió, and Dyonélio Machado's *Os ratos* (1935; The rats) about the southern city of Porto Alegre. According to Fernando Gil, these "novels of urbanization," by narrating the transformation of rural into urban environments, "articulate a temporal intertwining, between rural past and urban present, the result of which is the nullification of any horizon of social and existential expectation."[50] What Gil identifies as the genre of the novel of urbanization, in which *A cidade sitiada* could certainly be included,[51] grapples with broader social, economic, and environmental changes taking place during the Vargas era, from 1930 to 1945. Getúlio Vargas's rule started with a coup d'état in 1930 that put an end to the so-called Old Republic and met its demise in 1945 in the deep constitutional crisis of the Estado Novo, as the dictatorship installed by Vargas in 1937 was known. Although Vargas occupied the presidential seat again from 1950 to 1954, this chapter focuses on the period of his first government, during which most of Lispector's novel takes place.

In response to the international economic crisis of 1929, state reliance on industrialization as a basic component of economic growth characterized early developmentalism in Brazil during the Vargas era, and particularly during the Estado Novo period (1937–45).[52] As Ricardo Bielchowsky indicates, this shift stemmed from a number of factors, including awareness that the creation of an integrated industrial sector was viable; the centralization of mechanisms for providing financial resources for industrial production; state planning, in which federal and private forces work together; and economic nationalism.[53] These formed the basis of national developmentalism in the Vargas years. This scenario points to an accelerated process of urbanization, which, according to Milton Santos, accomplished a "true inversion in the place of residence of the Brazilian population" from the 1940s to the 1980s.[54] Even though urbanization intensified in the 1960s,[55] it was already underway in Lucrécia Neves's time, especially in metropolitan regions such as Rio de Janeiro.

Concentrated in more central areas of the city before the 1930s due to a lack of public transportation and urban regulation, Rio de Janeiro's industries moved gradually to the suburbs and nearby municipalities where they could find more adequate space, cheap labor, and better transportation conditions, even as the crash of 1929 and World War II increased demand for industrial goods. At the same time, federal support for industrialization and migration to the capital also grew.[56] As a consequence, empty lands, such as those on the outskirts of S. Geraldo, were typically among the areas rapidly taken up by factories as accelerated expansion was haphazardly pursued.[57]

Vargas was the first statesman in Latin America to adopt a developmentalist orientation, as Carlos Bresser-Pereira indicates. Somewhat later, continues Bresser-Pereira, "the notable Latin American economists, sociologists, political scientists, and philosophers who formulated this strategy in the 1950s came together in the Economic Commission for Latin America and the Caribbean (ECLAC) in Santiago, Chile, and in Instituto Superior de Estudos Brasileiros (ISEB) in Rio de Janeiro, Brazil."[58] The United Nations created ECLAC, or CEPAL in Portuguese and Spanish, in 1948, and it "played an essential role in conferring theoretical weight to ideas that, although they had been heard since the end of the nineteenth century, only became a research program with a more rigorous language and form in the 1950s."[59] Albeit with striking variations, developmentalist policies across Latin America generally focused on "the defense of: (a) industrialization, (b) pro-growth protectionism, and (c) nationalism, although this should be understood in a very broad sense,"[60] in addition to reinforcing the positivism so prevalent in the early decades of the republican regime in Brazil.[61]

Representing the basic principles of developmentalist thought in Brazil and other Latin American countries, these policies broadly indicate what the term *development* stands for in the second part of this book, from the viewpoint of national economic politics. Lispector witnessed this first moment of national developmentalism in Rio during the Estado Novo and later published *A cidade sitiada* around the time that developmentalism as a recognizable economic proposition and field of study was gaining momentum. In Brazil, one of developmentalism's major figures was the economist Celso Furtado, with whose work Lispector's novel has some points of contact.

Vargas-era industrialization, as Furtado explains in his 1959 classic, *A formação econômica do Brasil* (*The Economic Growth of Brazil: A Survey from Colonial to Modern Times*, 1963), was the result of demand for Brazilian products after the crisis of 1929, which altered the exchange rate for Brazilian currency, leading to a sharp increase in the price of imported industrial goods.[62] Coffee, despite becoming Brazil's major export after the country's independence from Portugal, entailed an economy that, as Furtado shows, strongly resembled that based on sugar, which was dominant in the colonial period.[63] Coffee fell sharply in the international market due to a drop in demand and the failure of state policies to keep prices artificially high after the crisis of 1929. In this context, the government gave Brazil's growing industrial sector a decisive boost that prevented the country from suffering more than it did from the economic crash.[64] Furtado, one of the main figures in the developmentalist wave so prevalent in Brazil and other Latin American countries in the late 1940s and 1950s, had already written similar, albeit less elaborated, theses on the causes of industrial growth in Brazil a few years before, in 1954, in a volume titled *A economia brasileira* (The Brazilian economy).[65]

In fact, the economist had more in common with Lispector than one might guess. Both went to the same school in Recife, Ginásio Pernambucano, then studied law in the same period at the same university, the University of Brazil (today's Federal University of Rio de Janeiro), then went to Italy in the final moments of World War II. Lispector went on to Bern, while Furtado went to Paris to pursue his Ph.D. Albeit writing from different angles, with different purposes, and in different genres, the two authors circulated in the same spaces, had a similar education and background, and I argue, explored the same context in *A cidade sitiada* and in work on industrialization in Brazil.

Furtado focuses on sweeping economic processes and, in the case of *A formação econômica do Brasil*, looks back at the country's history from its early colonial period in order to understand broader patterns and remnants of a colonial mind-set in twentieth-century Brazil. For her part, Lispector focuses on the sphere of everyday life and gives a detailed account of peoples, objects, and places, where constant allusions to historical specificities are coupled with a broader reflection on the nature, growth, and disappearance of cities. The industrialized goods that Furtado discusses are none other than the ones that populate S. Geraldo, and the factories that produce them are the same ones expelling women and horses from the city. In this sense, Lispector's novel and Furtado's work may be read as complementary—as two drastically different yet mutually illuminating views of the forces propelling industrialization and urbanization in Brazil during the 1930s and World War II. Furtado's broad panoramas, however, reveal neither the individual realms that were affected by these changes nor the nonhuman dimension that the novelist explored so deeply.

LISPECTOR AS A CHRONICLER OF EARLY DEVELOPMENTALISM

While a discourse of progress that, as the passage from Fonseca shows, married a positivist heritage to a defense of nationalism and economic growth through industrialization began to take hold in the Vargas era, the dominant narrative of this process came from the developmentalist thought fostered by CEPAL and carried out by a number of Brazilian economists and other members of the intelligentsia.[66] These individuals exercised a fundamental influence in the 1950s through governments that, as former president Juscelino Kubitschek's slogan makes clear, proposed the development equivalent of "fifty years in five" and exemplify, in the Brazilian context, Escobar's take on the discourse of development, discussed in the introduction to this book.

In parallel, another narrative of economic growth and environmental change through industrialization sheds a different light on the same context. It eschews the technical vocabulary of economic science while bringing to light the major transformations it outlines. It draws upon a broad imaginary of change and progress, made more acute in the Vargas years but already present since the 1889 foundation of the republican regime, for which "progress" already figured as a basic value. I'm talking, of course, about Lispector's novel. In narrating urbanization, *A cidade sitiada* revisits chapters of recent history but introduces a number of other actors that are traditionally left out. These are the nonhumans whose existence is rendered abstract in quantifications of growth and change, but which appear now as opaque figures whose singularity the human gaze cannot ignore, and which, as things imbued with a certain grammatical and narrative value, resist and challenge this same gaze. But they also include the young women who, like the horses, give impetus to urbanization as much as they later resist it and run away from it. This developing city, populated by a much wider range of beings than economic narratives can account for, reveals an overlooked and perhaps forgotten facet of development that few discourses are capable of conveying as well as fiction.

In *The Fictive and the Imaginary*, Wolfgang Iser proposes a triadic model for understanding fictionalizing acts: first, there is the real, or referential reality as understood by "thought systems, social systems, and world pictures";[67] second, an amorphous, neutral set of perceptions named the imaginary; and third, the fictive, which transgresses the boundaries between the first two categories and deforms them. In Iser's words,

> Consequently, there is a difference between the actual world and the world from which it is bracketed off, for the textual world takes its shape from the deformation of the referential fields of the text through selection and combination, which then relate the encapsulated elements and open them out into their potential multiplicity. . . . This simultaneous presence of the two [worlds] is caused by each of them making the other unreal: the textual world loses its function of designation, and the empirical world loses its objectivity. (229)

Through the diverging selection and combination of the elements that populate a narrative of development, Lispector deforms the field of developmentalist narratives specifically and narratives of progress more broadly. The impact of such reshaping, as Iser proposes, is mutual: while the referential fields of urbanization and industrialization are an integral part of *A cidade sitiada*, the novel arguably reveals the blanks, overlooked aspects, and incompleteness of the narratives so easily taken for the "real world" at the time. This novel is a transcultural materialist work in the sense Hoyos defines it: they "blur the line between nature and culture, defamiliarize objectifying language, [and] interrogate the power dynamics that affect human-nonhuman interaction."[68]

The fictional text "deforms" the real not only by increasing the number of participants in the urbanizing process but also by blurring the referents on which S. Geraldo is based. If, as shown above, the suburb draws from the real suburbs of Rio as well as from images of an idyllic albeit claustrophobic Bern and an agitated postwar Naples, the novel also puts the growth and fall of cities generally in perspective, as the following passage shows:

> Quando todas as cidades fossem erguidas com seus nomes, elas se destruiriam de novo porque assim sempre fora. Sobre os escombros reapareceriam cavalos anunciando o renascimento da antiga realidade, o dorso sem cavaleiros. Porque assim sempre fora.
>
> Até que alguns homens os prendessem a carroças, outra vez erguendo uma cidade que eles não entenderiam, outra vez construindo, com habilidade inocente, as coisas. E então de novo se precisasse de que um dedo apontado lhes desse os antigos nomes. Assim seria pois o mundo era redondo. (Lispector, *A cidade sitiada*, 88–89)

> When all the cities were erected with their names, they'd destroy themselves anew because that's the way it had always been. Upon the rubble horses would reappear announcing the rebirth of the old reality, their backs without riders. Because that's the way it had always been.
>
> Until a few men would tie them to wagons, once again erecting a city that they wouldn't understand, once again building, with innocent skill, the things. And then once more they'd need a pointing finger to give them their old names. That's how it would be for the world was round. (Lispector, *The Besieged City*, 88)

The biblical tone and the ironic closing, among other things, question the very meaning of the urban cycle of creation, destruction, and recreation. The *longue durée* of urban ascent and fall, present in few but significant passages such as this one, position the whole story of S. Geraldo's urbanization in a larger arc, in which the modernizing explosion described in the novel's closing pages already suggests a state of exhaustion to follow. Even though this state is never made explicit and only looms in the narrative as a potentiality, the reader is reminded of it and consequently sees S. Geraldo both as an account of environmental and social change in a Brazilian suburb and as an embodiment of other spaces and temporalities spectrally present. As with *Pedro Páramo*, this proleptic movement takes on catastrophic dimensions inasmuch as it gestures toward a potential postdevelopment scenario whose resources have been exhausted. Unlike in the Mexican novel, this catastrophic perspective only occasionally erupts in *A cidade sitiada*, rather than suggesting an alternative reading of a future embedded in images of the past, as in the case of Comala's devastated landscape.

Consequently, the deformation of the referents enacted by Lispector's novel not only shows up in the number and species of participants in urbanization but also announces a potential, perhaps inescapable, limit to developmentalism's primary assumptions, not so much as an economic practice but as a state policy with clear ideological contours. These assumptions include the possibility of infinite economic growth and the inevitable expansion of urban perimeters.[69] As deforestation advanced in the remnants of Atlantic forest in Rio and its neighboring states—partially to provide fuel for industrial activity, as Dean shows—the novel simultaneously narrates and questions the irreversibility of urban expansion and incorporation of suburban areas into urban and industrial perimeters. In fact, the almost fatalistic tone in which the above passage foretells the rise and fall of development precludes the possibility of nostalgia, sometimes hinted at but largely absent from the novel. If the feeling of nostalgia is attached to the perception of a teleology of progress, the construction of a nostalgic horizon in the novel becomes a task for potential readers who cherish the old lifestyles of Rio's neighboring towns rather than an explicit element in the plot.

Going beyond nostalgia, to link *A cidade sitiada* with the consequences of developmentalist thought and policy thus also means thinking of Lispector as a chronicler of an urbanizing Brazil. Though most present in *A cidade sitiada*, urbanization is also already evident in other early novels, such as *O lustre* and *A maçã no escuro*, which reflect on the country's impending transformation in the context of rural areas portrayed in ways that are clearly in dialogue with the regionalist fiction so prevalent in Brazil's literary production when these novels were published. In this sense, Lispector's work, which has so often been identified as breaking with regionalist fiction, in fact emerges from it and addresses many of the issues it left open concerning the imminent impact of urbanization.[70] Besides internal migrations from the countryside to the city such as those detailed at the end of Graciliano Ramos's *Vidas secas* (1938; *Barren Lives*; 1965), one of these issues is the very transformation of rural areas into suburbs and suburbs into parts of cities.

By narrating this transformation in S. Geraldo's environment in *A cidade sitiada*, not only does Lispector engage with this regionalist tradition, but she also reconfigures it by exploring the role of nonhumans and, to a lesser extent, the limits to growth, in the context of the specific transformations undergone by the suburbs of Rio in the Vargas years. In the novel, a sensibility to the ecology of things, to return to Bennett, provides new ways of interpreting processes that would otherwise be explained in socioeconomic terms by economists such as Furtado. Such is the potential of fictional discourse: it makes visible forgotten elements of changes that may be well remembered, and it brings to light "thinking things" that populate and make denser the layers of sociability enmeshed in the urbanizing suburb.[71] Mimesis thus does not exactly work as an imitation of reality but, in Luiz Costa Lima's terms, rather produces a mirage of it, which reveals aspects not yet seen.[72]

The previous chapters have discussed how environmental perceptions mediated by novels and other cultural materials have informed multifaceted, often conflicting views of certain rural and forested areas. Thus fictionality—not only of novelistic discourse but also of depictions of these places as quintessential evidence of the continent's marvelous nature and as guarantors of national identities—has shaped how these realities are described and represented. In contrast, *A cidade sitiada* presents new problems. Instead of focusing on nonurbanized areas, it dwells exactly on this rather violent, generalized, and apparently unstoppable (albeit circular) process of urban change. The novel, as would be expected in the case of a young woman writer living abroad, was not as well received, successful, or influential as those previously discussed. Yet, without relying on geographic specificity—S. Geraldo could be many places, after all—*A cidade sitiada* offers a powerful counternarrative to developmentalist euphoria that not only sheds new light on its caveats and limits but rearranges the actants in such processes. Here nonhumans surround humans almost as much as humans surround nonhumans. The ecological dimension of Lispector's work, especially in this novel, thus does not take into consideration any divide between nature and culture. It simply proposes a flow of actors in constant interaction. In this sense, while issues of social and racial inequality became more prominent in her later novels, such as *A paixão segundo G.H.*

and particularly *A hora da estrela*, Lispector, starting with her earlier novels, was "reassembling the social" in a quite different way than other socially engaged authors of the time, through the disruptive potential of mimesis to reveal unseen facets of otherwise well-mapped contexts.

PART III

The Rights of Nature, the Rights of Fiction

CHAPTER 5

Against Wind and Tide

Fiction, Ecology, and Politics in Mario Vargas Llosa's Amazon

In an interview with Raymond Leslie Williams in 2001, the Peruvian novelist Mario Vargas Llosa talked about how important his 1958 trip to the Peruvian Amazon was to him. He referred to the rain forest as "un mundo que era la aventura, que siempre me había seducido, fascinado como lector" ("a world that was adventure—a world that had always seduced and fascinated me as a reader"),[1] an impression confirmed by the number of novels he has dedicated to the region. His fascination with the place notwithstanding, Vargas Llosa has not shied away from statements that all but make evident his contempt for the indigenous populations living in the Amazon and conservation efforts that may block natural resource extraction. "En Ecuador hemos visto [indígenas] operando y además creando un verdadero desorden político y social" ("In Ecuador we've seen [indigenous peoples] taking action and even creating true political and social disorder"),[2] he said in an interview with journalist José Olmos for the Ecuadorean newspaper *El Universo* on his visit to Bogotá in November 2003. The statement was especially polemi cal because it came just a few weeks before indigenous groups and international NGOs filed a high-stakes lawsuit accusing Texaco, which had been bought by Chevron in 2001, of causing an environmental catastrophe in the Ecuadorean Amazon through decades of oil spills and negligence. The $19 billion dispute was historic as the first case in which a large corporation was held accountable for environmental crimes in a developing country.[3] In criticizing indigenous groups in Bolivia for fighting against the privatization of their gas reserves, Vargas Llosa compared indigenous activism to what he identified as a collectivism typical of totalitarian regimes, concluding, "Ninguna sociedad colectivista o impregnada con esa cultura es una sociedad que desarrolla, moderniza y alcanza la civilización" ("No collectivist society, or society permeated with this culture, is a society that develops, modernizes, and reaches civilization").[4]

Vargas Llosa, notably, was not a reclusive writer but one of the most engaged public intellectuals Latin America has seen in the past half century. He expressed his neoliberal positions ardently in numerous essays, newspaper articles, and talks.[5] He was a candidate for the Peruvian presidency in 1990 and even a favorite for the position until the final stage of the electoral campaign. In parallel, he remained a celebrated fiction writer with a prolific body of work, including novels, short stories, plays, and essays on literature, whose major consecration came with his receipt of the 2010 Nobel Prize in Literature. For critics and commentators, reconciling his literary work with his political activity and his profile as a public intellectual continues to be a challenging task. While many of his novels allude to aspects of his autobiography that might, in fact, trace the trajectory of his political views, he has repeatedly affirmed the fundamental independence of fictional truth, which, in his view, does not entail any form of ethical commitment to its referent.

The complex interconnections between Vargas Llosa's fictional work and his political views are especially evident in matters concerning the condition and fate of indigenous groups, mostly in the Amazon, but also in other parts of Peru and Latin America more broadly. While indigenous characters populate his Amazonian novels, from *La casa verde* (1966; *The Green House*, 1968) to *El sueño del celta* (2010; *The Dream of the Celt*, 2012), his public antagonism toward indigenous groups and indigenist movements is most developed in books such as *La utopía arcaica: José María Arguedas y las ficciones del indigenismo* (1996; The archaic utopia: José María Arguedas and the fictions of indigenism), which harshly criticizes the Indigenist tradition in Peru through the figure of the writer and anthropologist José María Arguedas. In the realm of fiction, *El hablador* (1987; *The Storyteller*, 1989) most intensely dramatizes debates over the results and future of Peruvian indigenous populations in an Amazonian context. In all these examples, environmental considerations are implicit and surface at specific moments. Vargas

Llosa's environmental thinking is increasingly visible in his writings on indigenous issues, particularly in Amazonian context. To a certain extent, the close connection between indigenous and environmental activism in Latin America toward the end of the twentieth century reveals a less overt yet undeniable thread of reflection on the state and fate of the jungle in Vargas Llosa's fiction and nonfiction.

The present chapter examines this environmental thought from the double perspective of Vargas Llosa's theories of fiction and the ethics of fiction that a rhetorical reading of his novels vis-à-vis his essayistic and political activity uncovers. In other words, I focus here on the less-studied presence of Amazonian forested environments through the challenges they pose both to literary representation in Vargas Llosa's novels and to an understanding of apparently contradictory statements on environmental issues in his fiction and nonfiction. My hypothesis is that some of these contradictions are, to a certain extent, explicable if we consider his views on fiction as they emerge from his essays and apply them to his literary work. By unveiling the environmental implications of Vargas Llosa's multifaceted oeuvre, this chapter investigates the relationship between aesthetics and politics as they transition from developmentalist to neoliberal axes.

Vargas Llosa's consistent defense of the ethical and ontological autonomy of the literary work, which does not necessarily owe anything to reality, does not entail an ethical stance toward the actual environments his fiction celebrates. On the contrary, a comparison of his theories of fiction, his fiction itself, and his political activity suggests that the fictional Amazonian forest is, in Vargas Llosa's view, self-sufficient and disconnected from any need to conserve this region in referential reality. To a certain extent, Vargas Llosa's case is exemplary in that, by strongly affirming fiction's autonomy and progressively denying, over the course of his career, any ethical commitment that novels might imply toward the realities they depict, his literary work initially seems at odds with his developmentalist posture. However, in spite of his careful defense of fiction's autonomy, Vargas Llosa is also an exemplary case because his own novels, especially later ones such *El hablador*, seem to continually question the separation on which he himself insisted between his work as a writer and his views as a public intellectual.

This chapter focuses mostly on two periods in Vargas Llosa's career. The first comprises the late 1960s and early 1970s, when his first Amazonian novel, *La casa verde*, was published and helped solidify his reputation after his first success, *La ciudad y los perros* (1962; *The Time of the Hero*, 1966). At this point, the representation of nature played a relatively significant role in his struggle to affirm the ontological independence of literary works from reality as way of grounding the "mimetic rupture," in Donald Shaw's terms, of the Boom narrative.[6] The second period revolves around the late 1980s and early 1990s, when *El hablador*, one of the most crucial novels for understanding his views on the Amazon with respect to both environmental issues and indigenous rights, was published on the eve of his presidential campaign. During and after his political failure, he continued to reaffirm the ethical independence of the fictional text, at the same time as his criticism of both Peru's historical Indigenismo and contemporaneous indigenous movements intensified.

EARLY ESSAYS AND THE BOOM

When the so-called Latin American Boom began taking shape in the mid-1960s, one of its major concerns was to affirm its own revolutionary quality—both aesthetic and, to a certain extent, political—which, proponents claimed, heralded the region's literary maturity. Often essays by Boom authors, such as Carlos Fuentes and José Donoso, marked the distance between their work and the waves of regionalist fiction across Spanish America in the first half of the twentieth century. As the introduction to this book shows, Boom writers attacked what they saw as the naive, imitative gestures of these genres, much as they mocked the threatening central role nature played in them. Such arguments suggested that acritical imitation was tightly linked with use of the environment as a structuring principle of narrative. Besides having published three major long novels in the 1960s, Vargas Llosa, as an active essayist and speaker, participated in these discussions as he helped shape a certain view of the *nueva novela hispanoamericana* vis-à-vis previous forms of novelistic writing in Spanish America.

Among his early essays on the topic, "Novela primitiva y novela de creación en América Latina" (1969; The primitive novel and the novel of creation in Latin America) and its variations treat Latin American nature as an aesthetic problem posed by the Boom authors in response to the *novelas de la tierra*.[7] What he calls the *novela primitiva* included the work of early twentieth-century novelists, from novels by Mariano Azuela to Miguel Ángel Asturias's early novel *El señor presidente* (1946; *The President*, 1963), covering, as expected, a number of modalities of regionalist fiction. Also as expected, the documentary dimension of these works and their social critique, as well as an apparent lack of concern for form, were targets for Vargas Llosa's attack.

Interestingly, some of these topics also appear in his reflections on his own fiction, as *Historia secreta de una novela* (1971; Secret history of a novel) shows. Most curious, however, is Vargas Llosa's conclusion that "el conflicto principal que ilustran casi todas ellas no es el de campesinos contra terratenientes, o colonizados contra colonizadores, sino el del hombre y la naturaleza" ("the principal conflict that nearly all these novels illustrate is not that of the peasants against the landowners, or the colonized against the colonizers, but rather that between man and nature").[8] The most significant shift from the primitive novel to the new novel thus reflects a reversal in this balance:

> En la novela primitiva, la naturaleza no sólo aniquilaba al hombre: también lo generaba. Ahora es al revés: el eje de la ficción ha rotado de la naturaleza al hombre, y son los tormentos de éste, de cuando en cuando sus alegrías, lo que Rulfo encarna en sus bandoleros harapientos y sus mujeres pasivas e indoblegables.
>
> In the primitive novel, nature not only annihilated man; it also generated him. Now it is the reverse; the axis of fiction has rotated from nature to man, and it is the torments of man, and from time to time his joys, that Rulfo incarnates in his ragged bandits and his passive and indomitable women. (Vargas Llosa, "Novela primitiva," 31)

What is specific to the *novela de creación*, we may conclude, is what could be called an amalgam of narrative anthropocentrism and an understanding of creative mimesis as the novel's independence from reality, of which *La casa verde* is a practical example. It is symptomatic that Rulfo is quoted as an example of the *novela de creación*, for here Vargas Llosa is not so much exposing a rift between urban and rural novels as highlighting an ontological turn in the way literature positions itself with regard to reality. The novel "ya no sirve a la realidad, ahora se sirve de la realidad" (31; "no longer serves reality, now it is served by reality").[9] Thus he includes amongst the "novelists of creation" Alejo Carpentier, whose technical virtuosity, Vargas Llosa contends, lends Carpentier's world its "intristic truth" (35). A confusion, however, appears here: nature seems at first to refer to the sublime nature of Romantic imagination,[10] which Vargas Llosa makes clear when he alludes to "una naturaleza magnífica y temible, descrita con minutia y tremolos románticos" (30; "a magnificent and fearsome nature, described with romantic minutia and tremolos"), but which is surreptitiously transformed into nature as a reality from which fiction must detach itself. This confusion is significant, as his later work echoes it.

Considering that Vargas Llosa has been concerned with the relationship between literature and reality for decades, this essay is but a portion of a larger theorization.[11] His main early theses on the topic underscore the nonconformist role of literature, whose mission should be to "agitar, inquietar, alarmar, mantener a los hombres en una constante insatisfacción de sí mismos" ("agitate, disturb, alarm, maintain men in a constant state of dissatisfaction with themselves"),[12] as he argued in his famous speech, "La literatura es fuego" (Literature is fire), given on his receipt of the Premio Rómulo Gallegos (Rómulo Gallegos Prize) in 1967. Works such as *García Márquez: Historia de un deicidio* (1971; García Márquez: History of a deicide) and *La orgía perpetua* (1975; *The Perpetual Orgy*, 1986)[13] present his theory of the inner demons the writer has to face in order to write and, most importantly for this essay, characterize certain fictional works as *deicidios*, or "total novels," that supplant the reality created by God: "Pero *Cien años de soledad* es una novela total sobre todo porque pone en práctica el utópico designio de todo suplantador de Dios: describir una realidad total, enfrentar a la realidad real una imagen que es su expresión y negación" ("But *One Hundred Years of Solitude* is a total novel above all else because it puts into practice the utopian plan of every supplanter of God: to describe a total reality, to face the real reality with an image that is its expression and negation").[14] In this radical insistence on the ontological independence of the literary text, Vargas Llosa argues that not all literature but particular novels—most notably *Cien años de soledad*—may reach the status of total novels, a concept that, as Mark Anderson shows,[15] he borrowed from Franco-Lithuanian author Romain Gary.[16] Yet for Vargas Llosa, the novel as a genre represents a means of rebelling against the harshness of reality by creating an alternative world. As Anderson shows, the realist, nonallegorical character of the *novela total* would "get as close as possible to the real in order to be able to transform it more efficiently."[17]

Interestingly, from his early writings on, Vargas Llosa has linked the creation of alternative realities with historical moments of crisis and hopelessness in which societies are on the verge of disappearance, such as in the essay *La novela* (The novel): "Es como si desde el punto de vista social e histórico ocurriera lo mismo, como si las novelas surgieran a fin de recuperar, de salvar, de rescatar de la nada a esas realidades que van a morir, que van a desaparecer, que van a cambiar, de rescatarlas y también de exorcitarlas" ("It is as if from the social and historical point of view the same thing happened, as if the novels arose in order to recover, to save, to rescue from nothing those realities that are going to die, that are going to disappear, that are going to change, to rescue them and also to exorcise them").[18]

If clear echoes of Georg Lukács's *Theory of the Novel* (1916) can be heard in this description of fiction as the expression of a disintegrating world that has lost its immanence to life, it also treats the novel as a means of conserving a world, even if in a nontangible dimension.[19] Accepting Vargas Llosa's argument that novels arise and become mature when a society faces the prospect of deep crisis and disappearance, fiction then transcends its rebellious character to effectively offer some image of totality—the lost totality of the epic perhaps—which might, to a certain extent, compensate for a broken reality and, just as importantly, exorcise it. Rather than an ability to change reality, this exorcising function suggests a purging of the trauma of loss and a transformation of past realities that now exist only in fiction, in a way that parallels what conservation projects often aim to do on a spatial axis: erase the sense of change by attempting to keep certain areas as they were before they were engulfed by developmentalist initiatives. *La novela* fundamentally addresses the rise of the novel in the West and its recent developments in Latin America and thus does not mention the possible role of fiction as conservation in the context of the changing world of the Amazon and its indigenous peoples. After his travels to the region in 1958 and 1965, he did express some concern about the impact of the Catholic Church and the Instituto Lingüístico de Verano (Summer Linguistic Institute) on indigenous peoples, but he did not make explicit the function of stories, oral or written, in these contexts.

Although Vargas Llosa's theses on fiction were never completely consistent and evolved over the decades, in this early period his ideas already suggest how environmental mimesis takes shape in his work: (1) through a relativization of nature as an overwhelming force, as it was portrayed to be in early twentieth-century regionalism; and (2) through an understanding of the novel as creating an independent, self-sufficient reality that performs a compensatory function with regard to a world in crisis.

If Avelar understood the celebratory tone of the Boom's fiction as way of compensating "not only for social underdevelopment [in a context of increasing technologization] but also for the loss of the auratic status of the literary object,"[20] another compensatory structure appears here: Vargas Llosa's desire for a Latin American novel simultaneously understood as modern and foundational—that is, with its auratic status reaffirmed—coexists with his fascination with an Amazonian jungle whose otherness in relation to national modernity is repeatedly declared. In other words, the framing of the Amazon as "a world that was adventure" legitimizes its conservation in fiction while minimizing the impact of the numerous transformations it underwent in real life.

LA CASA VERDE

Three years after Vargas Llosa's debut as a novelist with *La ciudad y los perros*, his second novel, *La casa verde*, helped solidify his position as a major writer of the *nueva novela*. Rather than being centered on an urban setting, such as the Lima of both his previous novel and the subsequent one, *Conversación en La Catedral* (1969; *Conversation in the Cathedral*, 1974), *La casa verde* unfolds over a much broader geographical and environmental span that, in some senses, evokes earlier pieces of regionalist fiction that he classified as *novelas primitivas*. The novel's numerous plots and subplots take place either in the Amazonian jungle (especially the small Catholic mission town of Santa María de Nieva but with important scenes on islands and in other localities) or in Piura, a city in the desert on the northern coast of Peru where the brothel known as the Green House, which lends the book its name, was built. The novel is set during the decline of rubber tapping extraction in the Amazon and Piura's gradual urban growth.[21] As such, the formal structure of *La casa verde*, with interwoven plots narrated in a nonlinear fashion, is a significant departure from *La ciudad y los perros* and advances some techniques that ultimately became Vargas Llosa's trademarks, such as the *vasos comunicantes* through which separate conversations are polyphonically enlaced.[22]

The role of nature in these plots, in which the forest is no longer a force "que sustituye y destruye al hombre" ("that replaces and destroys man"), is a telling example of how a *novela de creación* can be set "in the jungle" but not be "of the jungle." Both the Amazon and the sandy area around Piura present a degree of quick changeability and interference with human affairs that at some points seems to wink parodically at the reader familiar with the corpus of "primitive" regionalist fiction. At the beginning of the novel the character Aquilino notes, "Los que hacen mapas no saben que la Amazonía es como mujer caliente, no se está quieta. Aquí todo se mueve, los ríos, los animales, los árboles" ("People who make maps don't know that the Amazon is like a hot woman, she's never the same. Everything is on the move here, the rivers, the animals, the trees");[23] and the building of the Casa Verde is initially met with skepticism from those who believe that "la arena devoraría aquella mansión en poco tiempo, se la tragaría como a los viejos árboles podridos o a los gallinazos muertos" (98; "the sand would eat the house up in no time, it would swallow it up like the old rotten trees and the dead vultures," 67). The idea of a nature that swallows human structures—especially linked with the verb *tragar*, meaning "to swallow up," famously used in the last sentence of *La vorágine*—clearly alludes to the novelistic trend that perhaps most typifies the *novela primitiva*. And this is not its only occurrence: in a comment about how the surrounding vegetation destroyed a small village of huts, for example, Sergeant Delgado observes, in a Riveran fashion: "El monte ya casi se las ha tragado" (318; "The jungle's practically swallowed up these huts already," 238). Passages such as this attest to what Charlotte Rogers has identified as an intense dialogue between Vargas Llosa's jungle novels and the genre of the *novelas de la selva*.[24] I contend that *La casa verde*'s attempt to engage with this genre's tropes and motifs through parody shows precisely how Vargas Llosa's *novela de creación* differs from a *novela primitiva*.

In fact, descriptions of the rain forest in *La casa verde* are significantly shorter than in the *novelas de la selva*, and while water and profuse vegetation may affect human actions, they do not pose an existential threat to the characters. They do present obstacles to locomotion—"Así es la selva, hay que tener paciencia" ("That's the way the jungle is, you have to be patient"),[25] says Delgado—but, except in a few specific situations, the forest does not become an identifiable antagonist. In a sign of its departure from the Romantic sublime, the novel's descriptions of the jungle often take place not through the characters' gaze but rather through tangible perceptions of the forest as it interacts with the human body. This focus on bodies in their flesh and weakness, rather than on human eyes as transcendental filters of reality, turns the locus of attention away from the forest and toward its human inhabitants.[26] For example, when Fushía and Lalita run away into the wild, "los escoltaban jejenes, lluvias de zancudos, el canto ronco de los trompeteros y en las noches, a pesar del fuego y de las mantas, los murciélagos planeaban sobre sus cuerpos y mordían en lugares blandos" (267; "they were escorted by gnats, a rain of mosquitoes, the hoarse song of the trompetero birds, and at night, in spite of the fire and the blankets, the bats would swoop over their bodies and bite into the soft spots," 198–99).

Thus, *La casa verde* was primarily understood by its author and received by its critics in the context of the Boom's innovations, to the point that Gerald Martin, in 1989, called it Vargas Llosa's "most mature work, one of the greatest novels to have emerged from Latin America."[27] That nature was no longer a protagonist, that it did not occupy long pages of description, that instead an anthropocentric approach was achieved by emphasizing the jungle's effects on the human body: all these elements make up a "mature Latin American novel," which, for Vargas Llosa and other Boom writers, meant human characters taking the lead.

The young writer learned some decisive lessons while composing *La casa verde*, as the essay *Historia secreta de una novela*, published in 1971—the same year as *García Márquez: Historia de un deicidio*—shows.[28] Composed as a sort of reverse fan fiction, where fans of a novel do not build alternative outcomes but rather read of its origins,[29] Vargas Llosa narrates the autobiographical events—including two stints each in Piura and the Amazon during his childhood and young adulthood—that most influenced the settings of *La casa verde*, followed by an account of how he wrote the book. *Historia secreta* makes clear how aware Vargas Llosa was of avoiding the pitfalls he had identified a couple of years before. Living in Paris at the time of the novel's composition and consulting bibliographies on the region as well as visiting botanical gardens, he declares that "las lecturas amazónicas me vacunaron contra el vicio descriptivo" ("the Amazonian readings vaccinated me against the vice of description").[30] In other words, his novel's very thematic affinity with the novels of the jungle and colonial chronicles, and his close study of them, prevented him from yielding to the documentary impulse and, we might add, from allowing the forest to predominate over human characters. This explains why, in *La casa verde* as in some of his later novels, the descriptions of the Amazon are brief, perhaps crude, and never really similar to those of either colonial chronicles or the *novelas de la selva*, in spite of a shared setting and notwithstanding the dialogue Vargas Llosa establishes with those genres. These descriptions are not based on the detached eye contemplating the forest, but on constant interactions between humans and nature, in which smell, heat, discomfort, and insects come to the fore.

More than that, *Historia secreta* is effectively a key document showing how many of the tropes of and declarations about indigenous peoples that became explosive in Vargas Llosa's work in the late 1980s and 1990s were already present, sometimes almost in the same words, in this earlier period. After his first, decisive trip to the region, he notes, "Descubrí un rostro de mi país que desconocía por completo. . . . Allí descubrí que el Perú no solo era un país del siglo veinte, con abundantes problemas, desde luego . . . , sino que el Perú era también la Edad Media y la Edad de la Piedra" ("I discovered a face of my country that had been completely unknown to me. . . . There I discovered that Peru was not only a country of the twentieth century, with abundant problems, of course . . . , but that Peru was also the Middle Ages and the Stone Age").[31] Vargas Llosa here echoes Carpentier and the long-standing treatment of the forest as part of an earlier temporality defined in relation to a Eurocentric historiography. He maintained such views later, and especially in his speeches and articles as a politician and a public intellectual, they proved to be even more disturbing than in the context of his early novels.[32] In fact, passages like the one above call into question any assumption that Vargas Llosa's ethnocentrism with respect to Latin American indigenous populations was a byproduct of his ideological conversion from socialism to neoliberalism in the 1970s. Although less obviously, such opinions were already present in his work in 1971.

Regarding the opening scene of *La casa verde*, Vargas Llosa notes in *Historia secreta* that he does not approve of the forced acculturation of indigenous girls by nuns, which only enables their precarious insertion into and exploitation by nonindigenous societies later on. He also asserts that he does not idealize the living conditions of indigenous groups, unlike anthropologists, such as Mascarita in his 1980s novel, who "quisieran conservar a toda costa, fielmente intacta, la vida 'prehistórica' de las tribus para . . . 'estudiarlas mejor'" (34–35; "wanted to conserve at all costs, faithfully intact, the prehistoric life of the tribes in order to . . . 'study them better'"). Passages such as this show that themes already implicit in *La casa verde* cross Vargas Llosa's work and thought over decades, and that the history of this novel's reception, which celebrated it as a triumph of the *nueva novela* as well as a means for accessing an unknown Peru, later took on more problematic contours.

In its thematic and geographical breadth, as well as in stylistic choices such as nonlinear, entangled plots—the *cajas chinas*, as he called them—

and overlapping dialogue, *La casa verde* aspires to be a *novela total* that surpasses reality and ensures the maturity and richness of Latin American fiction. At the same time, while the understanding of fiction as conservation is not yet present in Vargas Llosa's thinking, the ethical independence of fictional discourse that he explored more deeply in the 1980s already appears in *Historia secreta*: "'La verdad real' es una cosa y la 'verdad literaria' otra y no hay nada tan difícil como querer que ambas coincidan" (69; "'The real truth' is one thing and the 'literary truth' is another, and there is nothing so difficult as wanting them to coincide"), he says toward the end of the book. As such, the threads weaving together Vargas Llosa's views of fiction in these two periods are already evident, and these threads would take on more problematic dimensions later, when the predicament of Amazonian indigenous peoples and environments became more publicly urgent.

ENVIRONMENTALISM, INDIGENISM, POLITICS

A few years after writing *Historia secreta*, in the late 1970s, Vargas Llosa gave a series of presentations about Peruvian novelist José María Arguedas that found their most developed form in the book *La utopía arcaica: José María Arguedas y las ficciones del indigenismo*. The epithet "archaic utopia" defines the thought of the influential Indigenist movement in twentieth-century Peru, and the book's critique converges on the polemical figure of writer and anthropologist José María Arguedas. The young Vargas Llosa carried on a friendly dialogue with Arguedas, though he had doubts about the latter's views on indigenous issues in the country, which contrasted with the idea that, in Antonio Cornejo Polar's words, the "modernity of the Andean countries depends upon their capacity for deindigenization," which Vargas Llosa defended.[33] Interweaving an account of Arguedas's life and works with a panorama of Peruvian Indigenist thought, this volume and the talks that preceded it constitute harsh criticism of what Vargas Llosa saw as a naively utopian project, albeit mixed with some admiration for Arguedas as a novelist.

At the core of Vargas Llosa's critique is what he characterizes as Arguedas's idealized portrayal of the Andean region's indigenous groups, in which "desindianizar a los indios . . . es un crimen todavía peor que explotarlos, discriminarlos y maltratarlos" ("to deindianize the Indians . . . is a crime still worse than exploiting, discriminating against, and mistreating them").[34] In this sense, Arguedas's desire to conserve Andean indigenous cultures makes him a "ecólogo cultural" (37; "cultural ecologist"), a telling classification given the attention that Vargas Llosa pays to the animated descriptions of nature in Arguedas's work and his lament for the environmental degradation of the town of Chimbote in his last novel—a lament, according to Vargas Llosa, closely connected to an aversion to modernization and technology echoed in his defense of indigenous cultures and societies.

In fact, Arguedas's perspectives on modernization and the results of cultural contact are markedly more nuanced than Vargas Llosa suggests. In his ethnographic work and other anthropological essays, for example, Arguedas lucidly describes the impact of economic modernization in predominantly indigenous areas in the *sierra*, often taking into consideration its positive impacts. He does worry about fast, violent cultural change prompted by politically and economically dominant nations, such as the United States and European countries, attempting to achieve cultural hegemony. On the other hand, he points to the cultural resilience of local communities and what might be "incolonizable" ("uncolonizable") in them.[35] If, for him, the penetration of Western culture into the *sierra* had historically been challenging because of the mountainous region's biophysical characteristics and "la resistencia cultural del indio" (*Formación*, 26; "the cultural resistance of the Indian"), in the twentieth century the lingering colonial mindset added another obstacle to the process that, in spite of its drawbacks, could lead Peru "hacia una nueva unidad, a cual será tan profunda y múltiple como la antigua" (27; "toward a new unity, which will be as profound and multiple as its ancient unity"). Together with the other essays that make up the volume *Formación de una cultura nacional indoamericana* (1975), these are some examples of how Arguedas's takes on modernization, albeit critical, were much more granular than they might seem at first.

Arguedas as a "cultural ecologist": the term *ecology* writ large enters here as a broader conservationist attitude that encompasses regions and cultures alike. And for somebody like Arguedas, who "describe este mundo arcaico y utópico, que él sabía condenado" ("describes this utopian and archaic world, which he knows to be condemned"),[36] the defense of this "archaic utopia" can only be fully expressed through the worlds constructed in fiction. The chapters devoted to analysis of Arguedas's literary works are thus also permeated by a vehement affirmation of their fictionality, complemented by Vargas Llosa's already well-established pronouncement that fiction is a world that has its own truth and does not find equivalents in referential reality.[37] Curiously, then, Vargas Llosa founds a significant portion of his critique of Arguedas on a slippage between two understandings of fiction: while he portrays the latter's Indigenist views as a fabrication and a lie, their expression in fiction still constitutes an autonomous world. These two understandings correspond to what Sara Castro-Klarén identifies as "persuasion," or the ability to produce a convincing argument in Aristotelian terms, and fiction as "verisimilitude," as "the art of storytelling or mythos,"[38] according to both of which Arguedas's novel *Todas las sangres* (1964; All the bloods) failed in Vargas Llosa's view.

In spite of its focus on the Andean world, from which *El hablador* quite strategically maintains some distance, *La utopía arcaica* constitutes in many senses an essayistic version of the thesis implied by that novel and already rehearsed in *Historia secreta*: that the difficulty, and indeed the inconvenience, of conserving a given reality, in its environmental, cultural, and social particularity, shape a utopian view of an archaic past that can only exist in fiction. In contrast with the *novela total* and Vargas Llosa's early attempts to portray literature as able to change or even supplant reality, he came to think that fiction is the only way in which such writers and dreamers may make their contributions meaningful and deserve the type of attention a volume such as *La utopía arcaica* grants them. Rather than changing reality or supplanting it, fiction offers an alternative realm that should instead remain imaginary, so as to open space for progress. Mimesis here must be understood in a far different fashion than the reverse mimesis analyzed in chapter 1, for example. Confined to its strictest sense as the representation of a certain reality, the mimetic gesture remains an intransitive exercise that ideally conserves the past in its pages without interfering with a process of "deindianization" assumed to be inevitable. Instead of being dynamically embedded in discussions of what reality is or might be, the text becomes a tomb. As such, any attempt to bring this "utopia" to the realm of the real automatically attaches to the very notion of fiction its worst connotation as a lie—dishonesty that reality needs to purge, as Plato's Republic expels its poets.[39] Jean Franco asks, in this sense, "why Vargas Llosa, an author who famously defended literature as a defiance to reality, criticizes Arguedas precisely on the grounds that his work does not correspond to reality."[40] With Arguedas as an emblematic example, this crucial ambiguity about the role and meaning of fictionality takes its most fraught form in Vargas Llosa's writings on indigenous and environmental issues.

To be sure, these and other works of his on the topic did meet with fierce resistance and criticism. The number of open letters online and in periodicals, as well as academic and nonacademic articles criticizing his defense of cultural assimilation and, to a lesser degree, his stance on environmental conservation, have steadily accumulated over the decades. They were particularly numerous around 2010, when Vargas Llosa won the Nobel Prize in Literature. One such criticism came from someone mentioned in *La utopía arcaica* because of his friendship with Arguedas toward the end of his life: Hugo Blanco, the indigenous activist who, in the late 1960s, organized a revolutionary movement in the Peruvian *sierra* in an attempt to establish a socialist regime like that of Cuba. Although a still-leftist Vargas Llosa then publicly condemned the death penalty (never carried out) to which Blanco was sentenced for revolutionary activity, he painted a critical portrait of Blanco as a radical Trotskyist leader in his 1996 volume. In 2010, Blanco, who had already criticized Vargas Llosa on other occasions, published an open letter accusing him of racism and citing the novelist's article in response to the indigenous massacre at Bagua in 2009, which, according to official reports, had ten indigenous (and twenty-three police) casualties, but which Blanco claims had as many as two hundred.[41]

The article that triggered Blanco's critique was "Victoria Pírrica," published in *El País* a couple of weeks after the massacre. The indigenous protests that led to the episode challenged an agreement between Peru and the United States for the extraction of natural resources in the Peruvian Amazon; thus, these protests had a decisive environmental dimension. Vargas Llosa laments Peru's withdrawal from this agreement in the aftermath of the massacre, claiming that it

> perseguían una necesidad imperiosa: atraer inversión privada y tecnología de punta hacia una región que tiene grandes reservas de gas, petróleo y muchos minerales y podría ser una fuente de prosperidad y modernización para ese país pobre que es el Perú, empezando, claro está, por quienes más ayuda necesitan: las comunidades nativas de la Amazonía.

> pursued a pressing need: to attract private investment and cutting-edge technology to a region that has large reserves of gas, oil, and many minerals, and could be a source of prosperity and modernization for that poor country that is

> Peru, beginning, of course, with those who need more help: the native communities of the Amazon.[42]

Environmental degradation was already a reality in the Amazon, he argued, but it occurred in an unregulated way. It remains a point of contention whether the agreement would have really curbed illegal exploitation, respected indigenous rights to lands, and had a smaller environmental impact than what was already taking place. Most important, however, is Vargas Llosa's unapologetic defense of cultural assimilation guided by transnational capital, which would bring "progress" to the country as a whole, regardless of its environmental costs and the keen awareness that protesting groups had of those.[43] While the issues at stake here are certainly not fictional, the message is clear and reinforces what Vargas Llosa had already said in *La utopía arcaica*: at least in the realm of reality, cultural and environmental conservation are utopian fallacies and real dangers, and their usually leftist "fictions"—here understood in its most negative sense as a synonym for lies and illusions, which, as Franco makes explicit, is a surprising move for an author so engaged with the specificities of fictional discourse—must be banned from the nonfictional realm.[44]

Although its main ideas were developed over decades, *La utopía arcaica* was published in 1996, three years after another nonfiction book by Vargas Llosa that delves deeply into Peru's recent history: not the intellectual and political history of Peruvian Indigenism, but the author's experience of his country's political life from his college years to the book's culmination, ending with his failed candidacy for the presidency in 1990.[45] In *El pez en el agua*, two main narrative lines develop in alternate chapters, showing how Vargas Llosa, albeit seen as an outsider in relation to party politics—"un pez fuera del agua" ("a fish out of water")[46]—had actually spent most of his life involved in political projects. From his leftist position in the 1950s and 1960s, he shifted toward neoliberalism in the 1970s, embraced it more thoroughly in the 1980s, and expressed it fully in his candidacy, via his ardent defense of privatization in opposition to the nationalization of the banks by then-president Alan García and the former leftist dictatorship of Juan Velasco Alvarado. Vargas Llosa advocated the creation of "un sistema en el que todos pudieran acceder al mercado, a la empresa y a la propiedad privada" ("a system in which everyone could have access to the market, to owing and running a business, and to private property"),[47] and his models were notably countries like Japan, South Korea, and Singapore, which Peru could copy and with which it could increase trade, as it had an advantage the Asian countries did not: "el petróleo y los minerales" (266; "petroleum and minerals," loc. 4457).

The Amazon appears minimally in *El pez en el agua*, indigenous and environmental issues even less, and *El hablador* is only mentioned early in the book, when Vargas Llosa notes that he was correcting the novel's proofs when he took the first steps toward what would become his candidacy (*El pez en el agua*, 33–34). Yet *El hablador* came out in 1987, close to the beginning of the campaign. Although other novels, such as *Pantaleón y las visitadoras* (1973; *Captain Pantoja and the Special Services*, 1978) and *La tía Julia y el escribidor* (1977; *Aunt Julia and the Scriptwriter*, 1982), were used as weapons against Vargas Llosa the candidate because of their sexual content (*El pez en el agua*, 81, 419), *El hablador* touched on aspects of the potential future president's plan for the Amazonian region and its population.

Before turning to *El hablador*, it is worth examining the curious role that his ecological agenda played in the electoral campaign and its complexities. The Amazon was at the center of the campaign as a locus for the expansion of narcotrafficking. A major element of Vargas Llosa's plan was "pacificación nacional" ("national pacification") directed at both the activities of the revolutionary group Sendero Luminoso (Shining Path), which terrorized the *sierra*, and narcotrafficking activity in the jungle. According to a text that Vargas Llosa presented at the Foro Economía y Agricultura (Agricultural and Economic Forum) a few months before the election, the coca plantations for the production of cocaine utilize

> tierras aptas para el cultivo, lo que acarrea una gravísima destrucción de recursos naturales, motivada por la tala de bosques y la erosión producida como consecuencia de ello. Debido a que la mayor parte de las áreas sembradas con coca pertenecen a tierras forestales, no es apropiado hablar de la sustitución de cultivos, sino más bien de la creación de alternativas para aproximadamente cien mil campesinos.
>
> land that is suitable for cultivation, which very seriously destroys natural resources due to the felling of forests and the resulting erosion. Because most of the areas planted with coca are forested land, it is not appropriate to speak of crop substitution, but rather of creating alternatives for approximately one hundred thousand peasants.[48]

It might seem surprising that Vargas Llosa would defend reforestation as a solution for areas cleared for coca cultivation rather than focus on a keyword of his plan for agriculture: productivity.[49] While he indeed attacked deforestation caused by narcotrafficking in "Victoria pírrica" and even in *El hablador*, his defense of reforestation seems to reflect a program devised by an organ of his own campaign: the Comisión del Medio Ambiente y Desarrollo Sostenible (Commission for the Environment and Sustainable Development). Led by Alfredo E. Ferreyros, it formulated for the prospective Vargas Llosa government a series of ambitious initiatives that presented environmental conservation not as an obstacle to development but rather as a strategy for inserting Peru into Western modernity—a modernity that the candidate sought, as Carlos Ivan Degregori argues, in an almost naive fashion.[50] The commission's plan opens as follows:

> La iniciación de una efectiva Gestión Ambiental por parte del Estado, que en el Perú nunca se ha dado, marcaría un hito de nuestra historia y nuestras relaciones internacionales se verían reforzadas dada la coyuntura mundial. Hoy en día el mundo desarrollado y las entidades de apoyo al desarrollo, inversión y fomento están especialmente interesados en proyectos donde el componente ambiental se enfatice o juegue un rol preponderante.
>
> The initiation of an effective Environmental Management by the State, which in Peru has never occurred, would mark a milestone in our history, and our international relations would be strengthened given the global situation. Nowadays, the developed world and the entities that support development, investment, and promotion are especially interested in projects in which the environment is emphasized or plays a preponderant role.[51]

Moreover, far from alienating indigenous groups as incapable of contributing to these conservation efforts, the plan recognized them as protagonists in its third proposal, Programa de Desarrollo Sostenido de la Amazonía (Program for Sustainable Development of Amazonia), whose objective was "trabajar estrechamente con las Comunidades Nativas, como precursores y conocedores de ese medio ambiente, para proyectos de investigación, fines de alimentación, medicinales e industriales" ("to work closely with Native Communities, as precursors and people who are familiar with that environment, on research projects and for industrial, medicinal, and nutritional purposes").[52]

These factors show that, even though his defense of the free market and private property were the most prominent facets of Vargas Llosa's campaign, it also invoked concerns about environmentalism and indigenous rights, which may seem surprising given the author's take on these issues elsewhere. While it remains impossible to know what would have happened had Vargas Llosa become president, these varying positions suggest a complex and sometimes contradictory dynamic by which the notions of development and modernity so insistent in Vargas Llosa's discourse took the form of plans for both maximum exploitation of oil and mineral resources, on one hand, and sustainable development with indigenous participation, on the other. Far from turning away from such tensions at work at the time of its publication, *El hablador* imbued them with more radical tones in the refracted space of fiction.

EL HABLADOR

Vargas Llosa's third novel set in the Amazon shares neither the multiple plots and formal complexity of *La casa verde* nor the comic style of *Pantaleón y las visitadoras*. Instead, it emphasizes, via an intensely dialogic structure, fundamental dilemmas about whether and how to integrate indigenous populations, especially groups with little to no contact with outsiders, into the nation. Involved in these debates is the management of the Amazon's natural resources and the impending threat of deforestation.

The two protagonists take diverging views on these subjects. On one hand, the first-person narrator—whom I call Mario here due to a number of biographical similarities with Vargas Llosa and to differentiate him from the storyteller, the other narrator[53]—defends the assimilation of Peruvian Indians as a process that is not only inevitable but actually good for them.[54] On the other hand, his school friend Saúl Zuratas, a promising Jewish anthropology student working with one of the most isolated groups in the Amazon, the Machiguenga, challenges his views. As Zuratas grows progressively more disappointed with the work of anthropologists and their influence on these communities, he abandons his studies and the narrator loses track of him. But Mario has reason to believe that Zuratas went to live among the Machiguenga and became one of the most cherished and protected figures in their culture: an *hablador*, a person who travels among the scattered members of the nomadic group telling stories. Albeit translated into English as "storyteller," the term *hablador* is more precisely a "talker," with negative connotations suggesting a careless character prone to gossiping, lying, and idle chatter. The term is clearly gendered: women are more often perceived as *habladoras*.[55] This ambiguity inflects a figure whom the narrator nevertheless defines in a serious tone as "la memoria de la comunidad" ("the memory of the community"),[56] "los vínculos aglutinantes de esa sociedad a la que la lucha por supervivencia había obligado a resquebrajarse y desperdigarse a los cuatro vientos" (106; "the connecting links of this society that the fight for survival had forced to split up and scatter to the four winds," 92). *Habladores* are those who conserve a common cultural knowledge and pass it along among the Machiguenga.[57]

The chapters alternate between recounting the plot and a series of shifting, confusing narrations of Machiguenga stories, until it ultimately becomes clear in the last chapter that Zuratas, the storyteller, is telling these stories and mixing Western Jewish allusions into them, such as references to Frank Kafka's protagonist Gregor Samsa and to Jesus Christ. It also becomes clear in the epilogue that, after seeing a photograph of an *hablador* with a large birthmark like Zuratas's, Mario decided to consider Zuratas an *hablador*, which allows the reader to retrospectively realize that the Machiguenga stories were part of Mario's own attempt to write about them.[58]

Unlike in the case of the Jewish diaspora, however, the ultimate threat to the Machiguenga's integrity emerges from the economic exploitation of Amazonian natural resources: rubber extraction or "sangría de árboles" ("tree-bleeding") in the relatively recent past, the remnants of such rubber-tapping activity, the oil industry, drug trafficking, and the expansion of the agricultural frontier. Departing from Vargas Llosa's position in the case of the Baguazo, the novel does not seem to differentiate between clandestine forms of exploitation and those permitted by law. The novel is in part nostalgic about the Machiguenga, who had piqued Vargas Llosa's interest since he first learned of them on his early trip to the Amazon, which he described in an affectionate way, as much as it evokes a certain "imperialist nostalgia," in Renato Rosaldo's words, which Misha Kokotovic uses to describe the attitude of both Vargas Llosa and the narrator.[59] Despite this nostalgia, the narrator states:

> ¿Qué proponía Zuratas, a fin de cuentas? ¿Que, para no alterar los modos de vida y las creencias de unas tribus que vivían, muchas de ellas, en la Edad de la Piedra, se abstuviera el resto del Perú de explotar la Amazonía? ¿Deberían dieciséis millones de peruanos renunciar a los recursos naturales de tres cuartas partes de su territorio para que los sesenta u ochenta mil indígenas amazónicos siguieran flechándose tranquilamente entre ellos . . . ? . . . No, Mascarita, el país tenía que desarrollarse. . . . Si el precio del desarrollo y la industrialización, para los dieciséis millones de peruanos, era que esos poco millares de calatos tuvieran que cortarse el pelo, lavarse los tatuajes y volverse mestizos—o, para usar la más odiada palabra del etnólogo: aculturarse—, pues, qué remedio. (*El hablador*, 31–32)

> What did he suggest, when all was said and done? That, in order not to change the way of life and the beliefs of a handful of tribes still living, many of them, in the Stone Age, the rest of Peru abstain from developing the Amazon region? Should sixteen million Peruvians renounce the natural resources of three-quarters of the national territory so that seventy or eighty thousand Indians could quietly go on shooting at each other with bows and arrows . . . ? . . . No, Mascarita, the country had to move forward. . . . If the price to be paid for development and industrialization for the sixteen million Peruvians meant that those few thousand naked Indians would have to cut their hair, wash off their tattoos, and become mestizos—or, to use the ethnologists' most detested word, become acculturated—well, there was no way round it. (*The Storyteller*, 21–22)

Not by chance has this passage frequently been recalled in critical pieces on the novel: it condenses in a few sentences decades of Vargas Llosa's thought, now transferred to Mario, about how Amazonian indigenous communities live in nothing short of a Stone Age, and their picturesque lifestyle must necessarily be disrupted, in spite of the good intentions of inherently misguided anthropologists and activists, in order to clear the way for the non-negotiable march of development. From an environmental perspective, the passage implies that the motive is ultimately not to acculturate indigenous peoples per se, but rather to develop and exploit the region, which their right to their lands would prevent, imposing a cost on the whole country. Although Vargas Llosa became even more emphatic in his later defenses of acculturation as a way to build a modern Peru, this passage, clear and concise, could be read as a self-parody of his own views, besides showing how similar Mario's opinions about environmental policies are to the author's. Yet, as this section shows, the fictional status of Mario's words is instrumental in the complex narrative structure of *El hablador*.

If similarities abound between Vargas Llosa and the narrator, so too do allusions to José María Arguedas via the figure of Zuratas—an analogy complicated by the way the novel displaces Arguedas's Andean Indigenist thought to the context of the Amazon. While Zuratas is so similar to Arguedas that the narrator characterizes his worldview as a "utopía arcaica" (91; "archaic [. . .] utopia," 78), he thinks the situation of indigenous peoples in the Andes, and therefore the Indigenist tradition in Peru, fundamentally diverges from that of indigenous groups in Amazonia. In Zuratas's words,

> No, no soy un indigenista a la manera de éstos de los años treinta. . . . [Y]o sé muy bien que para los descendientes de los incas no hay vuelta atrás. A ellos sólo les queda integrarse. . . . Ya ves, no soy un utópico. En la Amazonía, sin embargo, es distinto. No se ha producido todavía el gran trauma que convirtió a los incas en un pueblo de sonámbulos y vasallos. . . . Ahora ya sabemos la atrocidad que significa eso de llevar el progreso, de querer modernizar a un pueblo primitivo. Simplemente acaba con él. (114–15)
>
> No, I'm not an Indigenist like the ones of the thirties. . . . I know very well that there's no turning back for the descendants of the Incas. The only course left them is integration. . . . So you see I'm not being utopian. But in Amazonia it's different. The great trauma that turned the Incas into a people of sleepwalkers and vassals hasn't yet occurred there. . . . We know now what an atrocity bringing progress, trying to modernize a primitive people, is. Quite simply, it wipes them out. (99–100)

Passages like this one reveal a crucial rift between a defense of Amazonian Indians based on Andean Indigenism and the specificity of their situation: while Indians from the *sierra* have no option but to acculturate themselves, Indians from the *selva* can still be shielded from external modernizing forces. This passage in fact calls into question the inevitable temptation, present throughout criticism of *El hablador*, to read Zuratas's position exclusively through the lens of Andean Indigenism, or at least through the lens Vargas Llosa used to describe it. The identification of Zuratas with Arguedas and Andean Indigenism is, indeed, unavoidable yet imprecise. And it is telling that Vargas Llosa claimed in *La utopía arcaica* that Arguedas always expressed sympathy for the Instituto Lingüístico de Verano, whose activity among Amazonian Indians Zuratas decries as a mechanism of cultural assimilation and even Vargas Llosa himself distrusted, as *La utopía arcaica* shows.

A point of similarity between the real Arguedas and the fictional Zuratas, however, is the continuum between humanity and nature in their thought. Previous critical work on Arguedas, such as that of William Rowe,[60] identified this harmony, and Vargas Llosa reaffirmed it in *La utopia arcaica*, in spite of moments in Arguedas's fiction that disrupt it in states of ecological crisis, as Jorge Marcone notes in the case of the novel *El zorro de arriba y el zorro de abajo* (1971; *The Fox from Up Above and the Fox from Down Below*, 2000).[61] Zuratas, interestingly, uses this idea to environmentally justify the uniqueness of Amazonian Indians at the end of the previously quoted paragraph: "La relación del hombre y la naturaleza, por ejemplo. . . . Esa armonía que existe entre ellos y esas cosas nosotros ni sabemos lo que es, pues la hemos roto para siempre" (*El hablador*, 115; "The relationship between man and Nature, for instance. . . . We don't even know what the harmony that exists between man and those things can be, since we've shattered it forever," *The Storyteller*, 100). As such, Zuratas suggests that environmental conservation in the Amazon could enable the conservation of cultural forms and modes of existence already condemned in the Andes. A bifurcation of this position is evident in Vargas Llosa's own opinions: while the politician was not completely averse to reforestation, at least in areas deforested by narcotrafficking, the public intellectual stood firmly for acculturation, which he repeatedly portrayed as inevitable in widely read and translated essays such as "Questions of Conquest,"[62] and reaffirmed his favorable attitude toward exploiting rather than conserving natural resources in the Amazon.

Beyond Vargas Llosa's thought, the novel's reception was shaped by the upshots of significant transformations from the 1960s to the 1980s,[63] when the Peruvian Amazon was increasingly integrated into international circuits of capitalism in what Macarena Gómez-Barris has called "the extractive zone."[64] Besides the ideas, authors, and movements already mentioned in this book, rural and forest workers in the Brazilian Amazon led a number of grassroots movements that were part of what Joan Martínez Alier and Ramachandra Guha call the "environmentalism of the poor."[65] These environmental activists were brutally repressed, with rubber tapper and environmental leader Chico Mendes and others murdered by local landowners and extractive companies. According to Óscar Espinosa de Rivero, in the Peruvian Amazon, such movements, alongside development projects promoted by successive governments, inspired the creation of the first indigenous organizations dedicated to fighting for their territory and their culture.[66] This process began with the Federación Shuar (Shuar Federation), founded in 1964 in response to an indigenous massacre, and culminated with the establishment, in 1981, of the Asociación Interétnica de Desarrollo de la Selva Peruana (Interethnic Association of Development of the Peruvian Forest; AIDESEP), "which represents, on a national level, the interests of the majority of Amazonian indigenous peoples."[67]

Simultaneously, the 1980s saw the publication of literary works that gave indigenous voices almost unprecedent attention. In the Peruvian Amazon, César Calvo's *Las tres mitades de Ino Moxo* (1981, The Three Halves of Ino Moxo), a book based on interviews with shaman Ino Moxo, immerses readers into what Jorge Marcone calls "not only a representation of ayahuasca's mestizo shamanism, but a being of this very [Amazonian] cosmology."[68] Beyond Peru, in a volume published in Brazil, *Antes o mundo não existia* (1980; At That Time the World Did Not Exist), Umusi Pãrõkumu and Tõrãmu Kehíri narrate the mythology of the Desana-Kehíripõrã for a non-indigenous audience. Therefore, while the reception of *La casa verde* emphasized the technical virtuosity of its representation of indigenous peoples, such depictions were now associated with a series of pressing political issues that *El hablador* in fact dramatized in problematic ways.[69]

In this context, it is not surprising that a work as close to a novel of ideas as *El hablador*, with its crucial discussion of possible futures for Amazonian indigenous populations and the physical environments where they lived, moved critical discussion about Vargas Llosa's environmental representation from a mostly aesthetic plane to a broadly political and ethical one. What was at stake was not so much the possibility of formal innovation as the forests and peoples Vargas Llosa himself admired, disturbingly portrayed alongside an argument for cultural assimilation, deforestation, and urbanization. At a time when Vargas Llosa's literary persona was deeply attached to his role as a politician, the identification between *El hablador*'s author and narrator became especially significant.[70] A number of scholars have undertaken the task of understanding how this novel may have functioned rhetorically as part of Vargas Llosa's larger political agenda at the time,[71] even while a straightforward identification of Vargas Llosa the author with Vargas Llosa the politician and public intellectual remains, as many of these works show, difficult. Part of the problem is that the narrator identified with the author tells only half of the story, quite literally.

El hablador is composed of eight chapters, five of which are narrated by the narrator and three by the *hablador*, or Tasurinchi, who might be Zuratas. As these three chapters occupy 48 percent of the total number of pages, roughly half of the novel is devoted to narrating the legends, stories, and sometimes self-assessments of the Machiguenga, for whom discourses of deforestation and cultural assimilation are absent and would be foreign ideas met with hostility. While criticism of the novel has tended to emphasize the chapters in which the author's alter ego speaks, critics who focus on the Machiguenga, such as Lúcia Sá, have shown that there are discrepancies between Vargas Llosa's representation of the group and aspects of their referential reality—the most important of which is that the figure of the *hablador* does not exist among the real Machiguenga.[72] In the novel itself, perhaps the major obstacle to identifying the fictional *hablador* with a hypothetical indigenous figure is the revelation, toward the end of the book, that Zuratas is one of the *habladores*. This revelation takes place via an allusion to Jesus Christ so obvious that it could easily be considered a technical flaw in an otherwise brilliant writer, and that, for this same reason, makes the Western *hablador*'s intrusion clear enough that it unmistakably signals the writer's limitations in emulating an indigenous voice. In this unresolved state, Doris Sommer argues, "whatever rush toward modernity may be moving the plot and pushing Vargas Llosa's political pronouncements, whatever evacuation confronts us from the first page of the picture-book Indians, the novel *performs* a parity of attention span between tradition and modernity."[73]

The performance of a dual voice in the book thus conflicts with the broader rhetorical context in which the novel came out. But what is to be understood as voice here? Richard Walsh proposes three spheres in which narrative voice unfolds: (1) instance, or the broader task of narration or diegesis through which this voice constitutes "a representational act, not just a verbal one"; (2) idiom, which refers to discourses represented within the narration or mimetic voices in a Platonic sense, for example, the voices of characters in a dialogue; and (3) interpellation, which, borrowed from Louis Althusser, encompasses the ideological dimension of "double-voiced" discourses.[74] This third dimension, which can pervade both previous spheres, is expressed through the readers' ability to imaginatively align themselves with the "subject position of the discourse" (98). The positions of Mario, Zuratas, and the *hablador(es)* are clearly visible in the case of their idioms, yet there is no clear position on the level of instance. What is the ideological dimension of the novel as a representational act? Should it simply be equated with the positions Vargas Llosa has taken in other realms of intellectual activity, or should it include the ideological fissures implied by the double structure of alternating narrations (i.e., Mario's chapters and the *hablador*'s chapters)?

The novel's overall shape indeed converges to give prominence to Mario's narration, which is confirmed by Vargas Llosa's inability to fully represent an indigenous voice, as the references to Western culture in the *hablador*'s discourse reveal. But the intense, conflicted dialogism the novel stages cannot be resolved by framing it in the author's broader rhetoric as a politician and public intellectual, for the very representational act implied by giving the *hablador* and Zuratas voices in the novel challenges this straightforward correspondence.[75] In this sense, the whole novel is permeated by an interpellational dimension whose double-voiced discourse constantly connects to Vargas Llosa's positions in the extraliterary domain, whereas ideological ambivalence is kept on the level of idiom—the discussions between the narrator and Zuratas, for example—and in the rotation of narrative voice among the narrator, Zuratas, and the *hablador*. In other words, the complexity of *El hablador* is such that the mimesis of discourses inside the novel continuously undermines the ideological undertones of the broader diegetic level of instance (still following Walsh). Being "contingent and inherently protean in its rhetorical emphasis and focus, direction and misdirection,"[76] this narrative instantiation excludes any systematic equivalence between the narrator and Vargas Llosa, as the assumed ideological background of the novel is unsettled by the many voices that compose its idioms.

When it comes to an ethics of fiction, thus, *The Storyteller* offers an intriguing example of how, in James Phelan's words, "the technical choices of the narrative entail ethical consequences."[77] The different ethical situations stemming from the position in which readers are placed in a novel marked by a double-voiced discourse simultaneously seem to demand an ethical response and keep readers in an uncomfortably unresolved zone comparable, I contend, to the discomfort Phelan identifies in the blend of horror and sympathy implied by the dual focalization of Vladimir Nabokov's *Lolita* (130-131).

The consequent puzzle, for the purposes of this chapter, is whether the environmental defense that Zuratas and Tasurinchi articulate results in the novel itself suggesting any form of ethical commitment with regard to deforestation in the Amazon—and if this commitment stems from what Suzanne Keen calls an "empathic inaccuracy" that occurs when "authors evoke empathy unintentionally."[78] One important element in this equation, which resonates with Vargas Llosa's earlier work, is the role of storytelling in conserving Machiguenga worldviews and traditions, in creating a parallel plane on which the disintegrating world of the Amazon in the mid- to late twentieth century might still find a sense of wholeness and refuge. This is, as the next section proposes, a key element in understanding the relation between mimesis and environmental thought in Vargas Llosa's work of the 1980s and 1990s.

THE RIGHTS OF NATURE, THE RIGHTS OF FICTION

Far from being an accident in Vargas Llosa's fiction, *El hablador*'s lack of resolution reflects a broader set of concerns he expressed in that period. Especially in the late 1980s, when this novel's publication coincided with his increased activity as a reporter, public intellectual, and political commentator, and right before he reached a turning point with his presidential candidacy, his defense of fiction as possessing some form of unique truth became more insistent.[79] In this context, essays of his that evoke the semantic field of *lying* when referring to fiction abound: "El arte de mentir" ("The Art of Lying") and "El poder de la mentira" ("The Power of Lying"), for example, are versions of the same text.[80] Perhaps the central essay in this line, however, is "La verdad de las mentiras" ("The Truth of Lies").[81] Written precisely around the time of the presidential campaign in 1989 and the first in a book of essays with the same title published in 1990, this essay discusses his understanding of truth and lie in fictional discourse. The truth of fiction is not to be measured by its adherence to referential reality, the essay argues, but rather by its ability to create a fictional reality, which fundamentally depends on the quality of the work. In his words, "La novela es, pues, un género amoral, o, más bien, de una ética sui generis, para la cual verdad o mentira son conceptos exclusivamente estéticos" ("The novel is, then, an amoral genre, or, better, of a sui generis ethical stance, for which truth or lies are exclusively aesthetic concepts").[82] Fiction thus provides a richer life than reality—"porque la vida real . . . nunca ha sido ni será bastante para colmar los deseos humanos" ("La verdad de las mentiras," 19: "because real life . . . has never been nor will ever be enough to fulfill human desires")—insofar as it addresses "esa insatisfacción vital que las mentiras de la literatura a la vez azuzan y aplacan" (19; "that vital dissatisfaction that the lies of literature simultaneously stoke and placate"). Though Vargas Llosa focuses on novels by other authors in this essay and in *La verdad de las mentiras*, one might interpret it as an indirect response to the dilemma of *El hablador*. If, as Sara Castro-Klarén notes of the novel, "the autonomous existence of indigenous cultures is now an idea to be debated in the fictional and fictionalizing space of novelistic discourse,"[83] this fictionalization can be regarded not as a delegitimation of the past and present of the Machiguenga and other indigenous cultures but as an outcome of the disintegration these cultures will soon face, in Vargas Llosa's view, and from which the novel has no option but to ethically disengage itself.[84]

An overview of Vargas Llosa's positions on fiction in these two periods of his career thus reveals a myriad of varied yet interconnected perspectives on its role, its ontological status, and its relationship with reality. The first phase, most evident in his writings of the 1960s and early 1970s, is fundamentally concerned with the ontological independence of fictional works from reality, in which the very act of writing is conceived as an act of rebellion against that same reality—an act that could potentially change it but never depends on it. Two factors shaped this position; the first was the Boom narrative as a project of aesthetic innovation in Latin America, in reaction to the so-called *novelas primitivas* and what Vargas Llosa identifies as their subordination of fiction to social chronicle and to an acritical form of realism. The second factor was the alignment of Vargas Llosa and a number of Boom writers with socialism: fiction's rebellion against reality and the socialist rebellion against capitalism share, more than a common semantic field, an ability to shake up similar realities.

The *novelas de creación*, which include but are not limited to those of the Boom, would not submit to an imitative notion of mimesis but, while borrowing elements from reality, aimed to create worlds of their own. Literature was not denied a certain documentary value, especially for works, like those of Vargas Llosa, whose realist orientation and autobiographical elements are well known. However, this documentary value should not diminish a literary work's autonomy and its potentially transformative capacity. This capacity may at times lead to the work's power of subversion, a notion that might accommodate, for example, the defense of prose fiction's social commitment that Jean-Paul Sartre professes in *What Is Literature?* (1948).[85] In this first phase, the representation of the Amazon in *La casa verde* does fulfill documentary criteria insofar as it foregrounds elements of the jungle unknown to a large portion of its readers, while the novel also enjoyed a critical reception focused primarily on its formal innovations—namely, its complex, multifaceted structure with full use of Vargas Llosa's signature technique of interlaced dialogue.[86]

By contrast, the second phase, from the mid-1980s to the early 1990s, is marked by a more troubled relationship between Vargas Llosa's fictional works and his extraliterary activities. Public perception of him as a champion of right-wing politics and his contested conclusions in the Uchuraccay case increasingly raised suspicions about his views on indigenous peoples in Peru, in both the Andean and Amazonian regions, which only worsened in the 1990s and the 2000s.[87] Concurrently with these increased tensions, his essays on literature seemed to signal another version of his 1960s theorizations, reaffirming the independence of literary texts not so much in ontological as in ethical terms. By obeying its own regimen of truth, his fiction would not be subject to the same attacks that nonfiction texts endured.

In spite of this argument's clear importance as a response to those who used his fictional texts to question his political abilities during the campaign, such a separation is complicated by the very fact that his novels from the period, such as *Historia de Mayta* (1984; *The Real Life of Alejandro Mayta*, 1986) and especially *El hablador*, do deal with a series of nonfictional circumstances whose political dimensions only become more evident when they are dramatized in fiction. The rhetorical structure of the latter novel, for example, channels into a tense dialogism a fraught and fractured public debate about indigenous acculturation and environmental conservation in Peru, and does so by circumventing the Andean context to focus on the somewhat more delicate issue of the Amazon. Although Vargas Llosa's alter ego enjoys some predominance in the novel, both the juxtaposition of his narration with that of the *hablador* and his dialogue with Zuratas create fissures in his arguments that invite persistent questions. As such, Vargas Llosa engages intensely with controversial issues in his fiction at the same time as he dismisses, through his essays, any form of ethical commitment these same fictions might have with regard to the real dilemmas they portray. Though his essays by no means subscribe to another version of the subversive quality of literature—such as, for example, Martha Nussbaum's argument that novels form a literary imagination that shapes ethical choices and moral judgments in public life—his novels of the period seem tailored to enact the exact type of effect that his essays dismiss.[88]

A comparison between these phases of Vargas Llosa's career thus shows an enduring defense of literature as not serving reality, either because it creates its own reality as a form of *deicide* or because it remains impervious to notions of truth and falsehood while, as Mabel Moraña proposes, compensating "for the mediocrity of life."[89] The crucial point here is that the creation of such fictional worlds does not imply a need to protect the realities from which fiction borrows. Vargas Llosa's understanding of novels as ways of conserving a disintegrating reality in a time of crisis, which evolved in the 1960s, takes on a whole new dimension in *El hablador*. The *hablador*'s stories are quite explicitly the primary means of conserving intact a world on the verge of disappearance due to deforestation and acculturation—even though Zuratas's introduction of Western elements creates a fissure at the heart of the *hablador*'s function, constituting one of the novel's major postmodern ironies.[90] Moreover, the disappearing figure of the *hablador* and his stories were to be conserved, albeit imperfectly, in the very text of this typical product of modernity that is the novel.[91]

In this context, I propose that the ethical clash between Zuratas and Mario mirrors the ethical clash between a committed view of fiction in the 1980s and Vargas Llosa's professed position that fiction is independent from any exogenous notion of truth. When it comes to the environmental realm and the Amazon, this means that his fiction on the region, regardless of the sense of wonder it might convey, need not maintain any form of engagement with or responsibility toward its referential reality. Hence Vargas Llosa's fascination with the Amazon, which he has expressed numerous times, can coexist with his defense of deforestation. His aesthetic perception of the rainforest seems to have been completely encoded in his fictional rainforest. This could explain the coexistence, in Vargas Llosa's work, of his long-lasting appreciation of the jungle with the many projects and policies he has defended or proposed that threaten its environmental integrity as well as the well-being of indigenous communities living in the area.

To be sure, the problematic character of this disjunction becomes visible in the ethical double bind built into *El hablador*'s polyphonic structure. In *La casa verde* and even in *Pantaleón y las visitadoras*, deforestation is neither thematized nor generally perceived as a problem by critics. Something similar could be said of indigenous acculturation, even though, in *La casa verde*, indigenous girls are kidnapped to be educated in the Catholic mission of Santa María de Nieva—an episode that constitutes the author's attack on these and other "civilizing missions." Despite all these factors, in his essays Vargas Llosa maintained the mimetic independence of fiction, especially of the *novelas de creación*, which do not seem to need a truth other than their own. If we follow this reasoning, the conservation of the forest in the pages of his novels is dissociated from and markedly independent of the conservation policies the politician and public intellectual Vargas Llosa advocated for the referential Amazon, even if some components of his own novels continuously question the premises on which such a notion of conservation in fiction is based.

Unlike the other authors discussed thus far, Vargas Llosa's admiration for the Amazon is clearly superseded by his desire to see a "modern Peru" make use of its natural resources, at the same time as his fiction articulates a more nuanced and somewhat nostalgic position. In the 1980s, when indigenous and environmental struggles had become much more prominent in national and international arenas, and vocal defenses of these causes were beginning to find more listeners, writing about a place as emotionally charged as the Amazon almost automatically entailed the author's assumed empathy with the forest and an implicit defense of its conservation. Going "contra viento y marea" ("against wind and tide"), to quote his famous newspaper column, Vargas Llosa disrupts this assumption. While many readers around the world continue to read *El hablador* independently from the ethical concerns it raises, those familiar with Vargas Llosa's statements in the extraliterary domain cannot but reframe the novel's implications. In recent decades, the conflict between his multifaceted fictional work and his straightforward statements as a public intellectual has been an integral part of his presence on the literary scene and has made episodes such as his winning of the Nobel Prize in Literature in 2010 so contentious. Part of this broader controversy is his view of indigenous peoples and, at times, their connections to environmental struggles. A consideration of his longer history of theorization on literature and fiction, as well as his portrayals of the Amazon, may prove instrumental in elucidating the puzzling place he has occupied for decades.

Vargas Llosa and his works are thus a peculiar case in this book, yet an examination of the many tensions at work across his oeuvre is exemplary of key contradictions present in the work of the authors discussed in previous chapters. If Vargas Llosa marvels at the reality he portrays while failing to maintain the empathy toward this same reality that his readers would expect, these other authors also, often in a less explicit fashion, expressed a combination of nostalgia and admiration for the areas about which they wrote, even while their words or actions evinced, to varying degrees, some enthusiasm for the developmentalist orientation of the period. It is through these multiple positions that the similarly multiple facets of mimetic operations mediate and reshape the memory and conditions of these changing environments.

Conclusion

Guimarães Rosa, Carpentier, Rulfo, Lispector, Vargas Llosa: these are some of the major writers widely recognized as having shaped literary production in twentieth-century Latin America. Their work has generally enjoyed much attention both inside and outside their countries of origin; their novels have attracted broad readership, have been adopted in schools and adapted to film, and often figure as points of reference even for those who are unlikely to ever read the books themselves. These writers were all instrumental in fashioning the idea of a modern, international literature frequently deemed "universal," at the same time as they contributed to a renewed reading of and production of knowledge about local settings.

A great deal has been written about this group of highly canonical authors. As the critical corpus on them continues to grow, so does skepticism about their almost utopian modernism, discomfort with their often too white, too male-centered perspectives, and suspicion about the very possibility or convenience of establishing a Latin American canon that, like Boom literature writ large, is, in Brett Levinson's words, "a metonym for Latin American culture as a whole."[1] In fact, a transition "to an understanding of Latin American culture as established by other means, such as popular and mass culture, 'social movements' and/or testimonio" in a neoliberal marketplace raises the question of what it means to write about these authors today.[2] This book takes that question as a starting point: how can the very canonicity of these writers, with all the widely discussed implications and limitations of their work, be turned into a theoretical and methodological problem? How does their lasting influence prompt us to reconsider the relationship between mimesis and environmentalism and open up new avenues for understanding the role of fiction in increasingly delicate negotiations over how environments are perceived and managed? Following Byrnes, in short, "in what ways does aesthetic form shape how we see and act in the world?"[3] Throughout its pages, *Fictional Environments* has sought to underscore the ways in which, more than merely representing certain environments, the novels analyzed here participate in a broader ecology of discourses and practices through which the environments at stake are perceived. More often than not, these iconic fictional portraits have permeated the structures of feeling surrounding these areas and produced images of them taken as more real than reality itself.

As their reception has tightly linked the novels studied here to real places, their composition was also invariably shaped by a strong connection between the authors and the regions they depict. Either having lived in these areas in their youth or having repeatedly visited as adults, these writers had strong affective ties with these places and produced paratextual and other nonfictional materials about them; as such, they have a certain authoritative perspective on the areas depicted in their books. At the same time, these ties are situated within broader economic and social transformations that frame the very perception of an emergent national or regional modern fiction. Many of these authors participated, to varying degrees, in this desire for development, modernity, and progress, and some played an active role in these processes. Unlike later generations, who were much more skeptical of such changes, ambivalence marks this generation's relationship with environmental issues inside and outside their fiction: these authors at times seemed to embrace a developmentalist ethos and created lasting imagery of the mostly rural and forested areas about which they wrote. In this sense, *Fictional Environments* has aimed to capture some of the nuances of how environmental changes, as well as multifaceted views about them, were negotiated within and through the fictional realms of novels. This fundamental ambivalence—which encompasses enthusiasm about change and a blend of mistrust and nostalgia stemming from these very transformations—marks the atmosphere, or rather the *Stimmung*, of this moment, as "an all-embracing atmosphere and a subjectively experienced mood."[4]

While in later decades this relationship between textual space and environmental perceptions took on new complexity, these mid-twentieth-century novels also began to be displaced from their central spot by the progressive expansion of other novelistic and extranovelistic forms. The examples of Aridjis and the Grupo de los Cien, Rossi, and Kopenawa, briefly discussed in the introduction to this book, already point to some of these later developments. These writers evince a stronger and more explicit commitment to environmental activism and demonstrate the power of *testimonio* writing in the region, especially in postdictatorial and postwar contexts. In parallel, recent years have seen the growing popularity of other forms of environmental engagement in fiction writing, such as the emergence of horror stories and dystopias that feature environmental collapse and epidemics caused by pesticides and other human actions, for example. These more recent novels, when ecologically oriented, tend to have a straightforward connection with the environmental losses to which they refer, as a sense of urgency has been a given since the moment of their publication.

The particular relationship between such works and their referential realities constitutes a productive point of comparison for us, as early twenty-first-century readers, to investigate the intricacies of the less direct—yet not less effective—mimetic relations developed through the reception history of Guimarães Rosa, Carpentier, Rulfo, Lispector, and Vargas Llosa. After all, the fictional environments they created have been perceived differently and reshaped by successive generations of readers. Each of the five chapters in this book has detailed ways in which forms of mimesis have evolved in varying contexts as actual environments changed, taking into account how each novel's prestige played a role in these processes.

The strongest evidence of how fiction shapes referential reality certainly comes from projects that, to different degrees, aim to recreate environments as they are depicted in novels. This is the case, for example, with *Grande sertão: Veredas* and its impact in northwestern Minas Gerais, in what I termed a reverse mimesis. Although many of these projects emerged from extraliterary demands, the novel's image of the *sertão* remains the standard that referential reality should follow. A second, and more common, form of mimesis is the one at work in the case of *Los pasos perdidos*. Rather than having a direct, identifiable impact on a certain region, this novel participates in a larger series of environmental images of the Gran Sabana that, through a body of heterogeneous materials ranging from nineteenth-century travel accounts to children's movies, reinforces perceptions of the area as too precious not to conserve. It is another form of reverse mimesis, albeit a less direct one.

Rather than inspiring standards for what referential reality should be, the mimetic force of a novel such as *Pedro Páramo* stems from its ability to provide enduring images of certain areas that shape perceptions of them even as they change due to, for example, agricultural modernization. Here, mimesis takes the form of resilience and counterpoint while retaining a phantasmic quality. *Counterpoint* is also a key term for understanding the role of *A cidade sitiada* in the context of urbanizing and industrializing Brazilian cities in the 1930s and 1940s. Though less well known than the other works analyzed, this novel provides a powerful alternative to the developmentalist theses so prevalent in the period. Mimesis here, following Costa Lima's characterization, becomes a shadow, a folding of reality that unsettles and expands the scope of previous interpretations.

Finally, repeated affirmations of the autonomy of the literary work from reality, as in *La casa verde*, *El hablador*, and Vargas Llosa's nonfiction, constantly highlight the rift between representation and the represented reality. Especially in the 1980s, when environmental concerns and struggles for indigenous rights were becoming prominent, Vargas Llosa's persistent reworking of his 1960s theories sought to protect mimesis by making it intransitive and self-contained, at the same time as his views undermine the common assumption that writers should be systematically sympathetic to the conservation of forested areas about which they write.

As they have evolved in response to real and symbolic processes of environmental change in Latin America from the mid-twentieth century to the present, these specific forms of mimesis were not necessarily perceptible in the initial reception of these novels. Instead, they have taken new shapes across the decades as the expectations of reading publics have changed, with an increasing sense of loss and the growing urgency of ecological action. While the canonical status of these novels has prompted well-justified debates about the definition of and conditions for a literary canon in the region, their enduring presence among reading publics makes them fruitful sites of inquiry into how mimetic relations change in light of environmental transformations. In contrast with recent fiction that takes for granted the growing interest in environmental issues, these works continue to generate renewed understandings of how environments inspire fictions and fictions impact environments, with all their potentialities and ambivalences, on a deforesting continent.

Notes

INTRODUCTION

1. Homero Aridjis, "Declaración de 100 intelectuales y artistas contra la contaminación en la Ciudad de México," in *Noticias de la Tierra*, edited by Homero Aridjis and Betty Ferber (Barcelona: Random House Mondadori, 2012), 28; Homero Aridjis, "A Declaration by 100 Intellectuals and Artists Protesting Air Pollution in Mexico City," in *News from the Earth*, edited by Homero Aridjis and Betty Feber, translated by Betty Ferber (Simsbury, Conn.: Mandel Vilar, 2017), 9.

2. For an overview of Aridjis's environmental activism and the presence of environmental topics in his literary works, see Aridjis, "Los pájaros" ("The Birds"), in *Noticias de la Tierra*, 19–25.

3. For an ecocritical analysis of this novel, see Laura Barbas-Rhoden, *Ecological Imaginations in Latin American Fiction* (Gainesville: University Press of Florida, 2011), 127–38.

4. Rossi mentions these death threats, which ultimately prompted her to leave Costa Rica, in an interview with Sofía Kearns, "Environmental Issues in Costa Rica: An Interview with Ana Cristina Rossi." *Organization and Environment* 13, no. 2 (2000): 262–65.

5. According to Sterling Evans, "The resort was built, but thanks to people like Rossi and Cortés, with stricter environmental standards." Sterling Evans, *The Green Republic: A Conservation History of Costa Rica* (Austin: University of Texas Press, 1999), 230.

6. Marco Antonio Valentim develops the concept of *sobrenatureza*, or supernature, as "the form of cosmic-political agency" that includes the points of view of animals, plants, and spirits—and of which *A queda do céu* is exemplary. Marco Antonio Valentim, *Extramundanidade e sobrentureza: Ensaios de ontologia infundamental* (Florianópolis, Brazil: Cultura e Barbárie, 2018), 24.

7. Idelber Avelar, *The Untimely Present: Postdictatorial Fiction and the Task of Mourning* (Durham: Duke University Press, 1999), 28.

8. For an analysis of the contradictions between cultural modernism and social modernization in the region, see Néstor García Canclini, *Hybrid Cultures: Strategies for Entering and Leaving Modernity*, trans. Christopher L. Chiappari and Silvia L. Lopez (Minneapolis: University of Minnesota Press, 2005), especially chapter 2.

9. In this sense, these areas can be seen as "the undifferentiated supply of the available" that characterizes Martin Heidegger's concept of standing-reserve. William Lovitt. "Introduction," in *The Question concerning Technology and other Essays*, by Martin Heidegger, trans. William Lovitt (New York: Garland Publishing, 1977), xxix. For connections between this view of nature as standing-reserve and the metaphysical instrumentalism of sixteenth- and seventeenth-century Iberian thought on American natural resources, with a focus on mining, see Orlando Betancor, *The Matter of Empire: Metaphysics and Mining in Colonial Peru* (Pittsburgh: University of Pittsburgh Press, 2017), 321–45. This perceived endless availability manifests itself, for example, in the belief that the precious metals of the Potosí mines were self-generating.

10. Ángel Rama, *Writing across Cultures: Narrative Transculturation in Latin America*, ed. and trans. David Frye (Durham: Duke University Press, 2012), 44.

11. For some of the contestations as well as reconsiderations of Rama's theory, see, for example, Antonio Cornejo Polar, *Escribir en el aire: Ensayo sobre la heterogeneidad socio-cultural en las literaturas andinas*, 2nd ed. (Lima: Centro de Estudios Literarios "Antonio Cornejo Polar" and Latinoamericana Editora, 2003); Neil Larsen, *Modernism and Hegemony: A Materialist Critique of Aesthetic Agencies* (Minneapolis: Minnesota University Press, 1990), including the brief exposition of his critique in chapter 3; Alberto Moreiras, *The Exhaustion of Difference: The Politics of Latin American Cultural Studies* (Durham: Duke University Press, 2001); Silvia Spitta, *Between Two Waters: Narratives of Transculturation in Latin America* (Houston: Rice University Press, 1995); and Abril Trigo, "Shifting Paradigms: From Transculturation to Hybridity: A Theoretical Critique," in *Unforeseeable Americas: Questioning Cultural Hybridity in the Americas*, ed. Rita de Grandis and Zilà Bernd (Amsterdam: Rodopi, 2000), 85–111.

12. Published in book form only in 1982 but already formulated in articles and talks from the previous decade, Rama's theses on narrative transculturation remain, as Trigo notes, "a theory of the 70s, [if one considers the] erosion of the modernly utopian paradigms on which *transculturation* rested" in a postmodern context. Trigo, "Shifting Paradigms," 86, Trigo's emphasis.

13. Paulo Moreira, *Modernismo localista das Américas: Os contos de Faulkner, Guimarães Rosa e Rulfo* (Belo Horizonte, Brazil: Editora UFMG, 2012), 26. My translation.

14. Corey Byrnes, *Fixing Landscape: A Techno-Poetic History of China's Three Gorges* (New York: Columbia University Press, 2018), 5.

15. Lawrence Buell, *The Environmental Imagination: Thoreau, Nature Writing, and the Formation of American Culture* (Cambridge, Mass.: Harvard University Press, 1995).

16. Dana Phillips, *The Truth of Ecology: Nature, Culture, and Literature in America* (New York: Oxford University Press, 2003).

17. Buell responded to Phillips a couple of years later, when he revisited the topic of mimesis in environmental literature. While Buell notes the separation between text and context, he also states that "language never replicates extra-textual landscapes, but it can be bent toward or away from them." *The Future of Environmental Criticism: Environmental Crisis and Literary Imagination* (Malden, Mass.: Blackwell, 2005), 33.

18. In Morton's words, "The idea of nature is getting in the way of properly ecological forms of culture, philosophy, politics, and art." Timothy Morton, *Ecology without Nature: Rethinking Environmental Aesthetics* (Cambridge, Mass.: Harvard University Press, 2007), 1.

19. Christine Marran, *Ecology without Culture: Aesthetics for a Toxic World* (Minneapolis: Minnesota University Press, 2017), 10.

20. Antonio Candido, *Formação da literatura brasileira: Momentos decisivos*, 2nd ed. (São Paulo: Martins, 1964), 99. Unless otherwise noted, all translations from Portuguese and Spanish were made by Laura Colaneri.

21. Despite Candido's attention to this function of fiction, the lack of psychological depth he assigns to Brazilian Romantic novels, already problematic in the very corpus analyzed by the author, must be disregarded in the case of the corpus adopted in this volume.

22. Flora Süssekind, *O Brasil não é longe daqui: O narrador, a viagem* (São Paulo: Cia. das Letras, 1990).

23. Jens Andermann, *The Optic of the State: Visuality and Power in Argentina and Brazil* (Pittsburgh: University of Pittsburgh Press, 2007).

24. Thus, according to Gabriela Nouzeilles, "[the] celebration of the natural and the primitive, for a long time exclusive to elites, has lately become one of the most valuable commodities in the postmodern market." "Introducción," in *La naturaleza en disputa: Retóricas del cuerpo y el paisaje en América Latina*, ed. Gabriela Nouzeilles (Buenos Aires: Paidós, 2002), 28. My translation.

25. By Barthes's "reality effect," I refer to the number of "concrete details" in realism that, though apparently superfluous, as a "*direct* collusion of the referent and the signifier" (147, Barthes's emphasis), aim to convey the feeling of a naked "real" unfolding in front of the reader's eyes. The elements that produce a reality effect in the novels analyzed here are arguably different from those that populate the Flaubertian example Barthes analyzes. Roland Barthes, "The Reality Effect," in *The Rustle of Language*, trans. Richard Howard (Berkeley: University of California Press, 1989), 141–48.

26. Erich Auerbach, *Mimesis: The Representation of Reality in Western Literature*, trans. Willard Trask (Princeton, N.J.: Princeton University Press, 2003), 554.

27. Roland Barthes, *S/Z: An Essay*, trans. Richard Miller (Oxford: Blackwell, 2002), 80.

28. Barthes, *S/Z*, 55.

29. Maria Mäkelä, "Realism and the Unnatural," in *A Poetics of Unnatural Narrative*, ed. Jan Alber, Skov Nielsen, and Brian Richardson (Columbus: Ohio State University Press, 2013), 145.

30. In this sense, I follow John Searle when he states that "the author will refer to real places and events intermingling these references with the fictional

references, thus making it possible to treat the fictional story as an extension of our existing knowledge." John Searle, "The Logical Status of Fictional Discourse," *New Literary History* 6, no. 2 (1975): 331.

31. Richard Walsh, *The Rhetoric of Fictionality: Narrative Theory and the Idea of Fiction* (Columbus: Ohio State University Press, 2007), 36.

32. Walsh, *The Rhetoric of Fictionality*, 44.

33. Jacques Derrida, "The Double Session," in *Dissemination*, trans. Barbara Johnson (London: Athlone Press, 1981), 173–286.

34. Jean Baudrillard, *Simulacra and Simulation*, trans. Sheila Faria Glaser (Ann Arbor: University of Michigan Press, 1994), 6.

35. For an overview of this alleged early hostility to theory among ecocritics, see Alex Goodbody and Catherine Rigby's introduction to *Ecocritical Theory: New European Approaches* (Charlottesville: University of Virginia Press, 2011), a volume that, published in 2011, is itself an attempt at grounding ecocriticism in major theoretical and philosophical trends.

36. Cheryll Glotfelty, "Introduction," in *The Ecocriticism Reader: Landmarks in Literary Ecology*, ed. Harold Fromm and Cheryll Glotfelty (Athens: University of Georgia Press, 1996), xix.

37. As a result, fictional environments may, in certain circumstances, become simulacra in Baudrillard's sense, particularly when certain conservation policies aim at "concealing the fact that the real is no longer real, and thus of saving the reality principle." Baudrillard, *Simulacra and Simulation*, 13.

38. According to Heise, "In literary, visual, and musical representations of extinction [that follow elegiac and tragic modes], biological crisis typically becomes a proxy for cultural concerns: worries about the future of nature, on one hand, and on the other hand, hopes that a part of one's national identity and culture might be preserved, revived, or changed for the better if an endangered species could be allowed to survive or an extinct one could be rediscovered." Ursula Heise, *Imagining Extinction: The Cultural Meanings of Endangered Species* (Chicago: University of Chicago Press, 2016), 49. In this work, Heise provides an extensive study of the forms that engagement with endangered species has taken and the literary genres it has drawn upon, via laws, products, novels, and other works and actions.

39. All these variations render visible what Michael Taussig has called "the power of the copy to influence what it is a copy of" in *Mimesis and Alterity: A Particular History of the Senses* (New York: Routledge, 1993), 250. Moreover, they demonstrate another facet of the process of "maintaining sameness through alterity" (129) implied in the magic and cultural mimeses of the Cuna indigenous group in Panama, where a still identifiable relationship of similarity is pervaded, often quite slowly, by an awareness of alterity, an awareness of very specific contours, that goes beyond the distance of any copy from what is copied.

40. As Gunter Gebauer and Christoph Wulf put it, "Literary mimesis can itself flow back into social practice. . . . [L]iterature works with mimetic material; literature can become mimetic material." *Mimesis: Culture Art Society*, trans. Don Reneau (Berkeley: University of California Press, 1995), 23.

41. See Luiz Costa Lima, *Vida e mímesis* (Rio de Janeiro: Editora 34, 1995) and *Mímesis e modernidade: Formas das sombras*, 2nd ed. (São Paulo: Paz e Terra, 2003).

42. Alexa Weik von Mossner, *Affective Ecologies: Empathy, Emotion, and Environmental Narrative* (Columbus: Ohio State University Press, 2017), 48. As a counterpoint, as Jennifer Wenzel contends, literary works draw attention to certain areas and issues while keeping others invisible; to a certain extent, that is the case with cultural production that has foregrounded the Amazon and ignored the *cerrado*. In Wenzel's words, we must recognize "the work that literature and cultural imagining do *all the time* in naturalizing ideas about nature and shaping constituencies of caring and regimes of visibility, as well as their exclusions and occlusions." *The Disposition of Nature: Environmental Crisis and World Literature* (New York: Fordham University Press, 2020), 17.

43. Jean-Marie Schaeffer, *Why Fiction?* (Lincoln: University of Nebraska Press, 2010), 143.

44. Although Wolfgang Iser saw in the pastoral an ideal form for the emergence of the fictive, these narratives have a relationship with their readers that is often based on the assumption that some remnant of these countrysides, as well as of tropical forests, still exists. See Wolfgang Iser, *The Fictive and the Imaginary: Charting Literary Anthropology* (Baltimore: Johns Hopkins University Press, 1993), chapter 2.

45. Michel-Rolph Trouillot, *Silencing the Past: Power and the Production of History* (Boston: Beacon Press, 2015).

46. Andreas Huyssen, *Present Pasts: Urban Palimpsests and the Politics of Memory* (Stanford, Calif.: Stanford University Press, 2003).

47. Svetlana Boym, *The Future of Nostalgia* (New York: Basic Books, 2001), 10. As such, "nostalgia, as a historical emotion, is a longing for that 'shrinking space of experience' that no longer fits the horizon of expectations" (10).

48. According to Agamben, "Everything today can become a museum, because this term simply designates the exhibition of an impossibility of using, of dwelling, of experiencing." Giorgio Agamben, *Profanations*, trans. Jeff Fort (New York: Zone Books, 2007), 84. In other words, they are invulnerable to the use and consumption that characterize capitalist relations.

49. Forestry Department of the Food and Agriculture Organization of the United Nations, "Forest Resources Assessment: Terms and Definitions," p. 4, www.fao.org/3/a-ap862e.pdf.

50. For some widely accepted definitions, see Robin L. Chazdon et al., "When Is a Forest a Forest? Forest Concepts and Definitions in the Era of Forest and Landscape Restoration," *Ambio* 45, no. 5 (2016): 542.

51. Nophea Sasaki and Francis E. Putz, "Critical Need for New Definitions of 'Forest' and 'Forest Degradation' in Global Climate Change Agreements," *Conservation Letters* 2 (2009): 226–32.

52. Chazdon, "When Is a Forest a Forest?"

53. Robert Pogue Harrison, *Forests: The Shadow of Civilization* (Chicago: University of Chicago Press, 1992), 201.

54. Harrison, *Forests*, 199.

55. John McNeill, *Something New under the Sun: An Environmental History of the Twentieth-Century World* (New York: W. W. Norton, 2000), 236.

56. According to Michael Williams, "The 50 years between 1900 and 1950 saw a complete reversal of the eighteenth- and nineteenth-century pattern, where the temperate world had surpassed the tropical in terms of deforestation." *Deforesting the Earth: From Prehistory to Global Crisis* (Chicago: University of Chicago Press, 2010), 372.

57. M. Williams, *Deforesting the Earth*, 360–371.

58. See Candace Slater, *Entangled Edens: Visions of the Amazon* (Berkeley: University of California Press, 2002). Of special interest for the present volume is chapter 6, which describes some ways in which "'the Rain Forest' became synonymous with Amazonia" (134).

59. Shawn Miller, *An Environmental History of Latin America* (New York: Cambridge University Press, 2007), 194. As a result, "reports of its destruction suggest the final holocaust of paradise, snuffed, ironically, just as we claim to have come to our ecological senses" (194).

60. For an overview of this transition, see Claudia Leal, "From Threatening to Threatened Jungles," in *A Living Past: Environmental Histories of Modern Latin America*, ed. John Soluri, Claudia Leal, and José Augusto Pádua (New York: Berghahn, 2018), 115–37. According to Leal, it was mostly at the turn of the twentieth century that Latin American jungles and, most notably, the Amazon "entered into each nation's territory and self-definition in a subordinate position. They stopped being *terra incognita* and were now defined by their relationship with the central zones of the countries into which they were incorporated" (124).

61. Arturo Escobar, *Encountering Development. The Making and Unmaking of the Third World* (Princeton, N.J.: Princeton University Press, 1996), 39.

62. Fernando Mires, *El discurso de la naturaleza: Ecología y política en América Latina* (Santiago, Chile: Editorial Amerinda, 1990), 68. In Escobar's words, the "basic premise was the belief in the role of modernization as the only force capable of destroying superstitions and archaic relationships, without concern for the political, cultural, and social economic cost" (*Encountering Development*, 91).

63. Mires, *El discurso de la naturaleza*, 60.

64. Ramachandra Guha and Joan Martínez Alier, *Varieties of Environmentalism: Essays North and South* (London: Earthscan, 1997).

65. Rob Nixon, *Slow Violence and the Environmentalism of the Poor* (Cambridge, Mass.: Harvard University Press, 2011), 2.

66. For a recent overview of Latin America's environmental history in the twentieth century, see Claudia Leal, José Augusto Pádua, and John Soluri, *A Living Past: Environmental Histories of Modern Latin America* (New York: Berghahn, 2018). The idea of environmental loss due to resource exploitation, however, is already at work in classics of leftist thought in the region, such as Eduardo Galeano's *Las venas abiertas de América Latina* (Montevideo: Universidad de la República, 1987).

67. I borrow the concept "horizon of expectation" from Hans Robert Jauss to define the set of expectations and assumptions held by a given reading public before new works come out. In Jauss's words, "The horizon of expectations of

literature is differentiated from the horizon of expectations of historical life by the fact that it not only preserves real experiences but also anticipates unrealized possibilities, widens the limited range of social behavior by new wishes, demands, and goals, and thereby opens avenues for future experience." "Literary History as a Challenge to Literary Theory," *New Literary History* 2, no. 1 (1970): 33.

68. Amitav Ghosh, *The Great Derangement: Climate Change and the Unthinkable* (Chicago: University of Chicago Press, 2016).

69. For recent assessments of the implications, reach, and environmental history of the Anthropocene and the Great Acceleration, see, respectively, Christophe Bonneil and Jean-Baptiste Fressoz, *The Shock of the Anthropocene: The Earth, History and Us*, trans. David Fernbach (London: Verso, 2016); and John McNeill, *The Great Acceleration: An Environmental History of the Anthropocene since 1945* (Cambridge, Mass.: Harvard University Press, 2014).

70. Kate Soper, *What Is Nature? Culture, Politics and the Non-Human* (Malden, Mass.: Blackwell, 1995), 155.

71. Soper, *What Is Nature?*, 156.

72. For an ecocritical analysis of the colonial foundation text that is the diary of Christopher Columbus with a focus on the assumed immutability of the land and the prevalence of the color green in his descriptions of America, see Beatriz Rivera-Barnes, "To Discover, an Intransitive Verb: Christopher Columbus's First Encounter with the American Landscape," in *Reading and Writing the Latin American Landscape*, by Jerry Hoeg and Beatriz Rivera-Barnes (New York: Palgrave Macmillan, 2009), 9–24.

73. As Mary Louise Pratt shows in her study on Humboldt's transculturation of American knowledge to Europe, "Humboldt reinvented South America first as foremost as nature . . . a dramatic, extraordinary nature, a spectacle capable of overwhelming human knowledge and understanding." *Imperial Eyes: Travel Writing and Transculturation*, 2nd ed. (London: Routledge, 2008), 118. More recently, Andrea Wulf's *The Invention of Nature: Alexander von Humboldt's New World* (New York: Vintage Books, 2015) has examined Humboldt's contribution to modern ecology in both its scientific and cultural dimensions. This spectacular view of nature did not necessarily make aesthetic and utilitarian approaches to it incompatible for nineteenth-century Latin American Romanticism. A case in point is Esteban Echeverría, who, in his assessment of the Argentinian *desierto* outlined in a note to the reader of his 1837 long poem *La cautiva* (*The Captive*), states: "The desert is ours, our richest patrimony, and we must make an effort to extract from its bosom not only wealth for our own aggrandizement and well-being but also poetry for our moral delight and the enhancement of our national literature." *El matadero; La cautiva* (Madrid: Cátedra, 2006), 117, my translation.

74. Carlos J. Alonso, *The Spanish American Regional Novel: Modernity and Autochtony* (Cambridge: Cambridge University Press, 1990), 75.

75. For a more recent study of how *novelas de la selva* rewrite, often in a parodic fashion, tropes of colonial travel writing, see Lesley Wylie, *Colonial Tropes and Postcolonial Tricks: Rewriting the Tropics in the Novela de la Selva* (Liverpool: Liverpool University Press, 2009). I have analyzed the function of

nature as an antagonist in these genres in "Testando limites: Interdividualidade coletiva nos romances da selva e da seca," in *Mímesis e invisibilização social: A interdividualidade coletiva latino-americana*, ed. José Luís Jobim, Mariana Méndez-Gallardo, and Carlos Mendoza-Álvarez (São Paulo: É Realizações, 2016), 123–50. In a similar vein, Jens Andermann shows how this regionalist fiction, by bringing to the fore an "environmental insurrection" and establishing trans-species solidarity with exploited humans, showcases an alternative form of biopolitics and "anticipates the hypothesis we today known as 'anthropocene.'" *Tierras en trance: Arte y naturaleza después del paisaje* (Santiago de Chile: Metales Pesados, 2018, Kindle Edition), loc. 2626.

76. Concha Meléndez, "Tres novelas de la naturaleza americana: *Don Segundo Sombra*, *La vorágine*, *Doña Bárbara*," in *Signos de Iberoamérica* (Mexico City: Manuel Leon Sánchez, 1936), 96–97.

77. Pedro Grases, "De la novela en América," in *Escritos selectos* (Caracas: Biblioteca Ayacucho, 1989), 297.

78. Ángeles Mendieta Alatorre, *El paisaje en la novela de América* (Mexico City: Secretaría de Educación Pública, 1949), 36.

79. In 1984, Gerald Martin challenged "the idea that the New Novel was genuinely and overwhelmingly new" by considering it one of the "optical illusions" of the Boom. See "Boom, Yes; 'New Novel,' No: Further Reflections on the Optical Illusions of the 1960s in Latin America," *Bulletin of Latin American Research* 3, no. 2 (1984): 61.

80. Carlos Fuentes, *La nueva novela hispanoamericana* (Mexico City: Joaquín Mortiz, 1969), 9.

81. José Donoso, *The Boom in Spanish American Literature: A Personal History*, trans. Gregory Kolovakos (New York: Columbia University Press, 1977), 11. For Donoso, "with their entomologists' magnifying glasses, they were cataloging the flora and fauna, the tribes and the proverbs which were unmistakably ours" (15).

82. An example is Emir Rodríguez Monegal, editor of the influential literary magazine *Mundo Nuevo*. In a 1965 article, he starts his defense of the new novel in Latin America this way: "It is the cities that monopolize the attention of younger novelists" and not the older generations for whom "American nature and American landscape so dominated man, so crushed and moulded him, that the human individual disappeared." See "The New Novelists," *The Encounter* 25 (1965): 97. But the representatives of the "new novel" include a number of works not set in urban areas. This issue would remain unresolved in his book *Narradores de esta América* (Montevideo: Alfa, 1969), whose opening essay, originally published in 1952, starts by identifying "a false opposition between regionalist narrative and cosmopolitan or universal narrative" (39), then shortly afterward openly opposes critics who praise regionalism.

83. See Mariano Siskind's *Cosmopolitan Desires: Global Modernity and World Literature in Latin America* (Evanston, Ill.: Northwestern University Press, 2014) for an analysis of Latin American magical realism and its spread in world literature. It is also symptomatic, for example, that the literary movement known as McOndo, launched with an anthology of the same name (Barcelona: Mondadori, 1996) by Alberto Fuguet and Sergio Gómez, opened with a fierce

critique of the forceful identification between Latin American literature and magical realism. For a later commentary by Fuguet on the meaning of magical realism in the region, see "Magical Neoliberalism," *Foreign Policy*, Nov. 17, 2009, http://foreignpolicy.com/2009/11/17/magical-neoliberalism.

84. John Beverley, *Against Literature* (Minneapolis: University of Minnesota Press, 1993), 98.

85. Avelar, *The Untimely Present*, 32.

86. For a reading of the Boom as a literary market phenomenon and for views on the inclusion of writers who did not belong to the core group, such as the ones mentioned above, see Ángel Rama, "El *Boom* en perspectiva," in *Más allá del Boom: Literatura y mercado* (Buenos Aires: Folios Ediciones, 1984), 51–119. It was first published in a volume devoted to a reevaluation of the movement and its aftermath in Latin American literature. For a study on how the struggle for cultural hegemony in a Cold War context led to the internationalization of some of these writers' works, see Deborah Cohn, *The Latin American Literary Boom and U.S. Nationalism during the Cold War* (Nashville: Vanderbilt University Press, 2012).

87. I borrow this expression from a conference cycle of the same name that took place in the Casa de América, in Madrid in 2012, in which contemporary authors Rodrigo Fresán, Edmundo Paz Soldán, and Jorge Volpi talked about authors who published as the Boom gathered momentum but were not included in the trend: Juan Carlos Onetti, Clarice Lispector, and Jorge Ibargüengoitia, respectively. "Los olvidados del boom," accessed May 15, 2018, Casa América, http://www.casamerica.es/literatura/los-olvidados-del-boom.

88. These categories have recently been focuses of attention in ecocritical studies on Latin American literature. Recent titles that trace panoramic perspectives on the region's biomes include those by Beatriz Rivera-Barnes and Jerry Hoeg in *Reading and Writing the Latin American Landscape*, which offers an overview from Christopher Columbus to contemporary fiction; Laura Barbas-Rhoden's *Ecological Imaginations in Latin American Fiction*, divided mostly into geographical clusters, such as the Tierra del Fuego, the Amazon, Central America, and futuristic narratives; and Scott DeVries's *A History of Ecology and Environmentalism in Spanish American Literature* (Lewisburg, Penn.: Bucknell University Press, 2013), which combines chronological and thematic divisions.

CHAPTER 1

1. Albeit elected in 1963, Guimarães Rosa did not effectively become a member until 1967.

2. Pedro Bloch, "Pedro Bloch entrevista Guimarães Rosa," in *Pedro Bloch entrevista: Vida, pensamento e obra de grandes vultos da cultura brasileira* (Rio de Janeiro: Editora Bloch, 1989), 100. Unless otherwise noted, all translations are by Laura Colaneri.

3. Günter Lorenz, "Diálogo com Guimarães Rosa," in *Guimarães Rosa*, ed. Eduardo de Faria Coutinho (Rio de Janeiro: Civilização Brasileira, 1983), 84.

4. Clara Rowland, *A forma do meio: Livro e narração na obra de João Guimarães Rosa* (Campinas: Unicamp, 2011). Rowland discusses how Guimarães

Rosa's preoccupation with the materiality of his writings is intensely present in his published fiction through his attention to typographical projects, such as incorporating the design of a book's flaps into its content.

5. This attention has taken the form not only of the projects and works discussed in this chapter but also of occasional news media articles reassessing the current *sertão* vis-à-vis the fictional one, especially on commemorative dates such as Guimarães Rosa's centenary or the novel's publication anniversary. Examples include the series of articles exposing social and environmental changes and continuities by Leonencio Nossa, "Novas Veredas: O mapa do Grande Sertão nos 50 anos de morte de Guimarães Rosa," *O Estado de S. Paulo*, accessed Dec. 14, 2017,. http://infograficos.estadao.com.br/especiais/novas-veredas; an interview with Zito, a cattleman who met the author during his trips to Minas Gerais, by João Correia Filho in "Guia de Guimarães Rosa, vaqueiro narra viagem que inspirou *Grande sertão: Veredas*," *Revista Cult*, Nov. 17, 2017, https://revistacult.uol.com.br/home/vaqueiro-guia-guimaraes-rosa-sertao; and profiles of some of today's transgender residents of Minas Gerais as compared to the character Diadorim, by Gustavo Werneck in "Travessia," *O Estado de Minas Gerais*, Mar. 6, 2016, especiais.em.com.br/travessia. These and other pieces are part of an unusual media interest in keeping track of a region's changes in relation to its representation in a fictional work.

6. In standard Portuguese, *veredas* means "pathways" or "routes." In the semidry central plain of Brazil, however, it also defines certain hydric concentrations, akin to small linear oases or palm swamps, where trees such buritis can be found, as well as endemic flowers and birds. The *veredas* supply groundwater and are important for animal movements, to which their meaning as routes alludes. Guimarães Rosa describes the *veredas* to his Italian translator Edoardo Bizzarri: "Mas, por entre as chapadas, separando-as (ou, às vezes, mesmo no alto, em depressões no meio das chapadas) há as veredas. São vales de chão argiloso ou turfo-argiloso, onde aflora a água absorvida. Nas veredas, há sempre o buriti. De longe, a gente avista os buritis, e já sabe: lá se encontra água. A vereda é um oásis. Em relação às chapadas, elas são, as veredas, de belo verde-claro, aprazível, macio. Capim é verdinho-claro, bom. As veredas são férteis. Cheias de animais, de pássaros." ("However, between the plateaus, separating them (or, sometimes, even at the top, in depressions in the middle of the plateaus), there lie the *veredas*. They are valleys of loamy or mossy ground, where the absorbed water comes to the surface. In the *veredas* there is always a buriti. From afar, we can see the buritis, and we know: there we can find water. The *vereda* is an oasis. In relation to the plateaus, they are paths of beautiful bright green, pleasant, soft. The grass is green, good. The *veredas* are fertile. Full of animals, of birds.") João Guimarães Rosa, *Correspondência com seu tradutor italiano Edoardo Bizzarri*, 3rd ed. (Rio de Janeiro: Nova Fronteira, 2003), 22–23, my translation.

7. According to David Arrigucci, "The singularity of the novel, which is imposed right away upon the reader, depends upon the profound mix of narrative forms that composes it, intrinsically related with the jumbled world that is so disconcerting to the Narrator." "O mundo misturado: Romance e experiência em Guimarães Rosa," *Novos Estudos Cebrap* 40 (1994): 10.

8. An early attempt at mapping *Grande sertão: Veredas*'s toponyms was made in 1974, when Alan Viggiano proposed a bold and contested thesis: "Guimarães Rosa did not invent a single name, out of all the toponyms used in the saga of Riobaldo Tatarana." *Itinerário de Riobaldo Tatarana* (Brasília: Instituto Nacional do Livro, 1974), 21. Willi Bolle revisits the issue in a detailed study of the novel's cartography that, nevertheless, remains aware of and highlights its labyrinthine dimension. Bolle shows how Guimarães Rosa's fictional geography makes slight changes in the area's real geography for narrative purposes: "The fieldwork leads us, therefore, to verify empirically which are the principal procedures of fictional use of the geography on the part of the novelist: the techniques of fragmentation, disassembly, dislocation, condensation and reassembly." *grandesertão.br* (São Paulo: Ed. 34, Duas Cidades, 2006), 71.

9. João Guimarães Rosa, *Grande sertão: Veredas*, anniversary edition (Rio de Janeiro: Nova Fronteira, 2006), 287–88.

10. João Guimarães Rosa, *The Devil to Pay in the Backlands*, trans. James L. Taylor and Harriet de Onís (New York: Knopf, 1963), 261. The English translation does not include the remainder of this passage, which would be: "That's how it is. The sertão causes dizziness since dawn. Its immensities. Their soul."

11. Translated by Alison Entrekin. Unless otherwise stated, the translated passages of *Grande sertão: Veredas* come from Entrekin's in-progress translation of the novel, and thus might still be altered before it is published. I thank the translator for kindly making this unpublished material available to me.

12. According to Ettore Finazzi-Agrò in his work on the multiple implications of Guimarães Rosa's *sertão* in his modern epic, "The choice of the *sertão* as the only place of novelistic action allows its expansion beyond all spatial specifications, this specificity being recuperated in its own absolutization of the narrated place." *Um lugar do tamanho do mundo: Tempos e espaços da ficção em João Guimarães Rosa* (Belo Horizonte, Brazil: EdUFMG, 2001), 88.

13. In an early study, Manoel Cavalcanti Proença discussed how some natural elements gain a kind of narrative agency metaphorically attached to major characters and episodes: "The natural elements—*sertão*, wind, river, *buritis*—become living, active characters." "Trilhas no Grande Sertão," *Augusto dos Anjos e outros ensaios* (Rio de Janeiro: José Olympio, 1959), 159.

14. Lorenz, "Diálogo," 94.

15. Guimarães Rosa, *Correspondência com seu tradutor italiano*, 90.

16. Even in the numerous critical studies focused specifically on the metaphysical and mystical components of Guimarães Rosa's work, references to this insistent link between documentary and metaphysical elements are frequent. In her study of the mythical and philosophical roots of the novel, especially concerning the trope of evil, Kathrin Rosenfield notes: "The external scene—the geography of the *sertão*—appears as an emblem of the internal scene of human nature, imprisoned in the trap of cruelty and hate—now turned outward, now inward, reversing against itself." *Desenveredando Rosa: A obra de J. G. Rosa e outros ensaios rosianos* (Rio de Janeiro: Topbooks, 2006), 230. Francis Utéza reads the novel from a mystical, esoteric perspective, yet he notes: "The veredas oases, where the Minas Gerais and the Goiás rivers balance with liquid the dryness of the sertão, become paths that lead to knowledge, to the undifferentiated

beginning, to the Tao of the Chinese." *JGR: Metafísica do Grande Sertão*, trans. José Carlos Garbuglio (São Paulo: EdUSP, 1994), 56.

17. Guimarães Rosa, *Correspondência com seu tradutor italiano*, 90.

18. Such works are preserved in Guimarães Rosa's archive, held by the Institute for Brazilian Studies at the University of São Paulo.

19. Guimarães Rosa, *Grande sertão*, 542.

20. Lorenz, "Diálogo," 85. In part because I discuss Jacques Rancière's work below, it is worth noting that the author recently devoted a chapter to Guimarães Rosa's *sertão* as a space for the production of fiction: "The reference to the *sertão* as a place of natural storytelling must not deceive: fiction is the ability to start again, every time, the jump into the unbegun, to cross the threshold once more in order to enter a space where all sense of reality is lost, along with its identities and its landmarks." *Les bords de la fiction* (Paris: Seuil, 2017), 178. Translated by Guillaume Troïanowski.

21. Antonio Carlos Robert Moraes, "O sertão: Um 'outro geográfico,'" in *Geografia histórica do Brasil: Cinco ensaios, uma proposta e uma crítica* (Rio de Janeiro: Annablume, 2009), 89.

22. Haruf Salmen Espindola, *Sertão do Rio Doce* (Rio Doce, Brazil: EdUnivale, 2005), 73–74.

23. I have elsewhere shown how this semantic field attached to the *sertão* has been expressed in colonial writings, mostly in America and in Africa in "*Sertão Dentro*: The Backlands in Early Modern Portuguese Writings," *Portuguese Literary and Cultural Studies* 27 (2014): 254–72; and how postcolonial Lusophone African writers have negotiated the term's colonial connotations in connection with the multiplicity of meanings it has acquired in postindependence Brazil in "Transatlantic *Sertões*: The Backlands of Ruy Duarte de Carvalho and Mia Couto," *Ecozon@: European Journal of Literature, Culture and Environment* 8, no. 1 (2017): 79–97.

24. Nísia Trindade Lima analyzes the importance of the *sertão* as an interpretative category in the development of Brazilian social thought in the late nineteenth century and the first half of the twentieth century. See *Um sertão chamado Brasil: Intelectuais e representação geográfica da identidade nacional* (Rio de Janeiro: Revan, IUPERJ, 1999). For other works that discuss the role of the *sertão* in Brazilian thought, see Sandro Dutra e Silva, Dominichi Miranda de Sá, and Magali Romero Sá, *Vastos sertões: História e natureza na ciência e na literatura* (Rio de Janeiro: Editora Mauad X, 2015); Candice Vidal e Souza, *A pátria geográfica: Sertão e litoral no pensamento social brasileiro*, 2nd ed. (Goiânia: EdUFG, 2015).

25. Durval Muniz de Albuquerque Jr., *The Invention of the Brazilian Northeast*, trans. Jerry Dennis Metz (Durham: Duke University Press, 2014), 67.

26. Antonio Candido, "O homem dos avessos," in *Tese e antítese*, 4th ed. (São Paulo: T. A. Queiroz, 2002), 121–39. More recently, Willi Bolle has proposed reading *Grande sertão: Veredas* as a rewriting of *Os sertões* in *grandesertão.br*. For criticism of attempts to make *Grande sertão: Veredas* something close to an heir of *Os sertões*, see Silviano Santiago, *Genealogia da ferocidade: Ensaio sobre* Grande Sertão: Veredas, *de Guimarães Rosa* (Recife: Companhia Editora de Pernambuco [CEPE], 2017).

27. See Luiz Roncari's *O Brasil de Rosa: O amor e o poder* (São Paulo: Unesp, 2004) and *O cão do sertão: Literatura e engajamento* (São Paulo: Unesp, 2007) for studies of Guimarães Rosa's only apparently insular *sertão* and its relation to broader historical processes in Brazil, from the violence of the Old Republic in the late nineteenth century and early twentieth century, to the federal struggle to put an end to banditry during the Getúlio Vargas governments from 1930 to 1945. For an analysis of the power relations between the bandits of *Grande sertão: Veredas* and the development of a "politics of banditry" marked by violence, see Heloisa Starling, *Lembranças do Brasil: Teoria política, história e ficção em* Grande sertão: Veredas (Rio de Janeiro: Revan and IUPERJ, 1999), 46. For a historical contextualization of banditry and its ambiguities in early twentieth-century Brazil, see Walnice Nogueira Galvão, *As formas do falso: Um estudo sobre a ambiguidade no* Grande sertão: Veredas (São Paulo: Perspectiva, 1972).

28. Nísia Trindade Lima, "Brasília: A capital no sertão," in *Veredas de Brasília: As expedições geográficas em busca de um sonho*, ed. Nelson de Castro Serna (Rio de Janeiro: Instituto Brasileiro de Geografia e Estatística, 2010), 27.

29. As João Adolfo Hansen proposes, this multiplicity of discourses under the label of the *sertão* constituted a unique case in Brazilian literature up until that point: "For the first time in our literature, the *sertão* breaks out as sensible discourse." *Oo: A ficção da literatura em* Grande sertão: Veredas (São Paulo: Hedra, 2000), 33.

30. According to the 2017 Report of the Brazilian Tree Industry Association (Ibá), Brazil was the world leader in eucalyptus production, with 35.7m2 of hectares as of 2016. See Indústria Brasileira de Árvores, *Relatório Ibá 2017*, 32–33, www.iba.org/images/shared/Biblioteca/IBA_RelatorioAnual2017.pdf. Among Brazilian states, Minas Gerais was by far the biggest producer, accounting for 24 percent of the national production (32). Most of the state's production, nevertheless, fueled the charcoal industry (49), including eucalyptus plantations in the Andrequicé area.

31. Carlos Klink and Adriana Moreira, "Past and Current Human Occupation, and Land Use," in *The Cerrados of Brazil: Ecology and Natural History of a Neotropical Savanna*, ed. Paulo S. Oliveira and Robert J. Marquis (New York: Columbia University Press, 2002), 73–77.

32. Wendy Wolford, "Environmental Justice and Agricultural Development in the Brazilian *Cerrado*," in *Environmental Justice in Latin America: Problems, Promise, and Practice*, ed. David V. Carruthers (Cambridge: MIT Press, 2008), 221–22.

33. Roberto Cavalcanti and Carlos Joly, "Biodiversity and Conservation Priorities in the Cerrado," in Oliveira and Marquis, *The Cerrados of Brazil*, 351.

34. Cavalcanti and Joly, "Biodiversity and Conservation," 251.

35. Klink and Moreira, "Past and Current Human Occupation," 83.

36. Ricardo Machado et al., "Estimativas de perda da área do Cerrado brasileiro," *Conservação Internacional*, Brasília, June 2004, 7, http://cmbbc.cpac.embrapa.br/RelatDesmatamCerrado%20CIBrasil%20JUL2004.pdf.

37. For more information, see "Museu Casa Guimarães Rosa," *Cultura MG*, accessed Dec. 15, 2017, http://www.cultura.mg.gov.br/instituicoes/museus/museu-casa-guimaraes-rosa.

38. Marco Antônio Coelho, "A magia dos sertões desperta o Brasil," *Dossiê Guimarães Rosa: Estudos Avançados* 20, no. 58 (2006): 19–20.

39. For more information, see *Circuito Turístico Guimarães Rosa*, accessed Dec. 15, 2017, http://circuitoguimaraesrosa.com.br/.

40. As Carlos Jáuregui and Flávia Ayer indicate, the Miguilins Group is made up of storytellers who tell stories related to Guimarães Rosa's texts in an effort to popularize his work and make it available to an audience that would not read it. "Miguilins: Muita estória pra contar," *Projeto Manuelzão*, accessed Dec. 15, 2017, http://www.manuelzao.ufmg.br/festivelhas1/salaimprensa/miguilim.htm. The Path to the *Sertão* Group organizes weeklong hikes to a number of Rosian landmarks.

41. Information on this new initiative was provided to me via email by Marco André Malaquias, the circuit's manager, in 2019.

42. *Circuito Turístico Guimarães Rosa.*

43. Umberto Eco, "Travels in Hyperreality," in *Travels in Hyperreality: Essays*, trans. William Weaver (San Diego: Harcourt Brace, 1986), 4.

44. Marily da Cunha Bezerra and Dieter Heidemann, "Viajar pelo sertão roseano é antes de tudo uma descoberta!" *Dossiê Guimarães Rosa: Estudos Avançados* 20, no. 58 (2006): 11.

45. Pascale Casanova, *The World Republic of Letters*, trans. M. B. DeBevoise (Cambridge, Mass.: Harvard University Press, 2004).

46. Casanova, *The World Republic*, 147.

47. Álvaro Lins, "Uma grande estreia," in *Guimarães Rosa*, ed. Eduardo de Faria Coutinho (Rio de Janeiro: Civilização Brasileira, 1983), 237–42. For a reassessment of this attack on Lins's newspaper literary criticism, which critics such as Afrânio Coutinho, inspired by the New Criticism, deemed "impressionistic," see João Cezar de Castro Rocha, *Crítica literária: Em busca do tempo perdido?* (Chapecó: Argos, 2011).

48. Such anxiety about legitimizing Guimarães Rosa's work in an international canon often defined by European models, moreover, mirrors concerns repeatedly expressed by Guimarães Rosa himself. His predilection for authors such as Goethe, Thomas Mann, and Robert Musil, among others, goes hand in hand with his insistence, in a letter to his German translator, Curt Meyer-Clason, that his work has a "spiritual affinity" with the German language: "De todas, será a alemã a versão mais bem realizada, a melhor—tenho a certeza. Nada vale mais, em assuntos assim, que o parentesco anímico, as afinidades de espírito" ("Of all of them, German will be the most fully realized version, the best—I'm certain. Nothing is worth more, in such subjects, than a psychic kinship, an affinity of the spirit"). *Correspondência com seu tradutor alemão Curt Meyer-Clason (1958–1967)*, ed. Maria Aparecida M. F. Bussolotti, trans. Erlon José Paschoal (Rio de Janeiro: Nova Fronteira, Academia Brasileira de Letras, EdUFMG, 2003), 125.

49. Antonio Candido, "Literatura e subdesenvolvimento," in *A educação pela noite e outros ensaios* (São Paulo: Ática, 1989), 161.

50. See Nossa, "Novas veredas," for an updated description of these transformations in the context of Guimarães Rosa's geography.

51. Siskind, *Cosmopolitan Desires*, 8.

52. George Yúdice, *The Expediency of Culture: Uses of Culture in the Global Era* (Durham: Duke University Press, 2003), 25.

53. Santiago, *Genealogia da ferocidade.*

54. Jacques Rancière, *Dissensus: On Politics and Aesthetics*, ed. and trans. Steven Corcoran (New York: Continuum, 2010), 36.

55. Rancière, *Dissensus*, 152.

56. According to Jennifer Ladino's work on the multifaceted role of nostalgia in shaping environmental imaginaries and activist initiatives, "Nostalgia should not be dismissed as inherently conservative or reactionary. Rather, in some contexts, it can be a mechanism for social change, a model for ethical relationships, and a motivating force for social and environmental justice." *Reclaiming Nostalgia: Longing for Nature in American Literature* (Charlottesville: University of Virginia Press, 2012), 8. Although environmental justice remains a contentious topic in some of the initiatives analyzed in this chapter, it is a fundamental component of others.

57. *Projeto Manuelzão*, accessed Dec. 15, 2017, http://www.manuelzao.ufmg.br.

58. García Canclini, *Hybrid Cultures*. I use García Canclini's notion of hybrid cultures in a relatively broad way in order to encompass the aforementioned environmental factors and efforts.

59. Apolo Heringer Lisboa, "Imaginário do Projeto Manuelzão," in *Navegando o Rio das Velhas: Das Minas aos Gerais*, edited by Eugênio Goulart (Belo Horizonte, Brazil: Instituto Guaicuy, 2005), 55.

60. A similar dynamic can be seen in other projects, such as "OPARÁ—tradições, identidades, territorialidades e mudanças entre populações rurais e ribeirinhas no Sertão Roseano," hosted by the Montes Claros State University and aimed at providing a geographical and ethnographic perspective on areas that often coincide with the ones represented in Guimarães Rosa's works. Although the project's name refers to the author and their publications occasionally mention him, his works perform a mediating albeit not essential role in the project's general design. See João Batista de Almeida and Cláudia Luz de Oliveira, *Cerrado, gerais, sertão: Comunidades tradicionais nos sertões brasileiros* (São Paulo: Intermeios, 2012).

61. For a reading of *Grande sertão: Veredas* as an urban novel, see Willi Bolle, "Grande sertão: Cidades," *Revista USP* 24 (1994–95): 80–93.

62. Translation from Taylor and de Onís, *The Devil to Pay in the Backlands*, 252.

63. According to Monica Meyer, "The annotations of Guimarães Rosa reveal a concern for deforestation (which was increasing at the time), by pointing out a section of the Paraobeba/Sirga route, where it was possible to find 'a virgin bush (something already rare here)—in the majority *itapicurus*, large ones. *Vinháticos* too' (B1, p. 7)" *Ser-tão natureza: A natureza em Guimarães Rosa* (Belo Horizonte, Brazil: UFMG, 2008), 127.

64. A list of parks and their history is available at the website of the Chico Mendes Institute for Conservation, which manages Brazil's conservation units. For an overview of the results of conservation policies in the *cerrado*, see Roseli Senna Ganem, José Augusto Drummond, and José Luiz de A. Franco, "Conser-

vation Policies and Control of Habitat Fragmentation in the Brazilian Cerrado Biome," *Ambiente e Sociedade* 16, no. 3 (2013): 99–118.

65. This mission also informs some of the touristic activities in the area surrounding the park. For example, a local guide well known in the region, Elson Barbosa, knows by heart long passages from Guimarães Rosa's work, which he recites to both tourists and local communities.

66. Cesar Victor do Espírito Santo, dir., *Plano de manejo do Parque Nacional Grande Sertão Veredas* (Brasília: IBAMA/Funatura, 2003), 32, www.ibmbio.gov.br.

67. Geraldo Inácio Martins, "As tramas da des(re)territorialização camponesa: A reinvenção do território veredeiro no entorno do Parque Nacional Grande Sertão Veredas, norte de Minas Gerais," M.A. thesis, Federal University of Uberlândia, 2011).

68. Espírito Santo, *Plano de manejo*, 141.

69. In an informal survey with local inhabitants in August 2017, I was informed that, at the time, only five families still remained in the park, in the area belonging to the state of Bahia, because they have the paperwork to prove ownership over the land. Most removed families are not satisfied with the compensation they received, especially because the areas to which they were relocated have significantly less water supply than their original homes. The owner of the only large farm, known as Fazenda do Feltrim, originally located in the area that became the park, allegedly received a proportionally more advantageous financial compensation for the farm's removal. In spite of these problems, the general view of the park in nearby cities seems to be positive, due to both increased environmental awareness and the potential financial revenue from tourists and other visitors.

70. Roderick Nash, "The American Invention of National Parks," *American Quarterly* 22, no. 3 (1970): 726–35. A variation of this process, as William Cronon notes, has taken place in the tropical rain forests since the 1970s: "Protecting the rain forest in the eyes of First World environmentalists all too often means protecting it from the people who live there." "The Trouble with Wilderness; or, Getting Back to the Wrong Nature," in *Uncommon Ground: Rethinking the Human Place in Nature*, ed. William Cronon (New York: Norton, 1995), 82.

71. Marcus Colchester, "Salvaging Nature: Indigenous Peoples and Protected Areas," *Social Change and Conservation*, ed. Krishna B. Ghimire and Michel P. Pimbert (New York: Earthscan, 2013), 103.

72. For a defense of an understanding of state conservation policies that goes beyond the North American model, see Wilko von Hardenberg et al., eds., *The Nature State: Rethinking the History of Conservation* (London: Routledge, 2017).

73. "Decreto N. 1.713—de 14 de junho de 1937—Cria o Parque Nacional de Itatiaia," *ICMBio*, accessed Dec. 13, 2017. http://www.icmbio.gov.br/portal/images/stories/imgs-unidades-coservacao/itatiaia.pdf.

74. According to Freitas, "The exclusion of dwellers from national parks, although not initially codified in Brazilian law, was a staple of the discourse of national parks officials since the establishment of the first parks in the 1930s" Frederico Freitas, "Ordering the Borderland: Settlement and Removal in the

Iguaçu National Park, Brazil, 1940s–1970s," in *The Nature State: Rethinking the History of Conservation*, ed. Wilko von Hardenberg et al. (London: Routledge, 2017), 160.

75. José Augusto Drummond, "From Randomness to Planning: The 1979 Plan for Brazilian National Parks," in *National Parks beyond the Nation: Global Perspectives on America's Best Idea*, ed. Adrian Howkins, Jared Orsi, and Mark Fiege (Norman: University of Oklahoma Press, 2016), 210–34.

76. Such ambivalence can be seen in passages such as this one: "As características culturais da população tradicional são a representação original da região, formadas dentro de um espaço ambiental distinto e, também, único. A união concreta e veemente destes aspectos culturais e ambientais, retratada com fidedignidade e excelência por Guimarães Rosa, deu origem ao nome do Parque, uma vez que sua área abriga claramente tais características" ("The cultural characteristics of the traditional population are the original representation of the region, formed within a distinct and also unique environmental space. The vehement, concrete union of these cultural and environmental aspects, portrayed with dependability and excellence by Guimarães Rosa, gave rise to the name of the park, since its area clearly houses such characteristics"). Espírito Santo, *Plano de manejo do Parque Nacional Grande Sertão Veredas*, 14.

77. Rosa Amélia Pereira da Silva has observed that local populations in the Urucuia Valley, which is part of *Grande sertão: Veredas*'s geographical perimeter, have rarely read Guimarães Rosa's work, in spite of often being familiar with his name and stories from his works. Silva has been developing projects to foster the reading of the author's works in the region. "Nesta água que não para: Leitura de João Guimarães Rosa no Vale do Urucuia," Ph.D. diss., University of Brasília, 2014.

78. Alfred Gell, *Art and Agency: An Anthropological Theory* (Oxford: Oxford University Press, 1998), 15.

79. Edward W. Soja, *Thirdspace: Journeys to Los Angeles and Other Real-and-Imagined Places* (Oxford: Blackwell, 2000).

CHAPTER 2

1. Barbara Land and Myrick Land, *Jungle Oil: The Search for Venezuela's Hidden Treasure* (New York: Coward-McCann, 1957), 89.

2. Guillermo Zuloaga, *Petroleum Geography of Venezuela* (Caracas: Cromotip, 1957), 18.

3. Although these and other authors often use nomenclature in imprecise ways, the Gran Sabana is actually a small portion of the region to which they refer. It is a specific savannah area in the broader range of tepuyes known as the Guiana Highlands, the highest portion of the Guiana Shield. The Venezuelan portion of the shield spreads across two Venezuelan states, Bolívar and Amazonas, and belongs to a single Guianan Administrative Region for the purposes of the environmental policies of the National Institute of Parks. See Isabel Novo Torres et al., *Ciencia y conservación en el Sistema de Parques Nacionales de Venezuela: Una experiencia de cooperación interinstitucional* (Caracas: Altamira, 1997).

4. Canaima National Park's original area included the Angel Falls region, today known as the Western Section. In 1975, it incorporated the Gran Sabana proper, including Mount Roraima, on the border with Brazil and Guyana, which now belongs to the Eastern Section.

5. Lois Parkinson Zamora, *The Inordinate Eye: New World Baroque and Latin American Fiction* (Chicago: University of Chicago Press, 2006), 115. Due to space limitations, I will not discuss Carpentier's concept of the New World Baroque, on which Lois Parkinson Zamora focuses. In the paragraph to which this passage belongs, Parkinson Zamora shows how the ideas that eventually led Carpentier to the New World Baroque were already present in his work decades earlier.

6. For a more detailed account of these trips, see Roberto González Echevarría's *Alejo Carpentier: The Pilgrim at Home* (Austin: University of Texas Press, 1990), 170–74. According to Leonardo Acosta, the musician Hilario González, who accompanied Carpentier on the 1948 trip, noted that they were supposed to take a third trip more focused on the Andean region in 1950. *Alejo en tierra firme: Intertextualidad y encuentros fortuitos* (Havana: Centro de Investigación y Desarrollo de la Cultura Cubana Juan Marinello, 2004), 40–42. Unless otherwise noted, all translations are by Laura Colaneri.

7. Alejo Carpentier, *Los pasos perdidos*, 2nd ed. (Buenos Aires: Editorial Losada, 2004), 357; Alejo Carpentier, *The Lost Steps*, trans. Harriet de Onís (Minneapolis: University of Minnesota Press, 2001), xv.

8. Alejo Carpentier, "Un camino de medio siglo," in *Obras completas de Alejo Carpentier*, vol. 13 (Mexico City: Siglo XXI, 1990), 160.

9. According to Rogers, "For Carpentier, the promise of El Dorado becomes a means to first extol the marvelous qualities of the South American forest, many of which draw on his readings about the region, and then show its demise in the process of extractivism." Charlotte Rogers, *Mourning El Dorado: Literature and Extractivism in the Contemporary American Tropics* (Charlottesville: University of Virginia Press, 2019), 49.

10. Alejo Carpentier, *El reino de este mundo* (Madrid: Alianza Editorial, 2003), 14; "Prologue to *The Kingdom of this World*," *Review: Latin American Literature and Arts* 47 (1993): 31.

11. For more information on this prologue, see Alexis Márquez Rodríguez, *La obra narrativa de Alejo Carpentier* (Caracas: Universidad Central de Venezuela, 1970), xxvii.

12. As Anke Birkenmaier has demonstrated, Carpentier's interest in Haitian culture and folklore goes back to the late 1920s and evolved into a detailed knowledge of Haitian ethnology, which surpassed the scope of his 1943 travel. *Alejo Carpentier y la cultura del surrealismo en América Latina* (Madrid: Iberoamericana/Vervuert, 2006), 100. Instrumental in fostering this interest was his contact with the Haitian ethnologists at the Bureau d'Ethnologie Haitiene starting in the late 1930s (101).

13. González Echevarría, *Alejo Carpentier*, 167.

14. Alejo Carpentier, *Visión de América*, in *Obras completas de Alejo Carpentier*, vol. 13 (Mexico City: Siglo XXI, 1990), 274.

15. The complicated spatiotemporal dynamics of the novel analyzed in the following sections can be regarded as part of the author's larger exploration of

how to narrativize time. A notable example from this period is the backward chronology of the 1944 short story "Viaje a la semilla" (1963; "Journey Back to the Source," 1970).

16. Erich Auerbach, "Figura," in *Scenes from the Drama of European Literature* (Minneapolis: University of Minnesota Press, 1984), 53,

17. Considering the importance of Oswald Spengler's thought to Carpentier's during the 1930s and 1940s—and in the very conceptualization of the real maravilloso, as González Echevarría shows (*Alejo Carpentier*, 54–57, 122–25)—*The Decline of the West*'s influence on the novelist may also be perceived in these expressions of disillusionment.

18. According to DeLoughrey, the idea of "the island as isolate [worked] as a conceptual rubric as vital to a historical moment that brought together newly acquired island territories, the development of ecosystem concepts of closed space, and nuclear militarism that relegated these islands to laboratories." Elizabeth DeLoughrey, "The Myth of Isolates: Ecosystem Ecologies in the Nuclear Pacific," *Cultural Geographies* 20, no. 2 (2013), 172. These particularities notwithstanding, these tests can be read within a broader movement of manipulating natural processes for military (and sometimes civilian) ends. For an account of such initiatives in a Cold War context, see Jacob Darwin Hamblin, *Arming Mother Nature: The Birth of Catastrophic Environmentalism* (New York: Oxford University Press, 2013).

19. Alejo Carpentier, *Letra y solfa*, vol. 9, ed. Raumindo Respall Fina (Havana: Letras Cubanas, 2004), 130.

20. In fact, the quest for origins rather than for the future has been more prevalent in criticism on Carpentier's work, especially on *Los pasos perdidos*. See, for example, Claire Martin's *Alejo Carpentier y las crónicas de Indias: Orígenes de una escritura americana* (Hanover, N.H.: Ediciones del Norte, 1995) for a comparative study of Carpentier's work and the *crónicas de Indias*; and Eduardo González's *Alejo Carpentier: El tiempo del hombre* (Caracas: Monte Ávila, 1978) for a study of the origins of the narrative act, both with an autobiographical dimension.

21. See Acosta, *Alejo en tierra firme*; Antonio Benítez Rojo, *La isla que de repite: El Caribe y la perspectiva posmoderna* (Barcelona: Casiopea, 1998); and Roberto González Echevarría, *Alejo Carpentier*.

22. Alejo Carpentier, *Visión de Venezuela* (Caracas: Monte Ávila; Havana: Fundación Alejo Carpentier, 2014), 3.

23. A mention of "el mundo perdido" ("the lost world"), a probable allusion to Doyle, even appears in the handwritten travel notes Carpentier took as he saw the Gran Sabana from his airplane. I thank Charlotte Rogers, who recently found Carpentier's handwritten and typed travel notes at the Fundación Alejo Carpentier, for kindly making them available to me.

24. In his account of a conversation with Carpentier, Klaus Müller-Bergh notes about the novel's reception: "In the case of *Los pasos perdidos*, the indignation in Caracas was extraordinary. Many Venezuelan friends said that that was not right, that after *El reino de este mundo*, Carpentier had gotten lost in a confusing prose that mixed essay with philosophy" Alejo Carpentier, *Entrevistas*, ed. Virgilio López Lemus (Havana: Letras Cubanas, 1985), 491. Such prose,

interestingly, was the opposite of the clear, concise, and witty style of *Letra y solfa*'s articles.

25. The film adaptation was proposed by Power, who was also supposed to perform the protagonist role. According to Carpentier, Ava Gardner was considered for the role of Mouche (Carpentier, *Entrevistas*, 45). The project was relatively advanced, and shooting was scheduled to begin early in 1959, when Power's death prematurely ended it. Carpentier declared in an interview in *Carteles* that the project would continue in the hands of another director (54), but it was never finished.

26. I refer to Martí's *Sección constante*, published in *La Opinión Nacional* in 1881 and 1882. See Wilfredo Cancio, *Crónicas de la impaciencia: El periodismo de Carpentier* (Madrid: Colibrí, 2010), 233.

27. Ursula Heise, *Sense of Place and Sense of Planet: The Environmental Imagination of the Global* (New York: Oxford University Press, 2008), 21.

28. Fernando Coronil, *The Magical State: Nature, Money, and Modernity in Venezuela* (Chicago: University of Chicago Press, 1997), 389.

29. Derided by Boom authors as lacking quality and being too committed to representing local and picturesque details, the *novelas de la selva*, as well as closely related genres such as the *novelas de la tierra* and other branches of regionalist fiction, have recently enjoyed renewed interest as sites for discussion, questioning, and reassessment of colonial and neocolonial tropes about American forests. See, for example, Jennifer French, *Nature, Neo-colonialism, and the Spanish American Regional Writers* (Hanover, N.H.: Dartmouth College Press, 2005). For a critique of British neocolonialism and early environmental thinking in fictional works on the forest, see Wylie, *Colonial Tropes and Postcolonial Tricks*, on how *novelas de la selva* rewrite and parody, through varying means, colonial discourses about American nature.

30. See the introduction for further thoughts on the role of nature in early twentieth-century regionalist fiction, with an emphasis on the "novels of the jungle."

31. For the role of Richard Schomburgk's account in Carpentier's writing, see chapter 5 of Benítez Rojo's *La isla que se repite*, which proposes that the narrator's identification with Schomburgk and other proponents of "Western historical and cultural discourse" reinforces the European aspect of the narrator's identity over the Caribbean ones (211). Disagreeing with this centering of Richard Schomburgk's impact on Carpentier's writing, Acosta discusses the influence of Humboldt and Charles Darwin on his work (*Alejo en tierra firme*, 57–68). Carpentier's handwritten and typed travel notes reinforce the view of the jungle as "dramatic," "immense," and "virgin," which attests to how present these tropes were in his thought from the very first contact he had with it.

32. Cronon, "The Trouble with Wilderness," 69.

33. Fernando Aínsa, *Del topos al logos: Propuestas de geopoética* (Madrid: Iberoamericana/Vervuert, 2006), 54.

34. Aínsa, *Del topos al logos*, 78, my translation. Still according to Aínsa, the visualization of these "successive 'historical layers'" is also present in the Surrealism of André Breton." "Pasos perdidos, identidad encontrada: La edad

del paisaje en Alejo Carpentier," in *Alejo Carpentier ante la crítica*, ed. Alexis Márquez Rodríguez (Caracas: Monte Ávila, 2005), 201. See also Márquez Rodríguez, who describes the process in the following terms: "In such a way that the linear chronological sequence is, in reality, the referent of novelistic time, while there is in the novel a chronological sequence that we could call *ontic*, that is, a metaphysical time, opposed to the novelistic time, whose development is its inverse; or rather, a time that, instead of advancing, retreats. The sequence of this other time is also linear, but not in a positive sense; instead, it goes backward." *La obra narrativa*, 195, author's emphasis.

35. Gustavo Pérez Firmat described this process in the following terms: "Carpentier's narrator renounces analogy and accepts asombro, astonishment. But the fact that the narrator, even in the middle of his trance, finds a name for what he observes . . . suggests how frail and fleeting ecstatic trances really are. . . . [T]he attempt to move beyond culture always fails." "The Strut of the Centipede: José Lezama Lima and New World Exceptionalism," in *Do the Americas Have a Common Literature?* (Durham: Duke University Press, 1990), 329.

36. Mark Millington, "Gender Monologue in Carpentier's *Los pasos perdidos*," *MLN* 11, no. 2 (1996): 361–62.

37. Wylie, *Colonial Tropes*, 115.

38. Wylie, *Colonial Tropes*, 116.

39. Yet, Wylie warns the reader about the importance of not conflating author and narrator on this point: "The narrator's mystification of the feminine and the concomitant subtext of male hegemony are a source of much of the novel's irony, cleaving a rift between the narrator and the author which biographical criticism has not been able to bridge convincingly." *Colonial Tropes*, 117.

40. González Echevarría, *Alejo Carpentier*, 160.

41. As Leonardo Padura argues in his essay on the *real maravilloso* (mostly through a reading of Carpentier), "Without doubt, the resource most often used to show the marvelousness of the American reality is the dislocation of historic time, altered on this continent since the days of its discovery." *Lo real maravilloso: Creación y realidad* (Havana: Letras Cubanas, 1989), 48.

42. Morton, *Ecology without Nature*.

43. In this sense, as Rogers proposes, *Los pasos perdidos* can be read as a "meta-adventure novel" which parodies some of the genre's conventions. See Charlotte Rogers, *Jungle Fever: Exploring Madness and Medicine in Twentieth-Century Tropical Narrative* (Nashville: Vanderbilt University Press, 2012), 149.

44. George Handley discusses the eccentricity of humans in relation to a biological center in this novel. In his words, the real maravilloso as developed in *Los pasos perdidos* has a "more profound implication[, which] is that ethical experience between diverse human subjects and the natural world should remain intersubjective, multiplied and decentered by an awareness of the contingencies of the singular seeing I/eye." "The Postcolonial Ecology of the New World Baroque: Alejo Carpentier's *The Lost Steps*," in *Postcolonial Ecologies: Literatures of the Environment*, ed. Elizabeth DeLoughrey and George Handley (Oxford: Oxford University Press, 2011), 126.

45. Rogers, *Mourning El Dorado*, 80–81.

46. Although it is not mentioned in the "Nota" at the end of the novel, Carpentier identified the fictional place this way later, such as in an interview with Manuel Osorio in 1980 (Carpentier, *Entrevistas*, 484).

47. Coronil, *The Magical State*, 134.

48. V. Barzetti, ed., *Parks and Progress: Protected Areas and Economic Development in Latin America and the Caribbean* (Washington, D.C.: Interamerican Development Bank and IUCN, 1993).

49. Mario Gabaldón, *Parques nacionales de Venezuela* (Caracas: INPARQUES, 1992), 11–13.

50. As Gabaldón indicates, this area lost its national park status in 1975 (*Parques nacionales*, 13).

51. The convention's full title was Convención sobre la Protección de la Flora, de la Fauna y de las Bellezas Escénicas Naturales de los Países de América (Convention on the Protection of Flora, Fauna, and the Scenic Beauties of the American Countries). Gabaldón, *Parques nacionales*, 28, 21, 29, 22.

52. Novo Torres et al., *Ciencia y conservación*, 8.

53. See Alex Fergusson, *Venezuela, la cuestión ambiental y el desarrollo: Una señal de alerta* (Caracas: Ministerio del Poder Popular para Ciencia y Tecnología, 2008), chapter 3, for an overview of landmarks in environmental legislation and management, such as the 1976 environmental laws that, among other things, led to the establishment of the Ministerio del Ambiente y de los Recursos Naturales Renovables in 1977 and the environmental legislation in the 1999 Bolivarian Constitution.

54. According to Jorge Salazar-Carrillo and Bernadette West, from 1943 to 1957 "oil's potential contribution to the Venezuelan economy appeared to attain its peak." *Oil and Development in Venezuela during the Twentieth Century* (Westport: Praeger, 2004), 127.

55. Miguel Tinker Salas, *The Enduring Legacy: Oil, Culture, and Society in Venezuela* (Durham: Duke University Press, 2009), 84–85.

56. For an overview of the relationships between successive governments and US companies, see Tinker Salas, *The Enduring Legacy*, chapter 7.

57. Arturo Uslar Pietri, "Sembrar el petróleo," *Ahora* 1, no. 183 (1936), in *Sembrar el petróleo en Venezuela*, Universidad Simón Bolívar, published in November 2012, http://hemerotecavirtualsembrarpetroleo.blogspot.com/.

58. Novo Torres et al., *Ciencia y conservación*, 292.

59. Elena Raimúndez Urrutia and Nelson Ramirez, "Eficiencia reproductiva y niveles de aborto en especies de plantas de cinco comunidades naturales de la Cuenca Alta del Río Caroní (Parque Nacional Canaima) y efecto de cierto factores bióticos sobre estos parámetros reproductivos: Resutados preliminares," in Novo Torres et al., *Ciencia y conservación*, 306.

60. For a description of how environmental problems associated with human activity have impacted this fragile fertility, see Aldemaro Romero Díaz, *Canaima* (Caracas: Palmaven, 1992–93), 150–59.

61. Before he was elected president, a coup d'état had previously made Betancourt Venezuela's leader, from 1945 to 1948.

62. Rómulo Betancourt, "Empezamos a producir acero," in *Tres años de gobierno democrático* (Caracas: Impr. Nacional, 1962), 149.

63. Rómulo Betancourt, "Cultura a todo el ámbito de la patria: Inauguración de la Universidad de Oriente, Cumaná, 29 de mayo de 1960," in *Antología política, vol. 7 (1959–1964)*, ed. Aníbal Romero, María Teresa Romero, and Elizabeth Tinoco (Caracas: Fundación Rómulo Betancourt, 1991), 206.

64. Mildred Real et al. "Mejorando nuestra herencia: Informe Preliminar," *Unesco*, 2002, accessed Sept. 15, 2017, 25, https://whc.unesco.org/document/6991.

65. For a description of the Pemon and their "other Carib neighbors (Macuxi and So'to)" in relation to nonindigenous literature produced about the area, including Gallegos's *Canaima*, see Lúcia Sá, *Rain Forest Literatures: Amazonian Texts and Latin American Culture* (Minneapolis: University of Minnesota Press, 2004), 5.

66. Roberto González Echevarría, "Canaima y los libros de la selva," in *Canaima*, by Rómulo Gallegos, ed. Charles Minguet (San José: Editorial Universidad de Costa Rica, 1996), 503.

67. Alejo Carpentier, "Notes on the Trip to the Great Savannah," ed. and trans. Charlotte Rogers, *PMLA* 134, no. 5 (2019): 6. I thank Rogers for kindly making this work available before its publication.

68. Roberto González Echevarría, *Myth and Archive: A Theory of Latin American Narrative* (Cambridge: Cambridge University Press: 1990), 4, 3.

69. Sá, *Rain Forest Literatures*, 83.

70. Pratt, *Imperial Eyes*, 229.

71. Lawrence Buell, "Uses and Abuses of Environmental Memory," in *Contesting Environmental Imaginaries: Nature and Counternature in a Time of Global Change*, ed. Steven Hartman (Leiden: Brill, 2017), 96.

72. Luiz Costa Lima, *O redemunho do horror: Nas margens do Ocidente*, 2nd ed. (São Paulo: Perspectiva, 2011), 23.

73. For more information, see "The Forgotten Expedition," *Ruth Robertson*, accessed April 20, 2018, http://www.ruthrobertson.org/.

74. Raymond Williams, *Marxism and Literature* (New York: Oxford University Press, 1977), 134.

75. Beyond these films, the landscape of the Gran Sabana has populated Hollywood imaginations from Frank Marshall's *Arachnophobia* (1990) to a 1960 episode of the True Adventure TV series, featuring stereotypical explorer John M. Goddard, in which he presents the region in the episode "Lost Plateau of Angel Falls."

76. For a newspaper piece on this phenomenon, see Daniel García Marco, "Santa Elena de Uairén, la ciudad en la frontera de Venezuela y Brasil donde se enriquecen los 'talibanes' de la gasoline," *BBC Mundo*, Mar. 24, 2017, https://www.bbc.com/mundo/noticias-america-latina-39275772

77. The Cerro Autana Natural Monument was created in 1978.

78. It is true that, regarding a movie in which a man transports his house from the United States to Venezuela by attaching balloons to it, a realistic interpretation of *Up* might not find the depiction of the Gran Sabana its most significant challenge.

79. Alison Byerly, "The Uses of Landscape: The Picturesque Aesthetic and the National Park System," in *The Ecocriticism Reader: Landmarks in Literary*

Ecology, ed. Harold Fromm and Cheryll Glotfelty (Athens: University of Georgia Press, 1996), 57.

80. Diego Díaz Martín and Isabel Novo Torres, *Informe final de la evaluación del Parque Nacional Canaima, Venezuela, como Sitio de Patrimonio Natural de la Humanidad* (Caracas: INPARQUES, 2007), 11. See Díaz Martín and Novo Torres for a description of indigenous villages within the park's boundaries.

81. Luis Fernando Angosto Ferrández, "Mundo perdido, paraíso encontrado: Lugar, identidad y producción en la Gran Sabana, Venezuela," *Revista Colombiana de Antropología* 49, no. 1 (2013): 21.

82. Pierre Nora, "Between Memory and History: Les Lieux de Mémoire," *Representations* 26 (1989): 7–24. For a discussion of sites of memory as they relate to the environment, see Axel Goodbody, "A Sense of Place and Lieu de Mémoire: A Cultural Memory Approach to Environmental Texts," in *Ecocritical Theory*, 55–67.

83. Bernhard Gissibl, Sabine Höhler, and Patrick Kupper, *Civilizing Nature: National Parks in Global Historical Perspective* (New York: Berghahn Books, 2012), 9.

84. Thomas Pavel, *Fictional Worlds* (Cambridge, Mass.: Harvard University Press, 1986), 57.

85. Pavel, *Fictional Worlds*, 51.

86. Of course, the notion of remoteness does not apply to local populations. Yet, it does apply to Venezuela's political class and most of its population at the time, not to mention an international audience aware of this "lost world" but unable or unwilling to get there.

87. As Michelle Niemann notes in personal communication with me, "This point may be harder to see in the US tradition of environmental literature, since the literary images of pristine environments that have shaped and inspired our national parks are largely nonfictional, in work by John Muir, Henry David Thoreau, and so on. And Muir often wrote specifically to advocate for the preservation of certain places. But the fact that they appear in nonfiction texts does not make such representations of nature any less 'fictional' in the sense you mean—they are still literary and still often treat 'nature' as unchanging and ahistorical, or metaphysical and transcendent." Michelle Niemann, email, August 2019.

CHAPTER 3

1. Corn, beans, and squash are the most typical components of the Mesoamerican polyculture known as *milpa*. Usually practiced by small farms, this system's agrobiodiversity leads to proportionally larger crops that are more resistant to pests and diseases, and studies indicate, may be more resilient than monocultures in the face of climate change. Roland Ebel et al., "Manejo orgánico de la milpa: Rendimiento de maíz, frijol y calabaza en monocultivo y policultivo," *Terra Latinoamericana* 35 (2017): 149–60. For these reasons and the three crops' relatively varied nutritional value, *milpa* is "the foundation of food security in many Latin American rural communities." Miguel Altieri, Fernando R. Funes-Monzote, and Paulo Petersen, "Agroecologically Efficient

Agricultural Systems for Smallholder Farmers: Contributions to Food Sovereignity," *Agronomy for Sustainable Development* 32, no. 1 (2012): 4. For more information on the *huamil*, or the methods by which this combination of crops is typically cultivated, see Laura González Martínez, *Respuesta campesina a la revolución verde en el Bajío* (Mexico City: Universidad Iberoamericana, 1992), 153–62.

2. Angus Wright, *The Death of Ramón González: The Modern Agricultural Dilemma*, rev. ed. (Austin: University of Texas Press, 2005).

3. The period during which Porfirio Díaz ruled the country, from 1876 to 1910, until his ousting in the early stages of the Mexican Revolution, is called the Porfiriato.

4. I refer to Benedict Anderson's definition of the nation as a social construction whose members do not know each other yet are able to imagine themselves as part of the larger community of the nation. See *Imagined Communities: Reflections of the Origin and Spread of Nationalism* (London: Verso, 2006).

5. Gabrielle Schwab, *Imaginary Ethnographies: Literature, Culture, and Subjectivity* (New York: Columbia University Press, 2012), 15.

6. I use *Modernism* here in the Anglophone sense and not in the Spanish American one. For further explanation of the terms *Modernism*, *modernism*, *modernity*, and *modernization*, see note 48.

7. For a reassessment of how a canonical corpus was established in the 1960s and 1970s, see Rafael Olea Franco, "La novela de la Revolución mexicana: Una propuesta de relectura," *Nueva Revista de Filología Hispánica* 60, no. 2 (2012), esp. 479–90.

8. Max Parra, "Geografía y procesos culturales en la narrativa de la revolución mexicana (Azuela y Campobello)," in *Imagining the Mexican Revolution: Versions and Visions in Literature and Visual Culture*, ed. Tilmann Altenberg (Newcastle upon Tyne: Cambridge Scholars Publishing, 2013), 4. Unless otherwise noted, all translations are by Laura Colaneri. According to Danaé Torres de la Rosa, this process was interwoven with two factors: the nationalist atmosphere in which the Partido Revolucionario Nacional (National Revolutionary Party), later known as Partido Revolucionario Institucional (Institutional Revolutionary Party), was created, and an evolving publishing market in which the genre flourished but which also determined its paths, mostly via the mythification of revolutionary figures and events, even in novels critical or skeptical of them. See *Avatares editoriales de un "género": Tres décadas de la novela de la Revolución mexicana* (Mexico City: Bonilla Artiga, Instituto Tecnológico Autónomo de México, Iberoamericana/Vervuert, 2015).

9. Antonio Castro Leal, ed., *La novela de la Revolución mexicana*, 9th ed. (Mexico City: Aguilar, 1991).

10. Although Castro Leal did not include the novel, a later anthology, *Cuentos de la Revolución*, edited by Luis Leal and published in 1976, included short stories from *El Llano en llamas*. See *Cuentos de la Revolución*, 5th ed. (Mexico City: UNAM, 2010).

11. In his study of how Rulfo's work navigates regionalist and cosmopolitan trends, Emir Rodríguez Monegal states, "If [*Pedro Páramo*] were only that [the story of a landowner], Rulfo would not have added much to what Mexican

novelists of the Revolution had already written. But . . . beyond the extremely Mexican circumstances of *Pedro Páramo*'s story, there is a more basic, elementary story, one of man's most persistent myths." "Relectura de Pedro Páramo," in *La ficción de la memoria: Juan Rulfo ante la crítica*, ed. Federico Campbell (Mexico City: Era, UNAM, 2010), 129, my translation. See Mariana Frenk, his German translator, for a reading of *Pedro Páramo* in the spectrum of European and North American Modernist fiction. "Pedro Páramo," in Campbell, *La ficción de la memoria*, 44–54.

12. This is why Max Aub notes: "The primary characteristics of the narrative of the Revolution are no longer present in Rulfo . . . but he draws directly from it. . . . Rulfo is pure reconstruction, another world, but the air that he breathes, the breath of his characters is still the same, among other reasons because what he describes are country situations and, despite the time that has passed, on rural soil change is only relative." *Ensayos mexicanos* (Mexico City: UNAM, 1974), 110–11, my translation. Curiously, this engagement with the revolutionary novels' view of the countryside situates him at a threshold before the Green Revolution's effects were felt: "With him [Rulfo] a certain way of considering the Mexican countryside as still unharmed by machinery is ended" (111).

13. By "event," I mean the historical event in Hayden White's terms: an eruption that changes an ongoing system but can only be grasped at a later time, when this "later event can be plausibly represented in a narrative in which it is the fulfillment (or derealization) of the meaning having lain latent and now made manifest retrospectively in the earlier one." "The Historical Event," *differences: A Journal of Feminist Cultural Studies* 19, no. 2 (2008): 30.

14. Luis Harss, "Juan Rulfo o la pena sin nombre," in Campbell, *La ficción de la memoria*, 72–73.

15. For a description of the "zona rulfiana" where most of the author's works are set, see Gustavo Fares, *Ensayos sobre la obra de Juan Rulfo* (New York: Peter Lang, 1998), 73–79, though his scholarship was published before Rulfo's birthplace of San Gabriel recovered its original name after decades of being called Ciudad Venustiano Carranza. For an account of San Gabriel's history in connection with Rulfo's works, see Felipe Garrido, *Voces de la tierra: La lección de Juan Rulfo* (Mexico City: UNAM, 2004), 89–97.

16. Alberto Vital, *Noticias sobre Juan Rulfo 1784–2003* (Mexico City: UNAM, 2003), 117.

17. Vital, *Noticias sobre Juan Rulfo*, 118–19. Some references to his travels and hikes can be found in the letters he wrote to his wife Clara Aparicio. His membership in the Everest Club, for example, is noted in a letter from March 1, 1947. *Aire de las colinas: Cartas a Clara*, ed. Alberto Vital (Madrid: Debate, 2000), 63.

18. Vital, *Noticias sobre Juan Rulfo*, 135. For more information on Rulfo's fellowship at the CME and his long relationship with the center, see Sergio López Mena, *Los caminos de la creación en Juan Rulfo* (Mexico City: UNAM, 1994), 73–76.

19. Patrick Iber, "The Cold War Politics of Literature and the Centro Mexicano de Escritores," *Journal of Latin American Studies* 48 (2015): 250.

20. Iber, "The Cold War Politics," 255, 257.

21. For a study of the photographic work that Rulfo produced as part of the Papaloapan Commission, see Paulina Millán Vargas, "La difusión inicial de las fotografías de Juan Rulfo (1949–1964)," in *Nuevos indicios sobre Juan Rulfo*, ed. Jorge Zepeda (Mexico City: Fundación Juan Rulfo, 2010), 91–133. For a description of documents in his archive related to the commission, see Jorge Zepeda, "Rulfo en el Papaloapan: Algunos documentos," *La Jornada*, Nov. 12, 2006, http://www.jornada.unam.mx/2006/11/12/sem-jorge.html.

22. Víctor Jiménez, "Cronología de la obra y la vida de Juan Rulfo," in *Juan Rulfo y su obra: Una guía crítica*, ed. Víctor Jiménez and Jorge Zepeda (Mexico City: RM, 2018), 25–48.

23. Jiménez, "Cronología," 37.

24. Jiménez, *Juan Rulfo y su obra*, 332.

25. In a recent article, Bruno Bosteels reinterprets Rulfo's role as a modernizing agent, linking it to the simultaneous presence and disappearance of a Benjaminian storyteller immersed in a context of oral communication that permeates his fictional work. "Reading Rulfo between Benjamin and Derrida: End of Story," in *Mexican Literature in Theory*, ed. Ignacio M. Sánchez Prado (London: Bloomsbury, 2018), 111–37.

26. Juan Rulfo, *Juan Rulfo: Letras e imágenes*, ed. Víctor Jiménez (Mexico City: RM, 2002).

27. Joseph Sommers, "Los muertos no tienen tiempo ni espacio (un diálogo con Juan Rulfo), in Campbell, *La ficción de la memoria*, 517.

28. Fabienne Bradu shows how "in order to put things into relief (in space and time) everything must be placed on the same plane." *Ecos de Páramo* (Mexico City: CONACULTA, 2003), 55. On Comala's insularity, whose "atmosphere creates a hermetic space; [and] speech serves for the domination or transmission of a hegemonic ideology [that of the cacique] that suppresses, in spite of itself, all hope," see Alberto Vital, *Lenguaje y poder en* Pedro Páramo (Mexico City: Consejo Nacional para la Cultura y las Artes, 1993), 37.

29. Silvia Lorente-Murphy, *Juan Rulfo: Realidad y mito de la Revolución mexicana* (Madrid: Pliegos, 1988); Manuel Ferrer Chivite, *El laberinto mexicano en/de Juan Rulfo* (Mexico City: Editorial Novaro, 1972). This position is also corroborated by critics such as John Brushwood: "The continuation of the movement of the Revolution in Mexico seems to me to depend on the development of a deep understanding of Mexican reality. Rulfo has contributed notably to this end. . . . And even if, in some cases, the visible reality is not a typically Mexican social problem, the universal human reality discovered by the author also contributes to the Mexican act of self-discovery." *Mexico in Its Novel: A Nation's Search for Identity* (Austin: University of Texas Press, 1975), 33–34. As such, even when Rulfo's "universality" is emphasized, the very understanding of this condition is folded back into an exercise in Mexican self-interpretation.

30. Although environmental issues have not traditionally been part of the critical corpus on the *novelas de la Revolución*, recent work has paid attention to the role of the nonhuman world in the genre. Mark Anderson reads Agustín Yáñez's *Al filo del agua* (1947; *On the Edge of the Storm*, 1963) through Adorno and Horkheimer's take on the domination of nature and the revolt of nature. See "Was the Mexican Revolution a Revolt of Nature? Agustín Yáñez's Ecolog-

ical Perspective," *Revista de Estudios Hispánicos* 40 (2006): 447–67. Carolyn Fornoff analyzes human and nonhuman interactions in Rafael F. Muñoz's *Se llevaron el cañon para Bachimba* (1941; "They Took the Cannon to Bachimba"). In both cases, desertification and land erosion are part of environmental concerns that, as the authors show, are significantly more present in the genre than previously thought. See "The Nature of Revolution in Rafael F. Muñoz's *Se llevaron el cañon para Bachimba*," in Sánchez Prado, *Mexican Literature in Theory*, 93–110.

31. For an account of criticism on low productivity linked to land reform in the late 1930s and early 1940s, see Joseph Cotter, *Troubled Harvest: Agronomy and Revolution in Mexico, 1880–2002* (Westport, Conn.: Praeger, 2003), chapter 4; and Tore C. Olsson, *Agrarian Crossings: Reformers and the Remaking of the US and Mexican Countryside* (Princeton, N.J.: Princeton University Press, 2017), 131–38.

32. John H. Perkins, *Geopolitics and the Green Revolution: Wheat, Genes, and the Cold War* (New York: Oxford University Press, 1997), 108.

33. Olsson, *Agrarian Crossings*, chapter 5. In spite of their willingness to adapt, as Deborah Fitzgerald shows, "as a rule, the RF programme succeeded insofar as Mexican farmers and agricultural professionals shared with their American counterparts the same assumptions about and expectations for agricultural progress, and failed when such a parallel group did not exist." "Exporting American Agriculture: The Rockefeller Foundation in Mexico, 1943–53," *Social Studies of Science* 16, no. 3 (1986): 459.

34. González Martínez, *Respuesta campesina*, 302.

35. As Perkins states, "[Rockefeller] Foundation literature from the time paints a picture of helping subsistence farmers produce more food, which may have happened in some cases, but the Mexican government probably saw the foundation as helping transform Mexican agriculture away from subsistence farming toward the type of commercial farming that was compatible with a modern industrial state." *Geopolitics and the Green Revolution*, 112.

36. According to Olsson, "Since the Porfirian era, modernizing elites blamed campesinos' diet of corn, bean, and chilis for stunting their physical and intellectual development, even suggesting that the consumption of corn inherently produced backward, dark-skinned people in contrast to strong and virile wheat-fed Europeans." *Agrarian Crossings*, 150.

37. For a detailed account of how farmers negotiated the technologies of the Green Revolution alongside traditional methods, as well as rural exodus due to demographic pressure in the region of El Bajío, one of the historically crucial agricultural areas of Mexico, see González Martínez, *Respuesta campesina*. See David Clawson and Don Hoy for an example of the reasons why Nealtican's campesinos rejected the MAP's technologies, which included the relatively small size of corn kernels, a strict planting schedule that entailed higher risks in the event of crop failure, and dependence on outsiders for chemical fertilizers. "Nealticán, Mexico: A Peasant Community That Rejected the 'Green Revolution,'" *American Journal of Economics and Sociology* 38, no. 4 (1979): 379–80. For the predominance of wheat in determining the MAP's success, see Olsson, *Agrarian Crossings*.

38. Lane Simonian, *Defending the Land of the Jaguar: A History of Conservation in Mexico* (Austin: University of Texas Press, 2015), 96–97.

39. For an overview of water and soil management policies from 1940 to 1970, see Simonian, *Defending the Land*, 111–21.

40. Simonian, *Defending the Land*, 117. For more information on river basin and community forestry projects, and their impact on indigenous populations, see Christopher Boyer, especially chapter 5, according to whom, "In the forest sector, the PRI essentially became an environmental kleptocracy." *Political Landscapes: Forests, Conservation, and Community in Mexico* (Durham: Duke University Press, 2015), 167.

41. For an account of "the reorganization of public cases linked to the gestation and distribution of the improved seeds" (135) from the 1960s onward, after the Comisión del Maíz's end, see Gilberto Aboites Manrique, *Una mirada diferente de la revolución verde: Ciencia, nación y compromiso social* (Mexico City: Plaza y Valdés, Universidad de Guadalajara, 2002), esp. chapter 4.

42. Cotter, *Troubled Harvest*, 234.

43. Created in 1937, the cutting-edge Taller de Gráfica Popular was a leading collective in Mexico's printmaking industry at the time. As Stephanie Smith explains, it mobilized major Mexican artists, as well as a number of international interlocutors and foreigners living in Mexico. By coupling a realist style with a leftist agenda made explicit by its association with the Mexican Communist Party, the TGP was an important voice in the fight against fascism. Although it remained independent from the government, financial problems led the workshop to increasingly accept commissions from the governments of Ávila Camacho and Aleman in the late 1940s and early 1950s, around the time when these prints were produced. See *The Power and Politics of Art in Postrevolutionary Mexico* (Chapel Hill: University of North Carolina Press, 2017), chapter 5.

44. Helga Prignitz, *El Taller de Gráfica Popular en México 1937–1977*, trans. Elizabeth Siefer (Mexico City: Instituto Nacional de Bellas Artes, 1992), 320.

45. George Gray, "Blueprint for Hungry Nations; A Mexican-American Agricultural Project Demonstrates the Means of Multiplying the Food Output of Low-Yield Granaries," New York Times, Jan. 1, 1950, https://www.nytimes.com/1950/01/01/archives/blueprint-for-hungry-nations-a-mexicanamerican-agricultural-project.html.

46. "Mexican Agricultural Program," Revised Commentary for Film Prepared for the Rockefeller Foundation, Transfilm, Oct. 24, 1950, Rockefeller Archive Center, Mexican Field Office, Record Group 6.13 I.I, Series 1.3, Box 33, Folder 369, p. 1.

47. Cotter, *Troubled Harvest*, 225.

48. Among the semantic multiplicity that characterizes the linked terms *modernity*, *modernization*, and *Modernism*, the process at stake here resonates with the "dialectics between modernism and modernization" in Marshall Berman's formulation, according to which a broader process of economic modernization from the sixteenth to the eighteenth century gives rise in the nineteenth century to a modern sensibility that, in turn, fosters the varied artistic manifestations categorized under the umbrella of modernism. See *All That Is Solid Melts into Air: The Experience of Modernity* (London: Verso, 1982),

16. In Perry Anderson's synthetic formulation of Berman's work, modernity "is defined as the *experience* undergone within modernization that gives rise to modernism." "Modernity and Revolution," *New Left Review* 144 (1984): 109, Anderson's emphasis. The Modernist voice, for Berman, "is ironic and contradictory, polyphonic and dialectical, denouncing modern life in the name of values that modernity itself has created." *All That Is Solid*, 23. Although Rulfo's fictional works would not be considered modernist in the Spanish-American sense—that is, they were not part of the late nineteenth-century movement led by Ruben Darío—they do incorporate a voice that criticizes modernity from its own perspective, and in doing so they reveal a Mexican version of Berman's modern sensibility. See Rubén Gallo's *Mexican Modernity: The Avant-Garde and the Technological Revolution* (Cambridge, Mass.: MIT Press, 2005) for another facet of this modern sensibility in Mexico, one marked by artists' explicit enthusiasm for technology.

49. Marcos Natali, *A política da nostalgia: Um estudo das formas do passado* (São Paulo: Nankin, 2006), 89.

50. Kerstin Oloff, "The 'Monstrous Head' and the 'Mouth of Hell': The Gothic Ecologies of the 'Mexican Miracle,'" in *Ecological Crisis and Cultural Representation in Latin America: Ecocritical Perspectives on Art, Film, and Literature*, ed. Mark D. Anderson and Zélia Bora (London: Lexington Books, 2016), 81.

51. Oloff, "The 'Monstrous Head,'" 81.

52. Frederic Jameson, *The Political Unconscious: Narrative as a Socially Symbolic Act* (London: Routledge Classics, 2002), 66. Consequently, these perspectives, are "not immediately present as such, . . . but rather must [themselves] . . . always be (re)constructed after the fact."

53. Jameson, *The Political Unconscious*, 70.

54. In an interview given in the 1970s to Máximo Simpson, Rulfo explains that caciques existed in precolonial times and were later replaced by colonial *encomenderos*: "Así nació la encomienda y más tarde la hacienda con su secuela de latifundismo o monopolio de la tierra. . . . Pedro Páramo es un cacique de los que abundan todavía en nuestros países" ("And so was born the encomienda and later the hacienda, with its aftermath of *latifundismo* or land monopoly. . . . Pedro Páramo is a cacique of the type that still is common in our countries"). Vital, *Noticias sobre Juan Rulfo*, 200.

55. For how Rulfo uses what Amit Thakkar calls a "centrifugal irony" to satirize the resilience of the figure of the cacique in Mexico, see *The Fiction of Juan Rulfo: Irony, Revolution and Postcolonialism* (Woodbridge: Tamesis, 2012), chapter 6.

56. Ericka Beckman, "Unfinished Transitions: The Dialectics of Rural Modernization in Latin American Fiction," *Modernism/Modernity* 23, no. 4 (2016): 817.

57. According to Beckman, *Pedro Páramo* represents "always uneven and always unfinished transitions to capitalism that from the vantage of the mid-twentieth century could be grasped as a living hell." "Unfinished Transitions," 815.

58. For a reading of the idea of cheap nature—i.e., the assumption that natural resources are available at no cost—in the context of the Green Revolu-

tion, which yielded "cheap food," see Jason Moore, *Capitalism and the Web of Life: Ecology and the Accumulation of Capital* (London: Verso, 2016), chapter 10.

59. Victoria Saramago, "Ecos de piedras y ecos de palabras: Los espacios de *Pedro Páramo*," in *"Pedro Páramo": 60 años*, ed. Víctor Jiménez (Mexico City: Fundación Juan Rulfo and RM, 2015), 151–62.

60. This domination of nature that entails domination of people as involving two forms of control—one magical and the other rationalized—can be read through the lens of Theodor Adorno and Max Horkheimer in *The Dialectic of Enlightenment*, ed. Gunzelin Schmid Noerr, trans. Edmund Jephcott (Stanford, Calif.: Stanford University Press, 2002). The novel's universe is doubly instrumentalized by the magic influence of the cacique and the technical management of his lands.

61. For a study of how Borlaug became a "brand hero" for the Green Revolution, see James Sumberg, Dennis Keeney, and Benedict Dempsey, "Public Agronomy: Norman Borlaug as 'Brand Hero' for the Green Revolution," *Journal of Development Studies* 48, no. 11 (2012): 1587–1600.

62. Cotter, *Troubled Harvest*, 233.

63. Jorge Zepeda, *La recepción inicial de "Pedro Páramo," 1955–1963* (Mexico City: Fundación Juan Rulfo and RM, 2005), 136, Zepeda's emphasis.

64. Zepeda, *La recepción inicial*, 128.

65. Antonio Benítez Rojo, ed., *Recopilación de textos sobre Juan Rulfo* (Havana: Centro de Investigaciones Literarias Casa de las Américas, 1969). For an overview of Juan Rulfo's reception in Spanish America outside of Mexico, see Victoria Saramago, "Juan Rulfo leído por escritores y críticos latinoamericanos," in *Juan Rulfo y su obra*, 183–87.

66. Data on each print run can be found in Zepeda, *La recepción inicial*, 293. These figures refer to the average number of copies produced during each period, not to actual annual production.

67. For data on other editions of the novel in Spanish, as well as some translations, see Zepeda, *La recepción inicial*, 300–305.

68. Víctor Jiménez and Daniel Sada, "Juan Rulfo: La escritura y la preservación del enigma: Conversación con Daniel Sada," in *Tríptico para Juan Rulfo: Poesía, fotografía, crítica*, ed. Víctor Jiménez, Alberto Vital, and Jorge Zepeda (Mexico City: UNAM, 2006), 305.

69. I thank Víctor Jiménez for information on this topic.

70. For information on these and other adaptations, as well as Rulfo's activities in the film industry, see Douglas Weatherford, "Juan Rulfo y el cine," Juan Rulfo: Página Oficial, accessed Feb, 1, 2018, http://juan-rulfo.com/especial_cine.htm.

71. Larsen, *Modernism and Hegemony*, 67. For Larsen, "the consciousness of a 'cultural' identity in which all 'Mexicans' share the same quasi-genetic national traits offers a certain rationalization of the 'irrational' under conditions of post populist stalemate" (67).

72. Larsen, *Modernism and Hegemony*, 68.

73. Larsen uses the term *hegemony* in the Gramscian sense but with an important caveat in the Latin American case, in which the consolidation of state

power as the first step by which the bourgeoisie will struggle to attain the "*conquest of civil society*" (Larsen, *Modernism and Hegemony*, 73, Larsen's italics) constitutes an inversion of the process described by Gramsci. As a result, the hegemonic dimension of Rulfo's works is channeled through the apparent absence of a state that does not name itself while codifying "the meaning of its as yet prehegemonized domain under the general heading of 'culture'" (74), at the same time as it does not offer a "potential site of counterhegemonic agency" (76). Although I do see the cultural hegemony of Rulfo's work, understood as a cultural institution, as a condition for understanding the forms of agency I describe, I take issue with the absence, in Larsen's reading, of a more granular approach to the contradictory forces present in Rulfo's work that constantly offer counterpoints to the very means through which such hegemony takes shape in the first place. Larsen reformulated his position years later, in "Rulfo and the Transcultural: A Revised View," in *Determinations: Essays on Theory, Narrative and Nation in the Americas* (London: Verso, 2001), 137–42.

74. Jean Franco, for example, has read Comala's deadly narrative present as a locus for the fierce resentment of local populations over the intrusion of the state into their habits and affairs after the revolution: "Desvivir [the state in which the incestuous siblings classify themselves] has become the state of the subject in the secular nation state in which progress has come to a halt and religion is outlawed." *The Decline and Fall of the Lettered City* (Cambridge, Mass.: Harvard University Press, 2002), 135.

75. Raj Patel, "The Long Green Revolution," *Journal of Peasant Studies* 40, no. 1 (2013): 10.

76. Cotter describes early steps to internationalize the Green Revolution this way: "The [Rockefeller] foundation's program in Colombia began in 1950 and trained scientists from Ecuador, Peru, Central America, and Chile. By 1952 Indian and Israeli farmers grew MAP wheat and corn. The directors of the Point IV Program and the State Department decided that the MAP was an excellent model for Third World agricultural assistance programs, and in 1956 the foundation began one in India. . . . [I]n 1960 the foundation founded the International Rice Research Institute (IRRI) [in the Philippines]." *Troubled Harvest*, 248. For a comparative account of the Green Revolution in a number of countries, see Andrew Pearse, *Seeds of Plenty, Seeds of Want: Social and Economic Implications of the Green Revolution* (Oxford: Oxford University Press, 1980).

77. For an overview of the expansion of the Green Revolution under the aegis of Cold War policies, see Perkins, *Geopolitics and the Green Revolution*.

78. Vandana Shiva, *The Violence of the Green Revolution: Third World Agriculture, Ecology and Politics* (London: Zed Books and Third World Network, 1993).

79. Wright, *The Death of Ramón González*, 245.

80. Milagros Ezquerro, *Lecturas rulfianas* (Guadalajara: Universidad de Guadalajara, 2006), 65.

81. Raymond Williams, *The Country and the City*, 289.

82. See Raymond Williams, *The Country and the City*, chapter 24.

83. Mikhail Bakhtin, "Forms of Time and of the Chronotope in the Novel," in *The Dialogic Imagination: Four Essays*, ed. Michael Holquist, trans. Caryl Emerson and Michael Holquist (Austin: University of Texas Press, 2008), 217.

84. Bakhtin, "Forms of Time," 218.

85. Beckman, "Unfinished Transitions," 817, Beckman's emphasis.

86. Paul Goldberg, "Narco-Pastoral: Drug Trafficking, Ecology, and the Trope of the Noble Campesino in Three Mexican Narconovelas," *ISLE: Interdisciplinary Studies in Literature and Environment* 21, no. 1 (2016): 30–50.

87. Schwab, *Imaginary Ethnographies*, 15.

CHAPTER 4

1. Hélène Cixous, *Reading with Clarice Lispector*, trans. Verena Andermatt Conley (Minneapolis: University of Minnesota Press, 1990).

2. Gabriel Giorgi shows how the writing of *A paixão segundo G.H.* questions the meanings of bios, "returning to it the instance of an irreducible instability." *Formas Comunes: Animalidad, cultura, biopolítica* (Buenos Aires: Eterna Cadencia Editora, 2014), 112. Evando Nascimento's *Clarice Lispector: Uma literatura pensante* (Rio de Janeiro: Civilização Brasileira, 2012) analyzes the politics of gaze with respect to humans and things. Alexandre Nodari, writing about the first novel, reads G.H.'s condition as a form of "ontological hetareism" marked by her encounter with the earth and nonhuman forms, in "'A vida oblíqua': O hetairismo ontológico segundo G.H.," *O Eixo e a Roda* 24, no. 1 (2015): 139–54.

3. For an overview of this perceived rupture, see Carlos Mendes de Sousa, *Clarice Lispector: Figuras da escrita* (Braga, Portugal: Universidade do Minho, Centro de Estudos Humanísticos, 2000), 59–71.

4. Luís Bueno, *Uma história do romance de 30* (São Paulo: EdUSP, 2006), 18.

5. "Transcultural," here, refers to Fernando Ortiz's concept of transculturation, which, as Héctor Hoyos shows, addresses both "our historical and material situation," thus constituting a privileged site in the joint articulation of these two modalities of materialist theories. "A Tale of Two Materialisms," *Novel: A Forum on Fiction* 51, no. 1 (2018): 104. A more recent and through elaboration of this concept can be found in Héctor Hoyos, *Things with a History: Transcultural Materialism and the Literatures of Extraction in Contemporary Latin America* (New York: Columbia University Press, 2019).

6. While a thorough discussion of the conceptual distinction between objects and things is beyond the scope of this chapter, I maintain it here, insofar as, following Bill Brown, "the object-thing distinction . . . can become a way to caption, and a tool for apprehending, the unanticipated force of an object, no matter how banal that object may be" *Other Things* (Chicago: University of Chicago Press, 2015), 291. As the next section will show, placing objects in the subject position is a way through which objects reveal themselves as things precisely by taking advantage, on a grammatical level, of the subject-object distinction.

7. Clarice Lispector, *A descoberta do mundo* (Rio de Janeiro: Rocco, 1999), 411, 412. Unless otherwise stated, all translations are mine.

8. For an overview of this novel's early reception, and how initially negative reviews were counterbalanced by positive assessments, see Regina Pontieri, *Clarice Lispector: Uma poética do olhar* (Cotia: Ateliê Editorial, 2001), chapter 1. Sérgio Milliet, for example, criticized the novel's "rococo" style and noted "the writer's entanglement in her own web of precious images" (Milliet, quoted in Pontieri, *Clarice Lispector*, 38). In the same vein, Sérgio Buarque de Holanda noted the "less skilled dosage" of elements that could be found in her earlier novels (Buarque de Holanda, quoted in Pontieri, *Clarice Lispector*, 41). Other negative published reviews can be found in the author's archive at the Casa de Rui Barbosa in Rio de Janeiro, such as that of Wilson Martins, "Uma voz," *Suplemento Literário, O Estado de São Paulo*, Nov. 26, 1960, Arquivo Clarice Lispector, Fundação Casa de Rui Barbosa.

9. Lucia Villares, "Modernization and the Phantasmagoria of Commodities in Clarice Lispector's *A cidade sitiada*," *BHS* 87, no. 4 (2010): 473–87. In her Marxist reading of the novel, Villares shows how, in a context of increasing circulation of commodities, Lucrécia "merges into the landscape, becoming another of its objects" (474), and that this identification happens with objects that "have been deprived of their use-value and which become somehow magically animated" (480).

10. According to Benedito Nunes, "The environmental changes delimit the novelistic action, which begins with them and ends when they are completed. Lucrécia Neves's final desertion is part of an exodus of the inhabitants, who abandon the city in the moment that it loses its provincial character and the walls of time that surround it fall." *O drama da linguagem: Uma leitura de Clarice Lispector* (São Paulo: Ática, 1989), 33.

11. Clarice Lispector, *A cidade sitiada* (Rio de Janeiro: Rocco, 1998), 75; Clarice Lispector, *The Besieged City*, trans. Johnny Lorenz (New York: New Directions, 2019), 73.

12. Lispector, *A cidade sitiada*, 23; *The Besieged City*, 17.

13. Pontieri, *Clarice Lispector*, 20.

14. Lispector, *A cidade sitiada*, 92; *The Besieged City*, 92.

15. The depiction of the multiplicity of modern elements, contrasts, stimulations, and changes in urban space has been a constant theme in studies not only of High Modernist literature, but also of modernity at large. See, for example, Walter Benjamin's writings on Baudelaire in nineteenth-century Paris, for whom "the flâneur is someone abandoned in the crowd. He is thus in the same situation as the commodity" (*The Writer of Modern Life: Essays on Charles Baudelaire* [Cambridge, Mass.: Harvard University Press, 2006], 85), or the overview of urban experience in Modernist literature in David Kelley and Edward Timms, eds., *Unreal City: Urban Experience in Modern European Literature and Art* (New York: St. Martin's Press, 1985).

16. Nascimento, *Clarice Lispector*, 80. For Nascimento, "The very gaze has the dimension of a thing; besides that, things themselves stare at us, like the animals" (79).

17. Jane Bennett, *Vibrant Matter: A Political Ecology of Things* (Durham: Duke University Press, 2010), 3.

18. Lispector, *A cidade sitiada*, 47; *The Besieged City*, 43.

19. Brown, *Other Things*, 39.

20. Philippe Hamon, *Du descriptif*, trans. Guillaume Troïanowski (Paris: Hachette, 1993), 5.

21. Gérard Genette, *Narrative Discourse: An Essay in Method*, trans. Jane E. Lewin (Ithaca, N.Y.: Cornell University Press, 1983), 128.

22. Bruno Latour, *Reassembling the Social: An Introduction to Actor-Network-Theory* (Oxford: Oxford University Press, 2005), 72.

23. In his words, "When everything else has failed, the resource of fiction can bring . . . the solid objects of today into the fluid states where their connections with humans may make sense." Latour, *Reassembling the Social*, 82. Latour has a larger body of work on the issue upon which *Reassembling the Social* builds. For example, in his previous book, *Politics of Nature* (Cambridge, Mass.: Harvard University Press, 2004), he proposes replacing the distinction between subject and object with collectives of human and nonhuman actors as a way of solving the dilemmas faced by political ecology.

24. Another significant dynamic between humans and nonhumans that can be seen in other passages from Lispector's work arises from what Benedito Nunes has interpreted as a nausea, in the Sartrean sense, that takes place when "the revealed existence concretely presents itself. It is something throbbing, animated, in physical matter and in vegetative and animal organisms: its qualities are not only attributes of matter, but true ontological qualifications." *O dorso do tigre*, 2nd ed. (São Paulo: Perspectiva, 1976), 97. In fact, the examples that Nunes gives refer to encounters between human characters and the shocking texture of things. Nunes took up this discussion again later in *O drama da linguagem* (113–22).

25. Lispector, *A cidade sitiada*, 34; *The Besieged City*, 28.

26. According to Villares, "Modernization is depicted as something extremely concrete and visible, but at the same time as a force that works in a surreptitious way; a process that disrupts and disturbs the relationship between individuals, social groups and physical environment." "Modernization," 475.

27. Lispector, *A cidade sitiada*, 15; *The Besieged City*, 8.

28. A passage such as this one recalls Earl Fitz's argument that Lispector's characters are aware that "not even they can imbue their identities with the kind of perfect stability and meaning that we, adrift in an ever-changing and uncertain world, desire." *Clarice Lispector* (Boston: Twayne, 1985), 19. This awareness of the nature of language as "a self-referential system of signs" (19), nevertheless, meets exceptions when some characters see it as "a self-eliding illusion" (19)—in which category Lucrécia possibly belongs.

29. Nixon, *Slow Violence*, 2.

30. Curiously, the trope of the siege via which Lucrécia, horses, and others are expelled from the urban perimeter invokes the idea that some humans and nonhumans are to be discarded from the evolving town, though the novel does not touch on significant related issues of social and environmental vulnerabilities in urban spaces. One of them is the accumulation of garbage in landfills inhabited by what Gisela Heffes calls "hombres-basura" (garbage-men) in *Políticas de la destrucción, poéticas de la preservación: Apuntes para una lectura (eco) crítica del medio ambiente en América Latina* (Rosario: Beatriz Viterbo, 2013),

who live in "an invisible zone, fenced, that houses that ominous thing which is trash" (97), or "those spaces sought out by homeless and drug addicts" (Astrid Bracke, "Wastelands, Shrubs and Parks: Ecocriticism and the Challenge of the Urban," *Frame* 26, no. 2 [2013]: 13) as well as dumping grounds that, as Bracke proposes, must be part of an urban ecocriticism. These urban "heterotopias," to use Michel Foucault's term to define these countersites where real places are "simultaneously represented, contested, and inverted" ("Of Other Spaces," trans. Jay Miskowiec, *Diacritics* 16, no. 1 [1986]: 23), are not yet fully present in Lispector's novel, even though the expulsion of discardable elements from the conquered urban perimeter may point in this direction. In later moments of her career, Lispector did discuss forms of urban poverty, including Rio de Janeiro's favelas, as Marta Peixoto shows in "'Fatos são pedras duras': Urban Poverty in Clarice Lispector," in *Closer to the Wild Heart: Essays on Clarice Lispector*, ed. Cláudia Pazos Alonso and Claire Williams (Oxford: Legenda, 2002), 106–25.

31. Nixon, *Slow Violence*, 13.

32. In her discussion of the multiplicity of linguistic sources active in Lispector's work in connection with these recurring images of horses, Marília Librandi-Rocha proposes that "Lispector's *oeuvre* . . . is also *a variation of the centauric genius*, a definition par excellence of the type of (mixed) text she produced." *Writing by Ear: Clarice Lispector and the Aural Novel* (Toronto: University of Toronto Press, 2018), 176. For an analysis of the presence of animals and specifically the horse in Lispector's fiction, see Silviano Santiago, "Bestiário," in which he writes that the developmentalist context of the novel leads to "a certain objectivity that the novel's narrator exercised upon the theme of metamorphose of the human into animal." "Bestiário," *Instituto Moreira Salles: Cadernos de literatura brasileira: Clarice Lispector* 17–18 (2004): 219.

33. Clarice Lispector, "Seco estudo de cavalos," in *Onde estivestes de noite* (Rio de Janeiro: Editora Artenova, 1974), 51; "Dry Sketch of Horses," in *The Complete Stories*, trans. Katrina Dodson (New York: New Directions, 2015), 449. For a study of this text that pays special attention to revisions made between its publication in newspaper form and in a book, as well as its points of contact with Lispector's other works, see Simone Curi, *A escrita nômade em Clarice Lispector* (Chapecó: Argos, 2001), 91–126.

34. Lispector, *A cidade sitiada*, 58; *The Besieged City*, 55.

35. The horses' privileged role in these metamorphic descriptions has broader implications for the narrative, as Carlos Mendes de Sousa proposes: "If the act of othering leads to such a suggestive and emblematic identification, as we have read, one can speak of a notable multi-functionality or metamorphic ability. Lucrécia is the horses, but she is also the mason, the statue, and the city itself, that is, the builder and the built building itself; in short, the text makes itself in the absence of any constraining forces." *Clarice Lispector*, 185.

36. Val Plumwood, *Feminism and the Mastery of Nature* (London: Rutledge, 1993), 21.

37. Although ecofeminist authors discussed points of contact between the subjugation of women and animals in the 1980s and early 1990s, this topic came to be controversial and was usually avoided later in the 1990s as critics argued that asserting such parallels essentialized the categories of women and

animals. For an overview of this discussion, the backlash against it, and its present state, see Greta Gaard's "Ecofeminism Revisited," *Feminist Formations* 23, no. 2 (2011): 26–53.

38. Lispector, *A cidade sitiada*, 119; *The Besieged City*, 122.

39. "Estado da população / População de fato, na data dos recenseamentos gerais / Discriminação por Unidades da Federação / Distribuição da população presente / Segundo a situação do domicílio (quadros urbano, suburbano e rural) / 1°-IX-1940 e 1.°-VII-1950," *IBGE*, accessed July 4, 2017, http://seculoxx.ibge.gov.br. The categories of urban and suburban reflect the classifications of cities and villages, which, according to the Law 311 from March 2, 1938, are determined in the following fashion: cities are the heads of municipalities and give them their name; villages are districts within municipalities. Each municipality has one city (the urban area) and one or more villages (the suburban areas). See "Decreto-Lei N° 311, de 2 de março de 1938, Dispõe sobre a divisão territorial do país, e dá outras providências," *Câmara dos Deputados*, accessed July 5, 2017, www2.camara.leg.br.

40. It is curious to note that, in industrializing neighbor states such as São Paulo and Minas Gerais, suburbanization overtook urbanization: in both states, the suburban population nearby doubled, whereas the urban population increased by approximately 30 percent. Albeit weakly, this contrast seems to reinforce the location of S. Geraldo in the state of Rio.

41. Warren Dean, *With Broadax and Firebrand: The Destruction of the Brazilian Atlantic Forest* (Berkeley: University of California Press, 1995), 252. According to Dean, "It was estimated that, in 1948, wood and charcoal represented 79 percent of all energy consumed in Brazil. . . . In the Southeast, wood and charcoal burning was certainly not less than 50 percent of fuel for consumption, despite a significant amount of hydroelectric generation and the region's improved capacity to import fossil fuels" (254).

42. Henri Lefebvre, *The Production of Space*, trans. Donald Nicholson-Smith (Malden, Mass.: Blackwell, 2016), 86.

43. Olga Borelli, *Clarice Lispector, esboço para um possível retrato*, 2nd ed. (Rio de Janeiro: Editora Nova Fronteira, 1981), 130, 117, 110, 111.

44. In spite of her boredom, this was an important period in which, as Claire Varin shows, Lispector was living with some of the foreign languages she encountered both in her childhood in Brazil and in her years abroad. See *Línguas de fogo: Ensaio sobre Clarice Lispector* (São Paulo: Limiar, 2002), 51–101, for the theme of foreignness in her life and work.

45. Benjamin Moser, *Why This World: A Biography of Clarice Lispector* (New York: Oxford University Press, 2009), 180.

46. Moser compares Lucrécia's time in the big city with the period Lispector spent in Paris while living in Bern. In a more text-based analysis, such similarities between Lucrécia and Lispector are complicated by the sometimes satirical tone of the narrative. According to Earl Fitz, "The narrative voice of *A cidade sitiada* actually deprecates and at times satirizes Lucrécia herself, showing how the protagonist is not free of the very qualities, ideas, and habits that she disparages." *Sexuality and Being in the Poststructuralist Universe of Clarice Lispector: The Différance of Desire* (Austin: University of Texas Press, 2001), 76.

47. Olga de Sá has identified another type of siege in the novel, in the context of the uncertain and not rarely hostile reception that met the work of young women writers: "But there is a latent sub-text, in which the besieged city is the text, i.e., Clarice Lispector's very writing." *A escritura de Clarice Lispector*, 2nd ed. (Petrópolis, Brazil: Editora Vozes and EdPUC-SP, 1993), 71.

48. Bruno Carvalho, *Porous City: A Cultural History of Rio de Janeiro (from the 1810s Onward)* (Liverpool: Liverpool University Press, 2013), 12.

49. Giorgi, *Formas comunes*, 282. The rebellious component of this biopolitical order that Giorgi analyzes is, however, absent from S. Geraldo's inhabitants.

50. Fernando C. Gil, *O romance da urbanização* (Porto Alegre, Brazil: EDIPUCRS, 1999), 40.

51. Although, according to Gil, the genre tends to explore cities outside of the big metropolises, it is worth noting that S. Geraldo still keeps some forms of distance from what might be Rio de Janeiro.

52. Pedro Cezar Dutra Fonseca and Ivan Colangelo Salomão, "O sentido histórico do desenvolvimento e sua atualidade," *Revista de Economia Contemporânea*, special issue (2017): 5.

53. Ricardo Bielschowsky, *Pensamento econômico brasileiro: O ciclo ideológico do desenvolvimentismo* (Rio de Janeiro: IPEA/INPES, 1988), 293–295.

54. Milton Santos, *A urbanização brasileira* (São Paulo: Editora Hucitec, 1993), 29.

55. See Santos, *A urbanização brasileira*, chapter 3.

56. See Mauricio de Abreu, *Evolução urbana do Rio de Janeiro*, 4th ed. (Rio de Janeiro: Instituto Municipal de Urbanismo Pereira Passos, 2010), 96–106. According to Abreu, from 1930 on, "state support for manufacturing activity changed significantly the patterns of industrial localization, and as a consequence, suburban growth was also redirected, now privileging the areas served by these three railways (Leopoldina, Rio D'Ouro, and Linha Auxiliar)" (99).

57. Abreu, *Evolução urbana do Rio de Janeiro*, 103.

58. Carlos Bresser-Pereira, "National Developmentalism and Structuralism," in *The Oxford Handbook of Latin American Economics*, ed. José Antonio Ocampo and Jaime Ros (New York: Oxford University Press, 2011), 110.

59. See Fonseca and Salomão, "O sentido histórico," for a historical overview of developmentalist theses and policies.

60. Pedro Cezar Dutra Fonseca, "Gênese e precursores do desenvolvimentismo no Brasil," in *A Era Vargas: Desenvolvimentismo, economia e sociedade*, ed. Pedro Paulo Zahluth Bastos and Pedro Cezar Dutra Fonseca (São Paulo: Editora Unesp, 2011), 21–22.

61. Fonseca, "Gênese e precursores," 23.

62. Celso Furtado, *Formação econômica do Brasil*, 32nd ed. (São Paulo: Cia. Editora Nacional, 2005).

63. Celso Furtado, *A economia brasileira* (Rio de Janeiro: A Noite, 1954), 89–91.

64. Furtado, *A formação econômica*, chapters 30–33. In Furtado's words, "It is obvious, therefore, that, if the economy had only reacted passively to external stimuli, it would not only have faced a much deeper depression, but would not have recovered for the whole decade. The recovery, however, came quickly,

and was comparatively strong. Industrial production grew by about 50 percent between 1929 and 1937, and primary production for the domestic market grew by more than 40 percent in the same period" (210).

65. Curiously, this work was published by the same publisher as *A cidade sitiada*, A Noite (The Night). Although there is no space here for an overview of what Vera Cepêda classifies as a first phase in Furtado's work, to which the two books mentioned here belong, all his works from this moment, according to Cepêda, "have as their articulative center an interpretation about the past (the historical formation of underdevelopment) and an urgency about the possibility that the Brazilian economy might face disruption in the postwar period, a scenario that requires a political disposition to use heterodox tools of political economy, such as planning." Vera Alves Cepêda, "O lugar da teoria do subdesenvolvimento de Celso Furtado no pensamento político dos anos 1950," in *O moderno em questão: A década de 1950 no Brasil*, ed. André Botelho, Elide Rugai Bastos, and Glaucia Villas Bôas (Rio de Janeiro: Topbooks, 2008), 361.

66. For an overview of these discussions and of the concept of underdevelopment in Furtado's work, see Vera Cepêda, "O lugar da teoria."

67. Iser, *The Fictive and the Imaginary*, 305.

68. Hoyos, *Things with a History*, 200.

69. In fact, it would be interesting to contrast the stoic sense of eventual catastrophe in the passage above with popular theories of collapse stemming from exponential growth of population and its demands vis-à-vis the Earth's available resources, such as the best-selling *The Limits to Growth* (New York: Universe Books, 1972), by William Behrens et al., which challenge developmentalist theories such as those mentioned here.

70. Fitz, in this sense, has suggested reading *A hora da estrela*'s protagonist Macabéa and her boyfriend Olímpico "as later versions of Fabiano and Vitória, the two abused sertanejos who, fleeing the drought stricken Northeast in search of a better life in the big cities of Southern Brazil, drive the canonical novel *Barren Lives*, by Graciliano Ramos." "Lispector as a Northeastener Writer," *Review: Literature and Arts of the Americas* 49, nos. 1–2, (2006): 47. I propose a similar connection encompassing the larger context in which they are situated.

71. Albeit writing about Lispector's later works, Mattias Kärrholm touches on similar issues when he states that "both [Lispector and Louis Kahn] found a nontheoretical way of reassembling the material, a reshuffling within the given assemblages and networks through which they acted, experimenting in a process of seeing without (yet) understanding." "The Animistic Moment: Clarice Lispector, Luis Kahn, and the Reassembling of Materialities," *Lo Squaderno* 39 (2016): 74.

72. In Costa Lima's words, "The work of mimesis is unaware of a semantic layer that is, ultimately, ideally capable of fixing its meaning. Before the mirror, from the point of view of the senses, mimesis is mirage." *Mímesis e modernidade*, 257.

CHAPTER 5

1. Mario Vargas Llosa and Raymond L. Williams, "Diálogos: La invención de una realidad," in *Mario Vargas Llosa: Literatura y política*, by Raymond L.

Williams (Mexico City: Cátedra Alfonso Reyes [ITESM], Planeta, 2001), 94. Unless otherwise stated, translations are by Laura Colaneri.

2. José Olmos, "Vargas Llosa dice que indigenismo es un peligro democrático," *El Universo*, Nov. 11, 2003, https://www.eluniverso.com/2003/11/11/0001/8/8E389173D65C4B0BAE80101A0C5ACAD7.html?device=tablet.

3. For a detailed account of Texaco's presence in Ecuador and the trial, see Paul Barrett, *Law of the Jungle: The $19 Billion Legal Battle over Oil in the Rain Forest and the Lawyer Who'd Stop at Nothing to Win* (New York: Crown Publishers, 2014).

4. Olmos, "Vargas Llosa dice."

5. Mabel Moraña has explained this indeed prolific trajectory in the following terms: "In Vargas Llosa's case we have seen how *language* no longer works in just its literary function but also as a multimedia propagation of multiple, diversified, and all-encompassing enunciations that spread out and seek to control public space." *Arguedas / Vargas Llosa: Dilemmas and Assemblages*, trans. Andrew Ascherl (New York: Palgrave Macmillan, 2016), 121, Moraña's italics.

6. Donald L. Shaw, *Nueva narrativa hispanoamericana: Boom, posBoom, posmodernismo* (Madrid: Cátedra, 2008).

7. This essay was also published by *Marcha* in 1969, and under the title "En torno a la nueva novela latinoamericana" by *Río Piedras: Revista de la Facultad de Humanidades* in 1972.

8. Mario Vargas Llosa, "Novela primitiva y novela de creación en América Latina," *Revista de la Universidad de México* 23, no. 10 (1969): 30.

9. The author continued to hold this opinion throughout his life. In his memoirs *El pez en el agua* (1993; *A Fish in the Water*, 1994), for example, he reaffirms his dislike for early twentieth-century regionalist novels "porque en esos libros el paisaje tenía más importancia que las personas de carne y hueso . . . y porque sus autores parecían desconocer las más elementales técnicas de cómo armar una historia." *El pez en el agua: Memorias* (Barcelona: Seix Barral, 1993), 295. "Because in those books the background was more important than the flesh-and-blood characters . . . and because their authors apparently didn't know the first thing about how to put a story together." *A Fish in the Water* (New York: Farrar, Straus, and Giroux, 1994, Kindle Edition), loc. 4980. In a conversation at the University of Chicago on April 12, 2017, he confirmed to me that this remains his view on the subject.

10. In his influential early theorization of the sublime, Edmund Burke, in *A Philosophical Enquiry into the Sublime and Beautiful* (Abington: Routledge, 2008), emphasized the danger and incommensurability of nature while keeping the spectator safe from it. By identifying the ideological component of what would be from early on presented as a "universal" phenomenon, Kate Soper draws attention to the fact that in Burke's and Kant's theories of the sublime, "the explanation of our awe of nature draws on the idea of an inherent human mastery or transcendence of it." *What Is Nature?*, 230.

11. For studies of Vargas Llosa's theorizations of the novel in this early period and in connection with subsequent ones, see Blas Matamoro, "Escritores, escribidores y teoría de la novela," in *El autor y su obra: Mario Vargas Llosa* (Madrid: Universidad Complutense, 1990), 57–69; Belén Castañeda, "Mario

Vargas Llosa: El novelista como crítico," *Hispanic Review* 58, no. 3 (1990): 347–59; and Gesine Müller, "From 'The Novel' (1966) to 'The Art of the Novel' (2000): Readings of Vargas Llosa as Topos of Latin American Disenchantment," trans. Jessica Ernst Powell, *Literature and Arts of the Americas* 46, no. 1 (2013): 20–25.

12. Mario Vargas Llosa, "La literatura es fuego," in *Contra viento y marea, vol. 1 (1962–1972)* (Barcelona: Seix Barral, 1986), 179.

13. Mario Vargas Llosa, *García Márquez: Historia de un deicidio* (Barcelona: Barral Editores, 1971), 480. All of them point out the constitutive dilemma of his ideas on the role of literature, synthesized by Efraín Kristal in the following terms: "If literature is autonomous it need not contribute to socialist causes, but if it has to contribute to socialist causes it is not autonomous." *Temptation of the World: The Novels of Mario Vargas Llosa* (Nashville: Vanderbilt University Press, 1998), 24.

14. Although space constraints do not allow an extensive explanation, Ángel Rama and Vargas Llosa had an important debate on these issues in the Uruguayan periodical *Marcha* in 1972: the former criticized the romantic and eschatological resonances of the latter's ideas about the writer's demons and deicide. See Rama and Vargas Llosa, *García Márquez y la problemática de la novela* (Buenos Aires: Corregidor-Marcha, 1974).

15. According to Mark D. Anderson, "Gary developed many of the key concepts that resurface in Vargas Llosa's reflections on the total novel, including: those concepts regarding the autonomy of art from ideological instances . . . ; that the novel should constitute a total 'fictional universe' that does not claim to represent faithfully the real world . . . and yet rivals it in scope . . . ; and that the novelist 'plays God' within this fictional world." "Dissonant Worlds: Mario Vargas Llosa and the Aesthetics of the Total Novel," in *Critical Insights: Mario Vargas Llosa*, ed. Juan E. De Castro (Armenia, N.Y.: Grey House Publishing, 2014), 202.

16. Romain Gary's definition of the "roman total" is as follows: "The work slyly rules by its novelistic deceit assuming the guise of reality, it possesses the world and possesses itself wholly, unfettered by what inspired it: it is what I mean and will continue to mean by *total* novel." *Pour Sganarelle: Recherche d'un personnage et d'un roman* (Paris: Gallimard, 1965), 18. Translated by Guillaume Troïanowski. I thank Mark Anderson for a conversation on this issue.

17. Mark Anderson, "Dissonant Worlds," 205.

18. Mario Vargas Llosa, "La novela," in *Mario Vargas Llosa: La novela; José María Arguedas: La novela y el problema de la expresión literaria en el Perú* (Vte López: América Nueva, 1974), 40. In a handwritten note on this publication in the author's papers at Princeton University, he warns that this is a nonauthorized transcription of a recording of a talk he gave in Montevideo in 1966. As he never had the opportunity to revise it, it contains numerous repetitions and typos.

19. See Georg Lukács, *Theory of the Novel: A Historico-Philosophical Essay on the Forms of Great Epic Literature*, trans. Anna Bostock (Cambridge, Mass.: MIT Press, 1971).

20. Avelar, *The Untimely Present*, 31.

21. In her analysis of the novel's previous versions, Rogers concludes: "In the finished novel, Vargas Llosa's narrative technique evolves from one of overt exposition of specific historical and geographical entities to allusive references to vague peoples and places." Rogers, *Mourning El Dorado*, 141. Hence the difficulty in establishing clear-cut temporal and institutional reference points, in spite of overt mentions, for example, of the Instituto Lingüístico de Verano, which is even more prominent in *El hablador*.

22. For a study of how Vargas Llosa reconciles realist prose with a fragmented structure in the context of the 1960s, see Jorge Bracamonte, "'Rayuela' y 'La casa verde': Teorías del texto, teorías de lo real," *Revista de Crítica Literaria Latinoamericana* 27, no. 54 (2001): 91–109.

23. Mario Vargas Llosa, *La casa verde*, 2nd ed. (Madrid: Punto de Lectura, 2008), 64; *The Green House*, trans. Gregory Rabassa (New York: HarperCollins, 2005), 41.

24. Charlotte Rogers, "Mario Vargas Llosa and the *novela de la selva*," *Bulletin of Spanish Studies* 93, no. 6 (2016): 1043–60. As Raymond L. Williams proposes, "This jungle, however, is not the wild and uncontrolled vortex (or vorágine) of the criollista texts, in which human beings are devoured in an irrational chaos. Rather, it is a nature that Vargas Llosa constructs in the neutral mode of scientific discourse." "Natural and Built Environments: Toward an Ecocritical Reading of the Novels of Mario Vargas Llosa," in *Critical Insights: Mario Vargas Llosa*, 59.

25. *La casa verde*, 351; *The Green House*, 264.

26. In his comparative study of José María Arguedas and Mario Vargas Llosa, Ariel Dorfman notes that "nature, firmament for Arguedas, almost disappears in Vargas Llosa, even when half of *La casa verde* occurs in the jungle, the jungle is like a green house, like a green city, like a labyrinth full of streets and of cement, green, green." "José María Arguedas y Mario Vargas Llosa: Dos visiones de una sola América," in *Homenaje a Mario Vargas Llosa: Variaciones interpretativas en torno a su obra*, eds. Helmy F. Giacoman and José Miguel Oviedo (Long Island City: Las Américas, 1972), 142.

27. Gerald Martin, "Mario Vargas Llosa: Errant Knight of the Liberal Imagination," in *On Modern Latin American Fiction*, ed. John King (New York: Hill and Wang, 1989), 212. In the same vein, Julio Cortázar said in a letter about the novel that "the stupendous thing about the book . . . is that the description of nature, which is fundamental in the novel, is in that way fused with the action, so that one never realizes that you are showing to the reader what a clearing in the forest, a curve of the river, a street in the city is like." "Tres cartas a Vargas Llosa," *Letras Libres*, Oct. 31, 2007, https://www.letraslibres.com/mexico-espana/tres-cartas-vargas-llosa.

28. For an overview of *La casa verde*'s paratexts, see Luys Díez, "The Sources of *The Green House*: The Mythical Background of a Fabulous Novel," in *Mario Vargas Llosa: A Collection of Critical Essays*, ed. Charles Rossman and Alan Warren Friedman (Austin: University of Texas Press, 1978), 36–51.

29. Such a classification also reverberates with Vargas Llosa's famous observation that writing is like an inverted striptease, in which the author shows his demons rather than his charms. Mario Vargas Llosa, *Historia secreta de una novela* (Barcelona: Tusquets/Fábula, 2001), 11–12.

30. Vargas Llosa, *Historia secreta*, 66.

31. Vargas Llosa, *Historia secreta*, 29.

32. As María de las Mercedes Ortiz Rodríguez explains, "The writer uses here an idea that the anthropologist Johannes Fabian has developed as the concept of 'denial of coevalness,' a tendency through which anthropology has permitted itself to place the cultures it studies in a time distinct from the present of the researcher, thereby conceiving them as 'primitive.'" "La fisura irremediable: Indígenas, regiones y nación en tres novelas de Mario Vargas Llosa," *Antípoda* 15 (2012): 118.

33. Cornejo Polar, *Escribir en el aire*, 174. The author compares this position to José Carlos Mariátegui's view that "there is not one but rather many modernities" (174), including an Andean indigenous one. For an analysis of the "radical ethnocentrism" of *La utopía arcaica*, see Camilo Fernández-Cozman, "El etnocentrismo radical en *La utopía arcaica* y *La civilización del espetáculo*, de Mario Vargas Llosa," *Castilla: Estudios de Literatura* 7 (2016): 517–39.

34. Mario Vargas Llosa, *La utopía arcaica: José María Arguedas y las ficciones del indigenismo*, 2nd ed. (Mexico City: Fondo de Cultura Económica, 2011), 172.

35. José María Arguedas, *Formación de una cultura nacional indoamericana* (Mexico City: Siglo XXI, 1975), 188.

36. Vargas Llosa, *La utopía arcaica*, 340.

37. Sara Castro-Klarén also draws attention to the fact that Vargas Llosa's own meditation on Indigenism took shape in Anglophone universities where the very stakes and specificity of this tradition were much less familiar and, therefore, the polemical nature of his arguments would have been felt less intensely. "Disentangling the Knots: Vargas Llosa and José María Arguedas in *La utopía arcaica*," in *Critical Insights: Mario Vargas Llosa*, 71–88.

38. Castro-Klarén, "Disentangling the Knots," 77.

39. Plato, *Republic*, ed. and trans. Chris Emlyn-Jones (Oxford: Aris and Phillips, 2007). See Book X.

40. Jean Franco, "Alien to Modernity: The Rationalization of Discrimination," *A Contra Corriente* 3, no. 3 (2006): 14.

41. Hugo Blanco, "Carta abierta de Hugo Blanco a Mario Vargas Llosa," *Sin Permiso*, Nov. 28, 2010, http://www.sinpermiso.info/textos/carta-abierta-de-hugo-blanco-a-mario-vargas-llosa.

42. Mario Vargas Llosa, "Victoria Pírrica," *El País*, June 28, 2009, https://elpais.com/diario/2009/06/28/opinion/1246140013_850215.html.

43. In this sense, as Juan de Castro argues, Vargas Llosa's anger about indigenous communities' rejection of "civilization" is based on culture, not race. *Mario Vargas Llosa: Public Intellectual in Neoliberal Latin America* (Tucson: University of Arizona Press, 2011), 82. It is their choice of communal life, as opposed to individualism and neoliberalism, that prevents them from achieving "civilization" (84).

44. See William Rowe for an analysis of how Vargas Llosa established "his own person as the site of authority" at numerous points in his career. "Liberalism and Authority: The Case of Mario Vargas Llosa," in *On Edge: The Crisis of Contemporary Latin American Culture*, ed. George Yúdice, Jean Franco, and Juan Flores (Minneapolis: Minnesota University Press, 1992), 49.

45. In her assessment of Vargas Llosa's campaign in light of his political affiliations, Fabiola Escárzaga Nicté makes similar use of fiction's double meaning to attest that "Vargas Llosa was from the beginning of his career a very political writer, but as a politician turns out to be a creator of fictions." "La utopía liberal de Vargas Llosa," *Política y Cultura* 17 (2002): 227.

46. The title of this book alludes to "A Fish out of Water," an essay Vargas Llosa published in *Granta* in 1991 about his memories of the election, which served as a first step in the process of writing the book.

47. *Un pez en el agua*, 427; *A Fish in the Water*, loc. 7154. For an overview of Vargas Llosa's political and intellectual trajectory in the 1970s and 1980s leading up to his positions during the election, see Kristal, *Temptation of the World*, chapters 3 and 4. For a rather critical account of his increasing involvement in Peru's political life in the 1980s, see Mirko Lauer, *El sitio de la literatura: Escritores y política en el Perú del siglo XX* (Lima: Mosca Azul, 1989).

48. Mario Vargas Llosa, "Foro Economía y Agricultura," typed text of lecture given in Lima on January 30, 1990, Mario Vargas Llosa Papers, Princeton University, Box 41, Folder 2, 9–10.

49. Productivity was a common term in the agrarian policies that Vargas Llosa's team proposed to increase agricultural production not by cultivating more land but by introducing agrarian technologies following the model of the Green Revolution discussed in chapter 3. See Mario Vargas Llosa Papers, Princeton University, Box 42, Folder 7.

50. Vargas Llosa, according to Carlos Ivan Degregori, was the one who brought the term *modernity* to the center of the campaign, but through a "*naive*, ingenuous, and paradoxically premodern (almost magical) vision of modernity" in Europe and potentially in Peru, which nevertheless excluded popular and indigenous forms of modernity. Carlos Iván Degregori and Romeo Grompone, *Elecciones 1990: Demonios y redentores en el nuevo Perú, una tragedia en dos vueltas* (Lima: IEP Ediciones, 1991), 74, Degregori's italics.

51. *Resumen de los programas de la Comisión del Medio Ambiente y Desarrollo Sostenible*, coord. Alfredo E. Ferreyros, Mario Vargas Llosa Papers, Princeton University, Box 42, Folder 7, 1.

52. *Resumen*, 2.

53. Among these similarities is Vargas Llosa's decisive trip to the Amazon in 1958 on an expedition organized by the Instituto Lingüístico de Verano, which echoes Mario's. In calling the narrator Mario, I follow Doris Sommer, "About-Face: The Talker Turns," *boundary 2* 23, no. 1 (1996): 91–133.

54. Vargas Llosa challenges the characterization of this novel as an "autobiografía disimulada," ("disguised autobiography") in an interview with Ricardo Setti where he describes it as "una ficción en la que también hay unos elementos autobiográficos integrados con elementos de la imaginación" ("a fiction in which there are also some autobiographical elements integrated with elements from the imagination"). Mario Vargas Llosa and Ricardo A. Setti, *Sobre la vida y la política* (Buenos Aires: InterMundo, 1989), 72.

55. I thank Agnes Lugo-Ortiz for a conversation on the connotations of this term.

56. Vargas Llosa, *El hablador* (Lima: Alfaguara, 2008), 107; *The Storyteller*, trans. Helen Lane (New York: Farrar, Straus, and Giroux, 1989), 93.

57. As Emil Volek notes, "Just as Tasurinchi creates the world—'real' for the Machiguenga, but 'mythical' and 'magical' from the modern perspective—the novelist-god also creates, through the gift of the word, complex fictitious worlds." "*El hablador*: Del realismo mágico a la posmodernidad," in *Mario Vargas Llosa: Opera omnia*, ed. Ana María Hernández de López (Madrid: Pliegos, 1994), 111–12.

58. In this sense, Hedy Habra's *Mundos alternos y artísticos en Vargas Llosa* (Madrid: Iberoamericana/Vervuert, 2012) sees photography as the element connecting the separate worlds of each of the two narrators.

59. Misha Kokotovic describes this type of nostalgia as "the yearning felt by moderns for the vanished (and vanquished) cultures whose destruction was deemed a necessary and inevitable consequence of modernization." "Mario Vargas Llosa Writes Of(f) the Native: Modernity and Cultural Heterogeneity in Peru," *Revista Canadiense de Estudios Hispánicos* 25, no. 3 (2001): 463. For a less critical approach to the "nostalgic rational and written frame of the novel," see Véronique Bragard and Geneviève Fabry, "A Parrot without Feathers? Ventriloquy, Orality, and Nostalgia in Vargas Llosa's *The Storyteller* and Pauline Malville's *The Ventriloquist's Tale*," *Comparative Literature Studies* 53, no. 3 (2016): 473.

60. According to William Rowe, the relationship between humans and nonhumans in Arguedas's work is "essentially reciprocal: man is viewed in terms of nature, and nature is viewed in terms of man." *Mito e ideología en la obra de Arguedas* (Lima: Instituto Nacional de Cultura, 1979), 88.

61. Jorge Marcone, "Recuperar Chimbote, o la ecología menospreciada de 'Los zorros' de José María Arguedas," *Revista de Crítica Literaria Latinoamericana* 11, no. 79 (2014): 141–61.

62. Mario Vargas Llosa, "Questions of Conquest: What Columbus Wrought, and What He Did Not," *Harper's*, Dec. 1990, 45–53, https://harpers.org/archive/1990/12/questions-of-conquest/.

63. In spite of the author's polemical stances, as Jean O'Bryan-Knight proposes, "the work's appeal can be attributed, at least in part, to the timely nature of its setting and subject matter. *El hablador* features the Amazon jungle and its inhabitants, topics of special interest to readers who are becoming increasingly aware of ecological concerns as well as the plight of ethnic minorities whose needs conflict with perceived national interests." *The Story of the Storyteller: 'La tia Julia y el escribidor,' 'Historia de Mayta,' and 'El hablador' by Mario Vargas Llosa* (Amsterdam: Rodopi, 1995), 75.

64. According to Macarena Gómez-Barris, extractive zones are "what is submerged within local geographies that have been traversed by colonialism and extractive capitalism to show the ongoing force of the colonial encounter." *The Extractive Zone: Social Ecologies and Decolonial Perspectives* (Durham: Duke University Press, 2017), 2.

65. See Guha and Martínez Alier, *Varieties of Environmentalism*.

66. Óscar Espinosa de Rivero, "¿Salvajes opuestos al progreso? Aproximaciones históricas y antropológicas a las movilizaciones indígenas en la Amazonía Peruana," *Anthropologica* 27, no. 27 (2009): 123–68.

67. Espinosa de Rivero, "¿Salvajes opuestos al progreso?," 145.

68. Jorge Marcone, "Ecología de un sueño: chamanismo, ecumenismo y textualidad amazónicos en *Las tres mitades de Ino Moxo* de César Calvo." in *Migración y frontera: experiencias culturales en la literatura peruana del siglo XX*, ed. Javier García Liendo (Madrid: Iberoamericana/Vervuert, 2017), 330.

69. Among the urgent issues that are absent from both these novels and from *Lituma en los Andes* (1993; *Death in the Andes*, 1996), however, is the migration of Andean rural workers to the Amazon in the 1970s: "This agrarian conflict, which profoundly affected the cultural, political, social, and economic structures of Peru, appears in tangential manner, or does not figure at all, in the three works." Ortiz Rodríguez, "La fisura irremediable," 116.

70. For a study of the complicated dynamics between Vargas Llosa's fictional and nonfictional work with respect to indigenous issues, see Ignacio López-Calvo, "Going Native: Anti-indigenism in Vargas Llosa's *The Storyteller* and *Death in the Andes*," in *Mario Vargas Llosa and Latin American Politics*, ed. Juan E. De Castro and Nicholas Birns (New York: Palgrave Macmillan, 2010), 103–24.

71. José Castro Urioste shows how the indigenous voice, even in Zuratas's chapters, is erased by the use of "ventriloquized narrative." "Mario Vargas Llosa's *El hablador* as a Discourse of Conquest," *Studies in Twentieth Century Literature* 24, no. 2 (2000): 246. Kokotovic's "Mario Vargas Llosa Writes Of(f) the Native" reads the novel as a continuation of Vargas Llosa's clear defense of cultural assimilation in the essay "El nacimiento del Perú" (1986) and its variants. Sergio Franco metonymically connects the silence of photographs of the Machiguenga shown at an exhibition in Florence with the "silence of the native that dwells in the neocolonial unconscious of *El hablador*." "Tecnologías de la representación en *El hablador*, de Mario Vargas Llosa," *Revista Iberoamericana* 71, no. 211 (2005): 585. See also the passage by Castro-Klarén quoted in the next section.

72. Lúcia Sá, *Rain Forest Literatures*, 271.

73. Sommer, "About-Face," 101, Sommer's italics.

74. Richard Walsh, *The Rhetoric of Fictionality: Narrative Theory and the Idea of Fiction* (Columbus: Ohio State University Press, 2007), 89, 93, 100.

75. I agree with Yvon Grenier and Marteen Van Delden in their analysis of the relationship between literature and politics in Vargas Llosa, when they state that, although "Vargas Llosa's thought is organized largely binomially: fiction vs. reality, literature vs. politics," "within his literary work [nevertheless]—undoubtedly more so than in his political essays—these categories are fluid and opposites are reconciled and reemerge as coincidencia oppositorum." "The Private and the Public: Mario Vargas Llosa on Literature and Politics," in *Gunshots at the Fiesta: Literature and Politics in Latin America* (Nashville: Vanderbilt University Press, 2009), 214.

76. Walsh, *The Rhetoric of Fictionality*, 93.

77. James Phelan, *Living to Tell about It: A Rhetoric and Ethics of Character Narration* (Ithaca, N.Y.: Cornell University Press, 2005), 23.

78. Suzanne Keen, *Empathy and the Novel* (Oxford, New York: Oxford University Press, 2007), 137.

79. Raymond L. Williams proposes, in this sense, that this novel, as well as *¿Quién mató a Palomino Molero?* (1986; *Who Killed Palomino Molero?*, 1987) and *Lituma en los Andes*, "represent three approaches to the problem of truth." *Vargas Llosa: Otra historia de un deicidio* (Mexico City: Taurus, 2001), 253.

80. Mario Vargas Llosa, "El arte de mentir," *El País*, July 25, 1984, 9. Reprinted at *Dominical*, Aug. 12, 1984, 4–6. Mario Vargas Llosa Papers, Princeton University, Box 136, Folder 4; "El poder de la mentira," *Vuelta* 130 (September 1987): 54–56. http://www.letraslibres.com/vuelta/el-poder-la-mentira.

81. Mario Vargas Llosa, *La verdad de las mentiras: Ensayos sobre literatura*, 2nd ed. (Barcelona: Seix Barral, 1990).

82. Vargas Llosa, *La verdad de las mentiras*, 10.

83. Sara Castro-Klarén, "Monuments and Scribes: *El hablador* Addresses Ethnography," in *Structures of Power: Essays on Twentieth-Century Spanish-American Fiction*, ed. Terry J. Peavler and Peter Standish (Albany: State University of New York Press, 1996), 47.

84. As Kristal notes, this essay combines the influence of Georges Bataille with that of Karl Popper, which results in Vargas Llosa arguing "that the transgressions of literature can be useful to the health of an open society if the boundaries between the historical and the fictional are clearly demarcated." Kristal, *Temptation of the World*, 117. In this case, a possible use of literary discourse would be for the personal, intellectual, and spiritual self-fulfillment of its readers.

85. Jean-Paul Sartre, *What Is Literature?*, trans. Bernard Frechtman (London: Methuen, 1978).

86. Neil Larsen provides a sharp analysis of the *vasos comunicantes* in what he identifies as a form of narrative metalepsis that, albeit maintaining the modern form found in Gustave Flaubert, is applied to a context where "the material factors that would be required to successfully reproduce this—reified—social relation of public whole to private parts are lacking or withheld." "Mario Vargas Llosa: The Realist as Neo-Liberal," in *Determinations: Essays on Theory, Narrative and Nation in the Americas* (London: Verso, 2001), 164. Such disjunction leads to what Larsen terms a "dismodernity."

87. In 1983, Vargas Llosa accepted an invitation from the then-president of Peru, Fernando Belaúnde, to investigate the deaths of eight journalists and a guide in the Andean region of Uchuraccay. His report on the case mistakenly excused the armed forces' involvement and accused local communities of a crime resulting from their confusion of journalists with *guerrilleros* from the Sendero Luminoso. Mario Castro Arenas, Abraham Guzmán Figueroa, and Mario Vargas Llosa, "Informe sobre Uchuraccay," *Verdad y reconciliación*, accessed April 3, 2018. https://www.verdadyreconciliacionperu.com/admin/files/libros/376_digitalizacion.pdf. This is, according to Escárzaga Nicté, Vargas Llosa's "first approach to the Andean problematic" ("La utopía liberal," 228), and one that shows how confusion between fiction and reality in politics may have consequences unforeseen in novels (227).

88. Martha Nussbaum, *Poetic Justice: The Literary Imagination and Public Life* (Boston: Beacon Press, 1995).

89. Moraña, *Arguedas / Vargas Llosa*, 173. In Moraña's words, "Although the arguments that Vargas Llosa employs in defining the role and nature of the

task of literature have varied over time, the leitmotiv of this elaboration rests on the capacity of art to compensate for the mediocrity of life, to express opposition to the real world, and to elevate the perception of aspects of everyday experience that would otherwise be overlooked by the common man" (173).

90. Keith Booker argues thus that the failure of the modern novelist is the success of the postmodern one in this novel: "By undermining his narrator's efforts to achieve an alternative narrative form based on Utopian fantasies, Vargas Llosa prevents his own book from developing into an alternative fantasy of its own." *Vargas Llosa among the Postmodernists* (Gainesville: University of Florida Press, 1994), 138.

91. In this sense, Vargas Llosa's *hablador* clearly recalls Walter Benjamin's *storyteller* via their shared contrast with the novelist, i.e., the storyteller "tells [oral tales] from experience" (364), as opposed to the isolated novelist whose work appears only in the written book. Symptomatic of this similar function is the English translation of the two terms with the same word, *storyteller*, in spite of *hablador*'s connotation of "talker," as explained above. Walter Benjamin, "The Storyteller: Reflections on the Works of Nicolai Leskov," in *The Novel: An Anthology of Criticism and Theory 1900–2000*, ed. Dorothy J. Hale (Malden, Mass.: Blackwell, 2006), 363.

CONCLUSION

1. Brett Levinson, *The Ends of Literature: The Latin American "Boom" in the Neoliberal Marketplace* (Stanford, Calif.: Stanford University Press, 2001), 5.

2. Levinson, *The Ends of Literature*, 5.

3. Byrnes, *Fixing Landscape*, 168.

4. Hans Ulrich Gumbrecht, *After 1945: Latency as Origin of the Present* (Stanford, Calif.: Stanford University Press, 2013), 31. In this sense, it is significant that the post-1945 state of latency, of "downward movement" (*After 1945*, 31) that characterized the *Stimmung* of these postwar decades, as Hans Ulrich Gumbrecht has proposed, appears in a refracted fashion in the combination of enthusiasm and nostalgia embodied in the works and authors analyzed in this book, many of whom had firsthand experience of postwar Europe. Guimarães Rosa's *sertão*, as Gumbrecht shows, is a place where escape "is impossible because there is nowhere else to go" (55). The potential infinity that the novelist explored thus also renders visible the state of "no exit and no entry" (see *After 1945*, chapter 3) so recurrent in the literary production of the time. For a study on *Stimmungen* by Gumbrecht in a less time-specific context, see *Atmosphere, Mood, Stimmung: On a Hidden Potential of Literature* (Stanford, Calif.: Stanford University Press, 2012).

Bibliography

Aboites Manrique, Gilberto. *Una mirada diferente de la revolución verde: Ciencia, nación y compromiso social*. Mexico City: Plaza y Valdés, Universidad de Guadalajara, 2002.

Abreu, Mauricio de. *Evolução urbana do Rio de Janeiro*. Rio de Janeiro: Instituto Municipal de Urbanismo Pereira Passos, 2010.

Acosta, Leonardo. *Alejo en tierra firme: Intertextualidad y encuentros fortuitos*. Havana: Centro de Investigación y Desarrollo de la Cultura Cubana Juan Marinello, 2004.

Adorno, Theodor, and Max Horkheimer. *The Dialectic of Enlightenment*. Edited by Gunzelin Schmid Noerr. Translated by Edmund Jephcott. Stanford, Calif.: Stanford University Press, 2002.

Agamben, Giorgio. *Profanations*. Translated by Jeff Fort. New York: Zone Books, 2007.

"Agriculture Exposition in Cuernavaca (1954)." Rockefeller Foundation Photographs, Series 323, Box 91, Folder 1820. Rockefeller Archive Center.

Aínsa, Fernando. "Pasos perdidos, identidad encontrada: La edad del paisaje en Alejo Carpentier." In *Alejo Carpentier ante la crítica*, edited by Alexis Márquez Rodríguez, 199–224. Caracas: Monte Ávila, 2005.

———. *Del topos al logos: Propuestas de geopoética*. Madrid: Iberoamericana/Vervuert, 2006.

Albert, Bruce, and Davi Kopenawa. *A queda do céu: Palavras de um xamã yanomami*. São Paulo: Companhia das Letras, 2015.

Albuquerque, Durval Muniz de, Jr. *The Invention of the Brazilian Northeast*. Translated by Jerry Dennis Metz. Durham: Duke University Press, 2014.

Almeida, João Batista de, and Cláudia Luz de Oliveira. *Cerrado, gerais, sertão: Comunidades tradicionais nos sertões brasileiros*. São Paulo: Intermeios, 2012.

Alonso, Carlos J. *The Spanish American Regional Novel: Modernity and Autochtony*. Cambridge: Cambridge University Press, 1990.

Altieri, Miguel, Fernando R. Funes-Monzote, and Paulo Petersen. "Agroecologically Efficient Agricultural Systems for Smallholder Farmers: Contributions to Food Sovereignity." *Agronomy for Sustainable Development* 32, no. 1 (2012): 1–13.

Andermann, Jens. *The Optic of the State: Visuality and Power in Argentina and Brazil*. Pittsburgh: University of Pittsburgh Press, 2007.

———. *Tierras en trance: Arte y naturaleza después del paisaje*. Santiago de Chile: Metales Pesados, 2018. Kindle Edition.

Anderson, Benedict. *Imagined Communities: Reflections of the Origin and Spread of Nationalism*. London: Verso, 2006.

Anderson, Mark D. "Was the Mexican Revolution a Revolt of Nature? Agustín Yáñez's Ecological Perspective." *Revista de Estudios Hispánicos* 40 (2006): 447–67.

———. "Dissonant Worlds: Mario Vargas Llosa and the Aesthetics of the Total Novel." In *Critical Insights: Mario Vargas Llosa*, edited by Juan E. De Castro, 201–18. Armenia, N.Y.: Grey House Publishing, 2014.

Anderson, Perry, "Modernity and Revolution," *New Left Review* 144 (1984): 96–113.

Angosto Ferrández, Luis Fernando. "Mundo perdido, paraíso encontrado: Lugar, identidad y producción en la Gran Sabana, Venezuela." *Revista Colombiana de Antropología* 49, no. 1 (2013): 11–43.

Arguedas, José María. *Formación de una cultura nacional indoamericana*. Mexico City: Siglo XXI, 1975.

———. *Todas las sangres*. Lima: Editorial Horizonte, 1985.

———. "Reflexiones peruanas sobre un narrador mexicano." In *Juan Rulfo: Otras miradas*, edited by Víctor Jiménez, Julio Moguel, and Jorge Zepeda, 77–83. Mexico City: Fundación Juan Rulfo, Juan Pablos Editor, 2011.

Aridjis, Homero. "Declaración de 100 intelectuales y artistas contra la contaminación en la Ciudad de México." In *Noticias de la tierra*, edited by Homero Aridjis and Betty Ferber, 27–28. Barcelona: Random House Mondadori, 2012.

———. "A Declaration by 100 Intellectuals and Artists Protesting Air Pollution in Mexico City." In *News from the Earth*, edited by Homero Aridjis and Betty Feber, translated by Betty Ferber, 9–10. Simsbury, Conn.: Mandel Vilar, 2017.

———. "Los pájaros." In *Noticias de la tierra*, edited by Homero Aridjis and Betty Ferber, 19–25., Barcelona: Random House Mondadori, 2012.

Arrigucci, Davi. "O mundo misturado: Romance e experiência em Guimarães Rosa." *Novos Estudos Cebrap* 40 (1994): 7–29.

Aub, Max. *Ensayos mexicanos*. Mexico City: UNAM, 1974.

Auerbach, Erich. "Figura." In *Scenes from the Drama of European Literature*, 11–76. Minneapolis: University of Minnesota Press, 1984.

———. *Mimesis: The Representation of Reality in Western Literature*. Translated by Willard Trask. Princeton, N.J.: Princeton University Press, 2003.

Avelar, Idelber. *The Untimely Present: Postdictatorial Fiction and the Task of Mourning*. Durham: Duke University Press, 1999.

Bakhtin, Mikhail. "Forms of Time and of the Chronotope in the Novel." In *The Dialogic Imagination: Four Essays*, edited by Michael Holquist, translated by Caryl Emerson and Michael Holquist, 84–258. Austin: University of Texas Press, 2008.

Barbas-Rhoden, Laura. *Ecological Imaginations in Latin American Fiction.* Gainesville: University Press of Florida, 2011.

Barrett, Paul. *Law of the Jungle: The $19 Billion Legal Battle over Oil in the Rain Forest and the Lawyer Who'd Stop at Nothing to Win.* New York: Crown Publishers, 2014.

Barthes, Roland. "The Reality Effect." In *The Rustle of Language*, translated by Richard Howard, 141–48. Berkeley: University of California Press, 1989.

———. *S/Z: An Essay.* Translated by Richard Miller. Oxford: Blackwell, 2002.

Barzetti, V., ed., *Parks and Progress: Protected Areas and Economic Development in Latin America and the Caribbean.* Washington, D.C.: Interamerican Development Bank and IUCN, 1993.

Baudrillard, Jean. *Simulacra and Simulation.* Translated by Sheila Faria Glaser. Ann Arbor: University of Michigan Press, 1994.

Beckman, Ericka. "Unfinished Transitions: The Dialectics of Rural Modernization in Latin American Fiction." *Modernism/Modernity* 23, no. 4 (2016): 813–32.

Behrens, William W., III, Donella H. Meadows, Dennis L. Meadows, and Jørgen Randers. *The Limits to Growth.* New York: Universe Books, 1972.

Benjamin, Walter. "The Storyteller: Reflections on the Works of Nicolai Leskov." In *The Novel: An Anthology of Criticism and Theory 1900–2000*, edited by Dorothy J. Hale, 362–78. Malden, Mass.: Blackwell, 2006.

———. *The Writer of Modern Life: Essays on Charles Baudelaire.* Translated by Howard Eiland. Cambridge, Mass.: Harvard University Press, 2006.

Bennett, Jane. *Vibrant Matter: A Political Ecology of Things.* Durham: Duke University Press, 2010.

Benítez Rojo, Antonio. *La isla que se repite: El Caribe y la perspectiva posmoderna.* Barcelona: Casiopea, 1998.

Benítez Rojo, Antonio, ed. *Recopilación de textos sobre Juan Rulfo.* Havana: Centro de Investigaciones Literarias Casa de las Américas, 1969.

Berman, Marshall. *All That Is Solid Melts into Air: The Experience of Modernity.* London: Verso, 1982.

Betancor, Orlando. *The Matter of Empire: Metaphysics and Mining in Colonial Peru.* Pittsburgh: University of Pittsburgh Press, 2017.

Betancourt, Rómulo. "Empezamos a producir acero." In *Tres años de gobierno democrático*, 148–51. Caracas: Impr. Nacional, 1962.

———. "Cultura a todo el ámbito de la patria: Inauguración de la Universidad de Oriente, Cumaná, 29 de mayo de 1960." In *Antología política, vol. 7 (1959–1964)*, edited by Aníbal Romero, María Teresa Romero, and Elizabeth Tinoco, 204–7. Caracas: Fundación Rómulo Betancourt, 1991.

Beverley, John. *Against Literature.* Minneapolis: University of Minnesota Press, 1993.

Bezerra, Marily da Cunha, and Dieter Heidemann. "Viajar pelo sertão roseano é antes de tudo uma descoberta!" *Dossiê Guimarães Rosa: Estudos Avançados* 20, no. 58 (2006): 7–15.

Bielschowsky, Ricardo. *Pensamento econômico brasileiro: O ciclo ideológico do desenvolvimentismo.* Rio de Janeiro: IPEA/INPES, 1988.

Birkenmaier, Anke. *Alejo Carpentier y la cultura del surrealismo en América Latina*. Madrid: Iberoamericana/Vervuert, 2006.

Blanco Aguinaga, Carlos. "Realidad y estilo de Juan Rulfo." In *La ficción de la memoria: Juan Rulfo ante la crítica*, edited by Federico Campbell, 19–43. Mexico City: Era, UNAM, 2010.

Blanco, Hugo. "Carta abierta de Hugo Blanco a Mario Vargas Llosa." *Sin Permiso*, Nov. 28, 2010. http://www.sinpermiso.info/textos/carta-abierta-de-hugo-blanco-a-mario-vargas-llosa.

Bloch, Pedro. "Pedro Bloch entrevista Guimarães Rosa." In *Pedro Bloch entrevista: Vida, pensamento e obra de grandes vultos da cultura brasileira*, 99–103. Rio de Janeiro: Editora Bloch, 1989.

Bolle, Willi. "Grande sertão: Cidades." *Revista USP* 24 (1994–95): 80–93.

———. *grandesertão.br*. São Paulo: Ed. 34, Duas Cidades, 2006.

Bonneil, Christophe, and Jean-Baptiste Fressoz. *The Shock of the Anthropocene: The Earth, History and Us*. Translated by David Fernbach. London: Verso, 2016.

Booker, Keith. *Vargas Llosa among the Postmodernists*. Gainesville: University of Florida Press, 1994.

Borelli, Olga. *Clarice Lispector, esboço para um possível retrato*. 2nd ed. Rio de Janeiro: Editora Nova Fronteira, 1981.

Bosteels, Bruno. "Reading Rulfo between Benjamin and Derrida: End of Story." In *Mexican Literature in Theory*, edited by Ignacio M. Sánchez Prado, 111–37. London: Bloomsbury, 2018.

Boyer, Christopher. *Political Landscapes: Forests, Conservation, and Community in Mexico*. Durham: Duke University Press, 2015.

Boym, Svetlana. *The Future of Nostalgia*. New York: Basic Books, 2001.

Bracamonte, Jorge. "'Rayuela' y 'La casa verde': Teorías del texto, teorías de lo real." *Revista de Crítica Literaria Latinoamericana* 27, no. 54 (2001): 91–109.

Bracke, Astrid. "Wastelands, Shrubs and Parks: Ecocriticism and the Challenge of the Urban." *Frame* 26, no. 2 (November 2013): 7–22.

Bradu, Fabienne. *Ecos de Páramo*. Mexico City: CONACULTA, 2003.

Bragard, Véronique, and Geneviève Fabry. "A Parrot without Feathers? Ventriloquy, Orality, and Nostalgia in Vargas Llosa's *The Storyteller* and Pauline Malville's *The Ventriloquist's Tale*." *Comparative Literature Studies* 53, no. 3 (2016): 454–77.

Bresser-Pereira, Carlos. "National Developmentalism and Structuralism." In *The Oxford Handbook of Latin American Economics*, edited by José Antonio Ocampo and Jaime Ros, 110–29. New York: Oxford University Press, 2011.

Brown, Bill. *Other Things*. Chicago: University of Chicago Press, 2015.

Brushwood, John S. *Mexico in Its Novel: A Nation's Search for Identity*. Austin: University of Texas Press, 1975.

Buell, Lawrence. *The Environmental Imagination: Thoreau, Nature Writing, and the Formation of American Culture*. Cambridge, Mass.: Harvard University Press, 1995.

———. *The Future of Environmental Criticism: Environmental Crisis and Literary Imagination*. Malden, Mass.: Blackwell, 2005.

———. "Uses and Abuses of Environmental Memory." In *Contesting Environmental Imaginaries: Nature and Counternature in a Tome of Global Change*, edited by Steven Hartman, 95–116. Leiden: Brill, 2017.

Bueno, Luís. *Uma história do romance de 30*. São Paulo: EdUSP, 2006.

Burke, Edmund. *A Philosophical Enquiry into the Sublime and Beautiful*. Abington: Routledge, 2008.

Byerly, Alison. "The Uses of Landscape: The Picturesque Aesthetic and the National Park System." In *The Ecocriticism Reader: Landmarks in Literary Ecology*, edited by Harold Fromm and Cheryll Glotfelty, 52–68. Athens: University of Georgia Press, 1996.

Byrnes, Corey. *Fixing Landscape: A Techno-Poetic History of China's Three Gorges*. New York: Columbia University Press, 2018.

Calvo, César. *Las tres mitades de Ino Moxo*. Lima: PEISA, 2018.

Campbell, Federico, ed. *La ficción de la memoria: Juan Rulfo ante la crítica*. Mexico City: Era, UNAM, 2010.

Cancio, Wilfredo. *Crónicas de la impaciencia: El periodismo de Carpentier*. Madrid: Colibrí, 2010.

Candido, Antonio. *Formação da literatura brasileira: Momentos decisivos*. São Paulo: Martins, 1964.

———. "Literatura e subdesenvolvimento." In *A educação pela noite e outros ensaios*, 140–62. São Paulo: Ática, 1989.

———. "O homem dos avessos." In *Tese e antítese*, 121–39. São Paulo: T. A. Queiroz, 2002.

Carpentier, Alejo. "Viaje a la semilla." In *Cuentos completos*, 5th ed., 65–93. Barcelona: Editorial Bruguera, 1983.

———. *Entrevistas*, edited by Virgilio López Lemus. Havana: Letras Cubanas, 1985.

———. "Un camino de medio siglo." In *Obras completas de Alejo Carpentier, v. 13*. Mexico City: Siglo XXI, 1990.

———. *Visión de América*. In *Obras completas de Alejo Carpentier*, vol. 13, 274–94. Mexico City: Siglo XXI, 1990.

———. "Prologue to *The Kingdom of this World*." *Review: Latin American Literature and Arts* 47 (1993): 28–31.

———. *The Lost Steps*. Translated by Harriet de Onís. Minneapolis: University of Minnesota Press, 2001.

———. *El reino de este mundo*. Madrid: Alianza Editorial, 2003.

———. *Los pasos recobrados: Ensayos de teoría y crítica literaria*. Caracas: Biblioteca Ayacucho, 2003.

———. *Los pasos perdidos*. Buenos Aires: Editorial Losada, 2004.

———. *Letra y solfa*, vol. 9, *Variaciones*. Edited by Raumindo Respall Fina. Havana: Letras Cubanas, 2004.

———. *Visión de Venezuela*. Caracas: Monte Ávila; Havana: Fundación Alejo Carpentier, 2014.

———. "Notes on the Trip to the Great Savannah." Edited and translated by Charlotte Rogers. *PMLA* 134, no. 5 (2019): 1–8.

Carvalho, Bruno. *Porous City: A Cultural History of Rio de Janeiro (from the 1810s Onward)*. Liverpool: Liverpool University Press, 2013.

Casa América. "Los olvidados del *Boom*." Casamerica, Apr. 23, 2012. http://www.casamerica.es/literatura/los-olvidados-del-Boom.

Casanova, Pascale. *The World Republic of Letters*. Translated by M. B. DeBevoise. Cambridge, Mass.: Harvard University Press, 2004.

Carson, Rachel. *Silent Spring*. Boston: Houghton Mifflin, 1962.

Castañeda, Belén. "Mario Vargas Llosa: El novelista como crítico." *Hispanic Review* 58, no. 3 (1990): 347–59.

Castro, Juan de. *Mario Vargas Llosa: Public Intellectual in Neoliberal Latin America*. Tucson: University of Arizona Press, 2011.

Castro Arenas, Mario, Abraham Guzmán Figueroa, and Mario Vargas Llosa. "Informe sobre Uchuraccay." *Verdad y reconciliación*. Accessed Apr. 3, 2018. https://www.verdadyreconciliacionperu.com/admin/files/libros/376_digitalizacion.pdf.

Castro Leal, Antonio, ed. *La novela de la Revolución mexicana*. Mexico City: Aguilar, 1991.

Castro Rocha, João Cezar de. *Crítica literária: Em busca do tempo perdido?* Chapecó: Argos, 2011.

Castro Urioste, José. "Mario Vargas Llosa's *El hablador* as a Discourse of Conquest." *Studies in 20th Century Literature* 24, no. 2 (2000): 241–55.

Castro-Klarén, Sara. "Monuments and Scribes: '*El hablador*' Addresses Ethnography." In *Structures of Power: Essays on Twentieth-Century Spanish-American Fiction*, edited by Terry J. Peavler and Peter Standish, 39–57. Albany: State University of New York Press, 1996.

———. "Disentangling the Knots: Vargas Llosa and José María Arguedas in '*La utopía arcaica*.'" In *Critical Insights: Mario Vargas Llosa*, edited by Juan E. De Castro, 71–88. Armenia, N.Y.: Grey House Publishing, 2014.

Cavalcanti, Roberto B., and Carlos A. Joly. "Biodiversity and Conservation Priorities in the Cerrado." In *The Cerrados of Brazil: Ecology and Natural History of a Neotropical Savanna*, edited by Paulo S. Oliveira and Robert J. Marquis, 351–67. New York: Columbia University Press, 2002.

Cavalcanti Proença, Manoel. "Trilhas no Grande Sertão." In *Augusto dos Anjos e outros ensaios*, 151–241. Rio de Janeiro: José Olympio, 1959.

Cepêda, Vera Alves. "O lugar da teoria do subdesenvolvimento de Celso Furtado no pensamento político dos anos 1950." In *O moderno em questão: A década de 1950 no Brasil*, edited by André Botelho, Elide Rugai Bastos, and Glaucia Villas Bôas, 357–87. Rio de Janeiro: Topbooks, 2008.

Chazdon, Robin L., Pedro H. S. Brancalion, Lars Laestadius, Aoife Bennett-Curry, Kathleen Buckingham, Chetan Kumar, Julian Moll-Rocek lma, Célia Guimarães Vieira, and Sarah Jane Wilson. "When Is a Forest a Forest? Forest Concepts and Definitions in the Era of Forest and Landscape Restoration." *Ambio* 45, no. 5 (2016): 538–50.

Cixous, Hélène. *Reading with Clarice Lispector*. Translated by Verena Andermatt Conley. Minneapolis: University of Minnesota Press, 1990.

Clawson, David, and Don Hoy. "Nealticán, Mexico: A Peasant Community That Rejected the 'Green Revolution.'" *American Journal of Economics and Sociaology* 38, no. 4 (1979): 371–87.

Coelho, Marco Antônio. "A magia dos sertões desperta o Brasil." *Dossiê Guimarães Rosa: Estudos Avançados* 20, no. 58 (2006): 19–28.

Cohn, Deborah. *The Latin American Literary Boom and U.S. Nationalism during the Cold War*. Nashville: Vanderbilt University Press, 2012.

Colchester, Marcus. "Salvaging Nature: Indigenous Peoples and Protected Areas." In *Social Change and Conservation*, edited by Krishna B. Ghimire and Michel P. Pimbert, 97–130. New York: Earthscan, 2013.

Cornejo Polar, Antonio. "Mestizaje, transculturación, heterogeneidad." *Revista de Crítica Literaria Latinoamericana* 20, no. 40 (1994): 368–71.

———. *Escribir en el aire: Ensayo sobre la heterogeneidad socio-cultural en las literaturas andinas*. Lima: Centro de Estudios Literarios "Antonio Cornejo Polar" and Latinoamericana Editora, 2003.

Coronil, Fernando. *The Magical State: Nature, Money, and Modernity in Venezuela*. Chicago: University of Chicago Press, 1997.

Correia Filho, João. "Guia de Guimarães Rosa, vaqueiro narra viagem que inspirou *Grande Sertão: Veredas*." *Revista Cult*, Nov. 17, 2017. https://revistacult.uol.com.br/home/vaqueiro-guia-guimaraes-rosa-sertao/.

Corsi, Francisco. "O projeto de desenvolvimento de Vargas, a Missão Oswaldo Aranha e os rumos da economia brasileira." In *A Era Vargas: Desenvolvimentismo, economia e sociedade*, edited by Pedro Paulo Zahluth Bastos and Pedro Cezar Dutra Fonseca, 219–52. São Paulo: Editora Unesp, 2011.

Cortázar, Julio. "Tres cartas a Vargas Llosa." *Letras libres*, Oct. 31, 2007. https://www.letraslibres.com/mexico-espana/tres-cartas-vargas-llosa.

Costa Lima, Luiz. *Vida e mímesis*. Rio de Janeiro: Editora 34, 1995.

———. *Mímesis e modernidade: Formas das sombras*. 2nd ed. São Paulo: Paz e Terra, 2003.

———. *O redemunho do horror: Nas margens do Ocidente*. São Paulo: Perspectiva, 2011.

Cotter, Joseph. *Troubled Harvest: Agronomy and Revolution in Mexico, 1880–2002*. Westport, Conn.: Praeger, 2003.

Cronon, William. "The Trouble with Wilderness; or, Getting Back to the Wrong Nature." In *Uncommon Ground: Rethinking the Human Place in Nature*, edited by William Cronon, 69–90. New York: Norton, 1995.

Cunha, Euclides da. *Os sertões*. São Paulo: Ateliê Editorial, Arquivo do Estado, and Imprensa Oficial São Paulo, 2002.

Curi, Simone. *A escrita nômade em Clarice Lispector*. Chapecó: Argos, 2001.

de la Campa, Román. "Of Border Artists and Transculturation: Toward a Politics of Transmodern Performances." In *Latin Americanism*, 57–84. Minneapolis: University of Minnesota Press, 1999.

Dean, Warren. *With Broadax and Firebrand: The Destruction of the Brazilian Atlantic Forest*. Berkeley: University of California Press, 1995.

"Decreto-Lei N° 311, de 2 de março de 1938, Dispõe sobre a divisão territorial do país, e dá outras providências." *Câmara dos Deputados*. Accessed Jul. 5, 2017. www2.camara.leg.br.

Degregori, Carlos Iván, and Romeo Grompone. *Elecciones 1990: Demonios y redentores en el nuevo Perú, una tragedia en dos vueltas*. Lima: IEP Ediciones, 1991.

DeLoughrey, Elizabeth. "The Myth of Isolates: Ecosystem Ecologies in the Nuclear Pacific." *Cultural Geographies* 20, no. 2 (2013): 167–84.

Derrida, Jacques. "The Double Session." In *Dissemination*, translated by Barbara Johnson, 173–286. London: Athlone Press, 1981.

DeVries, Scott. *A History of Ecology and Environmentalism in Spanish American Literature*. Lewisburg, Penn.: Bucknell University Press, 2013.

Díaz Martín, Diego, and Isabel Novo Torres. *Informe final de la evaluación del Parque Nacional Canaima, Venezuela, como Sitio de Patrimonio Natural de la Humanidad*. Caracas: INPARQUES, 2007.

Díez, Luys A. "The Sources of *The Green House*: The Mythical Background of a Fabulous Novel." In *Mario Vargas Llosa: A Collection of Critical Essays*, edited by Charles Rossman and Alan Warren Friedman, 36–51. Austin: University of Texas Press, 1978.

Donoso, José. *The Boom in Spanish American Literature: A Personal History*. Translated by Gregory Kolovakos. New York: Columbia University Press, 1977.

Dorfman, Ariel. "José María Arguedas y Mario Vargas Llosa: Dos visiones de una sola América." In *Homenaje a Mario Vargas Llosa: Variaciones interpretativas en torno a su obra*, edited by Helmy F. Giacoman and José Miguel Oviedo, 135–60. Long Island City: Las Américas, 1972.

Doyle, Arthur Conan. *The Lost World*. New York: Hodder and Stoughton, George H. Doran, 1912.

Drummond, José Augusto. "From Randomness to Planning: The 1979 Plan for Brazilian National Parks." In *National Parks beyond the Nation: Global Perspectives on America's Best Idea*, edited by Adrian Howkins, Jared Orsi, and Mark Fiege, 210–34. Norman: University of Oklahoma Press, 2016.

Dutra e Silva, Sandro, Dominichi Miranda de Sá, and Magali Romero Sá. *Vastos sertões: História e natureza na ciência e na literatura*. Rio de Janeiro: Editora Mauad X, 2015.

Ebel, Roland, José Gonzalo Pozas Cárdena, Florencio Soria Miranda, and Jesús Cruz González. "Manejo orgánico de la milpa: Rendimiento de maíz, frijol y calabaza en monocultivo y policultivo." *Terra Latinoamericana* 35 (2017): 149–60.

Echeverría, Esteban. *El matadero; La cautiva*. Madrid: Cátedra, 2006.

Eco, Umberto. "Travels in Hyperreality." In *Travels in Hyperreality: Essays*, translated by William Weaver, 3–58. San Diego: Harcourt Brace, 1986.

Escárzaga Nicté, Fabiola. "La utopía liberal de Vargas Llosa." *Política y Cultura* 17 (2002): 217–40.

Escobar, Arturo. *Encountering Development. The Making and Unmaking of the Third World*. Princeton, N.J.: Princeton University Press, 1996.

Espindola, Haruf Salmen. *Sertão do Rio Doce*. Rio Doce, Brazil: EdUnivale, 2005.

Espinosa de Rivero, Óscar. "Salvajes opuestos al progreso? Aproximaciones históricas y antropológicas a las movilizaciones indígenas en la Amazonía Peruana." *Anthropologica* 27, no. 27 (2009): 123–68.

Espírito Santo, Cesar Victor do, dir. *Plano de manejo do Parque Nacional Grande Sertão Veredas*. Brasília: IBAMA/Funatura, 2003. www.ibmbio.gov.br.

Evans, Sterling. *The Green Republic: A Conservation History of Costa Rica*. Austin: University of Texas Press, 1999.

Ezquerro, Milagros. *Lecturas rulfianas*. Guadalajara: Universidad de Guadalajara, 2006.

Fabian, Johannes. *Time and the Other: How Anthropology Makes Its Object*. New York: Columbia University Press, 2014.

Fares, Gustavo. *Ensayos sobre la obra de Juan Rulfo*. New York: Peter Lang, 1998.

Fergusson, Alex. *Venezuela, la cuestión ambiental y el desarrollo: Una señal de alerta*. Caracas: Ministerio del Poder Popular para Ciencia y Tecnología, 2008.

Fernández-Cozman, Camilo Rubén. "El etnocentrismo radical en *La utopía arcaica* y *La civilización del espetáculo* de Mario Vargas Llosa." *Castilla: Estudios de literatura* 7 (2016): 517–39.

Ferrer Chivite, Manuel. *El laberinto mexicano en/de Juan Rulfo*. Mexico City: Editorial Novaro, 1972.

Finazzi-Agrò, Ettore. *Um lugar do tamanho do mundo: Tempos e espaços da ficção em João Guimarães Rosa*. Belo Horizonte, Brazil: EdUFMG, 2001.

Fitz, Earl. *Clarice Lispector*. Boston: Twayne, 1985.

———. *Sexuality and Being in the Poststructuralist Universe of Clarice Lispector: The Différance of Desire*. Austin: University of Texas Press, 2001.

———. "Lispector as a Northeastener Writer." *Review: Literature and Arts of the Americas* 49, nos. 1–2 (2006): 43–48.

Fitzgerald, Deborah. "Exporting American Agriculture: The Rockefeller Foundation in Mexico, 1943–53." *Social Studies of Science* 16, no. 3 (1986): 457–83.

Fonseca, Pedro Cezar Dutra. "Gênese e precursores do desenvolvimentismo no Brasil." In *A Era Vargas: Desenvolvimentismo, economia e sociedade*, edited by Pedro Paulo Zahluth Bastos and Pedro Cezar Dutra Fonseca, 21–50. São Paulo: Editora Unesp, 2011.

Fonseca, Pedro Cezar Dutra, and Ivan Colangelo Salomão. "O sentido histórico do desenvolvimento e sua atualidade." *Revista de Economia Contemporânea* 21, no. 2 (2017): 1–20.

Forestry Department of the Food and Agriculture Organization of the United Nations. "Forest Resources Assessment: Terms and Definitions." Rome: Food and Agriculture Organization of the United Nations, 2012. www.fao.org/3/a-ap862e.pdf.

Fornoff, Carolyn. "The Nature of Revolution in Rafael F. Muñoz's *Se llevaron el cañon para Bachimba*." In *Mexican Literature in Theory*, edited by Ignacio M. Sánchez Prado, 93–110. London: Bloomsbury, 2018.

Foucault, Michel. "Of Other Spaces." Translated by Jay Miskowiec. *Diacritics* 16, no. 1 (1986): 22–27.

Franco, Jean. *The Decline and Fall of the Lettered City*. Cambridge, Mass.: Harvard University Press, 2002.

———. "Alien to Modernity: The Rationalization of Discrimination." *A contra corriente* 3, no. 3 (2006): 1–16.

Franco, Sergio. "Tecnologías de la representación en *El hablador*, de Mario Vargas Llosa." *Revista Iberoamericana* 71, no. 211 (2005): 575–89.

Freitas, Frederico. "Ordering the Borderland: Settlement and Removal in the Iguaçu National Park, Brazil, 1940s–1970s." In *The Nature State: Rethinking the History of Conservation*, edited by Wilko G. von Hardenberg, Matthew Kelly, Claudia Leal, and Emily Wakild, 158–75. London: Routledge, 2017.

French, Jennifer. *Nature, Neo-colonialism, and the Spanish American Regional Writers*. Hanover, N.H.: Dartmouth College Press, 2005.

Frenk, Mariana. "*Pedro Páramo*." In *La ficción de la memoria: Juan Rulfo ante la crítica*, edited by Federico Campbell, 44–54. Mexico City: Era, UNAM, 2010.

Fromm, Harold, and Cheryll Glotfelty, eds. *The Ecocriticism Reader: Landmarks in Literary Ecology*. Athens: University of Georgia Press, 1996.

Fuentes, Carlos. *La muerte de Artemio Cruz*. Mexico City: Fondo de Cultura Económica, 1962.

———. *La nueva novela hispanoamericana*. Mexico City: Joaquín Mortiz, 1969.

Fuguet, Alberto. "Magical Neoliberalism." *Foreign Policy*, Nov. 17, 2009. https://foreignpolicy.com/2009/11/17/magical-neoliberalism/.

Fuguet, Alberto, and Sergio Gómez, eds. *McOndo*. Barcelona: Mondadori, 1996.

Furtado, Celso. *A economia brasileira*. Rio de Janeiro: A Noite, 1954.

———. *Formação econômica do Brasil*. 32nd ed. São Paulo: Cia. Editora Nacional, 2005.

Gaard, Greta. "Ecofeminism Revisited." *Feminist Formations* 23, no. 2 (2011): 26–53.

Gabaldón, Mario. *Parques nacionales de Venezuela*. Caracas: INPARQUES, 1992.

Galeano, Eduardo. *Las venas abiertas de América Latina*. Montevideo: Universidad de la República, 1987.

Gallo, Rubén. *Mexican Modernity: The Avant-Garde and the Technological Revolution*. Cambridge, Mass.: MIT Press, 2005.

Galvão, Walnice Nogueira. *As formas do falso: Um estudo sobre a ambiguidade no* Grande sertão: Veredas. São Paulo: Perspectiva, 1972.

Ganem, Roseli Senna, José Augusto Drummond, and José Luiz Franco. "Conservation Policies and Control of Habitat Fragmentation in the Brazilian Cerrado Biome." *Ambiente e Sociedade* 16, no. 3 (2013): 99–118.

García Canclini, Néstor. *Hybrid Cultures: Strategies for Entering and Leaving Modernity*. Translated by Christopher L. Chiappari and Silvia L. Lopez. Minneapolis: University of Minnesota Press, 2005.

García Marco, Daniel. "Santa Elena de Uairén, la ciudad en la frontera de Venezuela y Brasil donde se enriquecen los 'talibanes' de la gasolina." *BBC Mundo*, Mar. 24, 2107. https://www.bbc.com/mundo/noticias-america-latina-39275772.

Garrido, Felipe. *Voces de la tierra: La lección de Juan Rulfo*. Mexico City: UNAM, 2004.

Gary, Romain. *Pour Sganarelle: Recherche d'un personnage et d'un roman*. Paris: Gallimard, 1965.

Gavaldón, Roberto, dir. *La escondida*. Alfa Films, 1955.

Gebauer, Gunter, and Christoph Wulf. *Mimesis: Culture Art Society*. Translated by Don Reneau. Berkeley: University of California Press, 1995.

Gell, Alfred. *Art and Agency: An Anthropological Theory*. Oxford: Oxford University Press, 1998.

Genette, Gérard. *Narrative Discourse: An Essay in Method*. Translated by Jane E. Lewin. Ithaca, N.Y.: Cornell University Press, 1983.

Ghosh, Amitav. *The Great Derangement: Climate Change and the Unthinkable*. Chicago: University of Chicago Press, 2016.

Gil, Fernando C. *O romance da urbanização*. Porto Alegre, Brazil: EDIPUCRS, 1999.

Giorgi, Gabriel. *Formas comunes: Animalidad, cultura, biopolítica*. Buenos Aires: Eterna Cadencia Editora, 2014.

Gissibl, Bernhard, Sabine Höhler, and Patrick Kupper. *Civilizing Nature: National Parks in Global Historical Perspective*. New York: Berghahn Books, 2012.

Glotfelty, Cheryll. "Introduction." In *The Ecocriticism Reader: Landmarks in Literary Ecology*, edited by Harold Fromm and Cheryll Glotfelty, xv–xxxvii. Athens: University of Georgia Press, 1996.

Goldberg, Paul. "Narco-Pastoral: Drug Trafficking, Ecology, and the Trope of the Noble Campesino in Three Mexican Narconovelas." *ISLE: Interdisciplinary Studies in Literature and Environment* 21, no. 1 (2016): 30–50.

Gómez-Barris, Macarena. *The Extractive Zone: Social Ecologies and Decolonial Perspectives*. Durham: Duke University Press, 2017.

González Echevarría, Roberto. *Alejo Carpentier: The Pilgrim at Home*. Austin: University of Texas Press, 1990.

———. *Myth and Archive: A Theory of Latin American Narrative*. Cambridge: Cambridge University Press: 1990.

———. "*Canaima* y los libros de la selva." In *Canaima: Critical Edition*, edited by Charles Minguet, 503–14. San José: Editorial Universidad de Costa Rica, 1996.

González Martínez, Laura. *Respuesta campesina a la revolución verde en el Bajío*. Mexico City: Universidad Iberoamericana, 1992.

González, Eduardo. *Alejo Carpentier: El tiempo del hombre*. Caracas: Monte Ávila, 1978.

Goodbody, Axel. "A Sense of Place and Lieu de Mémoire: A Cultural Memory Approach to Environmental Texts." In *Ecocritical Theory: New European Approaches*, edited by Axel Goodbody and Catherine Rigby, 55–67. Charlottesville: University of Virginia Press, 2011.

Goodbody, Axel, and Catherine Rigby, eds. *Ecocritical Theory: New European Approaches*. Charlottesville: University of Virginia Press, 2011.

Grases, Pedro. "De la novela en América." In *Escritos selectos*, 295–301. Caracas: Biblioteca Ayacucho, 1989.

Gray, George. "Blueprint for Hungry Nations; A Mexican-American Agricultural Project Demonstrates the Means of Multiplying the Food Output of Low-Yield Granaries." *New York Times*, Jan. 1, 1950. https://www.nytimes.com/1950/01/01/archives/blueprint-for-hungry-nations-a-mexicanamerican-agricultural-project.html.

Grenier, Yvon, and Maarten Van Delden. "The Private and the Public: Mario Vargas Llosa on Literature and Politics." In *Gunshots at the Fiesta: Literature and Politics in Latin America*, 295–301. Nashville: Vanderbilt University Press, 2009.

Guha, Ramachandra, and Joan Martínez Alier. *Varieties of Environmentalism: Essays North and South*. London: Earthscan, 1997.

Guimarães Rosa, João. *The Devil to Pay in the Backlands*. Translated by James L. Taylor and Harriet de Onís. New York: Knopf, 1963.

———. *Noites do sertão*. 8th ed. Rio de Janeiro: Nova Fronteira, 2000.

———. *Manuelzão e Miguilim*. 11th ed. Rio de Janeiro: Nova Fronteira, 2001.

———. *Primeiras estórias*. Rio de Janeiro: Nova Fronteira, 2001.

———. *Correspondência com seu tradutor alemão Curt Meyer-Clason (1958–1967)*. Edited by Maria Aparecida M. F. Bussolotti. Translated by Erlon José Paschoal. Rio de Janeiro: Nova Fronteira, Academia Brasileira de Letras, EdUFMG, 2003.

———. *Correspondência com seu tradutor italiano Edoardo Bizzarri*. 3rd ed. Rio de Janeiro: Nova Fronteira, 2003.

———. *Grande sertão: Veredas*. Edição comemorativa. Rio de Janeiro: Nova Fronteira, 2006.

Gumbrecht, Hans Ulrich. *Atmosphere, Mood, Stimmung: On a Hidden Potential of Literature*. Stanford, Calif.: Stanford University Press, 2012.

———. *After 1945: Latency as Origin of the Present*. Stanford, Calif.: Stanford University Press, 2013.

Habra, Hedy. *Mundos alternos y artísticos en Vargas Llosa*. Madrid: Iberoamericana/Vervuert, 2012.

Hamblin, Jacob Darwin. *Arming Mother Nature: The Birth of Catastrophic Environmentalism*. New York: Oxford University Press, 2013.

Hamon, Philippe. *Du descriptif*. Paris: Hachette, 1993.

Handley, George B. "The Postcolonial Ecology of the New World Baroque: Alejo Carpentier's *The Lost Steps*." In *Postcolonial Ecologies: Literatures of the Environment*, edited by Elizabeth DeLoughrey and George B. Handley, 117–35. Oxford: Oxford University Press, 2011.

Hansen, João Adolfo. *Oo: A ficção da literatura em* Grande sertão: Veredas. São Paulo: Hedra, 2000.

Hardenberg, Wilko G. von, Matthew Kelly, Claudia Leal, and Emily Wakild. *The Nature State: Rethinking the History of Conservation*. London: Routledge, 2017.

Harrison, Robert Pogue. *Forests: The Shadow of Civilization*. Chicago: University of Chicago Press, 1992.

Harss, Luis. "Juan Rulfo o la pena sin nombre." In *La ficción de la memoria: Juan Rulfo ante la crítica*, edited by Federico Campbell, 61–88. Mexico City: Era/UNAM, 2010.

———. *Los nuestros*. Buenos Aires: Editorial Sudamericana, 1973.

Heffes, Gisela. *Políticas de la destrucción, poéticas de la preservación: Apuntes para una lectura (eco)crítica del medio ambiente en América Latina*. Rosario: Beatriz Viterbo, 2013.

Heidegger, Martin. *The Question concerning Technology and Other Essays*. Translated by William Lovitt. New York: Garland Publishing, 1977.

Heise, Ursula. *Sense of Place and Sense of Planet: The Environmental Imagination of the Global*. New York: Oxford University Press, 2008.

———. *Imagining Extinction: The Cultural Meanings of Endangered Species.* Chicago: University of Chicago Press, 2016.

Hoeg, Jerry, and Beatriz Rivera-Barnes. *Reading and Writing the Latin American Landscape.* New York: Palgrave Macmillan, 2009.

Hoyos, Héctor. "A Tale of Two Materialisms." *Novel: A Forum on Fiction* 51, no. 1 (2018): 101–16.

———. *Things with a History: Transcultural Materialism and the Literatures of Extraction in Contemporary Latin America.* New York: Columbia University Press, 2019.

Huyssen, Andreas. *Present Pasts: Urban Palimpsests and the Politics of Memory.* Stanford, Calif.: Stanford University Press, 2003.

Iber, Patrick. "The Cold War Politics of Literature and the Centro Mexicano de Escritores." *Journal of Latin American Studies* 48 (2015): 247–72.

IBGE. "Estado da população/População de fato, na data dos recenseamentos gerais/Discriminação por Unidades da Federação/Distribuição da população presente/Segundo a situação do domicílio (quadros urbano, suburbano e rural)/ 1°-IX-1940 e 1.°-VII-1950." Accessed Jul. 4, 2017. http://seculoxx.ibge.gov.br.

Indústria Brasileira de Árvores. *Relatório Ibá 2017.* www.iba.org/images/shared/Biblioteca/IBA_RelatorioAnual2017.pdf.

Instituto Chico Mendes. "Decreto N. 1.713—de 14 de junho de 1937—Cria o Parque Nacional de Itatiaia." Accessed Dec. 13, 2017. http://www.icmbio.gov.br/portal/images/stories/imgs-unidades-coservacao/itatiaia.pdf.

———. "Unidades de Conservação—Cerrado." Accessed Dec. 13, 2017. http://www.icmbio.gov.br/portal/unidadesdeconservacao/biomas-brasileiros/cerrado/unidades-de-conservacao-cerrado.

Instituto de Estudos Brasileiros, Universidade de São Paulo. *"Fundo João Guimarães Rosa."* Accessed Dec. 16, 2017. http://200.144.255.59/catalogo_eletronico/consultaUnidadesLogicas.asp?Tipo_Unidade_Logica_Codigo=1&Setor_Codigo=1&Acervo_Codigo=1&Numero_Documentos=.

Iser, Wolfgang. *The Fictive and the Imaginary: Charting Literary Anthropology.* Baltimore: Johns Hopkins University Press, 1993.

Jameson, Frederic. *The Political Unconscious: Narrative as a Socially Symbolic Act.* London: Routledge Classics, 2002.

Jauss, Hans Robert. "Literary History as a Challenge to Literary Theory." *New Literary History* 2, no. 1 (1970): 7–37.

Jiménez, Víctor. "Cronología de la obra y la vida de Juan Rulfo." In *Juan Rulfo y su obra: Una guía crítica*, edited by Víctor Jiménez and Jorge Zepeda, 25–48. Mexico City: RM, 2018.

Jiménez, Víctor, and Daniel Sada. "Juan Rulfo: La escritura y la preservación del enigma: Conversación con Daniel Sada." In *Tríptico para Juan Rulfo: Poesía, fotografía, crítica*, edited by Víctor Jiménez, Alberto Vital, and Jorge Zepeda, 303–25. Mexico City: UNAM, 2006.

Juan Rulfo: Homenaje nacional. Mexico City: Instituto Nacional de Bellas Artes, 1980.

Kearns, Sofía, and Anacristina Rossi. "Environmental Issues in Costa Rica: An Interview with Ana Cristina Rossi." *Organization and Environment* 13, no. 2 (2000): 262–65.

Keen, Suzanne. *Empathy and the Novel*. Oxford, New York: Oxford University Press, 2007.

Kelley, David, and Edward Timms, eds. *Unreal City: Urban Experience in Modern European Literature and Art*. New York: St. Martin's Press, 1985.

Klink, Carlos A., and Adriana G. Moreira. "Past and Current Human Occupation, and Land Use." In *The Cerrados of Brazil: Ecology and Natural History of a Neotropical Savanna*, edited by Paulo S. Oliveira and Robert J. Marquis, 69–88. New York: Columbia University Press, 2002.

Kokotovic, Misha. "Mario Vargas Llosa Writes Of(f) the Native: Modernity and Cultural Heterogeneity in Peru." *Revista Canadiense de Estudios Hispánicos* 25, no. 3 (2001): 445–67.

Kristal, Efraín. *Temptation of the World: The Novels of Mario Vargas Llosa*. Nashville: Vanderbilt University Press, 1998.

Kärrholm, Mattias. "The Animistic Moment: Clarice Lispector, Luis Kahn and the Reassembling of Materialities." *Lo Squaderno* 39 (2016): 71–77.

Ladino, Jennifer. *Reclaiming Nostalgia: Longing for Nature in American Literature*. Charlottesville: University of Virginia Press, 2012.

Land, Barbara, and Myrick Land. *Jungle Oil: The Search for Venezuela's Hidden Treasure*. New York: Coward-McCann, 1957.

Larsen, Neil. *Modernism and Hegemony: A Materialist Critique of Aesthetic Agencies*. Minneapolis: Minnesota University Press, 1990.

———. "Mario Vargas Llosa: The Realist as Neo-Liberal." In *Determinations: Essays on Theory, Narrative and Nation in the Americas*. London: Verso, 2001.

———. "Rulfo and the Transcultural: A Revised View." In *Determinations: Essays on Theory, Narrative and Nation in the Americas*, 137–42. London: Verso, 2001.

Latour, Bruno. *Politics of Nature: How to Bring the Sciences into Democracy*. Cambridge, Mass.: Harvard University Press, 2004.

———. *Reassembling the Social: An Introduction to Actor-Network-Theory*. Oxford: Oxford University Press, 2005.

Lauer, Mirko. *El sitio de la literatura: Escritores y política en el Perú del siglo XX*. Lima: Mosca Azul, 1989.

Leal, Claudia. "From Threatening to Threatened Jungles." In *A Living Past: Environmental Histories of Modern Latin America*, edited by John Soluri, Claudia Leal, and José Augusto Pádua, 115–37. New York: Berghahn, 2018.

Leal, Claudia, John Soluri, and José Augusto Pádua, eds. *A Living Past: Environmental Histories of Modern Latin America*. New York: Berghahn, 2018.

Leal, Luis, ed. *Cuentos de la Revolución*. 5th ed. Mexico City: UNAM, 2010.

Lefebvre, Henri. *The Production of Space*. Translated by Donald Nicholson-Smith. Malden, Mass.: Blackwell, 2016.

Levinson, Brett. *The Ends of Literature: The Latin American "Boom" in the Neoliberal Marketplace*. Stanford, Calif.: Stanford University Press, 2001.

Librandi-Rocha. Marília. *Writing by Ear: Clarice Lispector and the Aural Novel*. Toronto: Toronto University Press, 2018.

Lima, Nísia Trindade. *Um sertão chamado Brasil: Intelectuais e representação geográfica da identidade nacional*. Rio de Janeiro: Revan, IUPERJ, 1999.

———. "Brasília: A capital no sertão." In *Veredas de Brasília: As expedições geográficas em busca de um sonho*, edited by Nelson de Castro Serna, 17–34. Rio de Janeiro: Instituto Brasileiro de Geografia e Estatística, 2010.

Lins, Álvaro. "Uma grande estreia." In *Guimarães Rosa*, edited by Eduardo de Faria Coutinho, 237–42. Rio de Janeiro: Civilização Brasileira, 1983.

Lira, Miguel N. *La escondida*. Mexico City: Edición y Distribución Iberoamericana de Publicaciones, 1948.

Lisboa, Apolo Heringer. "Imaginário do Projeto Manuelzão." In *Navegando o Rio das Velhas: Das Minas aos Gerais*, edited by Eugênio Goulart, 53–71. Belo Horizonte, Brazil: Instituto Guaicuy, 2005.

Lispector, Clarice. "Seco estudo de cavalos." In *Onde estivestes de noite*, 49–58. Rio de Janeiro: Editora Artenova, 1974.

———. *A paixão segundo G.H.* 2nd ed. Madrid: ALLCA XX, 1997.

———. *A cidade sitiada*. Rio de Janeiro: Rocco, 1998.

———. *A maçã no escuro*. Rio de Janeiro: Rocco, 1998.

———. *Laços de família*. Rio de Janeiro: Rocco, 1998.

———. *A descoberta do mundo*. Rio de Janeiro: Rocco, 1999.

———. *O lustre*. Rio de Janeiro: Rocco, 1999.

———. *A hora da estrela*. Rio de Janeiro: Rocco, 2006.

———. "Dry Sketch of Horses." In *The Complete Stories*, translated by Katrina Dodson, 447–54. New York: New Directions, 2015.

———. *The Besieged City*. Translated by Johnny Lorenz. New York: New Directions, 2019.

Lorente-Murphy, Silvia. *Juan Rulfo: Realidad y mito de la Revolución mexicana*. Madrid: Pliegos, 1988.

Lorenz, Günter. "Diálogo com Guimarães Rosa." In *Guimarães Rosa*, edited by Eduardo de Faria Coutinho, 62–97. Rio de Janeiro: Civilização Brasileira, 1983.

Lousley, Cheryl. "Ecocriticism and the Politics of Representation." In *The Oxford Book of Ecocriticism*, edited by Greg Garrard, 155–71. New York: Oxford University Press, 2014.

Lukács, Georg. *Theory of the Novel: A Historico-Philosophical Essay on the Forms of Great Epic Literature*. Translated by Anna Bostock. Cambridge, Mass.: MIT Press, 1971.

López Mena, Sergio. *Los caminos de la creación en Juan Rulfo*. Mexico City: UNAM, 1994.

López-Calvo, Ignacio. "Going Native: Anti-indigenism in Vargas Llosa's *The Storyteller* and *Death in the Andes*." In *Mario Vargas Llosa and Latin American Politics*, edited by Juan E. De Castro and Nicholas Birns, 103–24. New York: Palgrave Macmillan, 2010.

Lovitt, William. "Introduction." In *The Question concerning Technology and other Essays*, by Martin Heidegger, translated by William Lovitt, xiii–xxxix. New York: Garland Publishing, 1977.

Machado, Dyonélio. *Os ratos*. 3rd ed. Rio de Janeiro: Civilização Brasileira, 1966.

Mäkelä, Maria. "Realism and the Unnatural." In *A Poetics of Unnatural Narrative*, edited by Jan Alber, Skov Nielsen, and Brian Richardson, 142–66. Columbus: Ohio State University Press, 2013.

Machado, Ricardo, Mário Ramos Neto, Paulo Gustavo Pereira, Eduardo Caldas, Demerval Gonçalves, Nazareno Santos, Karyn Tabor, and Marc Steininger. "Estimativas de perda da área do Cerrado brasileiro." Conservação Internacional, Brasília, June 2004. http://cmbbc.cpac.embrapa.br/RelatDesmatamCerrado%20CIBrasil%20JUL2004.pdf.

Marcone, Jorge. "Recuperar Chimbote, o la ecología menospreciada de 'Los zorros' de José María Arguedas." *Revista de Crítica Literaria Latinoamericana* 11, no. 79 (2014): 141–61.

———. "Ecología de un sueño: chamanismo, ecumenismo y textualidad amazónicos en *Las tres mitades de Ino Moxo* de César Calvo." In *Migración y frontera: experiencias culturales en la literatura peruana del siglo XX*, edited by Javier García Liendo, 315–35. Madrid: Iberoamericana/Vervuert, 2017.

Márquez Rodríguez, Alexis. *La obra narrativa de Alejo Carpentier*. Caracas: Universidad Central de Venezuela, 1970.

———. "Prólogo." In *Los pasos recobrados: Ensayos de teoría y crítica literaria*, *ix–l*. Caracas: Biblioteca Ayacucho, 2003.

Marran, Christine. *Ecology without Culture: Aesthetics for a Toxic World*. Minneapolis: Minnesota University Press, 2017.

Martin, Claire Emilie. *Alejo Carpentier y las crónicas de Indias: Orígenes de una escritura americana*. Hanover, N.H.: Ediciones del Norte, 1995.

Martin, Gerald. "Boom, Yes; 'New Novel,' No: Further Reflections on the Optical Illusions of the 1960s in Latin America." *Bulletin of Latin American Research* 3, no. 2 (1984): 53–63.

———. "Mario Vargas Llosa: Errant Knight of the Liberal Imagination." In *On Modern Latin American Fiction*, edited by John King, 205–33. New York: Hill and Wang, 1989.

Martins, Geraldo Inácio. "As tramas da des(re)territorialização camponesa: A reinvenção do território veredeiro no entorno do Parque Nacional Grande Sertão Veredas, norte de Minas Gerais." M.A. thesis, Federal University of Uberlândia, 2011.

Martins, Wilson. "Uma voz." In "*Suplemento Literário*," *O Estado de São Paulo*, Nov. 26, 1960. Arquivo Clarice Lispector, Fundação Casa de Rui Barbosa.

Matamoro, Blas. "Escritores, escribidores y teoría de la novela." In *El autor y su obra: Mario Vargas Llosa*, 57–69. Madrid: Universidad Complutense, 1990.

McNeill, John. *Something New under the Sun: An Environmental History of the Twentieth-Century World*. New York: W. W. Norton, 2000.

———. *The Great Acceleration: An Environmental History of the Anthropocene since 1945*. Cambridge, Mass.: Harvard University Press, 2014.

Meléndez, Concha. "Tres novelas de la naturaleza americana: *Don Segundo Sombra, La vorágine, Doña Bárbara*." In *Signos de Iberoamérica*, 89–101. Mexico City: Manuel Leon Sánchez, 1936.

Mendieta Alatorre, Ángeles. *El paisaje en la novela de América.* Mexico City: Secretaría de Educación Pública, 1949.

"*Mexican Agricultural Program.*" Revised Commentary for Film Prepared for the Rockefeller Foundation. Transfilm, October 24, 1950. Mexican Field Office, Record Group 6.13 I.I, Series 1.3, Box 33, Folder 369. Rockefeller Archive Center.

Meyer, Monica. *Ser-tão natureza: A natureza em Guimarães Rosa.* Belo Horizonte, Brazil: UFMG, 2008.

Millán Vargas, Paulina. "La difusión inicial de las fotografías de Juan Rulfo (1949–1964)." In *Nuevos indicios sobre Juan Rulfo*, edited by Jorge Zepeda, 91–133. Mexico City: Fundación Juan Rulfo, 2010.

Miller, Shawn W. *An Environmental History of Latin America.* New York: Cambridge University Press, 2007.

Millington, Mark. "Gender Monologue in Carpentier's *Los pasos perdidos.*" *MLN* 11, no. 2, Hispanic Issue (1996): 346–67.

Mires, Fernando. *El discurso de la naturaleza: Ecología y política en América Latina.* Santiago, Chile: Editorial Amerinda, 1990.

Moore, Jason. *Capitalism and the Web of Life: Ecology and the Accumulation of Capital.* London: Verso, 2016.

Moraes, Antonio Carlos Robert. "O sertão: Um 'outro geográfico.'" In *Geografia histórica do Brasil: Cinco ensaios, uma proposta e uma crítica*, 87–101. Rio de Janeiro: Annablume, 2009.

Moraña, Mabel. *Arguedas / Vargas Llosa: Dilemmas and Assemblages.* Translated by Andrew Ascherl. New York: Palgrave Macmillan, 2016.

Moreira, Paulo. *Modernismo localista das Américas: Os contos de Faulkner, Guimarães Rosa e Rulfo.* Belo Horizonte, Brazil: Editora UFMG, 2012.

Moreiras, Alberto. *The Exhaustion of Difference: The Politics of Latin American Cultural Studies.* Durham: Duke University Press, 2001.

Morton, Timothy. *Ecology without Nature: Rethinking Environmental Aesthetics.* Cambridge, Mass.: Harvard University Press, 2007.

Moser, Benjamin. *Why This World: A Biography of Clarice Lispector.* New York: Oxford University Press, 2009.

Müller, Gesine. "From 'The Novel' (1966) to 'The Art of the Novel' (2000): Readings of Vargas Llosa as Topos of Latin American Disenchantment." Translated by Jessica Ernst Powell. *Literature and Arts of the Americas* 46, no. 1 (2013): 20–25.

Nascimento, Evando. *Clarice Lispector: Uma literatura pensante.* Rio de Janeiro: Civilização Brasileira, 2012.

Nash, Roderick. "The American Invention of National Parks." *American Quarterly* 22, no. 3 (1970): 726–35.

Natali, Marcos. *A política da nostalgia: Um estudo das formas do passado.* São Paulo: Nankin, 2006.

Nixon, Rob. *Slow Violence and the Environmentalism of the Poor.* Cambridge, Mass.: Harvard University Press, 2011.

Nodari, Alexandre. "'A vida oblíqua': O hetairismo ontológico segundo G.H." *O Eixo e a Roda* 24, no. 1 (2015): 139–54.

Nora, Pierre. "Between Memory and History: Les Lieux de Mémoire." *Representations* 26 (1989): 7–24.

Nossa, Leonencio. "Novas veredas: O mapa do Grande Sertão nos 50 anos de morte de Guimarães Rosa." *O Estado de S. Paulo*. Accessed Dec. 14, 2017. https://infograficos.estadao.com.br/especiais/novas-veredas/.

Nouzeilles, Gabriela. "Introducción." In *La naturaleza en disputa: Retóricas del cuerpo y el paisaje en América Latina*, edited by Gabriela Nouzeilles, 11–36. Buenos Aires: Paidós, 2002.

Novo Torres, Isabel, Luis Gonzalo Morales, Carmen Teresa Rodríguez, Gladys Martínez, and Ildiko De Hertelendy. *Ciencia y conservación en el Sistema de Parques Nacionales de Venezuela: Una experiencia de cooperación interinstitucional*. Caracas: Altamira, 1997.

Nunes, Benedito. *O dorso do tigre*. 2nd ed. São Paulo: Perspectiva, 1976.

———. *O drama da linguagem: Uma leitura de Clarice Lispector*. São Paulo: Ática, 1989.

Nussbaum, Martha. *Poetic Justice: The Literary Imagination and Public Life*. Boston: Beacon Press, 1995.

Olea Franco, Rafael. "La novela de la Revolución mexicana: Una propuesta de relectura." *Nueva Revista de Filología Hispánica* 60, no. 2 (2012): 479–514.

Olmos, José. "Vargas Llosa dice que indigenismo es un peligro democrático." *El Universo*, Nov. 11, 2003. https://www.eluniverso.com/2003/11/11/0001/8/8E389173D65C4B0BAE80101A0C5ACAD7.html?device=tablet.

Oloff, Kerstin. "The 'Monstrous Head' and the 'Mouth of Hell': The Gothic Ecologies of the 'Mexican Miracle.'" In *Ecological Crisis and Cultural Representation in Latin America: Ecocritical Perspectives on Art, Film, and Literature*, edited by Mark D. Anderson and Zélia Bora, 79–98. London: Lexington Books, 2016.

Olsson, Tore C. *Agrarian Crossings: Reformers and the Remaking of the US and Mexican Countryside*. Princeton, N.J.: Princeton University Press, 2017.

Ortiz Rodríguez, María de las Mercedes. "La fisura irremediable: Indígenas, regiones y nación en tres novelas de Mario Vargas Llosa." *Antípoda* 15 (2012): 111–36.

O'Bryan-Knight, Jean. *The Story of the Storyteller: 'La tia Julia y el escribidor,' 'Historia de Mayta,' and 'El hablador' by Mario Vargas Llosa*. Amsterdam: Rodopi, 1995.

Padura, Leonardo. *Lo real maravilloso: Creación y realidad*. Havana: Letras Cubanas, 1989.

Pãrõkumu, Umusi, and Tõrãmu Kehíri. *Antes o mundo não existia: mitologia dos antigos Desana-Kehíripõrã*. São João Batista do Rio Tiquié e São Gabriel da Cachoeira: UNIRT/FOIRN, 1995.

Parra, Max. "Geografía y procesos culturales en la narrativa de la Revolución mexicana (Azuela y Campobello)." In *Imagining the Mexican Revolution: Versions and Visions in Literature and Visual Culture*, edited by Tilmann Altenberg, 3–17. Newcastle upon Tyne: Cambridge Scholars Publishing, 2013.

Patel, Raj. "The Long Green Revolution." *Journal of Peasant Studies* 40, no. 1 (2013): 1–63.

Pavel, Thomas. *Fictional Worlds*. Cambridge, Mass.: Harvard University Press, 1986.

Pearse, Andrew. *Seeds of Plenty, Seeds of Want: Social and Economic Implications of the Green Revolution*. Oxford: Oxford University Press, 1980.

Peixoto, Marta. "'Fatos são pedras duras': Urban Poverty in Clarice Lispector." In *Closer to the Wild Heart: Essays on Clarice Lispector*, edited by Cláudia Pazos Alonso and Claire Williams, 106–25. Oxford: Legenda, 2002.

Pérez Firmat, Gustavo. "The Strut of the Centipede: José Lezama Lima and New World Exceptionalism." In *Do the Americas Have a Common Literature?*, edited by Gustavo Pérez Firmat, 316–31. Durham: Duke University Press, 1990.

Perkins, John H. *Geopolitics and the Green Revolution: Wheat, Genes, and the Cold War*. New York: Oxford University Press, 1997.

Phelan, James. *Living to Tell about It: A Rhetoric and Ethics of Character Narration*. Ithaca: Cornell University Press, 2005.

Phillips, Dana. *The Truth of Ecology: Nature, Culture, and Literature in America*. New York: Oxford University Press, 2003.

Plato. *Republic*. Edited and translated by Chris Emlyn-Jones. Oxford: Aris and Phillips, 2007.

Plumwood, Val. *Feminism and the Mastery of Nature*. London: Routledge, 1993.

Pontieri, Regina. *Clarice Lispector: Uma poética do olhar*. Cotia: Ateliê Editorial, 2001.

Pratt, Mary Louise. *Imperial Eyes: Travel Writing and Transculturation*. London: Routledge, 2008.

Prignitz, Helga. *El Taller de Gráfica Popular en México 1937–1977*. Translated by Elizabeth Siefer. Mexico City: Instituto Nacional de Bellas Artes, 1992.

Raimúndez Urrutia, Elena, and Nelson Ramirez. "Eficiencia reproductiva y niveles de aborto en especies de plantas de cinco comunidades naturales de la Cuenca Alta del Río Caroní (Parque Nacional Canaima) y efecto de cierto factores bióticos sobre estos parámetros reproductivos: Resutados preliminares." In *Ciencia y conservación en el Sistema de Parques Nacionales de Venezuela: Una experiencia de cooperación interinstitucional*, edited by Isabel Novo Torres, Luis Gonzalo Morales, Carmen Teresa Rodríguez, Gladys Martínez, and Ildiko De Hertelendy, 305–12. Caracas: Altamira, 1997.

Rama, Ángel. "El *Boom* en perspectiva." In *Más allá del Boom: Literatura y mercado*, edited by Ángel Rama, 51–119. Buenos Aires: Folios Ediciones, 1984.

———. *Writing across Cultures: Narrative Transculturation in Latin America*. Edited and translated by David Frye. Durham: Duke University Press, 2012.

Rama, Ángel, and Mario Vargas Llosa. *García Márquez y la problemática de la novela*. Buenos Aires: Corregidor-Marcha, 1974.

Ramos, Graciliano. *Angústia*. 9th ed. São Paulo: Livraria Martins, 1964.

———. *Vidas secas*. 24th ed. São Paulo: Martins, 1970.

Rancière, Jacques. *Dissensus: On Politics and Aesthetics*. Edited and translated by Steven Corcoran. New York: Continuum, 2010.

———. *The Politics of Aesthetics: The Distribution of the Sensible*. Edited and translated by Gabriel Rockhill. London: Bloomsbury, 2013.

———. *Les bords de la fiction*. Paris: Seuil, 2017.

Real, Mildred, Jorge Rangel, Diego Díaz Martín, and Aníbal Invemón. "Mejorando nuestra herencia: Informe preliminar." Unesco, 2002. Accessed Sep. 15, 2017. https://whc.unesco.org/document/6991.

Resumen de los programas de la Comisión del Medio Ambiente y Desarrollo Sostenible. Coordinated by Alfredo E. Ferreyros. Mario Vargas Llosa Papers, Box 42, Folder 7, Princeton University.

Revueltas, José. *El luto humano*. Mexico City: Editorial México, 1943.

Rivera-Barnes, Beatriz. "To Discover, an Intransitive Verb: Christopher Columbus's First Encounter with the American Landscape." In *Reading and Writing the Latin American Landscape*, by Jerry Hoeg and Beatriz Rivera-Barnes, 9–24. New York: Palgrave Macmillan, 2009.

Rivera, José Eustasio. *La vorágine*. Mexico City: Editorial Porrúa, 1989.

Robertson, Ruth. "The Forgotten Expedition." Accessed Apr. 20, 2018. http://www.ruthrobertson.org/.

Rodríguez Monegal, Emir. *Narradores de esta América*. Montevideo: Alfa, 1969.

———. "Relectura de *Pedro Páramo*." In *La ficción de la memoria: Juan Rulfo ante la crítica*, edited by Federico Campbell, 121–35. Mexico City: Era/UNAM, 2010.

———. "The New Novelists." *The Encounter* 25 (1965): 97–110.

Rogers, Charlotte. *Jungle Fever: Exploring Madness and Medicine in Twentieth-Century Tropical Narrative*. Nashville: Vanderbilt University Press, 2012.

———. "Mario Vargas Llosa and the *novela de la selva*." *Bulletin of Spanish Studies* 93, no. 6 (2016): 1043–60.

———. *Mourning El Dorado: Literature and Extractivism in the Contemporary American Tropics*. Charlottesville: University of Virginia Press, 2019.

Romero Díaz, Aldemaro. *Canaima*. Caracas: Palmaven, 1992–93.

Roncari, Luiz. *O Brasil de Rosa: O amor e o poder*. São Paulo: Unesp, 2004.

———. *O cão do sertão: Literatura e engajamento*. São Paulo: Unesp, 2007.

Rosenfield, Kathrin. *Desenveredando Rosa: A obra de J. G. Rosa e outros ensaios rosianos*. Rio de Janeiro: Topbooks, 2006.

Rossi, Anacristina. *La loca de Gandoca*. 3rd ed. San José, Costa Rica: EDUCA, 1993.

Rowe, William. *Mito e ideología en la obra de Arguedas*. Lima: Instituto Nacional de Cultura, 1979.

———. "Liberalism and Authority: The Case of Mario Vargas Llosa." In *On Edge: The Crisis of Contemporary Latin American Culture*, edited by George Yúdice, Jean Franco, and Juan Flores, 45–64. Minneapolis: Minnesota University Press, 1992.

Rowland, Clara. *A forma do meio: Livro e narração na obra de João Guimarães Rosa*. Campinas: Unicamp, 2011.

Rulfo, Juan. *Aire de las colinas: Cartas a Clara*. Edited by Alberto Vital. Madrid: Debate, 2000.

———. *Juan Rulfo: Letras e imágenes*. Edited by Víctor Jiménez. Mexico City: RM, 2002.

———. *Pedro Páramo*. Edited by José Carlos González Boixo. 18th ed. Madrid: Cátedra, 2004.

———. *El Llano en llamas*. Mexico City: Fundación Juan Rulfo and RM, 2017.

Rulfo, Juan, and Máximo Simpson. "Entrevista a Juan Rulfo." In *Noticias sobre Juan Rulfo: 1784–2003*, by Alberto Vital, 199–206. Mexico City: UNAM, 2003.

Sá, Lúcia. *Rain Forest Literatures: Amazonian Texts and Latin American Culture*. Minneapolis: University of Minnesota Press, 2004.

Sá, Olga de. *A escritura de Clarice Lispector*. 2nd ed. Petrópolis, Brazil: Editora Vozes and EdPUC-SP, 1993.

Salazar-Carrillo, Jorge, and Bernadette West. *Oil and Development in Venezuela during the Twentieth Century*. Westport: Praeger, 2004.

Santiago, Silviano. *Genealogia da ferocidade: Ensaio sobre* Grande Sertão: Veredas, *de Guimarães Rosa*. Recife: Companhia Editora de Pernambuco (CEPE), 2017.

———. "Bestiário." *Instituto Moreira Salles: Cadernos de literatura brasileira: Clarice Lispector* 17–18 (2004): 192–223.

Santos, Milton. *A urbanização brasileira*. São Paulo: Editora Hucitec, 1993.

Saramago, Victoria. "*Sertão Dentro*: The Backlands in Early Modern Portuguese Writings." *Portuguese Literary and Cultural Studies* 27 (2014): 254–72.

———. "Ecos de piedras y ecos de palabras: Los espacios de *Pedro Páramo*." In *"Pedro Páramo": 60 años*, edited by Víctor Jiménez, 151–62. Mexico City: Fundación Juan Rulfo and RM, 2015.

———. "Testando limites: Interdividualidade coletiva nos romances da selva e da seca." In *Mímesis e invisibilização social: A interdividualidade coletiva latino-americana*, edited by José Luís Jobim, Mariana Méndez-Gallardo, and Carlos Mendoza-Álvarez, 123–50. São Paulo: É Realizações, 2016.

———. "Transatlantic Sertões: The Backlands of Ruy Duarte de Carvalho and Mia Couto." *Ecozon@: European Journal of Literature, Culture and Environment* 8, no. 1 (2017): 79–97.

———. "Juan Rulfo leído por escritores y críticos latinoamericanos." In *Juan Rulfo y su obra: Una guía crítica*, edited by Víctor Jiménez, 183–87. Mexico City: RM, 2018.

Sartre, Jean-Paul. *What Is Literature?* Translated by Bernard Frechtman. London: Methuen, 1978.

Sasaki, Nophea, and Francis Putz. "Critical Need for New Definitions of 'Forest' and 'Forest Degradation' in Global Climate Change Agreements." *Conservation Letters* 2 (2009): 226–32.

Schaeffer, Jean-Marie. *Why Fiction?* Lincoln: University of Nebraska Press, 2010.

Schwab, Gabrielle. *Imaginary Ethnographies: Literature, Culture, and Subjectivity*. New York: Columbia University Press, 2012.

Searle, John. "The Logical Status of Fictional Discourse." *New Literary History* 6, no. 2 (1975): 319–32.

Shaw, Donald L. *Nueva narrativa hispanoamericana: Boom, posBoom, posmodernismo*. Madrid: Cátedra, 2008.

Shiva, Vandana. *The Violence of the Green Revolution: Third World Agriculture, Ecology and Politics*. London: Zed Books and Third World Network, 1993.

Silva, Rosa Amélia Pereira da. "Nesta água que não para: Leitura de João Guimarães Rosa no Vale do Urucuia." Ph.D. diss., University of Brasília, 2014.

Simonian, Lane. *Defending the Land of the Jaguar: A History of Conservation in Mexico*. Austin: University of Texas Press, 2015.

Siskind, Mariano. *Cosmopolitan Desires: Global Modernity and World Literature in Latin America*. Evanston, Ill.: Northwestern University Press, 2014.

Slater, Candace. *Entangled Edens: Visions of the Amazon*. Berkeley: University of California Press, 2002.

Smith, Stephanie J. *The Power and Politics of Art in Postrevolutionary Mexico*. Chapel Hill: University of North Carolina Press, 2017.

Soja, Edward W. *Thirdspace: Journeys to Los Angeles and Other Real-and-Imagined Places*. Oxford: Blackwell, 2000.

Sommer, Doris. "About-Face: The Talker Turns." *boundary 2* 23, no. 1 (1996): 91–133.

Sommers, Joseph. "Los muertos no tienen tiempo ni espacio (un diálogo con Juan Rulfo)." In *La ficción de la memoria: Juan Rulfo ante la crítica*, edited by Federico Campbell, 517–21. Mexico City: Era/UNAM, 2010.

Soper, Kate. *What Is Nature? Culture, Politics and the Non-Human*. Malden, Mass.: Blackwell, 1995.

Sousa, Carlos Mendes de. *Clarice Lispector: Figuras da escrita*. Braga, Portugal: Universidade do Minho, Centro de Estudos Humanísticos, 2000.

Spitta, Silvia. *Between Two Waters: Narratives of Transculturation in Latin America*. Houston: Rice University Press, 1995.

Starling, Heloisa. *Lembranças do Brasil: Teoria política, história e ficção em* Grande sertão: Veredas. Rio de Janeiro: Revan and IUPERJ, 1999.

Sumberg, James, Dennis Keeney, and Benedict Dempsey. "Public Agronomy: Norman Borlaug as 'Brand Hero' for the Green Revolution." *Journal of Development Studies* 48, no. 11 (2012): 1587–1600.

Süssekind, Flora. *O Brasil não é longe daqui: O narrador, a viagem*. São Paulo: Companhia das Letras, 1990.

Taussig, Michael. *Mimesis and Alterity: A Particular History of the Senses*. New York: Routledge, 1993.

Thakkar, Amit. *The Fiction of Juan Rulfo: Irony, Revolution and Postcolonialism*. Woodbridge: Tamesis, 2012.

Tinker Salas, Miguel. *The Enduring Legacy: Oil, Culture, and Society in Venezuela*. Durham: Duke University Press, 2009.

Torres de la Rosa, Danaé. *Avatares editoriales de un "género": Tres décadas de la novela de la Revolución mexicana*. Mexico City: Bonilla Artiga, Instituto Tecnológico Autónomo de México, and Iberoamericana/Vervuert, 2015.

Trigo, Abril. "Shifting Paradigms: From Transculturation to Hybridity: A Theoretical Critique." In *Unforeseeable Americas: Questioning Cultural Hybridity in the Americas*, edited by Rita de Grandis and Zilà Bernd, 85–111. Amsterdam: Rodopi, 2000.

Trouillot, Michel-Rolph. *Silencing the Past: Power and the Production of History*. Boston: Beacon Press, 2015.

Uslar Pietri, Arturo. "Sembrar el petróleo." *Ahora* 1, no. 183 (1936), in *Sembrar el petróleo en Venezuela*, Universidad Simón Bolívar, November 2012. http://hemerotecavirtualsembrarpetroleo.blogspot.com/.

Utéza, Francis. *JGR: Metafísica do Grande Sertão*. Translated by José Carlos Garbuglio. São Paulo: EdUSP, 1994.

Valentim, Marco Antonio. *Extramundanidade e sobrentureza: Ensaios de ontologia infundamental*. Florianópolis, Brazil: Cultura e Barbárie, 2018.

Vargas Llosa, Mario. "Novela primitiva y novela de creación en América Latina." *Revista de la Universidad de México* 23, no. 10 (1969): 29–36.

———. *García Márquez: Historia de un deicidio*. Barcelona: Barral Editores, 1971.

———. "En torno a la nueva novela latinoamericana." *Río Piedras: Revista de la Facultad de Humanidades* 1 (1972): 129–40.

———. "La novela." In *Mario Vargas Llosa: La novela; José María Arguedas: La novela y el problema de la expresión literaria en el Perú*. Vte López, Argentina: América Nueva, 1974.

———. "La novela." Handwritten note. Mario Vargas Llosa Papers, Box 136, Folder 1, Princeton University.

———. *La orgía perpetua: Flaubert y Madame Bovary*. Madrid: Taurus, 1975.

———. "El arte de mentir." *El País*, Jul. 25, 1984, 9. Reprinted in *Dominical*, Aug. 12, 1984, 4–6. Mario Vargas Llosa Papers, Box 136, Folder 4, Princeton University.

———. *Historia de Mayta*. Barcelona: Seix Barral, 1984.

———. *La ciudad y los perros*. Barcelona: Seix Barral, 1985.

———. "La literatura es fuego." In *Contra viento y marea, vol. 1 (1962–1972)*, 132–37. Barcelona: Seix Barral, 1986.

———. "El poder de la mentira." *Vuelta* 130 (September 1987): 54–56. http://www.letraslibres.com/vuelta/el-poder-la-mentira.

———. *The Storyteller*. Translated by Helen Lane. New York: Farrar, Straus, and Giroux, 1989.

———. *La verdad de las mentiras: Ensayos sobre literatura*. Barcelona: Seix Barral, 1990.

———. "Questions of Conquest: What Columbus Wrought, and What He Did Not." *Harper's*, Dec. 1990, 45–53. https://harpers.org/archive/1990/12/questions-of-conquest/.

———. "Foro Economía y Agricultura." Typed text of lecture given at the Foro Economía y Agricultura, Lima, January 30, 1990. Mario Vargas Llosa Papers, Box 41, Folder 2, Princeton University.

———. "A Fish out of Water." *Granta* 36, Jun. 27, 1991. https://granta.com/a-fish-out-of-water/.

———. *El pez en el agua: Memorias*. Barcelona: Seix Barral, 1993.

———. *A Fish in the Water*. New York: Farrar, Straus, and Giroux, 1994. Kindle Edition.

———. *Historia secreta de una novela*. Barcelona: Tusquets/Fábula, 2001.

———. *The Green House*. Translated by Gregory Rabassa. New York: HarperCollins, 2005.

———. *Lituma en los Andes*. Barcelona: Planeta, 2006.

———. *El hablador*. Lima: Alfaguara, 2008.

———. *La casa verde*. 2nd ed. Madrid: Punto de Lectura, 2008.

———. "Victoria Pírrica." *El País*, Jun. 28, 2009. https://elpais.com/diario/2009/06/28/opinion/1246140013_850215.html.

———. *Conversación en La Catedral*. Madrid: Santillana, 2010.

———. *La utopía arcaica: José María Arguedas y las ficciones del indigenismo*. Mexico City: Fondo de Cultura Económica, 2011.

———. *El sueño del celta*. Barcelona: Penguin Random House, 2015.

———. *La tía Júlia y el escribidor*. Lima: Penguin Random House, 2015.

———. *Pantaleón y las visitadoras*. Barcelona: Penguin Random House, 2015.

Vargas Llosa, Mario, and Ricardo A. Setti. *Sobre la vida y la política*. Buenos Aires: Editorial InterMundo, 1989.

Vargas Llosa, Mario, and Raymond L. Williams. "Diálogos: La invención de una realidad." In *Mario Vargas Llosa: Literatura y política*, 73–108. Mexico City: Cátedra Alfonso Reyes (ITESM), Planeta, 2001.

Varin, Claire. *Línguas de fogo: Ensaio sobre Clarice Lispector*. São Paulo: Limiar, 2002.

Vidal e Souza, Candice. *A pátria geográfica: Sertão e litoral no pensamento social brasileiro*. 2nd ed. Goiânia: EdUFG, 2015.

Viggiano, Alan. *Itinerário de Riobaldo Tatarana*. Brasília: Instituto Nacional do Livro, 1974.

Villares, Lucia. "Modernization and the Phantasmagoria of Commodities in Clarice Lispector's *A cidade sitiada*." *BHS* 87, no. 4 (2010): 473–87.

Vital, Alberto. *Lenguaje y poder en* Pedro Páramo. Mexico City: Consejo Nacional para la Cultura y las Artes, 1993.

———. *Noticias sobre Juan Rulfo 1784–2003*. Mexico City: UNAM, 2003.

Volek, Emil. "*El hablador*: Del realismo mágico a la posmodernidad." In *Mario Vargas Llosa: Opera omnia*, edited by Ana María Hernández de López, 109–21. Madrid: Pliegos, 1994.

von Mossner, Alexa Weik. *Affective Ecologies: Empathy, Emotion, and Environmental Narrative*. Columbus: Ohio State University Press, 2017.

Walsh, Richard. *The Rhetoric of Fictionality: Narrative Theory and the Idea of Fiction*. Columbus: Ohio State University Press, 2007.

Wenzel, Jennifer. *The Disposition of Nature: Environmental Crisis and World Literature*. New York: Fordham University Press, 2020.

Werneck, Gustavo. "Travessia." *O Estado de Minas Gerais*, Mar. 6, 2016. especiais.em.com.br/travessia.

Weatherford, Douglas. "Juan Rulfo y el cine." Juan Rulfo: Página Oficial. Accessed Oct. 17, 2017. http://juan-rulfo.com/especial_cine.htm.

White, Hayden. "The Historical Event." *differences: A Journal of Feminist Cultural Studies* 19, no. 2 (2008): 9–34.

Williams, Michael. *Deforesting the Earth: From Prehistory to Global Crisis*. Chicago: University of Chicago Press, 2010.

Williams, Raymond. *The Country and the City*. New York: Oxford University Press, 1975.

———. *Marxism and Literature*. New York: Oxford University Press, 1977.

Williams, Raymond L. *Vargas Llosa: Otra historia de un deicidio*. Mexico City: Taurus, 2001.

———. "Natural and Built Environments: Toward an Ecocritical Reading of the Novels of Mario Vargas Llosa." In *Critical Insights: Mario Vargas Llosa*, edited by Juan E. De Castro, 55–70. Armenia, N.Y.: Grey House Publishing, 2014.

Wolford, Wendy. "Environmental Justice and Agricultural Development in the Brazilian *Cerrado*." In *Environmental Justice in Latin America: Problems, Promise, and Practice*, edited by David V. Carruthers, 213–38. Cambridge, Mass.: MIT Press, 2008.

Wright, Angus. *The Death of Ramón González: The Modern Agricultural Dilemma*. Rev. ed. Austin: University of Texas Press, 2005.

Wulf, Andrea. *The Invention of Nature: Alexander von Humboldt's New World*. New York: Vintage, 2015.

Wylie, Lesley. *Colonial Tropes and Postcolonial Tricks: Rewriting the Tropics in the Novela de la Selva*. Liverpool: Liverpool University Press, 2009.

Yáñez, Agustín. *Las tierras flacas*. Mexico City: Joaquín Mortiz, 1962.

Yúdice, George. *The Expediency of Culture: Uses of Culture in the Global Era*. Durham: Duke University Press, 2003.

Zamora, Lois Parkinson. *The Inordinate Eye: New World Baroque and Latin American Fiction*. Chicago: University of Chicago Press, 2006.

Zepeda, Jorge. *La recepción inicial de "Pedro Páramo," 1955–1963*. Mexico City: Fundación Juan Rulfo and RM, 2005.

———. "Rulfo en el Papaloapan: Algunos documentos." *La Jornada*, Nov. 12, 2006. http://www.jornada.unam.mx/2006/11/12/sem-jorge.html.

Zuloaga, Guillermo. *Petroleum Geography of Venezuela*. Caracas: Cromotip, 1957.

Index

FLASHPOINTS

1. *On Pain of Speech: Fantasies of the First Order and the Literary Rant*, Dina Al-Kassim
2. *Moses and Multiculturalism*, Barbara Johnson, with a foreword by Barbara Rietveld
3. *The Cosmic Time of Empire: Modern Britain and World Literature*, Adam Barrows
4. *Poetry in Pieces: César Vallejo and Lyric Modernity*, Michelle Clayton
5. *Disarming Words: Empire and the Seductions of Translation in Egypt*, Shaden M. Tageldin
6. *Wings for Our Courage: Gender, Erudition, and Republican Thought*, Stephanie H. Jed
7. *The Cultural Return*, Susan Hegeman
8. *English Heart, Hindi Heartland: The Political Life of Literature in India*, Rashmi Sadana
9. *The Cylinder: Kinematics of the Nineteenth Century*, Helmut Müller-Sievers
10. *Polymorphous Domesticities: Pets, Bodies, and Desire in Four Modern Writers*, Juliana Schiesari
11. *Flesh and Fish Blood: Postcolonialism, Translation, and the Vernacular*, S. Shankar
12. *The Fear of French Negroes: Transcolonial Collaboration in the Revolutionary Americas*, Sara E. Johnson
13. *Figurative Inquisitions: Conversion, Torture, and Truth in the Luso-Hispanic Atlantic*, Erin Graff Zivin
14. *Cosmopolitan Desires: Global Modernity and World Literature in Latin America*, Mariano Siskind
15. *Fiction Beyond Secularism*, Justin Neuman
16. *Periodizing Jameson: Dialectics, the University, and the Desire for Narrative*, Phillip E. Wegner
17. *The Practical Past*, Hayden White
18. *The Powers of the False: Reading, Writing, Thinking Beyond Truth and Fiction*, Doro Wiese
19. *The Object of the Atlantic: Concrete Aesthetics in Cuba, Brazil, and Spain, 1868–1968*, Rachel Price
20. *Epic and Exile: Novels of the German Popular Front 1933–1945*, Hunter Bivens
21. *An Innocent Abroad: Lectures in China*, J. Hillis Miller
22. *Form and Instability: East Europe, Literature, Postimperial Difference*, Anita Starosta
23. *Bombay Modern: Arun Kolatkar and Bilingual Literary Culture*, Anjali Nerlekar
24. *Intimate Relations: Social Reform and the Late Nineteenth-Century South Asian Novel*, Krupa Shandilya
25. *Media Laboratories: Late Modernist Authorship in South America*, Sarah Ann Wells
26. *Acoustic Properties: Radio, Narrative, and the New Neighborhood of the Americas*, Tom McEnaney

27. *The New Woman: Literary Modernism, Queer Theory, and the Trans Feminine Allegory*, Emma Heaney
28. *Civilizing War: Imperial Politics and the Poetics of National Rupture*, Nasser Mufti
29. *Late Colonial Sublime: Neo-Epics and the End of Romanticism*, G. S. Sahota
30. *Globalizing Race: Anti-Semitism, Empire, and the Politics of Scale in Modern French and European Culture*, Dorian Bell
31. *Domestications: American Empire, Literary Culture, and the Postcolonial Lens*, Hosam Mohamed Aboul-Ela
32. *Behold an Animal: Four Exorbitant Readings*, Thangam Ravindranathan
33. *Capital Letters: Hugo, Baudelaire, Camus, and the Death Penalty*, Ève Morisi
34. *Immaterial Archives: An African Diaspora Poetics of Loss*, Jenny Sharpe
35. *Figures of the World: The Naturalist Novel and Transnational Form*, Christopher Laing Hill
36. *Imperfect Solidarities: Tagore, Gandhi, Du Bois, and the Forging of the Global Anglophone*, Madhumita Lahiri
37. *Fictional Environments: Mimesis, Deforestation, and Development in Latin America*, Victoria Saramago